Also available at all good book stores

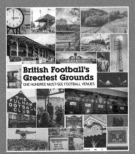

9781785316470

9781785313929

9781785315466

9781785318245

9781785315534

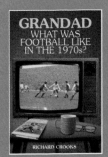

9781785312632

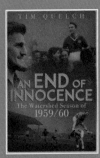

9781785317583

9781785317576

9781785316869

BEAUTIFUL BRIDESMAIDS

Gary Thacker

BEAUTIFUL BRIDESMAIDS
Dressed in
Oranje

The Unfulfilled Glory of Dutch Football

First published by Pitch Publishing, 2021

Pitch Publishing
A2 Yeoman Gate
Yeoman Way
Worthing
Sussex
BN13 3QZ
www.pitchpublishing.co.uk
info@pitchpublishing.co.uk

A CIP catalogue record is available for this book
from the British Library.

ISBN 978 1 78531 846 7

Typesetting and origination by Pitch Publishing
Printed and bound in India by Replika Press Pvt. Ltd.

CONTENTS

This book is dedicated to my wife Sue,
to Megan and Luke, Lydia and Gregory,
to my Beautiful Princess Dolores and
my gorgeous new granddaughter Polly.

It is also dedicated to all those who
always supported and believed in me

You are my strength.

And to those who only ever
doubted me.

You are my inspiration.

ACKNOWLEDGEMENTS

Many people have assisted in the production of this book.

The following have generously agreed to be interviewed, and allowed me to use their wise words:

- Jan-Willem Bult – Former player and KNVB qualified coach. International film and TV maker, football expert, initiator of Twitter @ Netherlands1974
- Jan-Hermen de Bruijn – Dutch football journalist, commentator and former owner and chief editor of the football magazine *ELF Voetbal*
- Alex Frosio – *Gazzetta dello Sport* journalist
- Raphael Honigstein – Author, journalist, broadcaster and presenter
- Nico-Jan Hoogma – KNVB (Dutch FA) director of top football.
- Ray Hudson – Former professional footballer, US football journalist and radio host
- Graham Hunter – European football journalist
- Abraham Klein – World Cup referee
- Rob Smyth – Author and *Guardian* journalist
- Michael Statham – Dutch football writer

- Dr Peter Watson – Teaching Fellow in the Department of Spanish, Portuguese and Latin American Studies, University of Leeds

Additionally, research for the book has been massively assisted by the following:

- Stuart Horsfield
- Mike Nasrallah
- Steven Scragg
- Aidan Williams

Finally, thanks to all at Pitch Publishing for their professionalism and dedication.

Sincere thanks to one and all.

FOREWORD

IF YOU get the opportunity to see a legend in the flesh, you do it. Back in March 1978, I was 21 years old, and since the early years of that decade had been an unashamed adherent to the doctrine of Total Football. I was seduced by the poetry of the Ajax team that dominated European club football, lifting the European Cup three times in succession.

The love deepened with the extravagant beauty, and ultimate fragility, of the bright flame of the Netherlands national team as they scorched the pitches of West Germany in the 1974 World Cup, before the fire became too fierce and their wings of wax melted. Football's Prometheus, Icarus in Oranje.

This was no one-night stand or clumsily fumbling embrace. This was a lasting bromance. We all lock on to some paradigm of play that we believe to be the true faith. In 1978 mine was – and remains – that having players with skill, that are comfortable on the ball with outrageous belief and commitment, regardless of the position they play, is the baseline requirement, and then you weave those talents into the fabric of a team.

Although second in my admiration to the titan that was Barry Hulshoff when they both sported Ajax's iconic red and white shirts, Johan Cruyff was the torch-bearer, guardian of the eternal flame kindled by Rinus Michels. By 1978, Cruyff had absconded from Amsterdam and decamped to the Camp Nou, to hook up with his old coach and reignite the passions of Barcelona's culés. Trophies had followed and, although unknown at the time, a new structure had been born that would change the club, and indeed European football, forever.

Cruyff had moved to Catalunya in 1973 and the 1977/78 season would be his last in Spain before what was almost a sabbatical year in California with Los Angeles Aztecs.

In March 1978, Barcelona had been drawn to play Aston Villa in the quarter-finals of the UEFA Cup. The Blaugrana – and Cruyff – were coming to the West Midlands. Living just north of Birmingham, this was my chance to go and see the great man in the flesh, to pay homage to one of the all-time great players. Was I going to miss the chance to watch the Dutch master paint some entrancing pictures in real life? Was I heck as like! Queuing for tickets was a cheap price to pay, as was the journey by foot, bus and train to get to Villa Park.

There I was in the crowd, just behind the home dugout, when Cruyff picked up the ball around halfway. With that unique style, he drove forward, swerving and gliding. Were his feet even touching the floor? I'm still not sure. On he went, evading rather than beating defenders, then drove a cross-shot into the far corner of the net. I stood up and cheered, enraptured by the moment. All around me, home fans scowled at my celebration, but still applauded the goal.

The pitch was wet and hardly like the snooker-table surfaces of today, but it was the perfect stage for Cruyff. Whilst others slogged on, heavy-legged, with damp, cold and fatigue clawing at aching muscles, he was the will-o'-the-wisp skating over the surface. Sometimes when you have high expectations of something anticipated, there's an almost inevitable anticlimax.

Not on that night. Not with Johan Cruyff. It wasn't the Grand Canyon, but it was mightily grand.

With eight minutes or so remaining, and Barcelona two goals clear, Cruyff – wearing No.9, rather than his iconic 14 – limped away to the dressing-room. Although their team had been unable to cope with his majesty, the Villa fans rose and applauded him off the pitch.

For me, that was enough. Along with more than a few disappointed home fans, I turned up my collar against the cold of the Birmingham night, and headed for the exits and the long, convoluted journey home. Walking away, I heard two roars suggesting a comeback from the home team that hadn't really looked on the cards for 80-odd minutes. The game ended in a 2-2 draw. Barcelona would progress after winning the second leg 2-1, but would lose in the semi-finals to PSV Eindhoven, the eventual winners. I didn't know it then, but a beautiful dream was on the cusp of passing into a lamented past, a legacy unfulfilled.

Three months later the Dutch, this time without Cruyff, but still with much of the flair echoing from 1974, would lose another World Cup Final to the country hosting the competition. As I turned my back on Villa Park, I little knew that the football I had come to so admire was destined to perish into ashes a few months later. When it happened, I felt cheated, frustrated and annoyed that the gods of football had denied the world a celebration befitting such beguiling football. It should have been 1974. It should have been 1978, but both were denied.

While football held a party, celebrating German efficiency and Argentine passion, a beautiful girl sat quietly in the corner, two silver, not gold, tears rolling down her cheeks, one for each lost final. There would be no celebration for the Beautiful Bridesmaid in Oranje. It wasn't to be her party. It wasn't my party either, but I'll cry if I want to.

INTRODUCTION

'The only people for me are the mad ones,
the ones who are mad to live, mad to talk,
mad to be saved, desirous of everything at the
same time, the ones who never yawn or say a
commonplace thing, but burn, burn, burn like
fabulous yellow roman candles exploding like
spiders across the stars.'[1]

CASTING HIMSELF in the personification of Sal Paradisie, Jack Kerouac expounds a philosophy desirous of passion and exhilaration; always the exceptional, never the mundane. Kerouac evokes a spiritual journey, an invitation to pursue belief, identity and an essential meaning for life. Eschewing the sheer ordinariness of a workaday world sated with consumerism, Paradisie and his fellow travellers, each of whom represent a kindred spirit in real life – Dean Moriarty (Neal Cassady), Carlo Marx (Allen Ginsberg), and Old Bull Lee (William S. Burroughs) – ache for something more, something exceptional, something sensational.

---

1   Kerouac, Jack, *On the Road* (New York: Viking Press, 1957)

When English referee Jack Taylor blew for full time on 7 July 1974, the Dutch team of flaring brilliance stood dejected. The bright Oranje flame of their football had scorched the tournament but, in the end, being the best team simply wasn't sufficient to deliver the trophy. A team that had entertained and entranced in equal measure, had sadly lost out at the very last. What had taken the Dutch so far had also doomed them to their fate. They had been magnificent, and the brilliance of their football had endeared them to so many fans, but their rewards were losers' medals.

Four years later, the same setting. With a different coach, team and an adapted philosophy, the width of a goalpost had denied them. Runners-up again. For the second time in successive tournaments, the Netherlands were left to watch in sad reflection as the World Cup hosts collected the prize. In Oranje shirts dampened by perspiration, the Dutch were bridesmaids again.

Succumbing to the hosts in the finals of successive tournaments was the most glorious of failures by, surely, the best team never to have won the World Cup. By the time they qualified again for a finals, a dozen years had passed and, so too, had the generation of players whose performances had thrilled so many.

For all the glory and acclaim that winners receive, love and affection doesn't always go to the victors. In football's four-yearly jamboree, whilst the bride is the star of the show, it's often the bridesmaid that everyone falls for. It's a World Cup legacy that taught us to cherish those who never make it to the altar.

Jack Kerouac isn't around to offer a better metaphor for the story of the glorious failures of the Netherlands at successive World Cups. Sal Paradisie could surely have accomplished the task with more eloquence than I, but *sans Paradisie*, I'll enthusiastically take up the baton. In 1974, I was a teenager innocently in search of my own footballing belief, identity and an essential meaning to the game. Beguiled by beauty, smitten by dreams and hopelessly in love, I found it in the Netherlands teams of 1974 and 1978. They were always On the Road, but never arriving. The journey was their boon, but also their bane.

At the World Cup, the teams that lift the biggest award football has to offer can go on to become the style-setters for a generation. It happened after 1966 with England dispensing with genuine wingers. The Brazilians did it on a number of occasions, but especially perhaps in 1970, when they infused the game with an injection of *Jogo Bonito* that made everyone want to play with such unfettered joy. And in 2010, Spain raised the banner for tiki-taka. Sometimes though, the tournament betrays us. The observer in love with the game is left unfulfilled. It fails us because the teams that should have triumphed, somehow didn't.

It happened in 1954 when Hungary, those cherry-red-shirted Magical Magyars, fell 3-2 to West Germany in a final doused in rain where, legend has it, the innovation of screw-in studs offered a steadier footing on a sodden pitch, allowing the Germans to stride purposefully forward and lift the trophy. 'Vorsprung durch Technik' as they never say in Budapest.

Hungary had won the Olympic title in 1952, scoring no less than 20 goals across the five games of the tournament, whilst conceding just two. In the following year, they dispelled any doubts about their majesty by handing out a comprehensive shellacking to England. In the years from 14 May 1950, until they lost 3-1 to Turkey on 19 February 1956, Hungary would play a half-century of games, winning 46, and drawing three. The only blot on their record, the sole defeat in 50 games across nearly six years, was the 1954 World Cup Final. Ferenc Puskás, Nandor Hidegkuti, Sandor Kocsis and the other members of the Magyar golden generation would take only silver medals.

Hungary were strong favourites in 1954, and their passage through the group stage suggested it would be a triumphal march towards a coronation. In the quarter-finals, they eliminated Brazil, scoring four goals, and then faced Uruguay in the semi-finals. A further four-goal haul took Hungary into the final, where they would face a German team they had thrashed 8-3 in the group stage.

Two goals inside the initial eight minutes, first by Puskás, and then Zoltan Czibor did little to dispel popular assumptions but, as with the Dutch 20 years later, despite taking an early lead, Hungary were destined not to reach the altar. In the semi-final, Puskás had sustained an injury to his ankle and the cloying surface of the rain-sodden pitch, plus the effects of further challenges, gradually slowed the 'Galloping Major' to a mere trot. His influence in the game would wane as time went on.

The Germans played themselves back into the contest and by midway through the first period, had drawn level. From that point on, with a mixture of good form and good fortune, goalkeeper Toni Turek and the frame of his goal somehow kept the increasingly frustrated Hungarians at bay until with just five minutes remaining, Helmut Rahn scored the winning goal. The team that excelled for more than half a decade, adored for their play, failed to win the biggest prize. When the Russian invasion of their country occurred two years later, the tragedy scattered their legendary team across the Continent. The Magnificent Magyars were lost, except to those who kept a place for them in their hearts.

In 1982 a Brazilian squad containing the elegant Socrates, the metronomic Júnior and the magical Zico – perhaps the true heir of Pelé – in the No.10 shirt among a glittering array of other stars, took on the task of restoring the Seleção's former glories. It was a team worthy of being world champions, but for all the recapturing of true Brazilian footballing heritage, they too would be loved for their artistry rather than their ultimate success. They swept effortlessly through the group stages, winning all of their games with relative ease. In the second stage, they defeated old rivals Argentina 3-1, but would fall to eventual champions Italy in a titanic and wildly entertaining 3-2 defeat, after twice battling back from being a goal down.

Four years later, in Mexico, under the German coach Sepp Piontek, the Danish Dynamite team exploded into the World Cup with outrageous dribbling and jet-heeled play that both bewitched and blew away opposition teams. Although comprising multi-skilled players throughout, it was the front pair of the team that epitomised the glory of this Denmark squad. Often described as a 'Beauty and the Beast' pairing, Michael Laudrup and Preben Elkjaer were a formidable combination. The former had extravagant skills, a dribble that saw him sway past opponents, the vision to bring others into the game with an ability to complete passes that very few others could even conceive of and a natural goalscorer's predatory instincts. It was Laudrup who christened the Danes 'Europe's answer to Brazil.'[2] If Laudrup was a string quartet, his partner was a rock and roll band. While possessing no little skill, Elkjaer was power, pace and passion. With a first instinct upon receiving the ball to turn and face his opponent, the belligerence of Elkjaer's forward play was the yin to Laudrup's yang. In combination, their play was explosive.

Thrown into a 'Group of Death' scenario, they faced Scotland, West Germany and Uruguay. A scrappy 1-0 victory over Scotland, thanks to a powerful strike by Elkjaer, was merely the forerunner. In the second game, they faced Uruguay and delivered the sort of artistic performance that should surely be destined for a run on a West End stage. Six goals against a sullen South American team were wonderful to watch. Elkjaer

2   Campomar, Andreas, *¡Golazo!: A History of Latin American Football* (London: Hachette UK, 2014)

notched a hat-trick, but the best goal was surely the graceful dart by Laudrup. It was a performance so enthralling that one Mexican commentator was compelled to comment that, 'Senors, Senores, you have just witnessed a public fiesta of football.' The Danes would go on to defeat a powerful West German team 2-0 to reach the quarter-finals, but fall foul of a misplaced back pass against Spain. Commentating on Danish television, Svend Gehrs would bemoan, 'But Jesper, Jesper, Jesper. That's lethal!' They would lose 5-1.

These are just three of the stories promoted over time of the 'should have, could have' laments when a team seemingly destined for glory falls short. Each would have their advocates, those who would promote these teams as the best never to have been crowned world champions. For all the worthiness of each, and perhaps other cases too, it's easier to argue that, after some 90 years of World Cup tournaments, the Dutch case is surely the strongest. No other team has played in three World Cup Finals and lost each time, twice to the hosts, twice in extra time and each time, tantalisingly, by the narrowest of margins. The Netherlands also hold the record of qualifying for the most World Cups without winning one. Add in the fact that in 1974 and 1978 they lost successive finals, and all that at a time when club sides from a country with a population of a shade less than 13.5 million had created a new paradigm of how the game should be played, and surely it's the saddest lament for all time.

There's something else about the Dutch in 1974 and 1978. This was not a story of prolonged success in World Cup tournaments. There was no pedigree for the Netherlands national team in the competition. Quite the reverse ... as David Winner describes in his book *Brilliant Orange*, 'Until the 1970s, Holland had an international record almost on a par with Luxembourg.'[3] Other countries perceived as major

3   Winner, David, *Brilliant Orange* (London: Bloomsbury, 2000).

powers at the 1974 and 1978 tournaments had long and proud records of achievement; many of them among the opponents faced by the Netherlands were previous finalists, and indeed, winners. Not so the team from the Low Countries.

Qualification for the 1974 World Cup, which came so perilously close to not happening, delivered their first appearance in the final stages for 36 years. They had qualified in both 1934 and 1938, but each time had been eliminated without winning a single game. Following their defeat in the 1978 final, they would not compete in a World Cup again for another 12 years. In more than 50 years between 1938 and 1990, the Dutch would only qualify for the final stages of the World Cup on two occasions.

Dutch football of that era is often referred to as being akin to a fire. The heat of the bright Oranje flame both scorched opponents and warmed the hearts of fans. Its incandescent brightness dazzled opponents and illuminated souls. Fires are powerful and can be all-consuming, but they are also brief, ephemeral, destined to fade away, leaving only ashes. After more than 30 dormant years, the Oranje spark ignited. The fire burnt so ferociously, then died away again. The story of how and why is a lament for the Netherlands national team of the 1974 and 1978 World Cups, and an unfulfilled legacy. It's the tale of 'Beautiful Bridesmaids Dressed in Oranje'.

PART 1

A Brief History of Oranje

From birth until the First World War

As with so many continental countries, football was introduced into the Netherlands by Britons taking the game with them on their travels. In this case, a group of English students studying in the Netherlands were the midwives, and the first Dutch football club, Haarlem Football Club, was formed in 1879 by Pim Mulier, who would later go on to found the 'Nederlandschen Voetbal-en Athletischen Bond' (NVAB) (Dutch Football and Athletics Association). This organisation evolved into the KNVB (Royal Dutch Football Association).

Despite its name, Haarlem's main sporting endeavours were in the field of rugby, and played games at weekends, in a field occupied by cows during the week, and a number of unobliging trees at all times. Clearly, the situation was less than ideal and in 1883, after many complaints from both injured participants and the parents of younger players fearing similar incidents, rugby was dropped in favour of what was seen as the far less physically intimidating game of association football. Now freed from its reputation for injuries, trauma, trees and cow pats, both the club and its new sport flourished, with membership of the NVAB booming.

Within Haarlem itself, Haarlemsche FC and Haarlemsche FC 'Excelsior' joined in.

From Amsterdam came Amsterdamsche Sportclub, Amsterdamsche FC 'RAP' and Voetbal-Vereniging 'Amsterdam'. Rotterdam also added three new clubs in the form of Rotterdamsche Cricket-en Football-Club 'Concordia', Rotterdamsche Cricket-en Football-Club 'Olympia' and Voetbalvereniging Rotterdam. The others were Delftsche FC and Haagsche Voetbal-Vereeniging. By 1895, however, the popularity of football had demanded exclusive attention. The athletics element of the organisation was jettisoned and the organisation was renamed as NVB, the Nederlandse Voetbal Bond. A decade later, a collaboration between the

Dutch banker, Cornelis August Wilhelm Hirschman, and French journalist Robert Guérin resulted in the Fédération Internationale de Football Association. Dutch football had an important hand in the founding of FIFA. Some 30 years later, the NVB was granted royal status and the organisation we know today as the KNVB (Koninklijke Nederlandse Voetbalbond) was born.

On 30 April 1905, the Netherlands national team played its first official fixture, facing Belgium in a one-off match for the Coupe Vanden Abeele in Antwerp. The Dutch recorded a 4-1 victory. Drawing 1-1 after 90 minutes, a period of extra time was played to decide the issue, during which Eddy de Neve added a further three goals to an earlier strike to make him the first Dutch player to score for his country; the first player to score a hat-trick; and the first player to score the winning goal in a cup final for the Netherlands. It so happened that, on that day, all of the goals were scored by the Dutch team, as the Belgian strike was an own goal by Ben Stom. During his brief career on the international stage, De Neve would play three times, scoring six goals. The template for the goalscoring legends of Dutch football to come was created by Eddy de Neve back in 1905.

The team of the time was coached by former part-time Sparta player, and full-time Rotterdam tailor, Cees van Hasselt. Four years earlier, Van Hasselt had organised a game against Belgium but, as it had not been officially sanctioned by the NVB, and selection of players was restricted to the area of South Holland, it was deemed to be an unofficial game, and is not included in international records.

Van Hasselt would remain in post until 1908, leading the Dutch in 11 games, six of which were won and five lost, with eight of the 11 against Belgium. He would be the only Dutchman to take charge of the national team until 1946, when Karel Kaufman took over at the end of the Second

World War. In between, nine British coaches would take charge of the team, including, briefly in October 1910, the legendary coach and visionary, Jimmy Hogan, for a game against Germany. Hogan had been appointed as coach of FC Dordrecht earlier the same year, and would stay with the club until 1912, despite thinking the attitude of many players in the Netherlands was 'primitive', as Norman Fox relates in *Prophet or Traitor: The Jimmy Hogan Story*, and that 'they drank like fishes and smoked like factory chimneys but were a jolly lot of fellows, intelligent and able to pick up the science of the game'.[4] It's a trait that would prove very useful many years down the line. The Netherlands triumphed 2-1. It was the first confrontation in a rivalry that would become as intense as any in international football.

Two years later, the Dutch faced England in an unofficial friendly game. By now, after sitting out the original invitation to join FIFA with typical isolationist arrogance, the FA, still staunchly amateur, had decided to indulge this strange continental enterprise, if only to lend it some legitimacy and dignity. Such haughtiness was only reinforced when the Dutch fell to an embarrassing 12-2 defeat. The game was memorable, however, for the fact that the Dutch wore what would become their trademark Oranje shirts for the first time. For the game against Belgium in 1905, and in all games preceding this one, they had worn a white shirt with a red, white and blue diagonal sash; colours taken from the Dutch flag. The design has also been worn on a number of occasions as a change strip in more contemporary times, for example, in the 2006 World Cup against Portugal.

By 1908, the Netherlands were ready for their first international competition and entered the Olympic Games. Van Hasselt had moved on and the team was led into the

4   Fox, Norman, *Propztor?: The Jimmy Hogan Story*, (Manchester: The Parrs Wood Press, 2003)

London Games by Edgar Chadwick, who had formerly managed the Haarlem and HVV Den Haag clubs in the Netherlands. The game was still in its nascent form at this level and, despite eight teams officially entering, only six competed. Hungary withdrew for political reasons due to the crisis in Bosnia, and Bohemia withdrew after losing their FIFA membership. With the Dutch scheduled to play the Hungarians, they received a bye to the semi-final where they faced hosts Great Britain at London's White City, on 22 October 1908.

The British team was, in fact, largely the England team, but wrapped in the Union Flag, rather than the Cross of St George. Having crushed Sweden 12-1 in the quarter-finals, they were in no mood to let up against the Dutch and notched a comfortable 4-0 victory, with West Ham United's Henry Stapley scoring all four goals. It was, however, a relatively close affair compared to the other semi-final, where Denmark crushed France 17-1. Such was the French embarrassment, they declined to play the bronze medal game against the Dutch, and returned home. Instead, Sweden were promoted in their stead, and the Dutch overcame their Scandinavian opponents 2-0 with goals from Jops Reeman and Edu Snethlage. Despite only limited tournament success in London – winning just a single game – the Dutch team returned home with medals that suggested they were the third best team on the planet, albeit that logic was produced from a competition involving only six countries, all from Europe.

Snethlage had been born in Ngawi, then part of the Dutch East Indies, now Indonesia, and in March 1909, opening the scoring during a 4-1 friendly victory over Belgium, became the Netherlands' accredited top scorer with seven goals. Completing his hat-trick in the same game, he raised that tally to nine. It was to be a short-lived accolade, though. Sixteen months later, Jan Thomée scored against Germany, taking his total to 11. The following year, another record was broken, but this one stands even up to the time of writing. On 2 April 1911, HVV Den Haag player Jan van Breda Kolff became the youngest ever player – just 17 years and 81 days old – to play for the Netherlands national team, when he debuted in a game against Belgium. He would score the second goal in a 3-1 victory, also meaning that he is the youngest player to score for the Oranje. As with Snethlage, Van Breda Kolff was born in the Dutch East Indies, in the city of Medan, Sumatra. Although the goal would be the only one of his international career, Van Breda Kolff played all four games in the Olympic tournament of the following year.

In 1912, the Dutch took their place at the Olympics in Sweden. Following the 1908 tournament, they had played 16 friendlies against varied opposition, losing only four times, each of them against England. With that record as encouragement, they would have entered the tournament with some confidence. That said, only one player retained his place in the squad from the previous Olympics, Sparta Rotterdam's Bok de Korver.

In Sweden, places had been allocated for 16 countries to compete, although only 11 actually took part. In a truncated first round, five teams received byes to the quarter-finals, with the Dutch needing extra time to get past the hosts, securing a 4-3 victory, thanks to an early extra-period goal by Jan Vos. In the quarter-finals, they defeated Austria 3-1, after being three goals clear inside the first 30 minutes. It meant a semi-final date against Denmark. A 4-1 defeat extinguished any hopes of further glory, but once again, the Dutch triumphed in the bronze-medal clash, trouncing Finland 9-0.

De Korver collected his second bronze medal, and would later go on to captain the Dutch team and accumulate 31 caps, a record at the time. In the following year, his last representing the Netherlands, De Korver would be part of a team that reached a landmark for the development and progress of Dutch football. Facing England at Houtrust, home of HVV Den Haag, on 24 March 1913, De Korver and his team-mates became the first Dutch side to defeat England. The Dutch had suffered the three worst defeats in their history against England – 2-12, 1-9 and 1-8 – but a brace by Huug de Groot gave the Oranje their first win over the English and ensured the Sparta Rotterdam player a place in the annals of the Dutch national team.

The following year saw Englishman Tom Bradshaw take charge for the home game against Belgium, in a one-off appointment as coach of the national team. The 2-4 defeat hardly encouraged his retention. In the same year, FIFA decreed that the 1916 Olympic football competition would also be considered the World Football Championship for Amateurs. That innovation would have to wait, though. By now, Scot Billy Hunter was coaching the team. He would be one of only two Scots to lead the Dutch – the other being Tom Sneddon in 1948 – and would be in charge for a mere four games, although the curtailment of his tenure had little to do with disappointing results. A 2-4 win in Belgium saw his reign off to a good start. Then a 4-4 home draw with Germany was followed by another victory over Belgium, this time at home. On 17 May, the Dutch lost 4-3 to Denmark. It was their final game before the conflagration of the First World War plunged the world into four years of tragedy. In so many ways, on the other side of those years, the world would be a very different place.

The inter-war years
The Netherlands wouldn't return to international football until 9 June 1919, marking their return with a 3-1 victory over Sweden. They were led by Englishman, Jack Reynolds. The former winger had enjoyed an itinerant playing career

in England, before moving into coaching after retirement, joining Swiss club, Fussballclub St Gallen 1879 in 1912. He had been due to take over the German national team in 1914, but war prevented him taking up the appointment, and after the resumption of football, the Dutch offered him the post of leading the Oranje. Between 1915 and 1925, Reynolds had been contracted to Ajax, and would share his national duties with the demands of club commitments. Following a two-year period with Blauw-Wit Amsterdam, he would return to Ajax in 1927, and stay there for the next two decades. Considered by some to be one of the early pioneers of Total Football at the club, he would lead Ajax to eight league titles and when, in the 1940s, a certain Rinus Michels played under him at the De Meer Stadion, the torch of Total Football was passed into safe hands.

By 1920, the Olympic football tournament resumed in Belgium. The Dutch would be led by another Englishman. Fred Warburton managed three Dutch clubs – Amsterdamsche FC, Hercules Utrecht and HVV Den Haag – before being offered the chance to take the national team to the Olympics, inheriting the role from Reynolds. He would stay in post until 1923.

By this time, England and the other home countries had decided to withdraw from FIFA, apparently in a fit of pique after seeing their power and influence within the organisation diminished by the rising number of members. Despite that, the Great Britain team were still allowed to compete in this Games, organised by FIFA, because it was thought unreasonable to deny them entry to the football when they were taking part in other Olympic sports. Doubtless, however, there may well have been a measure of *Schadenfreude* among the FIFA hierarchy when the Great Britain team was eliminated in the first round following a 3-1 defeat to Norway.

It would be the last tournament that a Great Britain team would decide to compete in until 1948. Professionalism was already a part of the game in a number of countries, with Belgium, the hosts for the 1920 tournament, among them. In 1923, the FA sought assurances that amateurism would be strictly maintained in the Olympic tournaments. The request was declined, thereby implicitly accepting the principle of an 'Open' tournament, allowing both amateurs and professionals to compete side by side. For the arch-traditionalists of the FA, this was a step beyond all reason. They picked up their ball and went home, sulking all the way. It was also the last tournament without South American teams, although Egypt had competed in 1920, breaking the European monopoly. If the British exit was less than auspicious, the Dutch, who remained amateur more through necessity than principle, would fare much better.

Again 16 places were allocated for the tournament but, despite the havoc endured in post-war Europe, only one country failed to take their allotted place. With the Polish–Soviet War still flaring, Poland's first-round tie with Belgium was awarded to the hosts in a walkover. On 28 August, the Dutch opened their campaign with a comfortable 3-0 victory over Luxembourg, taking them into a high-scoring quarter-final against Sweden. After 90 minutes, the scores stood at 4-4, but that was only after a late penalty by Japp Bulder kept the Dutch alive. The 24-year-old forward had just won the Dutch league title with his Groningen-based club Be Quick, and would score half of his total of six international goals in this tournament. The game was finally decided after 115 minutes when Jan de Natris scored the goal that put the Dutch into the final four. In the semi-final, however, they tumbled to defeat by three clear goals against the hosts.

The tournament was fated to end in farce though. The final pitted the Belgians against Czechoslovakia. All seemed fine when Robert Coppée converted a penalty after six minutes to give the hosts the lead. It was, however, the second goal, scored by Rik Larnoe, that ignited problems. The award of the goal by English referee John Lewis, supported by compatriot linesmen, C. Wreford-Brown and A. Knight, infuriated the Czechs and ten minutes later, with tempers at boiling point due to a perceived blatant bias by the referee, they walked off the pitch and refused to return and resume the game.

The Belgians were awarded the gold medal, with Czechoslovakia being disqualified, leaving the silver and bronze medal positions to be competed for in a strange knockout mini-tournament, which eventually saw the Dutch lose out 3-1 to Spain in what was the final to decide the tournament's runners-up. The silver medals therefore went to Spain and, for the third successive tournament, the Dutch went home with bronze medals. Despite a good measure of fortune, it would be difficult to dispute that, at least among the competing countries of continental Europe, they were performing consistently well in tournaments and were clearly a force in European football.

Three years later, on 25 November 1923, the Dutch invited Englishman Robert Glendenning to take charge of the national team for the friendly against Switzerland in Amsterdam. Born in County Durham, Glendenning had started his career with local club Washington United, before moving on to Barnsley where he played in the FA Cup Finals of 1910 and 1912. The former was lost to Newcastle United after a replay. The latter followed a similar pattern, but this time Barnsley triumphed over West Bromwich Albion in the replay, after Glendenning set up the winning goal for Harry Tufnell. After the First World War, he would briefly return to playing at Accrington Stanley, before retiring and moving into coaching. A 4-1 victory against the Swiss, with a team comprising many debutants, was clearly impressive enough, but following the game Glendenning would return to club football with Koninklijke HFC.

Two more brief appointments to coach the national team would follow, with Billy Townley in 1924 and John Bollington the following year. By 1925, however, Glendenning was reappointed. Initially, he shared his time between the national job and his position at the Haarlem club. With the 1928 Olympics in prospect, though, a full-time commitment was required and he took over the Oranje exclusively. He would stay in post until the Second World War. During his time in charge, as well as the 1928 Olympics, Glendenning would lead the team into two World Cup tournaments and 87 games in total, winning 36. Until 2017, when Dick Advocaat, then in his third term in charge of the Netherlands, recorded his 37th victory, no coach of the Dutch national team had won more matches than Glendenning.

The 1924 Olympic tournament in France had grown to include 22 teams, and a preliminary round was required to bring the number down to 16, allowing a knockout competition to proceed from there. Given the Dutch team's position as three-times bronze medal winners, they were excused this task and took their place in the first round proper against Romania on 27 May, skating to a comfortable 6-0 victory. Their quarter-final task against Ireland was a different matter, though, ending in a 1-1 draw after 90 minutes. Fourteen minutes into the extra period, Ocker Formenoy scored his second, and the deciding, goal to take the Dutch into the semi-finals, where they would be eliminated 2-1 by eventual champions Uruguay.

On 8 June, they faced their regular four-yearly task of securing bronze medals when they played Sweden. The game ended with a 1-1 draw, requiring a replay, which would take place the following day, ahead of the final. The first match had attracted a crowd of less than 10,000 but, with the Stade Olympique in Colombes full for the final, more than 40,000 watched the replay. Sweden won 3-1, and the Dutch fell into the unaccustomed position of fourth place, and went home without a medal.

The following year, during a friendly against Sweden, defender Harry Dénis played his 32nd international game for the Oranje, surpassing the number set by Bok de Korver. The HBS Craeyenhout player would go on to rack up 56 caps before retiring in 1930. His record would stand until 1937, when it was passed by Feyenoord's 'Puck' van Heel.

The next Olympic tournament held out a promise of success for the Dutch, with the competition held in the Netherlands. As well as Uruguay travelling across the Atlantic, the reigning champions were joined by Argentina, Chile, Mexico and the United States as the tournament took on a more global identity. Perversely, however, the success of attracting more countries and the growing worldwide popularity of the game would weigh against the Olympics, convincing FIFA that they no longer needed the support of the IOC. Two years later, they would launch their own competition as the World Cup was born.

Despite home advantage, the tournament was a disappointment for the Dutch. After a preliminary round meant 17 entrants were reduced to 16, ill fortune saw the hosts paired with the reigning champions. The Uruguayans were a much more accomplished team, and despite the support of almost 30,000 fans in Amsterdam's Olympisch Stadion, the South Americans comfortably accounted for the Dutch in a 2-0 victory, setting them on the way to retaining their crown. In what has often been disregarded by Olympic and football historians, however, the Dutch then took part in a type of repêchage competition, alongside Belgium, Chile and Mexico, for what was loftily described as the Consolation tournament.

A 3-1 win over the Belgians saw the Dutch into the final against Chile, who had been the first team eliminated from the competition when they lost 4-2 to Portugal despite leading

2-0 after 30 minutes, when the teams were reduced from 17 to 16. To round out what was surely a flawed concept anyway, the game ended in a 2-2 draw, after which lots were drawn to decide the winner. The Netherlands won the lottery, but the trophy was awarded to Chile. Has there been a stranger way to win a trophy, especially for a team who had been eliminated from a tournament before it had even truly begun?

Less than a year later, at FIFA's congress in Barcelona on 18 May 1929, the federation awarded the hosting of the first World Cup to Uruguay. There was an undeniable logic for this; as well as celebrating the country's centenary, the South Americans were also twice Olympic champions, and had been the first South American country to support FIFA's competition as part of the Olympics. But a number of other countries, including the Dutch, were less than enamoured by the decision. Alongside the Netherlands, Italy, Sweden, Spain and Hungary had also thrown their hats into the ring, hoping to be selected as hosts. For the most part, the football tournaments within the Olympic Games had been held by European countries, with the South Americans only latterly joining the party. The Dutch, especially, having hosted the Olympics and its football tournament in 1928, considered themselves prime candidates, but when it became clear that FIFA were swinging heavily in favour of Uruguay, all of the European countries withdrew their applications.

Whilst football at the Olympics had seen the Dutch largely prosper, as football moved into the era of the World Cup, the coming years would not be kind to them. The Oranje sun was setting, and a time in the footballing shadows awaited the Netherlands.

The inaugural World Cup went ahead without the Netherlands, and indeed most other European countries. For reasons ranging between cost of travel, concerns of time required, fits of pique for being denied as potential hosts and a marked reluctance to join in with something that looked destined to fail, only Yugoslavia, Romania, Belgium and France competed. The latter were somewhat compelled after political pressure from FIFA president Jules Rimet, who feared that if his own country opted out, it would be the death knell for the nascent competition. Uruguay triumphed, beating Argentina in the final and, more with an unsteady step, than a jaunty confident stride, the FIFA World Cup was born.

Four years later, the tournament was staged in Europe, as Italy became the Continent's first hosts. Both this tournament and the one that followed would be played out under the growing malevolent shadow of fascism that would later lead to the Second World War. With Mussolini in power in Italy, the second staging of a World Cup would seethe with political influence and intrigue.

After almost having to strong-arm countries to take part in the initial tournament, with 32 nations applying to compete in Italy, a qualification competition was required. The Dutch were placed into Group Seven, alongside perennial rivals Belgium, plus the Irish Free State. Each team would play twice, once at home and once away, with the top two teams qualifying. If it seemed an overly grandiose way of eliminating one of three teams, Group Eight was a far better example of that overcomplicated scenario. Germany and France were placed in a group alongside Luxembourg. The first couple of games saw the Grand Duchy entertain the Germans and then the French. After conceding 15 goals to their visitors, the final rubbers were abandoned as the hapless hosts could not qualify. It has the appearance of an elaborate exercise, but it was also an efficient way of both separating the footballing wheat from the chaff, and offering due respect to all entrants.

Things were even stranger in South America. Uruguay declined to defend their title, both because their attendance at Olympic Games held in Europe had not been reciprocated when they hosted the inaugural tournament, and the costs of travel. It left Argentina facing Chile, and Brazil playing Peru to decide which two countries would represent South America. Then, after thinking better of their application, both Chile and Peru withdrew, meaning there were no qualification games at all on the continent.

Back in Group Seven, the Dutch took a watching brief on 25 February 1934, as Belgium visited Dublin's Dalymount Park to face the Irish Free State. The growing stature of football was illustrated by an estimated crowd of 35,000, as a see-sawing game finished in a 4-4 draw. The result favoured the Dutch more than either of the participants. Eight days into April, the Irish visited the Olympisch Stadion, with the home team knowing that a victory would see them set fair for qualification.

Things looked to be heading in the right direction when Johannes Smit gave the home team the lead after 40 minutes. Three minutes later Johnny Squires, who had hit all four of the Irish goals against Belgium, equalised. Things got even worse after the break when Paddy Moore scored. Now it was the Irish looking well set to qualify. Three goals in just over quarter of an hour, though, two from Elisa Bakhuys and one from Leen Vente, swung things in favour of the Dutch.

With the Irish programme now complete and a single point accrued from a draw, the two points gained for the win meant qualification was assured for the Dutch. The result in Belgium would decide who joined them in Italy. Three weeks later, in Antwerp's Bosuil Stadion, the Belgians looked to be in pole position when Laurent Grimmonprez put them ahead early in the second period. By the time that Bernard Voorhoof notched the home team's second goal, though, strikes by Smit, Bakhuys and Vente had given the Dutch the lead. Bakhuys would add a fourth late on to seal the victory and put the Dutch in top position.

Perhaps perceived as mere icing on the Dutch cake at the time, that late goal from Vente against the Irish now assumed a vital importance. Had it not been scored, the records of the Belgians and Irish would have been identical, requiring a play-off to determine who would qualify. With goal average applied to the two teams tied on a single point each, that strike made all the difference and the Irish were eliminated. The qualifications were minor victories at best, however. A 4-5 home defeat for the Dutch in a friendly against France a couple of weeks before travelling to Italy seemed an ill portent for the competition, and so it proved. Both teams would be eliminated in the first round. The Belgians were comfortably beaten by Germany, and the Netherlands' first foray into World Cup competition came to an abrupt end as, despite goals from Smit and Vente in a spirited fightback, they lost 3-2 to Switzerland in the first round.

Between the end of the 1934 World Cup and the 1938 tournament, the Netherlands played a series of 15 friendlies across Europe, winning seven times. They suffered reverses only against Germany and England, until 1937, when they lost to Belgium in April and France in October, ahead of the qualifying games for the upcoming tournament held in France.

Like some recurring dream, the Dutch were again placed into a group with Belgium. This time, they were joined by Luxembourg. Denmark should also have been in the group, but had withdrawn. As had happened when Germany and France faced a similar proposition four years earlier, the minnows lost out to both teams, although the Belgians only scraped over the line 2-3. In late February of 1938, ahead of the final rubber of the group, the Netherlands entertained Belgium in a friendly at Rotterdam's Stadion de Kuip, coming away with a 7-2 victory, despite only being a single goal ahead at the break.

Two months later, in a much more even encounter, a 1-1 draw in Antwerp again sent both teams through to the finals.

The Dutch would play one more friendly before making the short journey to France. Some 50,000 crowded into the Olympisch Stadion for the visit of Scotland. Sadly, it would be a disappointing game for the home fans. With just three minutes remaining, the Scots were leading 0-3 and, if the late goal Vente scored offered any consolation, it was of the merest kind. Was this defeat the sort of warning that the loss to France had been four years earlier?

If the 1934 tournament was full of Italian symbolism for their fascist regime, the one in France had the impending dark cloud of the Second World War hanging over it. Austria had been subsumed into the German Reich meaning the *Wunderteam* would be absent and, with the Spanish Civil War still raging across the Pyrenees, and the German and Italian air forces involved in the bombing of civilians there, public hostility to a number of teams present was understandable and intense.

The first round of the tournament paired the Netherlands with Czechoslovakia in a game played at Le Havre's Stade Municipal on 5 June. Other than SK Zidenice's Oldrich Rulc, the opposition team was drawn exclusively from the clubs based in Prague. Six came from AC Sparta, and the remaining four from SK Slavia. Whether that club-orientated cohesiveness gave the Czechs any advantage is unclear, but after finishing goalless following the regulation 90 minutes, the Dutch capitulated in extra time, conceding goals to Josef Kostalek, Oldrich Nejedly, and Josef Zeman. They were again eliminated in the first round. The Dutch experience of World Cup football had been a salutary lesson and it would be a long time before things improved. In fact, for the next 36 years, the Dutch record in international football would deteriorate further.

A 2-2 draw in a friendly against Denmark saw out the year's fixtures in October, and across the following 18 months, a motley collection of results hardly suggested an upturn in fortunes. Victories over Hungary and Belgium, twice, were contrasted with some embarrassing returns. A 7-1 thrashing suffered against the Belgians in Antwerp and a 4-5 loss to Luxembourg, both coming in March 1940, were particular low points. Then, in what turned out to be their last game before war broke out, they beat Belgium 4-2 at the Olympisch Stadion, being four goals clear with just a quarter of an hour to play. The game saw the second cap of Abe Lenstra who, despite being robbed of possibly the best years of his career by the war, would go on to play 47 times for the national team, scoring 33 goals and becoming an icon of Dutch football in the late 1940s and 1950s. It was also the last game in which Glendenning would lead the team.

In May, Glendenning's team made the short journey to play against Luxembourg. The game never took place. On 10 May, German forces invaded the Netherlands. Glendenning returned to England, but died in November of that same year, aged 52. He was buried in Bolton, and the KNVB has maintained his headstone in honour of his contribution to Dutch football.

Post-war: 1946–72

Dutch international football resumed in 1946 when, with Karel Kaufman – the first Dutchman to take control of the side since Cees van Hasselt almost four decades earlier – in charge, they visited Luxembourg to play a friendly. Despite having a team containing six players making their first appearances for the Oranje, and only Henk Pellikaan having more than a dozen caps, they ran out 2-6 winners with RFC Xerxes's Faas Wilkes – who carried the nickname of The Mona Lisa of Rotterdam – scoring a hat-trick on debut. Kaufman would remain in charge until November 1946 when, playing their first game across the Channel since the Olympic Games of 1908, the Netherlands visited Huddersfield and were roundly beaten 8-2 by England, with Tommy Lawton scoring four times. The Chelsea striker would later remark on the amount of space he was allowed in the game. He took full toll, and the Dutch paid the full price. Before the war, Jesse Carver had been a defender with Blackburn Rovers and then Newcastle United in a ten-year career. When the conflict ended, then in his late thirties, he turned to coaching, first with Huddersfield Town before moving to the Netherlands with Rotterdam club, Xerxes in 1946. Faas Wilkes, hat-trick hero from the game against Luxembourg, coming from the same club, had benefitted from Carver's enlightened attitude to coaching, where work with the ball largely replaced the traditionally unwavering emphasis on physical exercises. The club made huge strides under Carver, and in 1947 he was invited to take over from Kaufman. He would stay in charge for two years and, across eight friendly games ahead of the London Olympics of 1948, lost only once.

Sadly, despite this excellent record, Carver could not inspire the Dutch to success on the competitive stage. After beating Ireland 3-1 in the preliminary round, the Dutch fell 4-3 after extra time to Great Britain in the first round. Carver would then move on and manage some of the biggest clubs in Serie A, over the next 15 years or so, including Juventus, Lazio, Torino, Roma and Internazionale. He was briefly succeeded by Scot Tom Sneddon, before Kaufman returned for a second, albeit somewhat brief, tenure. A third would follow in the 1950s. In 1949 the KNVB turned to Jaap van der Leck.

In 1950 Wilkes, who together with Abe Lenstra and Kees Rijvers was one of the 'golden trio' of Dutch football, signed for Internazionale. Lenstra would stay in the Netherlands, but Rijvers would also leave the country, signing for French club AS Saint-Etienne in the same year that Wilkes moved to Italy. The Dutch game would remain amateur for a few years longer, and the moves gave Wilkes and Rijvers the opportunity to cash in on their talents. Sadly for both players, and the Netherlands national team, it also meant that they were banned from representing their country. representing their country. That unfortunate situation persisted until the Dutch game finally went professional four years later. Rijvers would later coach the national team for three years from 1981.

In 1953, the Dutch region of Zeeland suffered terrible floods and a game was arranged in Paris between France and a team representing the best of Dutch football to raise funds for the victims. With typical authoritarian pique, the KNVB not only refused to lend the game authenticity by allowing the national team to play, it also offered up official opposition against the game taking place at all. Nevertheless, better counsel prevailed and the game went ahead. The accruing publicity and goodwill it created was a key factor in driving an unwilling KNVB, metaphorically kicking and screaming, into the professional era.

World Cup football returned in Brazil in 1950. The Dutch declined to enter, as would be the case four years later in Switzerland. It meant that Van der Leck would have a number of friendlies to play before the next major international competition, the Olympic Games of 1952 in Finland. During the former DOS Utrecht coach's time leading the team, it would be difficult to describe the Netherlands' games as staid and boring. In that run of friendlies, they conceded seven goals on three occasions, scored six once and five twice, incredibly losing two of those three games, and won only four in total.

It was hardly a surprise, therefore, when they were eliminated in the preliminary round of the Olympics; neither was the scoreline, as they succumbed 5-1 to Brazil. It would be the last Olympic tournament to which the KNVB would send a team. The game in the Netherlands became professional in 1954, although there was hardly an upswing in results. After 1952, the Dutch would choose not to enter one World Cup and the first European Championship, and failed to qualify for four World Cups and three European Championships. Jaap van der Leck left the national team in 1954 following three successive defeats; a 4-0 loss to Belgium, a 6-1 defeat in Sweden, followed by a 3-1 reverse in Switzerland. He returned to the Dutch club scene, where he would continue coaching top clubs until retirement in 1971 after four years with Willem II.

Kaufman returned for a single match, before Austrian Friedrich Donnenfeld served a similarly brief tenure. The much-travelled Donnenfeld bookended a run of three Austrians to coach the national team over the next 18 months or so, although only Max Merkel would serve for a significant number of games, losing only twice in ten matches. When Merkel left in 1956 to return to club football, Heinrich Muller took over for a game before Donnenfeld's second term in charge. Englishman George Hardwick then became head coach for five games but, aside from Merkel's relatively successful period, results were inconsistent at best. With the Olympics no longer an option, the next target was the 1958 World Cup, and the KNVB appointed the experienced Romanian coach Elek Schwartz to head the drive for qualification. Moving from Rot-Weiss Essen in West Germany, where he had enjoyed some moderate success, Schwartz would head the national team until 1964, across 49 games. Next to Glendenning's total of 86, Schwartz's reign would be the longest in the history of the Netherlands, and would remain so until the turn of the century.

On the face of it, that length of tenure suggests a successful period for Dutch international football, but that was hardly the case. At this stage, the game in the Netherlands was still in the doldrums and results under the Romanian varied enormously. A seven-goal mauling by the West Germans during a friendly in Cologne was a particular low point, but balancing that out against a victory over the newly-crowned world champions Brazil in 1963, illustrates the fluctuating fortunes of the team. In the Low Countries, expectations were also low, often with results to match.

Qualification for the World Cup in Sweden eluded the Dutch when they missed out in a qualifying group containing Austria and Luxembourg. With both teams beating the Grand Duchy home and away, the issue would be decided by the games against Austria. Hardwick's final game in charge had been a 3-2 defeat in Vienna. With ten minutes remaining, the Dutch led 1-2, but Karl Koller equalised for the hosts, and with time almost out, Karl Stotz converted a penalty to give the home side victory. The consequence was that in his second game in charge, after defeating Luxembourg 2-5, Schwartz would need to conjure a victory when the Austrians visited in September 1957. Despite Abe Lenstra, by now in the veteran stage of his career, equalising an early Austrian goal just past the hour mark, the required victory failed to materialise and the Dutch missed out.

Things were beginning to change in the Dutch club game, though. In 1959, Vic Buckingham was appointed to coach Ajax. Previously, he had spent six years at West Bromwich Albion, after taking over from Jesse Carver, when the former head coach of the Dutch national team left England for Italy and Lazio. Buckingham would win the Eredivisie title in 1959/60 with Ajax – averaging a more than impressive 3.2 goals per game. To round things off nicely, they defeated arch-rivals Feyenoord 5-1 in the game that confirmed that the title was going to Amsterdam. Dutch club football was still largely amateurish in outlook, despite having officially been professional for some time, but Buckingham could see great potential in the way they played. He was suitably impressed by the title triumph. 'I thought they were the best team in

Europe, even then,'[5] he said. Buckingham was often described as a man ahead of his time in the game, and the coronation he foresaw for his club would have to wait a decade or so.

'Their skills were different,' Buckingham mused, talking of the players at Ajax – a young Johan Cruyff, who was making his way through the ranks at the club, very much included. 'Their intellect was different and they played proper football ... I influenced them but they went on and did things above that which delighted me. For instance, two of them would go down the left side of the field passing to each other – just boom-boom-boom – and they'd go 30 yards, and two men would have cut out three defenders and created a vast acreage of space.'[6] The germ of the team that would conquer European club football was being tenderly nurtured by Buckingham.

In *Brilliant Orange*, David Winner contends that, 'Buckingham's philosophy was simple, and in that simplicity lay its beauty. "Possession football is the thing, not kick and rush," he asserted. "Long-ball football is too risky. Most of the time what pays off is educated skills. If you've got the ball, keep it. The other side can't score"'[7] Dutch football was eager to learn, and the Ajax side coached by Buckingham would lead the way. It wasn't quite the finishing school it would become. That would need to wait until Rinus Michels arrived, but as Cruyff would acknowledge later, Dutch football was learning lessons. Referring to Buckingham and Keith Spurgeon – who would succeed Buckingham when he returned to club football in England with Sheffield Wednesday in 1961 – Cruyff related that, 'They were open-minded but, tactically, you have to see where we were at that time. Football in Holland then was good but it was not really professional. They gave us some professionalism because they were much further down the

---

5   Winner, David, *Brilliant Orange* (London: Bloomsbury, 2000)
6   Wilson, Jonathan, *Inverting the Pyramid* (London: Orion, 2014)
7   Winner, David, *Brilliant Orange* (London: Bloomsbury, 2000)

road. But the tactical thinking came later with Michels. It started then.'[8]

That arrival wouldn't happen until 1965, however. After Spurgeon left, Austrian Joseph Gruber and Jack Rowley would coach the club, before Buckingham returned in 1964. If it was a less successful time in terms of trophies, however, other benefits would accrue, especially a young skinny boy who went by the name of Johan Cruyff, referred to by Buckingham as 'a useful kid'.[9] Buckingham granted that 'kid' his debut as a 17-year-old on 15 November 1964 in an away league game at Groningen. Ajax lost 3-1. Two months later, on 21 January 1965, with the club perilously close to the foot of the table, Buckingham left Ajax.

The new man in charge was Rinus Michels. Five years later, Buckingham, then at Barcelona, tried unsuccessfully to take Cruyff to Catalunya, but was stymied by the Spanish league's restrictions. Much as Michels had succeeded where Buckingham had been frustrated during his second term at Ajax, Michels would again succeed in completing the deal that Buckingham had seen blocked, when Cruyff moved to Barcelona in 1973. If the club scene was moving forwards as the 1960s progressed, however, the national team was lagging some way behind.

After giving the European Championship a miss in 1960, the next opportunity to qualify for a major tournament was the 1962 World Cup in Chile. Ahead of the qualifying competition, the Dutch were in a typically inconsistent run of form. That 7-0 loss to West Germany had been followed by a 7-1 victory over Norway merely weeks later. They had then lost three consecutive games, before a goalless draw against Netherlands Antilles broke the sequence. They had

8 'Everyone can play football but those values are being lost. We have to bring them back' *The Guardian*, 12 September 2014

9 Winner, David, *Brilliant Orange* (London: Bloomsbury, 2000)

then won twice, lost, won and then lost again before the qualifiers began.

Placed into Group Four alongside Hungary and East Germany, Dutch confidence would not have been high. With only one team to qualify, a 0-3 home defeat to the Hungarians in the opening rubber, on 16 April 1961, did little to change that feeling. This wasn't the magical collection of Puskás and his team-mates representing Hungary, but with established players such as Karoly Sandor and the thrusting talents of a young Florian Albert and Janos Gorocs, there was still too much talent for the Dutch. A 1-1 draw away to East Germany was insufficient to turn hopes around and when Hungary won 2-3 in East Berlin, the die was cast. Neither team could catch the Hungarians' six points, and the game where the Dutch should have hosted Hungary was deleted. Visa problems had complicated matters, but as the game was now only of academic importance anyway, there was little point in trying to resolve what seemed to be intractable political problems. The final rubber between East Germany and the Netherlands fell into a similar category, but this was played out, resulting in a 3-3 draw. The Dutch had failed to qualify, and very few were surprised.

If qualifying for the World Cup had proved to be beyond the Dutch, to do so for the second running of the European Championship, then officially called the European Nations' Cup would hardly be likely to offer an easier route. They had opted out of the original running of the tournament four years earlier but, with only four qualification spots open for the finals, any team hoping to progress would need to negotiate three rounds of matches, each with home and away legs.

In what was very much *de rigueur*, following their elimination at the qualifying stage for the 1962 World Cup, the Dutch had lost five of the seven friendly games they'd played, including an embarrassing 0-4 home defeat to

Belgium ... Their only victories had come in a 4-0 triumph over Northern Ireland, and a hardly competitive 8-0 romp against Netherlands Antilles. To claim that hopes were high as the qualifiers began in November 1962, therefore, would have been wide of the mark.

A preliminary round was required to whittle the entrants down to 16, allowing a couple of knockout rounds to establish the four teams who would progress to the semi-finals and final to be played in Spain. Not unreasonably, the Dutch were required to sing for their supper by playing Switzerland for a place in the first round proper. The first leg was played at the Olympisch Stadion on 11 November 1962, and more than 64,000 hopeful, rather than expectant, souls turned up to watch.

With 15 minutes left to play, qualification seemed to be slipping away. Tonny van der Linden had given the home team an early advantage, but the Swiss had drawn level through Charly Hertig just before the break. Now, with time drifting away, and the home leg to come, the Swiss were favourites. Sjaak Swart, then in the middle of a 17-year career with Ajax, restored the Dutch lead on 75 minutes, and another Ajax player, Henk Groot, scored a minute later. The following March, a 1-1 at the Wankdorf Stadium, Berne completed the progress. Hurdle one had been cleared.

With any number of much more taxing games possible, the Dutch were relieved to be paired with Luxembourg in the official first qualifying round. With the alternatives comprising Italy, France, Spain, Hungary and the Soviet Union, among others, a tie with the footballers of the Grand Duchy seemed like a more than favourable draw. Two single-goal friendly triumphs before the next stage augured well. A victory over France in April was followed up by that vastly encouraging win against Brazil the following month; after which, a home leg against Luxembourg appeared to be comfortable fare. The

Grand Duchy had only played one 'official' full international game in the two years before the match, a 3-1 defeat to the Soviet Union.

Within five minutes of kick-off the home crowd of around 36,000 could have been forgiven for expecting an easy victory as debutant Klaas Nuninga put the Dutch ahead, firing home from the edge of the area. The time between that strike and the Luxembourg equaliser by Paul May some 25 minutes later would, however, be the only time that the Dutch would have the lead across both legs of the tie. The home team struck the post twice in the second period, but the game ended in a disappointing draw.

The second leg was also held in the Netherlands, at Rotterdam's Stadion de Kuip. Luxembourg had agreed to forego home advantage in pursuit of greater financial rewards accruing from larger attendances than would have been possible at their home stadium.[10] The process would be repeated in succeeding years across similar qualifying encounters, and also some UEFA club competitions. Having the game staged in the same stadium where they had infamously defeated the Dutch 4-5 in a friendly in 1940 hardly seemed to pan out as a disadvantage, however.

With the opportunity of a second home game in order to correct the result of the first leg, expectation was still high in the Netherlands. Rumours began to circulate that the home players had eased down during the first leg, happily settling for a draw. The implied rationale was that the KNVB wanted to ensure a bumper crowd for the second leg. It feels like an unlikely scenario and may have been a mere 'plaster' to cover the wounds of an embarrassing result, but more than 42,000 attended the game anyway.

10   http://www.rsssf.com/tablesl/luxnedres.html

On 30 October, the teams met again. Strangely perhaps, Robert Heinz, the Luxembourg coach, made two changes to his line-up in attack, replacing goalscorer Paul May and Nicholas Hoffmann with Camille Dimmer and Henri Klein. The decision would bring generous rewards. Perhaps giving the lie to any talk of an engineered result in the first leg – or at least suggesting the head coach had no knowledge of it anyway – Schwartz also made changes. The first goal came after 20 minutes, but it was the visiting 'designated home team' that scored. Dimmer, an engineer by trade who was then playing for lower-league Belgian club Royal Crossing Club Molenbeek, justified his manager's enlightened decision and Luxembourg's prospects appeared brighter as they went ahead.

It took 15 minutes for the Dutch to find an equaliser through Pieter Kruiver. Kruiver had been part of an 'all change' front three from the first leg, including Peter Hendrik Petersen and, winning his third cap, Piet Keizer. Then just 21, Keizer would go on to enjoy success with Ajax, winning three European Cups, captaining them to the trophy in 1972, and playing a part in the World Cup campaign of 1974. This game wouldn't be an auspicious memory in such an outstanding career, however. Dimmer grabbed his second of the game midway through the second period and, despite increasingly frantic efforts to redress the balance, the Dutch were defeated. Any talk of having taken it easy in the first leg were now consigned to the column labelled, 'Who were you trying to kid" and the Dutch press illustrated the country's displeasure. 'Who are we going to play against now? San Marino? Andorra? Liechtenstein?'[11] *De Telegraaf* demanded the following day.

It was portrayed as a Halloween of a day for Dutch international football, but the fact that Schwartz remained in post for a further seven months was also a comment

11   *De Telegraaf* – 31 October 1963

on the general state of the game in the Netherlands. How embarrassing was the defeat? Perhaps on reflection, it may not have been as bad as the picture painted by the press. Luxembourg met Denmark in the next round for a place in the finals, earning two draws, 3-3 at home and 2-2 at home – actually in Luxembourg; the Danes were less of a financial draw than their near neighbours. Amsterdam was the chosen venue for the play-off game, but playing in the Netherlands failed to spark any Grand Duchy magic this time. Luxembourg lost 1-0 and the Danes progressed to Spain. Having beaten Malta, Albania and Luxembourg to do so, it's questionable whether any team before or since has had an easier passage to the last four of a European Championship.

The standing of Dutch football at the time was perhaps illustrated as their next three games were completed without recording a victory and, when the qualifying campaign for the 1966 World Cup began with a laboured 2-0 home victory over Albania, Schwartz was replaced by Denis Neville. The Englishman had begun his coaching career in Denmark with Odense Boldklub, before moving on to Atalanta in Italy and to Belgium with Koninklijk Berchem Sport, and then the Netherlands with Sparta Rotterdam and Holland Sport, before his dozen years as an itinerant club coach landed him the job with the Dutch national team. He lasted just over a year. It was not a glorious tenure, and after leaving in 1966, Neville moved back to England and managed Canvey Island. He was the 14th, and at time of writing, the last Briton to coach the Dutch national team.

Group Five of the World Cup qualifying competition comprised the Dutch, Switzerland, Northern Ireland and Albania and, when Neville took charge of the squad, the Dutch at least had those two points from the home victory over the Albanians on the board. Ahead of the return in Tirana, they played one of their regular friendlies against neighbouring

Belgium, going down to a late goal by Jef Jurion. The game was notable for the debut of DWS Amsterdam defender Rinus Israel who, two years later, would move to Feyenoord, earning the nickname Iron Rinus and legendary status with the Rotterdam club. He would win three league titles there, including a domestic double and lift the European Cup in 1970, as Dutch clubs began their domination of the Continent. His knee injury would also play a key part in the strategy of the Dutch at the 1974 World Cup.

In October 1964, the Dutch visited Albania and returned with another 2-0 victory. A goal from Hennie van Nee two minutes into the game and another by Frans Geurtsen two minutes before the final whistle was barely satisfactory. It was hardly a wildly encouraging result given the games ahead in the group, but the points were added to the table. Before the next rubber, a visit to Belfast, a couple of friendlies saw a 0-1 victory in Israel and a 1-1 draw at home to England. It meant that now on a run of four games without defeat, including three victories, there was some measure of confidence ahead of the Northern Ireland game in March 1965.

Some 25,000 fans crammed into Windsor Park to see if a team containing the blossoming talents of a 20-year-old George Best could deliver a victory. The Irish had already beaten the Swiss at home, and then lost to them in Lausanne, and had high hopes, but an early goal by Van Nee suggested Neville's team could add to their points haul. Five minutes later, though, Johnny Crossan equalised and, when Terry Neill added a second just after the hour, the game was done.

A few weeks later, the return game was played in Rotterdam and a 0-0 draw was far more valuable to the Irish than to a Dutch team whose aspirations of qualification had run into the buffers. In October, another 0-0 at home to the Swiss virtually killed off any lingering hopes and a 2-1 defeat in Bern not only delivered the *coup de grâce*, but also saw the end of

Neville. Finishing third in the group, albeit just three points from top spot, may have been par for the course in qualifying tournaments for the Dutch but, perhaps unrecognised at the time, a number of new faces were making their names, along with Swart, Keizer and Israel, who had already worn the Oranje shirt.

The new coach was the German, Georg Kessler. He had joined the KNVB the previous year. Kessler would be in charge of Dutch efforts to reach the finals of both the 1968 European Championship and the 1970 World Cup ... Despite later success in club football in the Netherlands, Belgium, Austria and West Germany, his efforts would fall into the same category as every other coach of the Netherlands national team seeking to qualify for those tournaments since 1938.

By the time Kessler began his term, significant things were happening in Dutch club football. After being appointed to take over from Buckingham at Ajax, Rinus Michels quickly turned a team struggling against relegation into a championship-winning outfit. Three successive Eredivisie titles were secured in 1965/66, 1966/67 and 1967/68, with another added in 1969/70. KNVB Cup triumphs in 1966/67, 1969/70 and 1970/71 also brought two domestic doubles. A few years later, Austrian Ernst Happel would not only take Feyenoord to domestic success, but also secure the European Cup. Michels and Happel were the two coaches that would guide the Oranje in the 1974 and 1978 World Cups, when Dutch football came so close to touching the sky. Back in 1966, however, that would have felt more like pie in the sky.

Kessler began with a 2-4 defeat to his native country, before successive wins sent the Dutch into the qualifying tournament for the 1968 European Championship on a relative high. They were placed into a group alongside Hungary, East Germany and Denmark. The Dutch campaign opened with a game against Hungary. Their opponents were coming off the back of an encouraging performance in the 1966 World Cup, and by this stage Florian Albert was at the height of his powers. He would be awarded the Ballon d'Or the following year.

More than 61,000 fans were in the Stadion de Kuip for the game, and were delighted to see the home team in a two-goal lead entering the final 20 minutes. The Hungarians had started well, and appeared the more threatening, but Miel Pijs's piledriver from distance gave the Dutch the lead ten minutes before the break. The second goal would herald more for the long-term future of the team than mere immediate concerns. With the Dutch looking the better team now, ten minutes after the restart a debutant once described as 'a useful kid' cut in from the left and fired home. 'Hello world. My name's Johan Cruyff!'

It should have locked the game out but, when experienced goalkeeper Eddy Pieters Graafland could only parry a shot, Dezso Molnar followed in to score. Nerves took hold as the visitors pressed for an equaliser. In a matter of two seconds, a shot rattled the bar and another was headed from the line, but a goal was coming. It arrived with three minutes remaining, as a header from Kalman Meszoly went in after being pushed against the bar. Had the Dutch held on for the win things could have been very different, but from that point on the fate of the group was always in Hungarian hands.

Two friendly defeats followed, first at home to Austria and then away to Czechoslovakia before the next qualifier. The latter of those two games saw another player destined for greater things enter the international fray as Wim Suurbier made his debut. A 2-0 victory over Denmark eased things a little, but only relatively. The Hungarians were galloping clear, racking up four successive wins that guaranteed them top spot. In contrast, the Dutch continued to labour; a 4-3 defeat in East Germany was followed by a 2-1 reverse in Budapest to eliminate all hopes of progress. A victory over East Germany, thanks to another Cruyff goal, hardly lifted spirits and the programme was completed with a 3-2 defeat in Denmark. A review of the team for that final group game though offered hope for the future; joining Cruyff, Keizer, Suurbier and Israel, the latter's Feyenoord team-mate, Wim Jansen, made his debut. The tousle-haired midfielder was another who would feature in the 1974 World Cup.

A run of half a dozen friendlies followed with typically mixed fortunes, although going into the first of the qualifiers for the 1970 World Cup, a record of only one goal in four games – and that in a home defeat to Belgium – suggested that qualification would be an uphill struggle. The goalless draw with Scotland on the last day of May 1968, however, saw two more stars of 1974 step forward as Rob Rensenbrink, then at DWS Amsterdam, but later of Anderlecht, and Feyenoord's Wim van Hanegem made their debuts.

In a group with Bulgaria, Poland and Luxembourg – following the catastrophe of 1963, even the prospect of facing the Grand Duchy looked problematical – the Dutch would kick off their campaign against the supposed minnows of the group. As in 1963, both games between the two would be played in the Netherlands. If that was considered an ill portent by some, such fears were allayed on 4 September 1968 when Feyenoord team-mates Jansen and Van Hanegem eased the Dutch to victory in what was designated as the away game. A 2-0 reverse in Sofia was less encouraging, but the Dutch got back into winning ways the following March completing the job in the official home game against Luxembourg with a 4-0 win. Tougher tasks awaited, though.

In May, Poland visited for their second game of the group, having already rattled in eight goals at home to Luxembourg. In a tight game that looked destined for a goalless draw, a last-minute goal by substitute Sjaak Roggeveen secured the points for the home team. Any Dutch momentum was quickly halted, however, in the return rubber four months later. Henk Wery's opening goal offered hope, but replies by Andrzej Jarosik and Wlodzimierz Lubanski saw Poland home and extinguished Dutch hopes. A home draw against Bulgaria, who topped the group, completed the programme, and to all intents and purposes brought the curtain down on Kessler's time at the head of the team.

He would be in charge for three friendlies before being replaced – a home defeat to England, a draw in the return game, and a 0-1 victory in Israel. In the first of those games, Kessler would give debuts to two more of Ajax's stars, Ruud Krol and Gerrie Muhren. Given that just a month earlier Feyenoord had won the European Cup, a team featuring a strong representation from the Rotterdam club and the burgeoning talents coming out of Ajax, defeating the Bulgarians should surely have not been beyond the talents of the Dutch. But, as David Winner described in *Brilliant Orange*, 'the Netherlands then had no tradition of even competing at the top level'[12] and they fell away.

Chosen to replace Kessler was Frantisek Fadrhonc. The 56-year-old Czech had been in Dutch club football since the early post-war years. Starting in Tilburg, he'd coached Willem II from 1949 to 1956, winning the league title in 1952 and 1955, Sportclub Enschede from 1956–62, and finally Go Ahead Eagles from 1962 until he was appointed by the KNVB in 1970. With no time for preparation, Fadrhonc was dropped right into the qualification battle for a place at the 1972 European Championship, in a group alongside Yugoslavia, East Germany and old friends, Luxembourg.

In the previous qualification campaign, the Dutch had been able to ease themselves into the fray with a couple of encounters against the minnows of the group. That option wasn't open to them this time, as they began with what always

12 Winner, David, *Brilliant Orange* (London: Bloomsbury, 2000)

looked like a key encounter, at home to Yugoslavia on 11 October. Despite falling behind to a first-half goal by Dragan Dzajic, a penalty from Israel, five minutes after the restart, secured a point. Exactly a month later, they fared worse in another key fixture, falling to a 1-0 defeat in Dresden, as Johan Neeskens wore Oranje for the first time. Three weeks later, a little hope was restored when a brace from Cruyff secured a 2-0 victory at home to Romania in a friendly. The Dutch would have to wait until February 1971 to resume their qualification campaign. By that time, though, East Germany's four points from successive victories and Yugoslavia's three put the Dutch total of a single point in the shade.

In the New Year, Luxembourg turned up at the Stadion de Kuip and faced a six-of-the-best spanking, as braces by Cruyff and Keizer were added to strikes from Willi Lippens and Suurbier. To be in with any realistic chance of hauling themselves over the qualification line, a win was required from the next game in Yugoslavia. As it was, though, a 2-0 defeat locked out any hopes of progress. The Dutch had just two fixtures remaining, at home to East Germany and the 'away' game with Luxembourg, played at Eindhoven's Philips Stadion, but before they played again Yugoslavia would have seven points with two games to play, both at home.

Six months after the defeat in Split, East Germany visited the Stadion de Kuip and, despite going a goal down, the Oranje ran out 3-2 winners. Although the game had little real impact on the qualification process, another player whose participation, or more precisely non-participation, in the 1974 World Cup would be pivotal made a goalscoring debut. The Ajax libero Barry Hulshoff had just turned 25 when selected for the game, and it would be his strike that equalised the early German goal. Piet Keizer scored the other two.

A few months earlier, along with his Ajax team-mates, Hulshoff had won the first of the three European Cup winners' medals he would collect with the club. A titan of a player, his career with the Oranje would be cut short by a knee injury that denied the Dutch his mighty presence in West Germany for the World Cup. A key piece missing from the Dutch jigsaw meant that their Total Football was anything but total. How valuable was Hulshoff to the Dutch? His international career ended in 1973, just two short years after his debut. A measure of his worth is that in 14 games, he scored six times – from the libero position of centre-back. Only nine goals would be conceded in those games, whilst 51 were scored by the Dutch; 11 of the 14 games were won, two drawn, and only one lost.

Six days after the Dutch win, Yugoslavia completed qualification with a goalless draw at home to the East Germans, and then surprisingly followed it up recording the same result against Luxembourg in a game of interest only to statisticians. An 8-0 romp in the last game of the programme, with Hulshoff scoring again in what was nominally the 'away' game against Luxembourg, rounded out another unsuccessful qualification campaign.

It meant that, since 1938, the Netherlands had failed to qualify for any major tournament, either World Cup or European Championship. That unenviable record would end with qualification for the 1974 World Cup. A country with a post-war pedigree of unmitigated failure would spark into life and, for six years or so, would be the planet's footballing guiding light. To appreciate how the success of two Dutch clubs had produced the nucleus of a team that would entrance the world in West Germany, and come so close again in Argentina, it's necessary to jump back a few years and examine the development and triumphs of Ajax and Feyenoord. The future was bright. The future was Oranje, and this was why.

PART 2

Double Dutch Dominance

The links that bind

The importance, or otherwise, of a link between the success of a country's clubs and its national team is a topic that many have debated. As, of course, have been the reasons why or why not such a link may exist. Why, for example, when English clubs dominated the European Cup in the mid-1970s and early 1980s, was this not reflected in England's performances in European Championships and World Cups? Any link there seems tenuous at best. A review of other countries, however, suggests that this was very much the exception, rather than the rule.

When Spanish football was pre-eminent as *La Roja* won successive European Championships in 2008 and 2012, sandwiching a World Cup victory in between, Barcelona were accruing two Champions League successes. From 2013, there also followed a sustained period of domination of continental football as Spanish clubs monopolised European success with five successive European champions coming from La Liga.

In May 1974, Bayern Munich picked up the crown as Europe's top club after CSKA Sofia had eliminated reigning champions, Ajax. Copying the success of the Amsterdam club, the Bavarians held the trophy for three successive seasons. That success came two years after West Germany had won the European Championship, and just a month or so before they took the bouquet as World Cup winners.

AC Milan trounced Johan Cruyff's Barcelona 'Dream Team' in the 1994 Champions League Final, and Italy would reach the World Cup Final in the USA a few months later. They would lose out on penalties to Brazil, but the lottery from 12 yards could so easily have gone the other way. Eleven years later, Milan would lose the Champions League Final against Liverpool and, two years later, return to the final to win it against the same team. In between those two seasons, the *Azzurri* would be world champions after beating France on penalties in 2006.

For the Dutch, the link between club and international success was also apparent. Before Ajax reached their first European Cup Final in 1969, no Dutch club had ever attained such exalted heights. From there, however, the following four finals would all feature Dutch clubs and each time the trophy would go to either Ajax or Feyenoord. This success was also feeding into momentum for the Oranje. After 38 years' absence from major tournaments, in 1974 and 1978 the Dutch national sides were the most beautiful of participants. As the Dutch clubs began to decline though – none would reach the final of the European Cup until 1988 – the Oranje also fell away from World Cup glory, not even qualifying for the tournament for another dozen years.

PSV Eindhoven would join Ajax and Feyenoord as the only Dutch clubs to be crowned as European champions in May 1988 as they overcame Benfica. Precisely one month later, the Dutch secured their first international trophy when, under Rinus Michels, they defeated the Soviet Union to win the European Championship. Such rare flowers blooming at the same time cannot surely be mere coincidences. It's an assessment that former player, certified KNVB coach and international film and television-maker, football expert, and initiator of the Twitter account @Netherlands1974, Jan-Willem Bult, concurs with. 'In general, I'd say that in the Netherlands we see the successes of the national team in 74 and 78 not separate from the successes of Ajax and Feyenoord in the same era.'[13]

Any consideration of the Dutch campaigns of 1974 and 1978, therefore, would be less than complete without an appreciation of how Dutch clubs came to dominate European football in the early 1970s. With the link between the two firmly established, there's one further fact to add. The coaches

---

13   Bult, Jan-Willem – Interview with the author

at the helm of each club when they reached their zenith were also the coaches of the Oranje at the two World Cup tournaments.

Ajax

Considered more to be hard-working and dedicated, rather than an extravagantly skilled player, Rinus Michels was a striker whose powerful play and heading ability made him a valuable team member at Ajax, rather than one of its stars. His career would range across the dozen years or so from the 1945/46 season, when he scored five goals on his debut during an 8-3 win over ADO Den Haag, to his final appearance, early in the 1957/58 season, when a back injury compelled his retirement. A total of 122 goals in 264 games, and a pair of league titles, in 1946/47 and 1956/57, suggest a worthy, rather than outstandingly successful, career.

Bobby Haarms was an Ajax team-mate of Michels from 1952 and assistant to him at the club from 1967 until he left for Barcelona in 1971. Haarms would stay with Ajax until 1981, briefly taking over as interim manager in 1974, when George Knobel left to take control of the national team, picking up the Oranje reins from Michels, following the 1974 World Cup.

For those only aware of Michels's authoritarian reputation – he was variously described as The Bull or The General in his managerial role – Haarms painted a different picture of the Michels he knew as a team-mate. He described him as an 'easy-going artist on the pitch, with a taste for practical jokes off it'.[14] When Haarms joined Michels as a coach, though, the change in attitude was obvious. 'He was completely different from when he was a player. The main thing with him now was discipline. Fantastic discipline.'[15] It wasn't the only change. The man who been a relative journeyman as a player would

14 Winner, David, *Brilliant Orange* (London: Bloomsbury, 2000)
15 Winner, David, *Brilliant Orange* (London: Bloomsbury, 2000)

become one of the world's most respected coaches, named as FIFA Coach of the Century in 1999.

The new adherence to discipline was a trait that players at the club also recognised. Piet Keizer had an uneasy relationship with Michels, and although they achieved great success together, the cold detachment of the coach in work matters made it difficult for some players to warm to him. Hulshoff was another who perhaps had more professional respect than affection for Michels. 'Sometimes you hated him,' he explained. 'You could sit with him in a restaurant and he would be nice and talk with you, and he would go on the pitch and be someone else.'[16]

Following retirement from playing, Michels had studied at the Sports Academy Amsterdam, taught gymnastics in a local school and coached an amateur team. When Buckingham was removed in 1965 with the club plagued by concerns of relegation, Ajax turned to their former player. Michels willingly answered the call. In his first game in charge, against MVV Maastricht, Ajax won 9-3. Although the initial impact was impressive, it hardly set the remainder of the season alight. Despite avoiding relegation, of the remaining 11 games, Ajax only won two more, drawing five and losing the others. Nevertheless, the relief of beating the drop was palpable, and the warm memory of those nine goals was enough to secure him in post. It was a first step on an epic journey that would take Ajax to the very pinnacle of European football.

For many, that journey began the day that Michels arrived but, for all that the club were at the wrong end of the table, it would be wrong to think that Buckingham had left Ajax in a tailspin of decline. He had inherited a team in trouble and a club in turmoil. He set to work behind the scenes to turn things around, and the improvement was already beginning to show

16   Winner, David, *Brilliant Orange* (London: Bloomsbury, 2000)

before Michels arrived. In his last seven games, Buckingham guided Ajax to four wins, one draw and two defeats. Michels would later declare the 'the starting point is of course the group of players you have to work with'[17] and, although changes to the team were inevitably required, some of the answers were already at the club. One player in particular.

Reflections on the history of football are full of the 'what if' conundrums. If circumstances had been different, how would the fickle caprices of fate have played out over the years? Often, it's difficult to perceive. On other occasions, however, there seems to be a predestined combination of factors, conspiring to guide someone along a path that delivers a blessed outcome. Such things cannot surely be assigned to the whims of mere chance. When a skinny ten-year-old Johan Cruyff joined the Ajax youth system in 1957, such a divine ploy was initiated. Had the youngster joined any other club, the history of football could have been very different ... if Cruyff would come to define Ajax, then just as definitively, in an act of perfect symbiosis, Ajax would nurture Cruyff.

Whilst at the club Cruyff fell under the beneficial care of coaches who would contribute to his development as a player, and also, in perfect symmetry, add to a growing ethos at the club. The man who first noticed the talents of the young lad kicking a ball in a playground near his house was Ajax youth team coach Jany van der Veen. A former Ajax player, whose career had briefly overlapped with that of Michels, before injury forced his retirement, Van der Veen would later return to the club, serving as a coach with a number of the junior teams, and was acknowledged as the man who first discovered, and then took the young Cruyff to Ajax.

The aspiring footballer, who would become the totem of the club's rise, and of the Oranje of 1974, would later talk of

17   Michels, Rinus, *Teambuilding: the road to success* (Spring City: Reedswain Incorporated, 2003)

his early influences, and describe Van der Veen as being the 'most important',[18] explaining he had a specific training regime that formed the basis of the player's footballing education. Van der Veen's emphasis on what Cruyff described as the 'five basic fundamentals of football: shooting, heading, dribbling, passing and controlling the ball',[19] taught him a lasting kinship with the ball. In the same year that Michels was preserving Ajax's top-tier status, the club's A1 side became national champions, with a team including Cruyff, Hulshoff and Suurbier, all of whom had been discovered by Van der Veen.

When Michels arrived, Cruyff was 18. His footballing education was about to progress from school to university. He possessed a rapacious appetite to learn, not that Michels was any kind university lecturer. Instead, he saw Cruyff, still the youngest player in the team, as the key element in plans to promote his beliefs and take Ajax to a position of prominence. Cruyff recalls how the coach would take him aside after training to discuss tactics and how the team should play.[20] It was a tutorial exclusively granted to the player who would become the new coach's disciple, trusted lieutenant and most ardent advocate. It was a pivotal time for both player and club as Michels launched them towards unheralded success … Ajax would take flight with wings of vivid colours as their Total Football was revealed in all its glory. Their play would illuminate Dutch football.

In his first full season, Michels took Ajax to the Eredivisie title, winning the league by seven points from Feyenoord, losing only a couple of games in the process. Cruyff would top score with an incredible 25 goals in 23 matches. What made the difference? As well as adding players to the team – Henk Groot was brought in from Feyenoord among other arrivals

18 Cruyff, Johan, *My Turn* (London: Macmillan, 2016)
19 Cruyff, Johan, *My Turn* (London: Macmillan, 2016)
20 Cruyff, Johan, *My Turn* (London: Macmillan, 2016)

– Michels also initiated a strict training regime, enforcing the discipline mentioned by Haarms, and deployed a 4-2-4 formation with an emphasis on attack. He also won over the players' loyalty by convincing the club to guarantee their wages. Despite nominally being professionals, most players had to undertake other jobs to supplement their earnings. Cruyff performed odd jobs at the printing works of *Sport World,* including occasionally standing on street corners to sell the magazine, and Swart and Keizer both ran shops. Team spirit clearly benefited from Michels's move.

The following season, the domestic double was achieved. Again, it was Feyenoord in second place, and although the gap to the runners-up was reduced to five points, the astounding total of 122 goals in 34 games – compared to Feyenoord, the next best, scoring 81 – screams of domestic domination, and a five-goal romp against the Rotterdam club illustrated the gap.

Across all competitions, Cruyff hit 34 goals in 33 games, Swart 31, Klass Nuninga and Groot 25. Suurbier was now established in the team and Hulshoff would feature in a third of the league games. The season also saw the arrival of Velibor Vasovic from Partizan Belgrade. The Serb would become an integral part of the club's success and skipper them to their first European triumph in 1971.

The European Cup also entered the crosshairs of Michels for the first time in that season. The previous year's title triumph had granted them an opportunity to measure their progress against Europe's elite clubs. In the first round, home and away victories against Turkish champions Besiktas eased progress to a meeting with Liverpool. It was as far as many – at least outside of the Netherlands, and probably even for some within – expected them to go.

A foggy Olympisch Stadion greeted the English champions on 7 December 1966. The De Meer Stadion was Ajax's official home ground, but big games were often transferred to the larger venue ... Liverpool turned out in an all-red kit and, for the only time in their history, the Dutch champions wore all white. It would be a particularly memorable occasion for the club. Around 150 seconds had been played when, following a throw-in, the ball was whipped into the visitors' box and a header found the back of the net. Cees de Wolf is widely credited with the goal, although other sources suggest Groot was the scorer. Fifteen minutes later, Swart gathered possession and accelerated forward, deceiving three Liverpool players as he scythed through the defence before squaring for Nuninga to shoot. In goal, Tommy Lawrence dived to block, but Cruyff put the rebound away. 'Liverpool are in dire trouble,' explained the BBC television commentator unnecessarily. Worse was to come.

As half-time approached, Tommy Smith fouled Cruyff, giving the home team a free kick. The shot from distance was fired in. Blocks and rebounds saw the ball cannon around in the area before Nuninga drove it home. The incredulous commentator now went into overdrive. 'Oh, my goodness me,' he exclaimed, maintaining the required dignity, before adding 'Oh, dear, dear, dear, dear.' The limits of his stiff-upper-lip mentality were being sorely tested. Other examinations of decorum would follow. When, still ahead of the break, Nuninga added the fourth after a flick by Cruyff, 'Oh, no,' was all he could manage.

By this stage, Suurbier had been limping for some while, but with the action concentrated at the other end of the pitch, it hardly seemed to matter. As the referee ended what had been an incredible display by the Dutch, the outcome was neatly summed up as an 'incredible score'. In the second period, a fierce free kick by Groot made it 5-0 with time almost up, before Chris Lawler dragged back a consolation goal in injury time. For many it was a shock result. Cruyff saw it differently, though, suggesting 'that everything Michels was putting in place was working. In a technical sense, the English champions were blown away.'[21]

Despite Bill Shankly expressing confidence that the deficit could be retrieved at Anfield, it wasn't to be. Cruyff scored twice, giving Ajax the lead each time, before Roger Hunt equalised on both occasions. The game ended 2-2. Ajax had eliminated Liverpool 7-3 on aggregate. It was a major milestone on the club's progress and established their pedigree on the European stage.

The quarter-finals paired Ajax with Dukla Prague and, after a disappointing 1-1 draw in Amsterdam, the second leg was lost when skipper Frits Soetekouw conceded an own goal from a corner in the final minute. Seeing his team dominate the Czechs, but lose out infuriated Michels. Soetekouw would never play for the club again. After the glory of defeating Liverpool, it was this defeat that had the greatest effect on the future of the club. Michels would ruthlessly hack at his team, disposing of players he considered as being ill-equipped for his requirements. Any naivety in the squad would not be tolerated.

It was now that Vasovic arrived, as Michels strengthened the heart of his defence with a purchase and a promotion. Partnering the Serb in the centre of the Ajax defence for the next four years or so would be Barry Hulshoff, promoted for the role. Vasovic was the experienced hand in the back line, Hulshoff eight years his junior. Vasovic was also acutely aware that the team he had joined had potential, but were far from the finished article. Quoted in *Brilliant Orange,* he said, 'But when we got Gerrie Muhren, Barry Hulshoff, Ruud Krol and Johan Neeskens in the team, and Heinz Stuy in goal, we changed the quality.'[22]

Despite the disappointment in Europe, another domestic double was achieved, and many of the players that Michels

---

21   Cruyff, Johan, *My Turn* (London: Macmillan, 2016)
22   Winner, David, *Brilliant Orange* (London: Bloomsbury, 2000)

added to the team would also be selected for the World Cup in 1974. The domestic season would also see Cruyff score what he describes as one of his most memorable goals. Playing against ADO Den Haag, a clearance fell to him as he attempted to tie up a sock. The ball was spinning when it landed at his feet, and as he struck it towards goal – with the string of the sock tie still in his hand – it described a poetic arc and flew into the net. In 1967/68, after being eliminated in the first round of the European Cup, another Eredivisie title offered a route back into the Continent's prime club championship.

The 1968/69 tournament would see their greatest progress so far. The league title was lost to Feyenoord, and an exit from the KNVB Cup in round three concentrated minds on Europe's top club competition. A first-round tie against Nurnberg could have been tricky, especially when Schorsch Volkert put the Germans ahead after five minutes, but a late equaliser from Cruyff calmed things, and a 4-0 win at the Olympisch Stadion eased the way to the second round, where Fenerbahce were eliminated with successive 2-0 victories.

The last eight paired Ajax with Benfica, and when the Dutch stumbled to a 1-3 first-leg defeat in Amsterdam, elimination was beckoning. The Ajax game plan had been hampered by a snow-covered pitch, compromising their normal pattern of play and leaving them vulnerable. The previous season's losing finalists were an outstanding team, though, comprising the talents of Eusebio and Jose Torres in attack and the wily Mario Coluna prompting from midfield, but Michels rallied his troops and, just past the half-hour mark in Lisbon, Ajax had scored three times without reply. Only a late goal from Torres squared the aggregate scores and secured a play-off. The game in Paris ended 0-0 after 90 minutes, but Ajax scored three times in the extra period to qualify for the semi-finals. Michels's team had shown they were building a resilience to add to their talents.

Alongside Ajax, the surviving clubs in the competition were reigning champions Manchester United, AC Milan and the Czech club Spartak Trnava, with the latter drawn against the Dutch champions. A 3-0 home win for Ajax almost certainly secured their place in the final, as Milan deposed of Manchester United. Although Ajax lost the second leg 2-0, the goals from the first leg were just sufficient to take them to their first European Cup Final, against the Italians.

If the games against Liverpool and Dukla Prague had been important in Ajax's development, this game would be a significant milestone, marking the progress achieved so far by Michels, but also indicating how far there was still to go. In a final dominated by the *Rossoneri*, the youthfulness of the Dutch squad was exposed by a team whose savvy had been case-hardened in the toughest league in the world. Milan ran out comfortable 4-1 winners. Hulshoff summed up the difference between the teams. 'They say sometimes you have to lose a final to win a final, and it's true. Later, we learned that if it was not going well for us, we could change ourselves in the game – we could change tactics. Against Milan, we could change nothing. They were too experienced. We were overwhelmed in every way. In every way they were better.'[23]

As with the defeat to Dukla Prague, Michels would change his team once more, removing those whose time had passed and bringing in new players. Before they would have the opportunity to again challenge the Continent's best clubs, however, their rivals from Rotterdam would seize the chance offered by their title-winning season of 1968/69 and become the first Dutch club to be crowned as champions of Europe.

---

23 Winner, David, *Brilliant Orange* (London: Bloomsbury, 2000)

Feyenoord

The success of Ajax and their players who featured in the World Cup squad of 1974 is often allowed to overshadow the triumphs of Feyenoord and their contribution to the Dutch campaign in Germany. The reality is that, although the Amsterdam club had six players in Michels's World Cup squad, Feyenoord had seven, albeit that every Ajax player saw action in the tournament, while only Willem van Hanegem, Wim Jansen, Wim Rijsbergen, Rinus Israel and Theo de Jong made appearances, and the latter two only as substitutes. The history books will nevertheless record that, as Dutch football climbed to the summit of the European game, it was Feyenoord that planted the first Dutch flag on the top of the mountain.

Much as other leagues across Europe are often perceived as duopolies – Real Madrid and Barcelona in Spain, Celtic and Rangers in Scotland, for example – often in the Netherlands from the 1960s to the mid-1970s, if Ajax didn't top the Eredivisie, odds were that it would be Feyenoord. In fact, between the 1959/60 and 1973/74 seasons only twice did the title go elsewhere. Ajax won it seven times, and Feyenoord six.

Although champions in both 1960/61 and 1961/62, it was perhaps the failed European Cup campaign of 1962/63, losing out to Benfica in the semi-finals, that launched the Rotterdam club into their golden era. Much as Ajax had learned valuable lessons from their various setbacks before moving on to greater success, so did Feyenoord. The domestic double was achieved in 1964/65, and then repeated in 1968/69.

The 1960s saw a series of success under Austrian managers. Franz Fuchs had delivered the 1960/61 and 1961/62 titles, and Willy Kment had produced the double-winning team of 1964/65. Then, after Dutchman Ben Peeters had coached Feyenoord to another double triumph in 1968/69, the club hierarchy decided that with a European Cup campaign in prospect for the following season, a stronger character was required to lead the club than the young Peeters, who returned to his role coaching a junior team. They decided to appoint another Austrian, Ernst Happel.

As a player Happel had missed the great Austrian *Wunderteam* by a decade or so, making his international debut in 1947 and taking part in the 1954 World Cup, where his team claimed third place. He moved into coaching in the early 1960s and enjoyed success with unfashionable ADO Den Haag in 1962, transforming the club into a consistent top-six team and winning the KNVB Cup in 1968, after defeating Ajax, before being snapped up by Feyenoord.

Happel would stay in Rotterdam until 1973, before moving to Spain for a largely unsuccessful season with Sevilla. A return to northern Europe and Bruges in Belgium was much more fruitful, bringing three successive league titles and a domestic double, before he was given a chance to take the Dutch national team to a World Cup finals in 1978. That was for the future, though. For the next few years, the competition between the two clubs, and Michels and Happel, would drive each other on to excellence and a level of success that would allow each to reap dividends when leading the Oranje.

Despite the success in securing the domestic double the previous season, Happel quickly sought to strengthen the Feyenoord squad for the European Cup campaign. If the club had aspirations of being serious contenders, a team that had dominated Dutch domestic football offered no guarantee of being strong enough to compete with the Continent's top club sides. In a dramatic change, he replaced goalkeeper and captain Eddy Pieters Graafland with 23-year-old Eddy Treytel, bringing in the younger man from neighbouring Rotterdam club Xerxes. By this time, Pieters Graafland was well into his mid-thirties and it seemed like Happel was ushering the erstwhile No.1 towards the exit. The veteran would return, though, and feature in one more moment of glory during the most important game in the history of the club.

Happel also signed Schalke midfielder Franz Hasil, and left-back Theo van Duivenbode from Ajax. With the emerging talent of Ruud Krol demanding a first-team place, Michels deemed Van Duivenbode surplus to requirements. At the time, it seemed a sensible move for all concerned. Had the defender held any particular grudge against Michels, however, he would take full toll, not only by collecting a European Cup winners' medal in his first term in Rotterdam, but also by scoring the late winning goal at the Stadion de Kuip in February 1969, as his new club defeated his old one in his first *Klassieker* wearing Feyenoord colours.

Happel already had the services of 'Iron Rinus' and coupled with Theo Laseroms they presented a formidable defensive barrier at the heart of the Feyenoord back line. In midfield, three players would be key to the success of Happel's reign. A native of Rotterdam, Coen Moulijn had been with the club since 1955, and to many fans was simply known as Mr Feyenoord. Already approaching his mid-thirties when Happel arrived, the new manager recognised the value of both the experience and talent of the left-winger, plus the kinship he had with the fans who, in modern parlance, considered him to be 'one of their own'. By the time the 1974 World Cup came around, Moulijn would have been retired for two years, having won his last cap for the Oranje in 1969. Two other members of Happel's Feyenoord midfield would, however, be key elements in the Dutch squad.

Wim Jansen was a defensive midfielder player, both for Feyenoord and the Oranje. The man who would later coach Glasgow Celtic in the season when they denied Rangers a tenth successive league title, was already a Dutch international when Happel arrived at the club, having made his debut in 1967 in a European Championship qualifying match in Denmark.

The dogged defensive commitment of the unassuming Jansen is perhaps aptly reflected in the fact that, across 65 games for the national team, he would only score a single goal. It came in the qualifying campaign for the 1970 World Cup, when he netted the opening goal in Luxembourg's nominally home game in the group. Fittingly, it was played at the Stadion de Kuip. Also, providing a neat link, the other player who scored for the Dutch in that game is the other key midfielder in Happel's team.

For many Feyenoord fans, it is Wim van Hanegem who should be regarded as the greatest ever Dutch player, rather than Johan Cruyff. Given both the rivalry between the clubs, and a natural allegiance to another hero of *De club aan de Maas,* such opinion is unsurprising, and whilst there are many differences in style between the two players, each were extravagant talents. The history of Dutch football could well have been quite different had a rumoured transfer taken place. In 1968, the 24-year-old Van Hanegem was playing at the small Rotterdam club Xerxes. The Ajax chairman had spotted the midfielder and told Michels that he was planning to bring him to the club. Whether due to the prospect of having a player he had not selected being merely presented to him as a *fait accompli,* or for more tactical reasons, the coach reportedly rejected the option, apparently declaring that the player was 'Too slow and too one-dimensional.' The chairman relented, and the prospect of two of the greatest Dutch midfielders playing for the same club side slipped away, forever to be buried in the file labelled, 'What Might Have Been'.

Feyenoord clearly disagreed with the Michels assessment, and signed the player who would win the domestic double in his first season, add two more league titles later and, in his second term, lift the European Cup. Later, Van Hanegem would be christened 'De Kromme' (The Crooked) by Feyenoord fans, some say for his ability to curl passes with unerring accuracy, others less kindly suggest it was because of his bandy legs. He would play more than 250 games for Feyenoord, striking over 50 goals from midfield and creating many others, despite his admitted lack of pace. It's something he hardly tried to conceal. Quoted in *The Guardian*, he confessed that, 'As a player, they never had to run after me after a goal. I didn't have the speed for that.'[24]

Michels was a man of firm convictions, but was it an error born of arrogance that prevented Van Hanegem teaming up with Cruyff at Ajax? The latter would acknowledge one of the Feyenoord legend's key talents, in an unusually self-deprecating way confessing that, 'Van Hanegem has one advantage over me. When I have a bad game, I'm useless. When Van Hanegem has a bad game, he rolls up his sleeves and starts tackling.' It's also worth noting that future team-mate, and regular partner alongside the midfielder in the Netherlands national team, Wim Rijsbergen had no doubts about Van Hanegem's ability. 'He had the best left foot I've ever seen,'[25] he explained. Many years later, Johnny Rep would draw another distinction. 'They could both be pretty extreme. But Van Hanegem is fine when you know him. Cruyff is more distant. If you get in bad with him, he'll never speak with you.'

It's worth noting that reports suggest Happel originally had a similar opinion to that of Michels about signing Van Hanegem. The story goes that the club hierarchy instructed the new coach that, if he wanted to sign Hasil, he would have to take Van Hanegem as well. Perhaps less secure in his role as the new manager than Michels was in Amsterdam, Happel conceded. It was a decision he never had cause to regret, until the selection for the 1978 World Cup squad, at least. Van Hanegem and his new coach would develop a kinship of ideas as the player's ability to dictate the pattern of games became an

24   https://www.theguardian.com/football/2001/apr/10/sport.comment1
25   Football's Greatest International Teams, *Sky Sports*, 2010

increasingly valuable asset for Happel. Final vindication would be seen on 6 May 1970, when Jansen, Hasil and Van Hanegem formed the midfield trio of the Feyenoord team that defeated Celtic 2-1 in the European Cup Final. The team that Happel developed had strong echoes of their manager – solid and determined, but also with the tactical flexibility that allowed formations and patterns of play to be adapted as required. It would bring great success in Europe, and also regain the Eredivisie title in 1970/71.

Before that, though, in his first term in Rotterdam, the league title would be lost to Ajax, with Happel's club five points adrift of the new champions, although their defensive record, only conceding 22 goals across 34 games, was the best in the league. Success in Europe, however, would reduce the significance of such brief domestic issues.

The European Cup campaign began with a tie against Icelandic club Knattspyrnudeild Knattspyrnufelag. Both legs would be played in Rotterdam, and in the first, nominally the home leg for the Icelandic club, Happel's team rattled in a dozen goals. Ruud Geels scored four times and Swedish striker Ove Kindvall netted a hat-trick. The Swede had been with Feyenoord since 1966, arriving under Willy Kment. Initially, the move appeared likely to founder as Kindvall struggled to adapt to the professional game in the Netherlands after moving from the more sedate amateur Swedish league. Despite a somewhat less than auspicious opening, the Scandinavian recruit would attain legendary status with Feyenoord.

'The football was so different from what I was used to, and I didn't understand what they were saying,'[26] Kindvall would lament. Things would get better, though, when young Dutch coach Ben Peeters succeeded the Austrian. The double was secured and Kindvall prospered. 'You have to find your

26   Enquist, Anna, *Hard Brood* (Amsterdam: De Arbeiderspers 2016)

way in such a team, know who those guys are, how they are. It was winter and it was so wet! We do not play in the winter [in Sweden], and it is not wet with us either. I don't like playing football in the mud.'[27] Kindvall would go on to score 129 goals in 144 league appearances for the club, but one goal in particular would guarantee him a permanent place in the hearts of Feyenoord fans.

Happel's arrival signalled a new role for Kindvall. Instead of dropping deeper to become more involved and linking play, the Austrian insisted that his striker should stay up front, and save his energies for scoring goals. The move would pay dividends both in this European competition, and the following domestic season, and Kindvall finished as the league's top scorer.

Kindvall bagged another brace when the teams met again at the same stadium, and a further four goals were added to the aggregate victory. The second round would offer a much sterner test. AC Milan had brushed aside the young Ajax team to win the trophy in the previous season and, when the *Rossoneri* were paired with the new champions of the Netherlands, many expected the same outcome. Happel decided on an unexpected plan to contain the reigning champions, and hopefully allow his team to triumph.

It was widely accepted that if Feyenoord were to progress, Van Hanegem and Jansen would need to negate the influences of Giovanni Lodetti and Gianni Rivera. Happel deployed Jansen, his most effective defensive asset in midfield, to mark Rivera, identifying the winner of the previous season's Ballon d'Or as Milan's key player. The consequence was, however, that Van Hanegem would need to press Lodetti. Keeping tabs on Milan's *regista* was hardly suited to the one-paced Dutchman, but with Jansen subduing Rivera, Milan's play would be unsettled. It also meant that Van Hanegem, being in a forward role, would be in prime position to attack any space left by Angelo Sormani if the full-back failed to track back quickly when possession was lost. The plan worked and, in the dying minutes of the return leg, that space would prove to be decisive.

When the teams met for the first leg at the San Siro on 12 November, a goal from Nestor Combin inside the first ten minutes looked to have set them on the road to their expected success. Conceding an early goal spelt danger for Happel's team. Concede again and they would have a mountain to climb back in Rotterdam. A mistake by goalkeeper Treytel nearly brought that second goal, as he scuffed a goal kick straight to Rivera. Fortunately, Israel recovered quickly enough to head the cross clear. Other chances would follow as the Italians pushed for another goal. In a typically attacking position Sormani should have scored when through from the left with just Treytel to beat, but he dragged his shot wide, and Feyenoord held on. At the end of the game, a single-goal deficit meant they were still in the tie, if only just.

Two weeks later, it took the rarest of scorers to open Feyenoord's account. Jansen found himself just inside the Milan penalty area and, whether it was a mis-hit cross, or the most delicate of chipped shots, as the ball left his right foot it arced over Cudicini in the Milan goal, striking the far post and falling into the net. Milan's advantage had lasted all of six minutes. The Italians were nothing if not resilient, however, and despite pressing, the Feyenoord forwards struggled to find another breakthrough. With just three minutes to play, it was another unlikely goal – albeit not unlikely scorer – that sealed the win. Space vacated by Sormani allowed possession to develop on the Feyenoord flank, and a cross found Van Hanegem running into the box. Although his header was near to Cudicini, the ball slipped past the goalkeeper and into the net. Van Hanegem would score many valuable goals in his career, but few would be with his head, and none would be as important as the one that eliminated the European champions.

Feyenoord were into the quarter-finals and would face East German club Vorwarts. In a mirror of the Milan tie, they lost the first leg away to a single goal, but then turned things round back in Rotterdam as strikes from Kindvall and Wery put them into the last four. Avoiding the British clubs – Celtic and Leeds United – Feyenoord were pitted against Polish champions Legia Warsaw. Both legs of the tie would be played in appallingly adverse weather conditions. On 1 April, again drawn to play the away leg first, Feyenoord visited the Polish capital, where heavy rain had turned the Stadion Wojska Polskiego pitch into more mud than grass. As both teams slogged through the heavy conditions, chances were few and far between, and goals non-existent. Rain also dominated the leg in Rotterdam. At least there was more grass than mud on the Stadion de Kuip surface, but the preponderance of umbrellas in the crowd suggested conditions would deteriorate further as the game progressed.

Fortunately, the first home goal came early, as Van Hanegem added another rare header to his collection of goals, nodding in at the far post from a free kick. The goal of the game, however, came from Hasil, who hammered home a volley from 25 yards on the half-hour mark to double the lead. The deteriorating conditions were hardly helpful to any hopes of a Polish fightback, and Feyenoord were through to the European Cup Final, where they would meet Celtic.

A couple of weeks before the final, Feyenoord played an Eredivisie game against Ajax. It would be a fixture of major significance for both clubs. On 26 April 1970, Happel took his team to the De Meer Stadion. Ajax were in pole position to regain the Dutch title and also into the semi-finals of the KNVB Cup. A win against second-placed Feyenoord would almost lock out the title but, with 20 minutes remaining, the visitors were leading 1-3. Kindvall had given Feyenoord an early advanatage, before Swart equalised midway through the first period. The lead had been restored by Hasil and, when Wery scored on 70 minutes, Feyenoord looked likely to throw the title chase open. The visitors' fluid 4-3-3 formation had seen them dominate Ajax's staid 4-2-4, and reports suggest it was this occasion that convinced Michels that if he was to develop his team as he wished, a change to 4-3-3, a system that would lend itself much more easily to Total Football, would be required.

The game convinced the coach to sign Johan Neeskens from RCH Heemstede to make his system work. The league and cup double were secured and the stage was set for Ajax to dominate the Continent's club football for the next few years. It would also have ramifications for Feyenoord's pursuit of European glory. Happel watched in frustration as, with the game apparently won, two mistakes by goalkeeper Treytel allowed Ajax to scrape a 3-3 draw, as first Cruyff then Suurbier capitalised. With the European Cup Final so close, Happel had a choice to make.

Israel had inherited the captain's armband when Pieters Graafland had been displaced and the commanding defender had become not only a key player for Happel, but also someone he would take into his confidence about team selection and tactics. On this occasion, though, the defender had been kept in the dark on the coach's thoughts and, despite Happel's mind being made up days earlier, it wasn't until the eve of the final that his captain was informed that it would be Eddy Pieters Graafland, then well past his 36th birthday, rather than Treytel in goal for the final. Somewhat surprised by what he considered to be a drastic and impetuous decision, he asked the coach for time to consider the matter. Happel was happy to grant his skipper all the time he wanted. Both men knew, however, that once Happel's mind was made up, there would be no changing it.

On 6 May the teams took the field to contest the 1970 European Cup Final at Milan's San Siro. Once again, it was Happel's 4-3-3 formation, full of fluidity and movement, against a 4-2-4 as deployed by Jock Stein. Happel's tactics allowed him to push the hard-working Moulijn up against full-back David Hay. The 33-year-old winger had suffered a slight injury in training the day before the game, following a mistimed challenge from Israel, but nothing would prevent the veteran from playing on his club's greatest day. Happel's plan was to diminish the effect of Hay, cut the service to danger man Jimmy Johnstone, and limit the winger's influence on the game. As with the plan devised to defeat Milan, Happel's ploy worked to perfection. Starved of possession, Johnstone struggled to affect the game, and Feyenoord flourished.

Despite Feyenoord having much of the early game, it was Celtic who scored first. Tommy Gemmill put the Scots ahead, firing in after a free kick was tapped short to him just on the half-hour. Although the shot was struck hard and low, any attempts to save the shot by Pieters Graafland were hardly helped by the strange positioning of Italian referee Concetto Lo Bello, who placed himself behind the defensive wall, and directly in line with Gemmill's shot. Justified Dutch complaints came to naught. It mattered little, though. A mere two minutes later, a cross into the Celtic box saw a period of head tennis concluded when Rinus Israel nodded firmly past Evan Williams to equalise.

That's how things stayed into half-time and throughout the second period, despite the Dutch striking a post. Into extra time and, as both teams began to tire, chances came more frequently, but any winning strike was proving elusive. Just three minutes remained when a Dutch free kick was played towards the Scottish penalty area. With Kindvall closing in behind him, Celtic skipper Billy McNeill back-pedalled frantically into the area to get into a position to head clear, but the flight of the ball deceived him. Stumbling, he reached up a hand, in an attempt to palm the ball away. There was clear contact, and certainly enough to warrant a penalty, but seeing the ball running on to Kindvall, the referee paused before blowing. The Swedish striker wrote his name into the history books of Netherlands football as he delicately clipped the ball over Williams and into the net. Feyenoord became the first Dutch club to win the European Cup. It had hardly been a classic encounter, but the players, fans and coach of the Rotterdam club cared little for that. Recognising the success of Happel's patterns of play, Stein later conceded that, 'Celtic has not lost to Feyenoord. I have lost to Happel.'

Any debut season can be a trial, and one with so much unprecedented success can be a double-edged sword. After winning the country's first major continental club title, a hangover could have been expected in Rotterdam. The following season, though, Happel would regain the title and add the Intercontinental Cup to Feyenoord's trophy cabinet, unofficially making them the best club team in the world, after they defeated Estudiantes of Argentina.

The bar had now been set so high that a fall from such an exalted position was almost inevitable. A shock first-round defeat to little-known Romanian club UT Arad that derailed any hopes of a successful defence of their European crown was difficult to take. To make matters worse for Feyenoord fans, it would be Ajax who took over their mantle as Europe's top club. Kindvall left to return home to Sweden, and Feyenoord struggled to replace their main source of goals. Inevitably, as success and confidence drained away, times became harder, and unrest followed. In 1973 Happel left the Dutch club football scene for a brief stay in Spain, before returning to northern Europe and Bruges, where those three successive

Belgian titles, including one domestic double, were sufficient to propel him back into the attention of the KNVB.

Happel's legacy at Feyenoord was clear. It would be wrong to say that his time at the club had invented Total Football, but it had certainly influenced its development, and his contribution to the success of the game in the Netherlands should not be understated. After leaving Feyenoord, it would be four years before he re-enters this story. In 1977, he was invited to take over the Dutch national team targeting the 1978 World Cup. Before that though, Feyenoord would rise again, and another generation of players would feed into their particular story, and that of the Netherlands national team.

Ajax again

As the Rotterdam club conquered Europe's premier club competition, Ajax were compelled to seek solace in the Inter-Cities Fairs Cup. A decent run took them to the semi-final and a tie against Arsenal. Moving into April 1970, things were looking brighter for Michels. Top of the Eredivisie, into the quarter-finals of the KNVB Cup and semi-finals of a European competition – the final couple of months of the season held out great promise. Despite disposing of local rivals DWS to reach the last four of the domestic cup, TS Eliot's poetic assertion that 'April is the cruellest month'[28] was shown to be prophetic.

Travelling to north London on 8 April, a comprehensive three-goal defeat left Ajax with a difficult task in Amsterdam the following week, and a single goal by Gerrie Muhren was insufficient to turn things around. Four days later, Ajax visited Utrecht to play struggling VV DOS in a league game and took out their frustration with seven goals. When DWS were beaten 1-2 a few days later, the loss to Arsenal was beginning

28   Eliot, TS, *The Waste Land* (New York: Boni & Liveright 1922)

to look like an unfortunate blip on the Ajax journey to success. A roadblock was waiting though.

It was now that the game with Feyenoord mentioned previously took place. Michels watched as his team were dominated by the club who would, shortly afterwards, ascend to the European crown. His two-man midfield of Nico Rijnders – who would tragically collapse and die whilst playing for Bruges on 16 March 1976 – and Muhren was overrun by Happel's fluid 4-3-3, and the Rotterdam club were clearly the dominant force, despite the home team salvaging a fortunate draw. There's a Dutch phrase, 'Meten is weten' (Measuring things brings knowledge). Michels took the necessary knowledge from the game, and sought to fine-tune his squad. The musical metaphor was not alien to Michels. Neeskens would be added, and Total Football would sound all the sweeter for the change … The league and cup double was secured and, the following season, Ajax embarked on a European journey that would take the club to legendary status.

The new season would also see new faces make their mark in the Ajax shirt. German-born goalkeeper Heinz Stuy had been signed from Telstar in 1967, but had only played nine times in the 1968/69 season. That would increase to 13 the following year, and by the time Ajax started the 1970/71 season, he was the undisputed first choice. Often overlooked, cast into the shadows of his more illustrious team-mates, following Ajax's three European Cup successes, Stuy would hold the record for most consecutive minutes unbeaten in European Cup finals at 270, until Sepp Maier passed it in 1976, accumulating 276; albeit thanks to a replay in the first of Bayern Munich's finals. It meant that Stuy remained the only goalkeeper to play in three European Cup finals and not concede a goal.

Neeskens joined in July 1970, and immediately took his place in Michels's new three-man midfield. He would play

48 games across all competitions in his first season with the club. Only Stuy would play more with 49. German defender Horst Blankenburg moved from 1860 Munich in December 1970 and, although he only featured in a dozen or so games in that first term, he would eventually displace Vasovic, who retired in January 1971, and become the long-term partner of Hulshoff. As with Stuy, Blankenburg is also often considered to be one of the more peripheral figures of the great Ajax team, but it was his defensive ability and application that allowed Hulshoff to develop into a powerful libero. Hulshoff would later explain that, 'When I came out [with the ball] Vasovic would take my place, and later Blankenburg did the same thing. We were so strong it was no longer a risk, we never felt we were taking a risk.'[29]

Arie Haan had signed in October 1967 from the amateur club WVV 1896 for 3,000 guilders. The midfielder was following in the footsteps of Klaas Nuninga. At the time, it was the set fee for a player moving from amateur football to a professional club. (In 2002, the guilder was replaced by the euro at an exchange rate of 2.2 guilders = 1 Euro. Even taking inflation into account, the amount is trifling when measured against the success Haan enjoyed with Ajax.) Haan had just turned 19, and he would have to wait for his chance to break into the first team. Along with Blankenburg, he would come off the bench in the 1971 European Cup Final – and score the second goal – but be a fixture in the team for the next two triumphs and, in 1974, provide Michels with a typically Total Football solution to a perplexing problem after Blankenburg turned down the chance to do so.

Finally, a player who would star in two European Cup triumphs and feature in both the 1974 and 1978 World Cups also joined the club during this season. Johnny Rep moved into

29   Winner, David, *Brilliant Orange* (London: Bloomsbury, 2000)

the Ajax youth structure in early January 1970, but wouldn't join the first-team squad until 12 months later, and his debut would have to wait until the early days of 1971/72. From there, though, his blond flowing locks and teen-idol looks would mark him out as an iconic part of both the Ajax and Dutch teams.

Michels now had his team ready, and Total Football was about to sweep across Europe. After their early days of success, teams had now built seemingly impenetrable walls of packed defenders to counteract the threat offered by Ajax. Encouraging players to switch positions intelligently opened up a further dimension to create space and pull defensive shapes apart. As the coach explained, 'In the fourth and fifth year [of my time at Ajax] I tried to find guidelines that meant we could surprise a little of those walls. I had to let midfield players and defensive players participate in the building up and in the attacking. It's easy to say, but it's a long way to go because the most difficult thing is not to teach a full-back to participate in attacking – because he likes that – but to find someone else who is covering up. In the end, when you have the mobility, the positional play of such a team makes everyone think, "I can participate too, it's very easy." And then you have reached the top, the paramount of the development.'[30]

Or, to put it another way, reaching back to that musical metaphor again, Michels said, 'Football coaches have often been compared to conductors. Every musician plays his own role and instrument in an orchestra. It is not only the task of the conductor to ensure that every one of the individual musicians is able to contribute, he must also ensure that the result is harmonic. It is the important prerequisite to achieve a unique performance, which is greater than the sum of the individual achievements of all musicians together.'[31]

30   Winner, David, *Brilliant Orange* (London: Bloomsbury, 2000)
31   Michels, Rinus, *Teambuilding: the road to success* (Spring City: Reedswain Incorporated, 20031)

Ajax's return to the European Cup began against Albanian champions 17 Nentori, and the positional flexibility was clearly having an effect as Ajax led 2-0 at the hour mark, with both goals coming from right-back Suurbier. A 2-0 victory in Amsterdam got the show on the road but, overall, it was a pedestrian performance, rather than one that offered up great promise. Cruyff was absent for both legs, sidelined by a groin injury sustained against Bruges in the final pre-season friendly. Dick van Dijk replaced him, but Muhren wore Cruyff's No.9 shirt.

In the next round, Ajax played at home in the first leg against Swiss side Basel. A 3-0 victory, again without Cruyff, suggested an easy task in the return game. Before that, however, came one of those legendary occasions that you just hope has been honestly recorded. Cruyff would return for the next but one game, an Eredivisie fixture against PSV Eindhoven. Then, still only 23, but already the key member of the squad, legend has it that, on his return, although still retaining his own place, Muhren offered the No.9 shirt to Cruyff. He declined, however, returning it and declaring that it would be wrong to take the shirt from him. Cruyff then reached for the next unallocated shirt in the pile. He picked up No.14. Muhren scored the winning goal in that game wearing No.9, and Cruyff would for ever more be known for that No.14.

Sporting his new number, Cruyff returned for the away leg in Switzerland. Basel scored from a penalty ten minutes before half-time, but any undue concerns were quickly put to rest as Rijnders and Neeskens netted second period goals to secure victory, qualification for the last eight and a meeting with the previous season's beaten finalists, Celtic. If Stein's team were in the mood for some revenge against a Dutch club after their loss to Feyenoord, it looked like some measure of satisfaction would be achieved, as the first leg in Amsterdam remained goalless with an hour played. Things would then change dramatically, however.

A long punt downfield from Stuy was wonderfully flicked on by Neeskens to find Cruyff clear on goal. A right-foot finish closed out the move. It had hardly been the epitome of Total Football but it opened the door. Seven minutes later, as Cruyff stood over a free kick on the edge of the Celtic box, Hulshoff came running past him to power a shot into the bottom corner of the net. Two goals may well have been enough but, in the final minute, after drifting out to the left, as Keizer slotted into the central role he had vacated, Cruyff cut inside, drifted past a man and played the ball into the feet of the erstwhile left-winger. With an elegant turn, Keizer slipped past his marker and fired high into the net. A single goal by Jimmy Johnstone on 14 March was all the Scots could muster in the home leg. It was the first goal Stuy and his back line had conceded in a competitive fixture since a 5-1 victory against Go Ahead Eagles on 7 February. In the same period, they had found the back of their opponents' net no less than 17 times. Ajax were into the semi-finals. They were scoring goals and hardly conceding at the other end. The omens looked good. The semi-final against Atletico Madrid, however, would be a stern test.

Visiting the Estadio Vicente Calderon on 14 March, Ajax were faced by a team that had won the La Liga title by a single point from Athletic Bilbao, with both Barcelona and Real Madrid trailing well behind. Coached by Frenchman Marcel Domingo, Atletico boasted the firepower of Jose Eulogio Garate and Luis Aragones. For all that goalscoring potential, it was midfielder Javier Irureta who gave the home side the lead just before the break. They would maintain the advantage until full time. Ajax would need to overcome the deficit two weeks later in Amsterdam.

Another goal for the Spanish champions in Amsterdam would mean that Ajax needed three, but it was the Dutch who scored the early goal. Bursting forward from midfield, Cruyff skimmed past one challenge before being crudely upended some 35 yards from goal. Keizer struck the free kick with such venom that it was still rising when it crashed into the Madrid net, with goalkeeper Rodri comprehensively beaten.

Rodri and his defenders, though, refused to capitulate under pressure. In the previous league season, they had only conceded 22 goals across the 30-game programme. They would make Michels's team work for any further goals. With just 12 minutes remaining, extra time was beckoning, when a speculative shot from Suurbier squirmed past Rodri to put Ajax in front. A third goal from Neeskens confirmed that Ajax would follow in Feyenoord's footsteps and reach the European Cup Final. Two years previously, it was a young, immature Ajax that had been comfortably beaten by AC Milan. This time, now with a more rounded team, things would be different. There was a downside to the match, though, as Ruud Krol suffered a broken fibula, effectively ending his season. The defender's injury opened the door for Horst Blankenburg to take his place in the following games, but in the final Michels would come up with a different solution.

Following the win over the Spaniards, Ajax went six Eredivisie games unbeaten, winning five of them in pursuit of Feyenoord. They also won the KNVB Cup, beating Sparta Rotterdam 2-1 on 20 May, but a 3-1 home defeat to Happel's team a week before the European Cup Final, despite leading 1-0 at half-time, both scuppered any hope of the league title, and concentrated minds on lifting the big trophy.

In front of more than 83,000 fans at Wembley stadium on 2 June 1971, Ajax faced Greek champions Panathinaikos in the European Cup Final. The team coached by Hungarian legend Ferenc Puskás were, and at the time of writing remain, the only Greek team to reach the final of European club football's premier competition, but it would be wrong to consider them as easy opposition. As well as having the tall and muscular Antonis Antoniadis, whose ten goals would make him the tournament's top scorer, to lead their line, they had displayed both tenacity and character to reach the Wembley showpiece. Victory over Everton in the last eight and Red Star Belgrade in the semi-final, had both been achieved on away goals, the latter after a storming 3-0 home leg turned around a 4-1 defeat in Belgrade.

With Krol unavailable, Michels left Blankenburg on the bench, instead opting to deploy the versatile Neeskens as an emergency defender. It was a typical Michels solution to an issue he would also face three years later in the World Cup, where he would come up with a similar answer. As events panned out, though, both the German defender and Arie Haan came on just after the break, replacing Rijnders and Swart. By that time, Ajax had been ahead for almost 40 minutes.

With just five minutes on the clock, Hulshoff strode forward in typically powerful fashion and arrowed a pass out to Keizer on the left flank. Gliding past Aristidis Kamaras, the winger then crossed for Van Dijk to head home, cleverly wrong-footing goalkeeper Ikonomopoulos, glancing the ball inside the far post. For the remainder of the game, Ajax would control most of the possession and, with Hulshoff negating the danger of Antoniadis and Vasovic sweeping up any odd danger that escaped his partner, the Greek team looked beaten before Haan's killer blow was delivered in the dying minutes.

A goal worthy of the Michels philosophy, it came from an intricate move only slightly compromised by a deflected finish. Neeskens weaved between two tiring Greeks, and played the ball into midfield. A pass then found Cruyff driving towards the box from the right before flicking a neatly disguised pass to the running Haan, whose shot was half-blocked, deceiving Ikonomopoulos and finding the net. Five minutes later, English referee Jack Taylor ended the game and Ajax had their first European Cup. Three years later, Taylor would also play a major part in the Oranje's biggest day so far.

The game marked a milestone in the story of Dutch football. It was both a moment of triumph for Michels, and a fitting end to his journey in Amsterdam. After returning for the final league fixture of the season, a 4-1 win over Go Ahead Eagles, he left the club. For all the success Ajax had enjoyed, they were hardly one of the financial powerhouses of Europe's footballing elite, and Michels was seduced away by the siren calls of Barcelona.

Ajax were left in a precarious position, although some of their players were less upset by the news than others. Legend has it that Piet Keizer jumped on a nearby table and danced when he was told the coach was moving to Spain. The two men had endured a difficult and often strained relationship, the result of which would play out in Germany three years later. Regardless of in-house discord, the club's success had been built by the man who was now leaving.

At such times, clubs can easily stumble off in the wrong direction and see their hard-won progress melt away, but the appointment of Romanian Stefan Kovacs was inspired, and after what now seems a strange period when he was almost removed by the club after perceived lapses of style, a players' rebellion, led of course by Cruyff, put such ill-considered talk away, and Ajax prospered anew. Kovacs arrived from Steaua Bucharest, where he had won one league title and two domestic cups in three seasons. It was hardly an overwhelmingly inspiring CV, but aside from his time as a player with the club, very much the same could have been said about the appointment of Michels.

A legend has attached itself to the appointment of Kovacs. The club apparently took the view that, with the Michels philosophy now ingrained in the players, the next coach would be fairly peripheral to how the team played, and that success would follow as a matter of course. *The Guardian* reported that they drew up a list of 15 possible coaches, and chose Kovacs because he was the least expensive option.[32] It sounds naïve in the extreme, but sometimes fortune smiles on those who perhaps need it the most, and that certainly seemed the case here ... Even after the appointment, Kovacs felt that his time in Amsterdam may be brief, buying a return rather than one-way ticket when he travelled to the Netherlands. The second portion of that ticket wouldn't be required for a while, however.

Many have considered that Kovacs was merely following the template left by his predecessor, and any success he enjoyed was more down to what he didn't do than what he changed as coach. That, however, is grossly unfair. His ways were different, and there was a need to first conquer a belief amongst the squad that the new coach was unworthy of the club and his exalted position as the heir to Michels. As is so often the case with a group of Dutch footballers, opinions of the new coach differed. As with the old adage about economists, you could probably put three Dutch footballers in a room and end up with five different opinions – and each one would be held passionately.

Muhren, for example, had reservations. 'Kovacs was a good coach, but he was too nice. Michels was more professional. He was very strict, with everyone on the same level. In the first year with Kovacs we played even better because we were good players who had been given freedom. But after that the discipline went and it was all over. We didn't have the same spirit. We could have been champions of Europe for ever if we'd stayed together.'[33] Others, however, were more positive, feeling that the new regime, far less restrictive than that of the authoritarian Michels, actually helped the squad to develop.

---

32 The man who took Ajax to new heights and the brink of destruction, *The Guardian*, 8 January 2008

33 Winner, David, *Brilliant Orange* (London: Bloomsbury, 2000)

Rep, for example, perhaps influenced by youthful exuberance, suggested that, 'The players were fed up with the hardness and discipline of Michels.'[34]

Two issues initially faced the new man. The ill-fated Rijnders was sold to Bruges and Vasovic announced his retirement. Instead of seeking expensive replacements, however, Kovacs slid Blankenburg in alongside the established Hulshoff, the quietly efficient technician, alongside the ebullient titan. Haan would be established in midfield, as would Neeskens, relieved of any further requirement to play in the back line, as Krol, now recovered, became established as the nominal defender of the left flank. Not only was the Ajax team assuming the familiar look that would take them on to greater success, the nucleus of the Dutch team for the 1974 World Cup was also taking shape.

The Romanian was astute enough, though, to recognise that having Cruyff on his side was key, and he focused on that, making the club icon the centrepiece of his strategy. It's often a thin line to tread when one player is recognised as being more than the first among equals; especially when that player had the dominant personality of Cruyff. Rep would later assert that Cruyff's influence over the coach was detrimental to the team, asserting that Kovacs did not have the guts[35] to select him in front of Swart until Cruyff gave his assent to the move. Perhaps such sentiment was merely an aggrieved player venting his frustration. Other reports suggest that Kovacs understood how to handle his captain. Ahead of one game, Cruyff was complaining of a knee injury, saying that he couldn't play. The coach produced a 1,000 guilders banknote, and rubbed it therapeutically on the apparently injured knee, suggesting that the action would solve the problem. Cruyff apparently smiled, agreed and played.

34   Winner, David, *Brilliant Orange* (London: Bloomsbury, 2000)
35   Winner, David, *Brilliant Orange* (London: Bloomsbury, 2000)

Whatever the fluctuating opinions of his players, the new coach's plan prospered ... Kovacs grafted his own approach on to the Michels philosophy, the club's run of success continued, and their style of play flourished. In *The Guardian*, Jonathan Wilson said, 'Ajax almost certainly produced their most eye-catching football under Kovacs.'[36] Cruyff didn't demur from such an assertion, confirming that, 'the results show that Kovacs was not wrong.'[37]

In his first term with the club, Kovacs led Ajax to a domestic double and also returned them to the European Cup Final to defend their trophy, although strangely, their progress was almost halted by a boardroom decision to remove him. Taking a single goal lead to face Benfica at Lisbon's Estadio da Luz, Ajax delivered a disciplined performance to return with a goalless draw sending them to a final, held at arch-rivals Feyenoord's Stadion De Kuip. Ajax had qualified as holders, but with Happel's team winning the Eredivisie title, the Netherlands had two clubs in the competition. In the previous round, however, the Portuguese champions had trounced Feyenoord 5-1, easily overturning a single-goal deficit from the leg in Rotterdam. Ajax wouldn't fall to the same fate.

Back in domestic football, Ajax had also recently beaten Feyenoord 5-1 in a league game in Rotterdam, were five points clear at the top of the Eredivisie and had reached the KNVB Cup Final. At such times, Dutch football has a tendency to turn success into a crisis, and so it was here. Concerned that recent displays, and in particular the dogged goalless draw in Portugal, was not worthy of the club and its self-perception, the club hierarchy began to doubt the wisdom of their appointment. Additionally, amid rumours of ill-discipline amongst the players, Han Grijzenhout, an assistant coach, and

36   The man who took Ajax to new heights and the brink of destruction, *The Guardian* – 8 January 2008
37   Wilson, Jonathan, *Inverting the Pyramid* (London: Orion, 2014)

the club doctor John Rollink reported that Kovacs had lost control of the players. It reads like some kind of footballing 'palace coup', but the board were apparently swayed and, after holding a 'crisis' meeting, resolved to dismiss Kovacs.

There may well have been merit in the reports passed to the club's hierarchy, but the players were content both with the progress the club had made and, perhaps more pertinently, the enhanced freedom offered by Kovacs after the suffocating strictness of Michels. Led, inevitably, by Cruyff, they made their feelings clear to the board and the decision was reversed. Perhaps conversely, the reversal actually proved the validity of the accusations, and the power of the players. A few weeks later, however, any concerns of style were dismissed as an exuberant performance against Internazionale not only retained the European Cup, but also confirmed that the dominant paradigm of European club football was now Total Football. Catenaccio was summarily dismissed.

It had been an entrancing display, as David Winner enthused in *Brilliant Orange*. 'I was hooked … Ajax played with a gorgeous, hyper-intelligent swagger. They ran and passed the ball in strange, beguiling ways, and flowed in exquisite, intricate, mesmerising patterns around the pitch. They won 2-0 but it could have been five or six. Ajax were like beings from a different, more advanced football civilisation. They were warm and fun to watch. They were clearly wonderful.'[38]

The physical appearance of the Ajax players in the final also offered up a nice metaphor for the direction of travel of their football. Whilst Michels had been strict and organised, preferring his players to look smart, almost to a man in this game – Stuy being the notable exception – the players all had long hair, very much in keeping with the mood of the rebellious nature sweeping across Europe. At his first training

---

38 Winner, David, *Brilliant Orange* (London: Bloomsbury, 2000)

session with the club, the story goes, a player asked Kovacs, 'How do you like the length of our hair?' Perhaps sensing an opportunity to distance himself from Michels and accrue favour with his squad, the Romanian apparently replied, 'I've been employed as a coach, not a hairdresser.' Whether the story is true or not is hardly the point; the spirit had changed, and the more relaxed attitude of the new coach clearly fed through to his players. If Michels had created Total Football, it was Kovacs who gave it free rein to flourish. As Cruyff later said, 'Our team was ready to take part in making decisions.'[39]

Despite this, it was two very un-Total Football goals that won the trophy. Firstly, Cruyff profited from a mix-up between goalkeeper Ivano Bordon and one of his defenders, allowing a cross to drop to the Dutchman to steer into an empty net, and then a header, by the same player, from a corner. Conversely, one particular moment of magic is often overlooked. Although two years later, he presented the move to the world in the biggest football tournament on the planet, it's often missed that Cruyff gave a tantalising glimpse of his 'turn' in the final against Inter. Sad to say, though, this freedom, belief and, some may say arrogance, that had made the team great, would also be their curse. It was a cautionary tale, regrettably unheeded, for what would occur in Germany two years later.

Next season produced another glorious haul of silverware. After their victory in the 1971 European Cup, Ajax had opted out of the Intercontinental Cup games against the champions of South America. In September 1972, however, a 1-1 draw in Argentina against Independiente was followed up with a 3-0 home victory to replicate the achievement of Feyenoord. Dutch football was becoming lord of all it surveyed.

In early 1972, another trophy was added when the European Super Cup was lifted, defeating Scotland's Rangers

39   Wilson, Jonathan, *Inverting the Pyramid* (London: Orion, 2014)

both home and away. The Eredivisie was secured with plenty to spare. Ajax won 30 of their 34 games, scoring 102 goals and topping the league by 13 points. By now, however, the true measure of the club was in the Continent's most prestigious club tournament. Ever since Real Madrid's run of five consecutive titles in the early days of the competition, both Benfica and Inter had won, and then retained, the title. To lift themselves above these achievements, Ajax needed to go one better, and show that they should be considered alongside the legendary Spanish club. As fate would have it, each of their ties in the 1972/73 tournament would be significant, one for establishing legendary status, the other two for holding ill portents of the future.

After receiving a bye in the first round, Ajax faced CSKA Sofia, running out comfortable 6-1 aggregate winners. Almost a year later, in the 1973/74 tournament, a 2-0 defeat in the Bulgarian capital would see the Dutch club lose a European Cup tie for the first time in almost four years. By this time, Kovacs and Cruyff would have left – the former to take over as national manager of France, and the latter to join his old coach and mentor in Barcelona. It would be the end of an era.

In the quarter-finals, they faced Bayern Munich and, in what was one of the final glorious flourishes of the team, destroyed the club that would inherit their crown as champions of Europe the following year. A 4-0 victory was more than enough to overcome a 2-1 defeat in Munich. The scoreline paints a picture of enduring domination, but the story of the game itself suggests something a little different, and was perhaps an indication of what was to come.

German author, journalist, broadcaster and presenter, Raphael Honigstein, explains why. 'By 1974 [elements of Total Football], changing positions to avoid marking for example, had already taken hold in Germany. In the 1973 game between Bayern and Ajax, you see a lot of the German players doing things that would have been seen as intrinsically Dutch at the time. … Defenders going forwards, people moving around. So, a lot of the Dutch football had already been adopted by the better German teams. You had to go where your marker didn't want to be. So, it was less a big philosophical construct, but more the consequence of having skilled players. Breitner playing left-back and midfield. Beckenbauer, a midfield player, playing in defence. These things were happening at Bayern and in Germany at the time, but they just never had the same kind of philosophical underpinnings. So, the story became that the Dutch were the team that do it, and everything else had to be different.[40]

Perhaps the result allowed the Dutch to think otherwise. The following season would offer some validation of Raphael Honigstein's assessment, but for now Ajax continued towards their third European triumph. The final four pitched them into a confrontation with a Real Madrid side keen to re-establish their credentials. Leading 2-0 inside the final five minutes in Amsterdam, a useful lead looked to be secured for the second leg, but a late goal for the visitors by Pirri changed all that. The tie was in the balance again.

The new rulers of Europe overcame the old aristocrats, however, with an exceptional performance at the Estadio Santiago Bernabeu, capped by a 1-0 win thanks to a goal from Muhren, and an elaborate piece of control and ball-juggling by the same player. After controlling a 50-yard pass from Krol, he flicked the ball up in the air, two, three times, before cradling it on his foot. Was it arrogance? Some would argue so. Others would contend, though, that it was confidence and self-assurance; an expression of joy in ability. The new order was confirmed. 'It was the moment when Ajax and Real Madrid changed positions,' said Muhren much later. 'Before then it

40   Raphael Honigstein – Interview with the author.

was always the big Real Madrid and the little Ajax. When they saw me doing that, the balance changed.'[41]

The final was another game against the champions of Italy. This time it was the Old Lady of Turin who turned up in Belgrade to try and usurp the new order ruling European football. Due to the similarity of first-choice shirts, Ajax played in all-red. If they looked different however, their football still shone like a beacon. In typically contrary fashion, however, it was another header that won the game. With five minutes played, Blankenburg, supporting the attack, curled a cross to the far post where Rep outjumped his marker to loop a header past Dino Zoff.

For most of the remaining time, the champions comfortably held the Juventus forwards at bay with Hulshoff shackling the dangerous Altafini. 'Juventus were so frightened,' Rep remembered. 'We were surprised. A good team but they did nothing. They seemed satisfied to lose 1-0. We were waiting for them. Come! But nothing. For the public, I'm afraid, it was a very bad game.'[42] The victory margin could have been wider, but Zoff smothered a powerful long shot from Haan – something he would fail to do five years later in Argentina – and a Hulshoff header hit the bar.

At the final whistle, it was Cruyff, wearing an exchanged Juventus shirt, who became the third Ajax captain to lift the European Cup, following Vasovic in 1971 and Keizer in 1972. Four days later, they would travel to Tilburg to face Willem II. In what was both a celebration and perhaps also a wake, Ajax rattled up a 7-2 win, with Cruyff scoring twice. He would play two more Eredivisie games in the new season, before leaving for Catalunya, to rejoin Michels. His final game would be a 6-1 rout against FC Amsterdam on 19 August 1973. He would provide assists for three of the first five Ajax goals, but scored

41   Wilson, Jonathan, *Inverting the Pyramid* (London: Orion, 2014)
42   https://www.theguardian.com/football/2001/apr/10/sport.comment1

the sixth himself, running clear before nutmegging goalkeeper Jan Jongbloed on 70 minutes. He was then substituted, and the crowd at the De Meer offered up both thanks to their talismanic player and concern about the club's fortunes without Cruyff.

The following season, without the coach and iconic player, a decline set in. The club brought in George Knobel from MVV Maastricht to take over from Kovacs. His tenure would be both short and largely unsuccessful, although an astonishing 6-0 home victory against AC Milan, following a 1-0 defeat in Italy, did secure the European Super Cup. It would be their only trophy that season. Later, Knobel would leave to replace Michels at the head of the national team following the 1974 World Cup.

That loss to CSKA Sofia ended Ajax's European dominance, but worse was to follow. A serious knee injury to Hulshoff midway through the first half of an Eredivisie game against NAC Breda on 10 February denied the club of the defender's services, and the season fell away. The injury would also prevent Hulshoff taking part in the Dutch World Cup squad a few months later, ending his international career, and hugely restricting a talent that was in full bloom. Exit from the KNVB Cup in the semi-final and a third place in the league was a poor return compared to the riches of previous years. Meanwhile, Feyenoord were experiencing something of a revival.

Feyenoord again
With Ajax in decline, it was Feyenoord who came to the fore again, winning the Eredivisie title in 1973/74. After Happel left in 1973, Ad Zonderland briefly took charge until Wiel Coerver was appointed. The man now famed for his Coerver Method coaching schools led the team to the title, and also added the UEFA Cup in the same year. After triumphing over

VfB Stuttgart in the semi-final, 4-3 on aggregate, Feyenoord faced Tottenham Hotspur in the two-legged final. A 2-2 draw in north London, thanks to a late goal by Theo de Jong, opened up the tie and a 2-0 victory at home in Rotterdam, with strikes from Rijsbergen and Peter Ressel, secured the trophy.

Coerver had guided the club to glory largely working with the same squad that Happel had left, including all of the Feyenoord players that would go to the World Cup – Eddy Treytel, Rinus Israel, Wim Jansen, Wim Rijsbergen, Harry Vos, Wim van Hanegem and Theo de Jong – the only Feyenoord player to score in the World Cup for the Dutch. Rijsbergen, the most junior member at 22 years of age, had joined in 1971.

The links that bind again

As the Ajax team drifted apart, the club wouldn't be champions of the Netherlands again until 1977. 'The biggest problem was that everything was so easy,' recalled Rep. 'It was such a good team. The players had won everything. They needed another challenge, another team, another club. We had won everything.'[43] Despite the domestic reverse, however, the work of Michels and Kovacs had produced a core of players that would excel for the Oranje. In Rotterdam, a similar situation was apparent. Following Coerver's success in winning both the Eredivisie title and the UEFA Cup in 1974, Feyenoord, who officially changed the name of the club from the Dutch spelling Feijenoord in the same year, would not win another trophy until 1980.

The years of rivalry and success both domestically and across Europe would hardly be squandered, though. Surely an unintended happy consequence of that glorious half-dozen

43   Winner, David, *Brilliant Orange* (London: Bloomsbury, 2000)

or so years, when the football of Ajax and Feyenoord became so successful, was the production and development of an outstanding group of players for the Oranje. Although with different coaches across the two clubs, they had been schooled in a way of playing that not only brought out the best in them, but also created a conviction that they could not only compete with the very best, but also overcome them.

Along the way, they had captivated many young fans who were developing a love of the game at the time, but there was always one main star. A young boy in Scotland who would grow up to become a European football journalist, Graham Hunter, was no exception. 'By 1974 I had been pretty much captivated … Cruyff, from the first moment I saw him, whether it was his balance, his slenderness, his angular face, his unusual haircut, his grace … my eye was hypnotically drawn towards Cruyff.'[44]

The Ballon d'Or holder, who would win the prize again later that same year, would have a stage and cast worthy of star billing in the upcoming World Cup, as Hunter suggests. 'I'd been particularly enchanted by Rensenbrink and to some degree Johnny Rep, I very much liked Neeskens. The way Neeskens looked, as skilled as he was, a worker and a turbine in the midfield […] It just totally fixated me that Johan Cruyff and Johan Neeskens were so different in everything that they did, but they were a partnership for club and country.'[45] The value of Neeskens to the Dutch machine, and his partnership with Cruyff, was immense, as *Gazzetta dello Sport* journalist Alex Frosio confirmed, describing him as the 'Perfect incarnation of that kind of football: eclectic, athletic, perfect partner for Cruyff.'[46]

44   Hunter, Graham – Interview with the author
45   Hunter, Graham – Interview with the author
46   Frosio, Alex – Interview with the author

In 1972, the Netherlands entered the qualifying competition for the World Cup in West Germany as a country with an international record that would roughly rank them alongside the likes of Luxembourg. By the time they reached the tournament in 1974, however, they had a group of players well accustomed to success at the highest of club levels, and the player lauded as the best on the planet. The contrast was strange but, in the realms of Dutch football, strange things were hardly unusual. All that was needed now was to qualify and to have the right coach in charge for the tournament. The destination was clear, but there would be a few bumps along that road.

PART 3

The 1974 World Cup

Qualification

Despite Fadrhonc's failure to lead the Oranje to the European Championship of 1972, he was retained for the run to the next World Cup. If his squad of players had been merely maturing up to the turn of the decade, by the time the qualification process for 1974 began late in 1972, there was clearly a wealth of experienced talent to select from.

After the failed European campaign, Fadrhonc led the Dutch in four friendly games. Wins at home against Scotland and Peru, together with successful visits to Greece and Czechoslovakia, suggested things may well be on the upswing. Only qualification for the next World Cup would confirm that, though.

The Dutch were placed into a group alongside Belgium, Norway and Iceland, with only the group winners progressing. It always looked like the games with their neighbours and regular opposition would be the deciding factor – and so it proved. By the time the Dutch played the first of their qualifying games on 1 November 1972, the Belgians had already recorded home and away wins over Iceland and won 2-0 in Oslo. It meant, therefore, that if they could then complete the run by beating the Norwegians at home, a game scheduled for October 1973, the Netherlands would need to both repeat their neighbours' victories, preferably with a better goal difference, fare better in the head-to-head confrontations, or probably both. There was little room for error.

Despite still being goalless after the first half-hour, a thumping 9-0 win at home to Norway was the sort of start both Fadrhonc and his players needed to set them off in hot pursuit of the Belgians. A couple of weeks later, they were to visit Antwerp for the first of those key matches. For both of the opening games, unsurprisingly, the Oranje selection was dominated by players from Ajax and Feyenoord. For the game in Belgium, eight of the eleven starters came from those two clubs. Only established goalkeeper Jan van Beveren from PSV Eindhoven, and the young pair of Den Haag defender Aad Mansveld and MVV Maastricht forward Willy Brokamp, both winning their third caps, disturbed the duopoly. A goalless draw felt like a highly satisfactory result with which to end the year for the Dutch. Jean Thissen striking a post for the home team was as near as anyone came to breaking the deadlock.

Moving into 1973, they played two more friendlies before resuming the qualification campaign. In March, a largely experimental side, featuring a first cap for Rene van de Kerkhof, plus second appearances for Arie Haan and FC Twente's Jan Jeuring, but without Cruyff, travelled to Vienna to face Austria. A 1-0 defeat would not have caused too many concerns, given the players selected – and those omitted. A couple of months later, a much more recognisable team, with Rep making his debut, defeated Spain 3-2 at the Olympisch Stadion. It took the debutant a mere dozen minutes to announce his arrival with a goal.

The serious business returned in August and across three weeks, the Oranje eliminated Belgium's early advantage by defeating Iceland 5-0 and then 8-1 – the latter match should have been a 'home' game for Iceland, but was transferred to Deventer – before returning from Oslo with a vital 1-2 victory thanks to a late goal from Hulshoff. Cruyff had given the Oranje an early lead, heading home inside seven minutes, but a disputed goal with 13 minutes left brought the game level again as Harry Hestad appeared to kick the ball from Van Beveren's hand before firing into an empty net. A neat back-heel by Cruyff, however, opened up the chance, and the big defender scored with the composure of a seasoned striker. In October, Belgium defeated Norway 2-0 in Brussels to leave their visit to Amsterdam as the deciding rubber.

Although the Belgians had yet to concede a goal in the qualification process, the fact that the Dutch had notched 24 times against Belgium's 12 meant that the visitors would need to win the final game on 18 November to qualify. Any other result would see the Dutch reach a major tournament for the first time since the World Cup of 1938. As things transpired, that record came oh-so-close to being extended.

Ahead of the game, the Dutch had problems. When were things ever different? Five weeks earlier they had entertained Poland in a friendly, achieving a fairly unimportant 1-1 draw. Just after the break, however, established first-choice goalkeeper Van Beveren was injured, and had to be replaced by FC Twente's Piet Schrijvers. The PSV keeper would not recover in time for the big game, and Schrijvers was retained. There would be further consequences for Van Beveren later.

Rob Rensenbrink had made his debut for the Oranje back in 1968 as a DWS Amsterdam player, before moving to Bruges in Belgium the following year, and then on to Anderlecht in 1973. He had last played for the national team in a 1-0 win in Israel in 1970 but, almost three years later, he would return for his ninth cap, replacing Piet Keizer as a substitute in the Poland game. Often disregarded by many of his international team-mates as someone who had made his name after moving to the less competitive Belgian league, from this point his presence would be vital in the next two World Cups. To date he had failed to score for the Oranje, but he was a player who seemed to save his goals for the biggest of occasions and, five years after making his return to the national team, would come so close to taking the Oranje all the way to the altar on the biggest day. Aside from Schrijvers, Rensenbrink, plus of course Cruyff, who was now with Barcelona, and Aad Mansveld, were the only other non-Ajax players in the line-up for the key game.

As was suggested by his team's exemplary defensive record so far, Belgium's coach, Raymond Goethals, was naturally cautious and set up his formation and tactics not to concede, hoping to score once and then close down the game. The prospect of getting overrun by the Dutch in an end-to-end basketball match was hardly enticing and, for much of the game, the visitors defended stoically, rarely pressing.

Chances came the way of the Dutch, but Christian Piot remained unbeaten in the Belgian goal and, when Rep unaccountably sent a side-foot volley wide from six yards with just the goalkeeper to beat, the clearest chance of the game had passed. In a rare sortie upfield, the Belgians even managed to strike a post with Schrijvers beaten. It seemed strange that the visitors, who needed a goal, remained in earnest defence, and as time slipped by their hopes were surely drifting away. A draw would suffice for the Dutch.

Patience is a virtue they say and in the last minute, Belgian patience seemed to have been rewarded. The opportunity came from a free kick out on the left flank. It was surely their last chance, as defenders piled into attacking positions to support the forwards. Skipper Paul van Himst stood over the ball surveying his options as the referee signalled for the free kick to be played. As he struck the ball, in a well-drilled ploy, the Dutch defenders moved out, seeking to catch the attackers offside. It was a risky more.

Van Himst played the ball with the outside of his right foot, causing it to arc towards the Dutch six-yard line before drifting away. Deceived by the flight, Schrijvers had advanced to intercept and then been caught hopelessly out of position as the ball flew past him towards an unmarked Jan Verheyen, advancing towards the far post. With the goalkeeper flapping helplessly, a right-foot volley turned the ball home. It was the ultimate smash and grab. The Belgians had mugged the Dutch in their own backyard, and the Oranje had missed out on a major tournament again.

As Dutch heads dropped, though, Schrijvers raised an arm. He alone had noticed the linesman on the far side of the pitch with his flag in the air. Referee Pavel Kazakov could do little but accept the advice of his linesman; the offside ploy had worked. The goal was disallowed. Shortly after the full-time whistle went and the Dutch had their all-important point. It would be them rather than Belgium going to West Germany. Later, replays of that last-minute incident showed how fortunate the Dutch had been, as Rob Smyth wrote in *The Guardian*. 'It wasn't even close: when the free kick was taken, Verheyen was being played onside by at least three defenders. It was a Total Scandal.'[47] Maybe so, but it was Total Football that had got the Dutch to that point and, had they not progressed, the world would have been denied the opportunity of seeing one of the greatest sides never to win the World Cup fail so magnificently.

For all Belgian laments, no amount of hand-wringing would change things. The Oranje may have been one of the more fortunate guests to be turning up for the party, but they would still be the undisputed belles of the ball. Despite his assertion that they were fortunate to qualify, in *The Guardian* Rob Smyth also celebrated the fact that they were there. 'For the Holland players, life would change for ever in West Germany the following summer. So would football. With their hippie chic, Holland freed the minds – and manes – of an insular sport, yet if they had not made it there would have been no Total Football, no pom-poms and pomposity, no instant friendship between football and the cerebrum, no empowerment for future generations of Dutch players. Cruyff would have joined Barry Ferguson on the list of great players never to appear at the World Cup, and a great West German side would have got the credit they deserved.'[48]

---

47 The forgotten story of ... how Cruyff and co almost missed out on the 1974 World Cup, *The Guardian*, 10 February 2009

48 The forgotten story of ... how Cruyff and co almost missed out on the 1974 World Cup, *The Guardian*, 10 February 2009

Before the team arrived in Germany, however, in typical Dutch fashion, everything would be thrown in the air. Frantisek Fadrhonc would be denied to opportunity of joining in the fun. Well, not quite. In essence, he was demoted to merely being a member of Michels's coaching team. Even that, however, most reports suggest was little more than a sinecure. Although the former head coach would travel to West Germany with the squad, his relationship with Michels was bordering on the non-existent, and he was more a tourist than a contributing member of the party.

It's worth mentioning here, though, that there are suggestions from some that Fadrhonc enjoyed a better relationship with Michels than is usually accepted. Given that the new man supplanted him, however, it feels unlikely. There would be long and heated debate about the squad. Personal feuds had to be played out, and even the shirts that the team would wear caused conflict. This was Dutch football after all. Why keep things calm when you can brew up a storm?

Preparation

Cruyff had now spent a season in Catalunya with Barcelona, renewing the relationship with Michels. The La Liga title had been gained for the first time in 14 years and, had it been necessary, Cruyff's iron-clad belief in Michels and his systems of play had been reinforced. It's impossible to know whether the possibility of Michels usurping Fadrhonc and taking charge of the Dutch squad for the World Cup had ever been discussed in conversations between the two, but, given the outcome, it is difficult to believe that it wasn't.

Three months ahead of the tournament, the Czecho-slovakian coach was unceremoniously removed, with Michels being handed the reins. Cruyff, who had been less than fully convinced of Fadrhonc's tactics and team selection throughout the qualifying competition, was delighted with the move, declaring that, 'it was very important to me. Perhaps even crucial.'[49] With a core of players educated in the Ajax philosophy, and a Feyenoord contingent schooled by Happel, the Dutch would play very much in the style Cruyff wanted. Despite the harsh treatment meted out to Fadrhonc, it's difficult to describe it as a poor decision.

Much as his club playing career had been less than stellar, Michels had hardly set the world alight when appearing for the Oranje. In five appearances, all under the coaching regime of Van der Leck, ranging from a debut 4-1 defeat to Sweden on 8 June 1950 to a 3-1 reverse in Zurich against Switzerland on 30 May 1954, which was also Van der Leck's final game, the Netherlands had lost every game in which Michels had appeared … As with the coaching success at Ajax, however, the hope was that where he had been acceptable on the field, he would be exceptional as a coach. The problem was that the time available to get things right was very truncated, with a host of issues to resolve. Inevitably, a number of them involved Cruyff.

The captain of the national squad had never been reluctant to pursue his case where financial considerations were concerned. An entirely reasonable stance, but one that often led to conflict with club, coach, national association and occasionally with team-mates. A case in point, ahead of the tournament, was a bitter row between the squad and the KNVB regarding bonuses that would surely have had Cruyff's hand guiding it. There was also, however, a more personal issue also involving money. Cruyff had a deal with German sportswear company Puma. They supplied him with Puma King boots and other kit. In exchange, he had committed not to wear anything produced by the firm's arch-rivals Adidas. Although both companies are based in Herzogenaurach,

49   Cruyff, Johan, *My Turn* (London: Macmillan, 2016)

Germany, the rivalry is both familial and long-standing, dating back to the early post-war years. In 1948, after working together for many years, the two Dassler brothers, Rudolf and Adolf fell out, parted ways, and each formed their own sportswear business. Adolf created Adidas, inspired by his own name, and Rudolf formed Puma.

Traditionally, the Oranje shirt had never carried a manufacturer's logo, regardless of the company supplying it. The world was now awakening to the rapacious appetite of corporate power, however, and in the days of worldwide television exposure, such things were bound to be compromised. The KNVB signed a deal for the team to wear Adidas shirts during the World Cup, and the design would encompass three clear black stripes – the distinctive trademark of Adidas – running from shoulder to cuff on the sleeves.

Cruyff was insistent that he could not wear the shirt if that was the case. He was clearly also irritated that the deal had been concluded without consultation with the squad and how it may affect them. 'They thought that they didn't need to,'[50] Cruyff would later explain, 'because the shirt was theirs. "But the head sticking out of it is mine," I told them.'[51] The influence of Cruyff is illustrated by the fact that the resolution was to supply him with shirts carrying only two stripes, rather than the three that the other players would wear, and the same would apply to shorts and socks. It satisfied both player and Puma.

Ironically, the team facing the Oranje in the final would also be sponsored by Adidas. Whilst the Germans had those three stripes on the sleeves of the light blue tracksuits that the coaches and substitutes wore, their white shirts carried no markings. One is left to wonder why the KNVB agreed to them being on the Oranje shirts, when clearly a deal could have been struck without them. Was it a financial decision?

50   Cruyff, Johan, *My Turn* (London: Macmillan, 2016)
51   Cruyff, Johan, *My Turn* (London: Macmillan, 2016)

Was there a larger cheque available if they agreed to carry the stripes? If so, perhaps Cruyff's stance was wholly reasonable anyway. Strangely enough, four years later other, albeit perhaps less celebrated, players wearing Oranje would have a similar solution.

Squad selection also proved troublesome. That injury sustained by Hulshoff in February denied Michels and the Netherlands the services of the Ajax libero. It left a gaping hole.

Mop-haired and bearded with the trademark socks around his ankles, bereft of shin pads, he had worked his way into the Ajax team under Michels, although it was always an uneasy relationship. Hulshoff's personality was much like his playing style, individual and with a spirit abounding to perform the extraordinary. Take a picture of Virgil van Dijk at his imperious best, add in the passing ability of Zidane, sprinkle in the defensive determination of Franco Baresi, with a dash of the shooting power of Cristiano Ronaldo, and you have an idea of his prowess. The Ajax libero strode around the pitch like some giant, committed to right the wrongs of the game. With three European Cup victories to his name, he was the complete article when the 1974 tournament rolled around. At 27, Hulshoff was primed to play a full part in delivering the ultimate prize in world football to the Netherlands.

Dutch football journalist and, for 25 years, owner and chief editor of the football magazine *ELF Voetbal*, Jan-Hermen de Bruijn, offered this description: 'Hulshoff looked like a Viking, with a sword and an axe, but he really was a very skilful player, but he was so completely unlike all the other Ajax players. Almost from the first moment, opponents thought, because of the way he looked, that he was dangerous, that he was a hitman … so he had tremendous help from his reputation.'[52] As the jigsaw pieces fell on to the table when the

52   De Bruijn, Jan-Hermen – Interview with the author

squad assembled in West Germany, however, Ajax's bearded Viking was missing.

It was a major dilemma for the coach. Israel would have been the obvious replacement, but by this time he was 32, and a number of injuries had also eaten away at his powers. Ironically, given the reason for Hulshoff's absence, a recent knee problem for the Feyenoord skipper had also rendered serious doubts about his fitness. Playing regularly across such a high-profile tournament seemed untenable, but Michels included him anyway, as a back-up plan.

There was also talk of Hulshoff's Ajax central-defensive partner Horst Blankenburg being approached. The problem was that Blankenburg was German. Nevertheless, as the player had never represented his homeland, and with the Bayern Munich pairing of Franz Beckenbauer and Hans-Georg Schwarzenbeck automatic selections for the German national team, such a development was unlikely to occur. The Dutch authorities reportedly agreed to fast-track nationality papers through if Blankenburg was minded to apply. A proud German, he understandably refused the offer.

ADO Den Haag's Aad Mansveld had made his debut in August 1972 during a friendly against Czechoslovakia and established a partnership with Hulshoff. Both seemed destined to feature strongly in the World Cup, but the final qualifying game, the 0-0 draw against Belgium, would be the last time they played together. A knee ligament injury in March 1974 put paid to those hopes, and Mansveld would never play for the Oranje again. A new approach would be required.

With the search for a libero proving increasingly difficult, Michels opted for a solution that would be replicated by another Barcelona manager more than three decades later. When faced with the loss of Carles Puyol, Pep Guardiola chose to deploy midfielder Javier Mascherano alongside Gerard Pique. Guardiola had played during Cruyff's tenure in charge in Catalunya. Lessons had been learned. In a similar approach, Michels decided to play Arie Haan as the libero, and paired him with the Feyenoord full-back Rijsbergen, in an untried central-defensive partnership.

Haan would play as an advanced libero, in front of the young Feyenoord defender, and Krol and Suurbier would be the nominal full-backs. It was a gamble on Haan, still only 25 years old, being able to utilise his game nous to fill any gaps in his defensive technique, alongside a relatively inexperienced partner. It was a typically Total Football solution. Neeskens had been tried in the role, but stripping him out of the midfield and breaking up his partnership with Cruyff was considered too expensive a price to pay. Initially, Haan was reluctant to take on the role, but was eventually persuaded. The decision would also have an effect on the selection of the goalkeeper for the tournament.

Had Michels been able to call on his first-choice central defenders and goalkeeper, free from concerns about injuries, it would have been Hulshoff and Israel playing in front of Van Beveren. The Dutch team would have been far stronger in defence, but the open play encouraged by the inclusion of Haan at centre-back enabled Total Football. Without that, it might never have happened. 'Important things always happen by a lot of coincidences, and this was the most massive coincidence because, in goal and in central defence, the first seven, eight, nine players who were all better than what played in Germany were not available.'[53]

Another Ajax player, and likely candidate for inclusion in the squad, would also be unavailable. Gerrie Muhren's son was ill, and the midfielder opted out of the trip to Germany to be with him. There were plenty of other quality midfield options for Michels to choose from, though. The absence of Hulshoff

53   De Bruijn, Jan-Hermen – Interview with the author

and Muhren were beyond the control of Michels, but another was largely attributable to a stubborn stance by the coach and player in question, with Cruyff having more than a small say in the solution.

In all successful squads, the position of goalkeeper is key. An outstanding shot-stopper can be the difference between success and failure. In Jan van Beveren, the Netherlands had an experienced and accomplished performer, but since the injury in the game against Poland he had been absent from consideration for the Oranje. Typically, as a goalkeeper, Van Beveren had too much bravery for his own good. In late 1973, he injured his groin during a match against Ajax. Despite severe pain, he chose to remain on the pitch. The injury prevented Van Beveren from playing for the remainder of the season, in which PSV won the KNVB Cup. Now with the World Cup looming the player who had been the number one choice for the No.1 shirt – despite declaring himself fit and ready to play – was told that he had to prove the point to his new coach.

Short of time to hone his squad, Michels had arranged a pre-tournament friendly against German club SV Hamburg, and insisted that the goalkeeper should play to prove his fitness. Van Beveren was now 26, and felt that rather than play in that game and risk further damage to his injury, it would make far more sense to use the time to ensure that he was fully fit for the opening game of the tournament against Uruguay. As a compromise though, he suggested that he play one half of the game. Michels was unimpressed by the player's apparent refusal to comply with the coach's requirement. A row broke out and Van Beveren was not considered for the squad. He wouldn't play for the Oranje again for two years, and never again under Michels.

Schrijvers of FC Twente and Treytel of Feyenoord were included in the squad, but who would be No.1? When the decision became known, to describe it as something out of left field would be a wild understatement. It was neither of them. FC Amsterdam's Jan Jongbloed was 33, and had picked the ball out of his net half a dozen times in Cruyff's last game for Ajax. It was, however, to the player with only a single cap, and that a dozen years before, for only the final five minutes in a 4-1 friendly defeat to Denmark, that Michels turned.

Despite the limited time on the field 12 years earlier, as he replaced the injured Piet Lagarde, even five minutes had been too long for Jongbloed to keep a clean sheet. Going into the World Cup, the Netherlands' first-choice goalkeeper would have precisely five minutes of international experience behind him, and had conceded in that precious little time. A friendly against Argentina in the month before the tournament started would see the beginning and completion of his reintroduction to the international game ahead of the tournament. If anyone, 12 months before the Oranje played their first game of the World Cup, had suggested that the goalkeeper and two central defenders would be Jongboed, Rijsbergen and Haan, they would have invited ridicule.

To many it seemed like a strange decision to even include such a player in the squad. Jan-Hermen de Bruijn certainly did. 'He was by far also not the best goalkeeper in Holland.'[54] To nominate him as first choice looked beyond strange. The apparent rationale was that, although Van Beveren was accepted as being the better goalkeeper, Jongbloed was more accomplished with his feet, often leaving his area to deploy himself as a 'sweeper-keeper'.

Reports suggested that Cruyff had been influential in the decision. A passage from his autobiography hardly disputes such an assertion. 'In our style of play, there was no room for a goalkeeper who never came off his line,' he confirmed. 'That was why Jongbloed was chosen over Jan van Beveren.

---

54   De Bruijn, Jan-Hermen – Interview with the author

The great thing was that in his youth Jongbloed had been an attacker. As a goalkeeper he didn't just like joining in he was also very good at it.'[55] It's important to recall that goalkeepers were still allowed to pick up backpasses. It meant that the only advantage Jongbloed's footballing ability would offer was on the occasions he would venture outside his penalty area.

Although that may to some extent explain his selection ahead of Van Beveren, can the same be said of Schrijvers and Treytel? Was the choice simply down to Cruyff's preference? Wim van Hanegem may have had doubts, but understood the rationale for the selection. 'There's no denying that Jongbloed could play football, he could. But he wasn't a great goalkeeper. For the style of football we played, however, he was the best, especially when we played offside.'[56] As the tournament got under way, the Feyenoord midfielder's logic was shown to be sound. Similar to the occasion in the final qualifying game, when video evidence strongly suggested that Belgium's goal should have stood, the Dutch would repeatedly not only deploy a group pressing tactic, but also a 'mass rush' offside ploy, with players sprinting out of defence to leave any number of tardily dallying forwards snared in their trap.

Many years later, Graham Hunter interviewed Haan and Van Hanegem, and explained how they related the principle to him. 'They played a massive high line, that they squeezed up,' Hunter related. 'They were playing a ten-man press ... In retrospect it was ... unbelievable the way they played ... It was a style of football that you just didn't see in Britain.'[57] It was certainly entertaining, and Jongbloed fitted the system like a hand in a goalkeeper's glove. 'In his early days, Jongbloed would even sometimes run up to the midway line to intercept

55 Cruyff, Johan, *My Turn* (London: Macmillan, 2016)
56 Football's Greatest International Teams, Sky Sports – 2010
57 Hunter, Graham – Interview with the author

counter-attacking play,'[58] Jan-Hermen de Bruijn explained. A goalkeeper capable of covering the empty space that such a ruse left unguarded was a tempting option.

Given Jongbloed's age and club experience, however, it's worth noting that he was a first-team choice for his club when Michels was searching for a new goalkeeper for Ajax in 1967. Indeed, Jongbloed had been part of the team that secured the Eredivisie title for DWS in 1963/64, so he was hardly an unknown.

Jongbloed would go on to be selected in the Netherlands squads for the 1976 European Championship and the 1978 World Cup finals. Schrijvers would keep him out of the team in 1976, but the 1978 World Cup was a different story. Jongbloed played in the opening group phase, and Schrijvers in the second one, before the veteran returned for the final after Schrijvers was injured against Italy. For a goalkeeper with such a limited international CV in early 1974 to play in two World Cup finals was a notable renaissance.

The goalkeeping issue was rife with controversy. To many it demonstrated the unhealthy amount of influence that Cruyff could exert on Michels; to others it merely emphasised the commitment to playing a brand of football that the players excelled at. Suffice to say that Van Beveren's PSV team-mates in the squad, the Van de Kerkhof twins and Pleun Strik, may well have been in the former group. Other than when the older Van de Kerkhof replaced the clearly unfit Rensenbrink in the final, the PSV players would take a watching brief from the bench – none of the other players from the Eindhoven club would play in the tournament. Perhaps there was little adverse effect in the short term, but a simmering resentment would linger for years to come, costing both Van Beveren and the Oranje dearly.

58   De Bruijn, Jan-Hermen – Interview with the author

Almost regardless of anything else, in *Mapping the Pitch: Football Coaches, Players and Formations Through the Ages*, Edward Couzens-Lake said that Michels knew that delivering the 'best Cruyff' would benefit the entire squad, and give the Oranje the optimum chance of success. That could only be achieved by keeping the skipper happy and allowing him the freedom to play that his skills demanded. Some have argued that Michels found it almost impossible to 'shackle Cruyff into any given formation or position on the field, choosing instead to hand him his shirt and let him get on with things however he saw fit',[59] as Couzens-Lake asserts. That may be an oversimplification, but the latitude afforded to the captain far outweighed that offered to any others in the squad. As Michels once conceded, 'Without Cruyff, I have no team.'[60] The allocation of squad numbers offers a neat summary. While all of the other players were allocated from 1 to 22 in alphabetical order, Cruyff was allowed to keep his No.14 shirt – with just two stripes on the sleeves. Such gestures were hardly sufficient for Michels to keep his star happy, however. A further complication arose with regard to Cruyff's relationship with a former Ajax team-mate.

After captaining Ajax to their second European Cup, Piet Keizer had handed the captaincy over to Cruyff. Then, at the end of the 1973/74 season, with Kovacs gone and George Knobel in charge, a vote had been arranged amongst the players as to who they wanted to be skipper for the coming season. Cruyff had suggested he carry on in the role, but was surprised to hear that a rival candidate had been put forward in Keizer. Cruyff felt that the move was fuelled by resentment, and 'a form of jealousy I had never experienced before'.[61]

---

59 Couzens-Lake, Edward, *Mapping the Pitch: Football Coaches, Players and Formations Through the Ages* (Aarchen: Meyer & Meyer Sport, 2015)

60 Squire, David, *The Illustrated History of Football* (London: Random House UK, 2017)

61 Cruyff, Johan, *My Turn* (London: Macmillan, 2016)

If Cruyff was resentful that there was even going to be a vote, the fact that he lost out in the ballot to Keizer was the final straw. 'It was a terrible shock. I immediately went to my room, phoned Cor Coster [his father-in-law and agent] and said he needed to find a new club for me straight away. That was it. I had suffered the kind of injury that you can't see with the naked eye. The blow was particularly severe because we weren't just fellow players but also close friends.'[62] The move to Barcelona followed.

Whilst there's a clear sense of betrayal in Cruyff's words, some would argue that, far from being the reason he left the club, Keizer's captaincy was, at most, merely the trigger, a convenient event upon which to hang the cause for something that was becoming increasingly inevitable anyway. Whatever the truth, there was discord between the erstwhile team-mates. Keizer was an outstanding player, but Cruyff was overwhelmingly the key element in Michels's plans. It remained a difficult circle to square. Potentially denying his team of Keizer's services would be a big decision for Michels. Whilst Cruyff overshadowed every other Dutch player, Keizer was not bereft of advocates. The famous Dutch journalist Nico Scheepmaker once famously argued that, 'Cruyff is the best, but Keizer is the better one.'[63]

Whether through a desire to placate Cruyff, or merely to better accommodate the Total Football philosophy, Michels decided to go for a 4-3-3 formation that was better suited to including Rob Rensenbrink, rather than Keizer. The new Ajax captain would occupy the bench for most of the tournament, only starting in the goalless draw against Sweden in the initial group phase. It was the only change that Michels made to his starting line-ups throughout the competition, and was

62 Cruyff, Johan, *My Turn* (London: Macmillan, 2016)
63 https://www.ajaxdaily.com/2017/piet-keizer-cruyff-is-the-best-but-keizer-is-the-better-one/

quickly rectified for the following game. As with so many things involving Cruyff, however, whatever the arguments, they hardly diminished his respect for a player. When selecting his best-ever XI, in *My Turn*, only two players made it from the Ajax and Netherlands team. One was full-back Ruud Krol. The other? Piet Keizer.[64]

The oft-quoted mantra that any squad seeking success needs to be bound together and bereft of disputes applies to all squads in all major competitions – except the Dutch. That is especially the case for the squad of 1974. With unavoidable absences to key players, disputes over selection, arguments between players, resentment about the captain having too much influence, and even how many stripes should be on their shirts, Michels could be painted as that other famous Dutch boy with insufficient fingers to plug all of the holes in the dyke. Instead, he was the man in charge of the most talented collection of players assembling in West Germany to contest the World Cup. Across the next four weeks his team would speak for the young, the burgeoning, the talented, those who choose not to conform, and those who chose exuberance over the mundane.

David Winner, author of *Brilliant Orange,* put it this way: 'Holland's '74 team is somehow the Summer of Love, Sergeant Pepper, Altamont and the death of John Lennon all in one four-week period. You get the whole thing – the peak, the summation of this movement that's been developing since the mid-60s in Holland which embodies some of the ideals of the youth movement of later in the decade and you have this team where Ruud Krol – this hard defender, is wearing hippie love beads in a World Cup Final.'[65]

64   Cruyff, Johan, *My Turn* (London: Macmillan, 2016)
65   https://www.the42.ie/holland-1974-world-cup-tragedy-1488354-Mar2016/

The tournament

The semi-final teams from the tournament in Mexico four years earlier were selected as seeds for the 1974 World Cup, with each placed into a different group. Four pots were then organised geographically, labelled as Western European, Eastern European, South American and the Rest of the World. Leaving aside an odd anomaly, such as the Swedes being placed in the last of those groups in order to preserve their status as seeds, the rationale was to ensure a reasonable spread of continental interest across the four groups. To ensure this, it was decided that Argentina and Chile could not be placed in a group headed by the seeded teams of Brazil or Uruguay. Unlike 1970, but in line with 1978 and 1982, there would be two group stages to establish the finalists, rather than an initial group stage followed by a series of knockout games.

The draw took place on 5 January 1974 and, after all the complications, deliberations and shuffling had been completed, the Netherlands were placed into Group Three, alongside Uruguay, Sweden and Bulgaria. Statistically, a review of previous global tournaments would hardly have suggested the Dutch as being outstanding favourites to top the group, but the country that until the 1970s, 'had an international record almost on a par with Luxembourg'[66] now had a team bristling with outstanding talents. Bulgaria had arrived in Germany after topping a relatively weak group, with only Portugal offering any real opposition. Both the South Americans and Swedes had only qualified by the narrowest of margins, booking their places on goal difference. Any over-inflated idea the Dutch had about the group being a comfortable stroll, however, was perhaps tempered by the fact the Oranje were only there by an equally, if not – given the events of the final qualifying game against Belgium – even more, tenuous thread.

---

66   Winner, David, *Brilliant Orange* (London: Bloomsbury, 2000)

The opening game took place on 15 June at the Niedersachsenstadion, home of Hannover 96 in front of 55,000 fans. Michels selected a starting XI that would change only once across the course of the tournament. Jongbloed had the gloves and, apparently just as importantly, the boots as well. In front of him, the Ajax pair of Krol and Suurbier were the nominal full-backs, with Rijsbergen and Haan in the centre. The midfield comprised the Feyenoord pairing of Jansen and Van Hanegem, alongside Neeskens. Cruyff had the middle of the front three, but inevitably with a licence to roam, with Rensenbrink on one flank, and Rep, the tyro forward from Ajax, on the other.

The Dutch bench was occupied by Schrijvers as the reserve goalkeeper, defender Kees van Ierssel from FC Twente, midfielders Theo de Jong from Feyenoord and Bruges's Ruud Geels, who wore the No.1 shirt but never saw a moment of action in the tournament, plus Keizer. Although Hannover was more than 270km (168 miles) from the Dutch border, the chants from the crowd ahead of kick-off certainly suggested many thousands had made the trip to Lower Saxony.

In Scotland, a ten-year-old Graham Hunter also remembered watching the game on his family's new Grundig colour television, something he compared to feeling like having a Rolls-Royce outside. The television granted the boy a glimpse into a new world of football, one alien to his experiences. 'Holland in that orange strip … and the Uruguay strip. It was an arresting clash of colours. Colours that you didn't really see in Scottish or British football.'[67] Such experiences can define a life's obsession.

There was a feverish atmosphere inside the stadium, Jan-Hermen de Bruijn recalled; something a little alien to the players sporting the Oranje shirt. 'The Dutch national team,

67   Hunter, Graham – Interview with the author

before the finals, was not loved by the crowds. When they played in Hannover though [against Uruguay], instead of the expected two or three thousand Dutchmen, there were 25,000, and half of the stadium was Oranje. This never happened before, when the national team played, all 25,000 fans sang, that lifted the players enormously.'[68]

Just seven minutes after kick-off, with the Uruguayans hardly having been able to break out of their own half, the Oranje flame was lit. Rijsbergen coolly played the ball to a deep-lying Van Hanegem, who then fed Haan advancing from the backline precisely as Michels would have required from the midfielder-cum-centre-back. A pass to Suurbier on the right was moved on to Cruyff. Accelerating, he beat one man, then swayed past another, irresistibly attracting two more defenders towards him, before playing the ball wide to the right flank, where Suurbier had moved into a right-wing position, allowing Rep to drift inside. Using the space created by Cruyff's elegantly magnetic sally forward, Suurbier moved the ball on to his left foot before crossing. The ball arced towards the six-yard line where the repositioned Rep's blond hair flicked it home. It was a goal of simplicity, grace and superb interplay. Cruyff once declared that 'Playing football is very simple, but playing simple football is the hardest thing there is.'[69] With that goal, the Oranje had proven they could do that 'simple' thing well – very well indeed.

For much of the next 25 minutes or so, the Dutch assumed total command of the game, probing for weaknesses in the massed ranks of the Uruguay back line. The South Americans 'were organised, they were tough',[70] Graham Hunter remembered. Had they set up to play so deep, or been

68   De Bruijn, Jan-Hermen – Interview with the author
69   Johan Cruyff: The best quotes on the Dutch master, *The Independent,* 24 March 2016
70   Hunter, Graham – Interview with the author

compelled to do so? In fact, it took until the half-hour mark for Jongbloed to touch the ball in any meaningful way, as he punched an optimistic cross clear. At the other end, the Oranje players were taking turns to run forward and threaten. Cruyff time and again, Van Hanegem often, Neeskens with power, Rep cutting in from the right, Suurbier doing the same, and even Jansen joining in the karaoke-esque ploy of giving everyone a turn to perfrom. Michels's orchestra was playing beautifully.

By the break, both Rensenbrink and Krol had joined the ensemble, with the other full-back, Suurbier, perhaps having the best chance to add to the lead when he skewed his shot wide from about five metres after a deft header by Cruyff had found the defender once more in the opposition box. A single-goal lead can often be precarious, but with Jongbloed almost redundant at the other end, it looked like the definition of an oxymoron, the most secure of slender leads.

If the South Americans' coach Roberto Porta was hoping that his half-time team talk would change things, he was to be disappointed. Midway through the second period, the nearest to another goal had been when Rep just failed to squeeze a cross from Cruyff over the line, as goalkeeper Ladislao Mazurkiewicz foiled him. It was increasingly clear that the unchanging flow of the game was becoming frustrating for the Uruguayans, and a yellow card for Juan Carlos Masnik, for an apparent stamp on Neeskens' ankle, heralded a breakdown in discipline that shortly afterwards would all but confirm victory for the Dutch.

On 65 minutes, midfield enforcer Julio Montero was dismissed by Hungarian referee Károly Palotai. The fairly limited television coverage of the day missed the incident. Some reports suggest it was for a late studs-up challenge on Rensenbrink, others say that a punch to the stomach of the Dutch player was the cause. It may have been either, neither

– or indeed both – the effect was the same, regardless. With 11 players on the pitch, Uruguay had yet to muster a shot on target. Their chances of doing so now seemed even more remote. Not long afterwards, the ball fell to Rensenbrink around the penalty spot, clear of any marking defender, but a wild shot over the bar squandered the opportunity. It may have been the moment that Michels decided to insert Keizer in the Anderlecht's player's place for the next game.

The second goal nearly came when Cruyff pulled down a cross from Rensenbrink to fire home, but Palotai disallowed the strike, deciding that the Barcelona player's foot was dangerously high as a defender sought to head the cross away. Then Jansen struck the foot of a post with the goalkeeper beaten. It would take until four minutes from time for the second goal and, when it came, simplicity was the key once more. A delicately clipped pass from Van Hanegem put Rensenbrink in behind the Uruguay back line, compelling Mazurkiewicz to narrow the angle. A simple pass to the unmarked Rep waiting centrally allowed the 20-year-old to collect his second goal of the game and seal the win.

In the closing minutes, Cruyff, Rep and then Neeskens could all have added to the scoreline, but it was hardly necessary. Defensively the Dutch had rarely been troubled. Rijsbergen was tidy, Haan unruffled, while Krol and Suurbier spent much of their time in advanced positions. On the odd occasions when Uruguay tried to force the pace, that well-drilled offside ploy often caught five or six offenders out of position, or a flurry of pressing Oranje shirts tackling in packs disrupted the momentum. As the tournament progressed, the tactics would become an established feature of the Dutch defence. In the entire game, Uruguay hadn't had a shot worthy of the name, let alone one on target.

The game ebbed away in a strange atmosphere. It had hardly been a contest at all following Rep's early goal. From the seventh minute, the Dutch had strutted and strolled, confidence in overdrive. Cruyff commented that, 'Of course we had self-belief that we could do something brilliant, but in truth we'd never expected that a team from a South American country, one we regarded as a bigger and more established footballing nation, mightn't be able to keep up with us.'[71] Perhaps the early goal did the Dutch no favours, and they were fortunate that such arrogance brought no penalty, but it was a dangerous game to play, and sometimes there's a price to pay. At the final whistle, with the late afternoon sun casting a shadow from the stand halfway across the pitch, the Netherlands had played sunshine football. The Uruguayans had been put in the shade. But where precisely did the truth lie? Were the Dutch that good, or were Uruguay that poor? We'd need to wait another four days to find out. A young Graham Hunter in Aberdeen had no doubts though. 'To watch them, to see them win so gracefully. That was me hooked on them.'[72] He wasn't on his own.

On 19 June, the Netherlands returned to action travelling to Dortmund to face Sweden in the Westfalenstadion. Michels made the only change to his regular starting XI across the entire tournament. Rob Rensenbrink had hardly been a passenger in the game against Uruguay, and it was his dart behind the back line, and astute cutback for Rep that set up the second goal. For the game against the Scandinavians, however, he was left out in favour of Keizer. It should be remembered that the decision to play the Anderlecht player ahead of the Ajax captain must have been a close call, with perhaps the simmering distrust between current and former captains of the Amsterdam club the deciding factor. If such a personality clash was involved, Michels pushed it to the back of his mind as he set in place the front three that

---

71 Cruyff, Johan, *My Turn* (London: Macmillan, 2016)
72 Hunter, Graham – Interview with the author

had overcome Juventus in the 1973 European Cup Final for Ajax.

If the Uruguay game had been something of a stroll against a team considered to be outdated in approach compared to the Dutch – 'They were doing things we'd given up doing five or six years ago,'[73] claimed Cruyff – the game against Sweden would be a different matter. Georg Ericson's team were well-organised and had earned their qualification after a play-off against Austria in what came to be known in the country as the 'Snömatchen'. With Gelsenkirchen serving as the neutral venue in November 1973, the game was in doubt following a heavy snowfall. Already an adjunct to the regular qualification process, however, there was pressure to complete the fixture. The game went ahead and the Swedes' Nordic experience may have served them well, as they overcame the Austrians 2-1.

The goals in that game had been scored by Roland Sandberg and Bo Larsson, and the team Ericson selected to face the Dutch had a core of players case-hardened by experience in Europe's top leagues. The former was playing in the Bundesliga with FC Kaiserslautern and following the tournament would be joined in the Rhineland-Palatinate city by goalkeeper Ronnie Hellstrom. Defender Bjorn Andersson was also earning his living in Germany, playing for the newly crowned European champions Bayern Munich. Midfielder Inge Ejderstedt was a team-mate of Rensenbrink at Anderlecht and captain Bjorn Nordqvist was at PSV Eindhoven, as was star forward Ralf Edstrom. The burly striker would give Rijsbergen an uncomfortable time.

Sweden would qualify from the initial groups and lead West Germany at half-time in the second group phase before losing to two late goals, and eventually finish the tournament ranked in fifth position. They would also complete the initial group

---

73   Cruyff, Johan, *My Turn* (London: Macmillan, 2016)

section without conceding a goal, a fact that underscores the frustrating time the Oranje endured on the evening of 19 June.

In the first two minutes of the game, the difference from the opening encounter with Uruguay was clear, the Swedes having two shots on target. Two more than the South Americans managed in the entire game.

In the first quarter of an hour, though, it was still the Dutch dominating. The Swedish back line was drilled and organised, plus they still carried a threat on the break, but there was always the thought that a goal was on the way. Cruyff had repeatedly drifted out to the left, tormenting right back Jan Olsson, offering a taste of something special to follow, before playing in dangerous crosses. Always dangerous, one precisely found its mark, but Neeskens's volley from beyond the far post was the nearest they had come to a goal as the game approached the midway point of the first half.

At least this game offered Jongbloed the chance to show that he was more than a mere 'libero in gloves'. A clever free kick by the Swedes allowed a free shot on the turn from ten metres, but the goalkeeper instinctively stuck out a left hand to block the shot. If the defence had a comfortable time against the less threatening Uruguayans, in this game Michels would see how his revamped back line held up under pressure. Then came the moment for which the game will always be remembered.

Rep swept the ball wide to Cruyff, positioned out on the left once more and controlling the ball facing the touchline. Twenty-two minutes had been played and Olsson closed to prevent the Dutch captain's advance. It was a moment frozen in time. With his back to goal and the defender behind him, Cruyff shaped to play the ball inside with his right foot. Instinctively, Olsson jabbed out a left leg to block the pass that never came. Instead of completing the pass, Cruyff had hooked his leg back and dragged the ball behind his left leg, spun and chased after it, leaving Olsson three metres behind and feeling like the dupe in a conjurer's act. Despite that early *hors d'oeuvre* a couple of years ago in the European Cup Final against Inter, the main dish had now been served at football's top table. The Cruyff Turn had been born.

Jan Olsson was 32 at the time, and vastly experienced, with a dozen years as a professional footballer on his CV. In that moment, though, his name was forever etched into the annals of football, not for his excellence, but for the fact that, so badly was he sent the wrong way by the move that, not only did he need to buy a ticket to get back into the stadium, he first needed to hail a taxi to get back there. Many years later, he recalled his reaction. 'My team-mates after the game, we looked at each other, they started to laugh and I do the same. I laughed then and I laugh now. It was very funny. He was a world-class player. I do my best but I was not a world-class player. The players in my team, they all laugh because they know me – we laughed together in the changing-room because everyone saw what a player he was. What more could we do?'[74]

It was a 'hands up' moment of contrition, but also a recognition and celebration of being even a bit-part support as one of the all-time great players delivered a magical moment on the biggest stage of all. 'I do not understand how he did it. It was a fantastic sequence,' Olsson said. 'I thought I was going to take the ball. I still cannot understand. Now when I see the video, every time I think I have got the ball. When he is about to kick the ball, I am sure I am going to take it, but every time he surprises me. I loved everything about this moment. After the game I thanked him for the match and said congratulations. Even though it was 0-0, it was right to say congratulations.'[75]

74 'Sweden's Jan Olsson pays tribute to Johan Cruyff, his great tormentor' *The Guardian,* 24 March 2016.

75 'Sweden's Jan Olsson pays tribute to Johan Cruyff, his great tormentor' *The Guardian,* 24 March 2016.

In that final sentence there's an unintended lament for Dutch football. Those few seconds as Olsson searched his pockets for the taxi fare, and Cruyff scampered away with the ball, like some street vagabond having picked the pocket of a dull-witted aristocrat, serves as a microcosm of the Oranje in the tournament. After leaving Olsson bewitched and bewildered, an outside-of-the-foot cross led to nothing. Impudent skill, balletic movement, other-worldly aura and a wanton desire to 'burn, burn, burn like fabulous yellow roman candles exploding like spiders across the stars'[76] brought no tangible reward. The ball was cleared and the game was played out as a goalless draw. It was a moment of rare beauty, but a forlorn one for all that. Olsson later admitted that he regretted not asking for Cruyff's shirt after the game. He wasn't the only one feeling unfulfilled.

Had the move led to a goal, perhaps the game would have been different, but it didn't, and for much of the remaining time, the pattern remained the same. The Dutch were in control, but the Swedes were never out of the game, despite them sinking further back in defence as the second half ebbed away and the prize of a draw appeared ever brighter on the horizon. A Van Hanegem header, scrambled off the line with Hellstrom beaten, just past the hour mark, was probably the nearest to a breakthrough for the Dutch. Michels brought on Theo de Jong for Van Hanegem inside the last 20 minutes, but it brought little reward. At the full-time whistle, it wasn't difficult to discern which team was happier with the result. The Dutch didn't win, but Jan-Hermen de Bruijn suggested that 'they played probably their second-best game of the tournament. They forgot to score, but they played really brilliantly.'[77]

76   Kerouac, Jack, *On the Road* (New York: Viking Press, 1957)
77   De Bruijn, Jan-Hermen – Interview with the author

The game had been a test for Michels, but probably one that his team would benefit from in the long run. The win against Uruguay had inevitably topped up the already inflated confidence levels of his team. The game against Sweden would have concentrated their attention more on the job to be done. In the final games of the group, Sweden would go one better than the Dutch, putting three goals past Uruguay. It was now left to the Netherlands to show which performance was their true measure – the arrogant dismantling of Uruguay, or the frustrating stalemate against Sweden.

In a strange twist, not untypical of events in the Dutch camp having the potential to cause unrest, during the day following this game it was announced that Johan Neeskens had signed for Barcelona. He would be joining Cruyff and Michels at the Camp Nou at the end of the year. The now soon-to-be former team-mates of the midfielder at Ajax apparently knew little of the move ahead of the announcement. Such things can disrupt any squad's harmony, but this was the Netherlands and it meant just one more pebble dropped into a pool already full of ripples. Michels just needed to ensure his team would surf the waves, rather than see their aspirations washed away by them. The game against Bulgaria was now key.

As far as Michels was concerned, the decision to bench Rensenbrink for Keizer had hardly been a roaring success. To be fair to the Ajax captain, he was far from being the only disappointment. A number of the Dutch forwards could have been said to be misfiring in the game. Rep had hardly starred either, but when the team was announced for the Bulgaria game, back in the Ruhr valley, the Anderlecht forward was reinstated at Keizer's expense.

Sunday 23 June was a bright sunny day, and the afternoon's fixture would produce some suitably illuminating football. Inside the first 20 seconds, Neeskens had a shot that Bulgarian goalkeeper Stefan Staykov could only collect at the second attempt. A few minutes later, he wouldn't be so fortunate. Before that, though, Jongbloed was required to show his footballing dexterity, racing from his area to hack clear when a blocked clearance fell behind his back line. Four minutes in, Cruyff cut in from the left. His movement was too quick for the defender, and a clumsy challenge sent the Dutchman to the turf. Australian referee Tony Boskovic had no doubt, resolutely pointing to the penalty spot. The Bulgarian protests seemed to be obligatory rather than convincing and, after the area was cleared, Neeskens smashed home the penalty. Oranje celebrations were quickly quelled, however, as Boskovic had identified encroachment by the Dutch and Neeskens was invited to repeat his success. He stepped up and calmly did so. Jan-Hermen de Bruijn recalled the moment as deeply significant for the team 'They scored very early with Rep, then they started hunting the ball with Arie Haan ... and in that first half Total Football was born [for this team].'[78]

Another early goal. What now? Whereas Rep's strike against Uruguay had almost lulled the game into a period of stupefied somnambulance, this time it seemed to enliven the Dutch. Rep, Cruyff, and particularly Van Hanegem, began running through the Bulgarian midfield with driving intent. A second goal didn't quickly follow, but when Neeskens joined in to fire just past the upright, still inside the first quarter of an hour, it so nearly did ... The urgency missing from the Uruguay game, and the cutting edge absent against Sweden were both to the fore here. A superb ball from Rijsbergen saw the restored Rensenbrink weave inside and then outside his defender before firing perilously close to Staykov's far post.

On the midway point of the first period, a slip in the Dutch defence opened up a rare chance for Bulgaria, but Jongbloed

78   De Bruijn, Jan-Hermen – Interview with the author

smothered Georgi Denev's tame effort. Five minutes later, as the Dutch seemed to pause for breath and rethink, a free kick for Bulgaria out on the left flank was swung in by Hristo Bonev and struck the bar with Jongbloed flapping helplessly. Whether it was intentional or not is open to debate, but regardless, it was the nearest either team had come to a goal since Neeskens buried his penalty 20 minutes or so earlier.

As if to suggest that they were now finding their feet, a few minutes later the Bulgarians threatened again. Denev cut inside from the left and fed Pavel Panov, but his scuffed shot was comfortably saved by Jongbloed. Van Hanegem was cautioned and then Cruyff followed him into the notebook. Was the tension rising as the second goal remained elusive? Inside the last ten minutes of the half it was the Netherlands pressing again as Cruyff fired powerfully in, but the ball only found the welcoming arms of Staykov.

Niggling fouls by both teams seemed to prevent the game gathering any sort of consistent rhythm and it was no surprise that the next goal came from another infringement. In the final minute of the half, a quick throw-in from Krol set Rensenbrink off, cutting in from the left flank. Inside, the unexpected figure of Jansen loomed up, unmarked. The ball was fed inside and, just as the midfielder was about to shoot, he was unceremoniously felled by Stefan Velichkov. A yellow card and spot kick were the obvious outcomes. Again, complaints were merely customary. Neeskens stepped up for a third time. He smashed it home for a third time. Seconds later, the referee ended the half.

There was insufficient time between the goal and the break to see the effect it would have on the game but, as the second period got under way, the Netherlands looked to drive home their advantage. Cruyff and Rep both had efforts go close inside the first 120 seconds. Whether for tactical reasons, injury or because a first-half yellow card meant possible trouble afterwards, Van Hanegem was removed for the second period. The fact that Michels sent on defender Rinus Israel rather than a like-for-like midfielder suggests it was the former. Locking down the advantage made eminent sense as a win confirmed qualification.

Such apparent caution was so nearly deemed unnecessary when a cross from Jansen found Rensenbrink unmarked in front of goal. A couple of twists and turns and a shot against the upright kept the game alive, though. While the introduction of the Feyenoord stopper certainly added steel to the Dutch play, the loss of the driving runs of Van Hanegem also reduced their attacking threat. But they still controlled the game, and Rensenbrink became a regular threat to the Bulgarian defence. It looked increasingly like a question of how many the Oranje would win by.

Rensenbrink threatened. Cruyff was denied at the last by a desperate challenge. Then, inside the final 20 minutes, a challenge on Rep inside the area looked like a third spot kick when the referee blew. Perhaps concerned by the potential notoriety of having awarded three penalties in a single game, he decided on an indirect free kick for obstruction. It mattered little. A weak header from the crossed ball allowed Rep to volley the third goal. It was now 'game over' and the Dutch were back in swagger mode, as the chants echoed around the stadium … A Neeskens volley was acrobatically tipped over the bar by Staykov as the setting sun illustrated how the light was going out on Bulgarian hopes.

Suurbier, Rep, Rensenbrink and Cruyff had efforts, but the next goal would strangely come at the other end, albeit from a Dutch foot. A break down the left and cross deceived Jongbloed and, bracketed by two forwards, Krol turned the ball into his own net as he tried to clear. Michels replaced Neeskens with De Jong, and ten minutes later the substitute restored the three-goal lead. Cruyff crossed and the Feyenoord midfielder threw himself forward to score with a diving header. It rounded out an impressive display.

The performance, the goals and the thrilling football now opened the floodgates. In the stadium tens of thousands were wearing Oranje and cheering their team. Back in the Netherlands as well, as David Winner described, Oranje Fever was captivating a country that, '...having been largely indifferent to their national team when the competition began – had become a nation of passionate armchair fans. This was the first World Cup to be televised in Holland; and as totaalvoetbal bemused and overwhelmed one opponent after another, sales of colours TVs rocketed.'[79] The group ended with the Netherlands topping the standings with five points, the Swedes also qualified. Both Bulgaria and Uruguay went home. This was about to get serious.

Traditionally, following the initial group stage, a knockout process followed, reducing the qualifiers to a final two who would then meet in the final. The 1974 tournament, however, saw FIFA inaugurate the concept of extending the groups into a second stage; two groups, each comprising four teams, with the winners of each advancing to the final, and the runners-up competing in the play-off for third place. Although the rationale may have been to allow each team to maintain an active presence in the competition for longer, there was always the prospect of unexpected initial group outcomes producing unequal second-phase groups. Although to some extent that happened, only a surprise result in one of the other group games avoided an outcome that may have persuaded the governing body to abandon the idea for future tournaments. Well, after 1982, that is.

Along with the Netherlands and Sweden the qualifying teams were East and West Germany from Group One,

---

79   Winner, David, *Brilliant Orange* (London: Bloomsbury, 2000)

Yugoslavia and Brazil from Group Two, together with Poland and Argentina from Group Four. It meant that the teams that reached the last eight were as widely expected. The order in which they finished, however, was less the case, and that was the criteria that determined the composition of the second-phase groupings. East Germany's defeat of their brethren from the other side of the divided country meant that they topped Group One, rather than the hosts. Yugoslavia's nine-goal romp against Zaire outgunned Brazil and saw them top Group Two. Poland's 3-2 defeat of Argentina did the same for Group Four, although as the succeeding games confirmed this was a true reflection of form between the two teams.

It all meant that the concept of having two group winners and two runners-up in each second-phase group, theoretically logical, produced unexpected results. Group A was made up of the Netherlands, Argentina, East Germany and Brazil, while Group B had West Germany, Poland, Sweden and Yugoslavia. Had the game between the two Germanys gone the other way, though, Michels's team would have faced the ultimate 'group of death' and faced Brazil, Argentina and West Germany. The hosts, therefore, were presented with a less onerous task, facing Poland, Sweden and Yugoslavia. Of course, as it turned out, the Oranje would still have to play West Germany anyway, albeit after the hosts so nearly missed out against the outstanding Poles on a swimming pool of a pitch.

With the wisdom of hindsight, it looked like avoiding the hosts was a minor break of sorts for Michels and his players, although it may not have felt like it at the time. For a squad brimming with confidence following the display against Bulgaria, and the front three of Rensenbrink, Cruyff and Rep now firing, the Dutch would have feared no one. Their opening second-phase encounter was against Argentina on 26 June at the Parkstadion in Gelsenkirchen. This was the same stadium where the Swedes had overcome Austria to book their place in West Germany when heavy snow left the pitch whited out. There wouldn't be snow this time, but as the game progressed, there would be rain, and lots of it. None of it would pour on the Oranje parade, however.

The South Americans had hardly impressed to date. Following their defeat to the Poles, they had overpowered Haiti, winning by seven goals, and then drawn with Italy. Qualification came via the narrowest of goal-difference margins placing them above Italy. Had they not enjoyed the romp against the Haitians, they would not have progressed. Their reward would be to have the Dutch tear them asunder.

A mere couple of minutes into the game, Cruyff so nearly controlled a high through pass on the edge of the Argentine box, but the ball was scampered clear. When a similar opportunity presented itself ten minutes or so later, the outcome was very different. Chances were appearing and Rensenbrink fired powerfully, but Daniel Carnevali tipped the shot over the bar. Already, the Argentines were being pushed on to the defensive. From the corner, the ball was pulled back to Krol. The defender drove in a shot, but dragged it wide of the near post. A clipped pass from Jansen found Cruyff free in the box, but the offside flag saved Argentina. A goal was clearly on the way, and Cruyff on the end of a through ball looked the obvious route. Another astute pass broke the back line again. This time Rensenbrink galloped clear. Again, the flag. It was a close decision, but probably accurate.

Eventually, the run was timed to perfection and the flag offered no escape. Van Hanegem clipped the ball forward as Cruyff ran across, and then into, the penalty area. With an elegance that disguised the technical complexity, his right foot reached into the air and plucked the ball under his spell. A further step, as Carnevali advanced, allowed him to slip by the lunging goalkeeper, carefully avoiding a trailing right leg, and roll the ball into the unguarded net with his left foot. The balance was gymnastic, the poise balletic, the finish graceful. Poetry in motion. Which other player, which other team, of that or almost any era, could conjure up such a goal? 'Something in the way [he] moves...'[80] as James Taylor would might have serenaded. The right arm raised, slapping the air in celebration, was classic Cruyff, as was the goal.

The floodgates were open. Not scoring more was simply inconceivable. Seconds later, Rensenbrink was nearly through on goal. Surely there were more Oranje shirts on the pitch than Argentine ones? Everywhere the South Americans were outnumbered. Even when possession was lost, the Dutch players swarmed around the ball hustling and harrying, bullying opponents off the ball, before sweeping forwards again. Jansen and Krol exchanged passes, once, twice, three times as they raided down the left. The latter crossed, but found no one. The ball rolled on unimpeded out to the right flank. Rep gathered, to Neeskens, to Cruyff as Neeskens ran forward and Cruyff found him unerringly, advancing beyond the Argentine defence. A pass was pulled back to Van Hanegem, who somehow got the ball stuck under his feet, and it was desperately cleared.

This was football from the gods. The Dutch were Hermes, wing-heeled delivers of goals. The Argentines were mere mortals in comparison, as rapt as the crowds in the stadium and the millions watching on television. *Gazzetta dello Sport* journalist Alex Frosio was watching with delight. 'They played a football nobody had seen before. No roles, no positions: I would say socialism applied to football, even if some are more equal than others, Cruyff for example.'[81]

80   'Something in the way she moves' from James Taylor's debut album, *James Taylor* 1968
81   Frosio, Alex – Interview with the author

A through ball once more. Rep like a knife slicing through the defence to collect. He rounded Carnevali and pulled the ball back to Jansen, who slid in to shoot, but a defender blocked on the line. Less than 20 minutes had been played, but the Dutch could have been four or five goals clear already. Suurbier and Cruyff opened up the defence from the left. Cruyff closed in on the overworked Carnevali and feigned to shoot before rolling the ball back to Neeskens who crashed it high into the net. Another marginal offside decision ruled the strike out. If anyone was working as hard as the Argentine goalkeeper it was the official with the flag lining the left flank of the South Americans' defence.

Another pass through the inside-right channel, and it was Jansen's turn to gallop into space, draw Carnevali out wide and skate past him. The goalkeeper recovered to block the cross and concede a corner. Getting to his feet, he berated his defenders for allowing so many gaps. It was hardly their fault, though. They only had 11 players. It clearly was far from enough.

As the corner was played in, Carnevali flapped at the ball, diverting it towards the edge of the area from where Krol had fired wide earlier. This time, there was no escape. The ball detonated from the defender's right foot and arrowed home – 2-0 after 25 minutes. The game was surely over already, but one question remained. How many were the Dutch going to score? Perhaps the question should have been better phrased. How many do they want to score? For ten minutes or so, they seemed happy that two was enough. Perhaps it was merely a pause, though. As half-time approached, Cruyff was nearly clear, then Rensenbrink was, but rare poor control cost him the chance. At the break Argentina would have been elated that no more had been conceded.

Early in the second period, the floodlights came on as the evening darkened. The football played by the Netherlands, however, was bright enough to light up the darkest of hours, as they continued to dominate. Studied possession was interspersed with bursts of attacking verve. Slow, slow, quick, quick, slow. The Argentines were compelled to dance to the Oranje tune as Michels's orchestra played majestically. The rain began to fall but, as Krol later related, it hardly mattered. 'It was typical Dutch weather. It was raining. In Holland we play a lot in the rain. So, it suited us.'[82] As with the Dutch dominance, the rain would become a consistent feature for the remainder of the game. The sky seemed to weep for the team toiling without hope or reward. 'Don't Cry for Me Argentina'.[83]

Into the last quarter of the game with players finding it difficult to keep their feet on the slickened surface. Only the Dutch grasp on the game remained unaffected, as the fatigue tearing at South American muscles and increasing feelings of resignation nagging their souls allowed more spaces to develop. Cruyff nearly added a third as he burst into the area but, with the pitch so wet, perhaps walking on water was beyond even him, and Carnevali jabbed out a foot to divert his shot wide.

A couple of minutes later, though, a precise cross from the left by Cruyff found Rep beyond his defender as the ball dropped for him to head inside the post. On the bench, Michels waved his arms in the air. Five minutes from the end, Suurbier limped off to be replaced by Israel, but there was still one more goal to come. Argentina escaped when Cruyff scampered past an exhausted and demoralised Perfumo breaking into open space, only to be halted by a desperate rugby tackle. Inside the final seconds, Carnevali blocked Van Hanegem's shot as he advanced on goal, but the ball scooted out to Cruyff who volleyed home from an acute angle.

82   Krol, Ruud, Football's Greatest International Teams, Sky Sports, 2010
83   'Don't Cry for me Argentina', Julie Covington, *Evita*, 1976

It had been a startling performance, suggested David Winner, 'their most electrifying to date'.[84] In Spain, *Marca* would later describe it as being 'as close to producing a perfect performance as anyone in footballing history'.[85] It seems a little strange to say, but there was a general appreciation that the four-goal defeat was something of a let-off for Argentina. Both teams had their squad numbers allocated alphabetically, and both were standing on the same area of grass. Other than that, there seemed little similarity between the teams. They were clearly playing the same game at entirely different levels.

Four years later, however, with both teams having so many different personnel, Argentina would take revenge, beating the Dutch in the 1978 World Cup Final. There's a sad symmetry about that. The year before Ajax lost their crown as European champions, they defeated Bayern Munich 4-0, only to see the Bavarians crowned as champions next time around. Fate always seemed to have an individually perverse sense of irony where Dutch football was concerned.

In the group's other game, played in Hannover at the same time, Brazil defeated East Germany 1-0 in an uninspiring triumph thanks to a typical Rivellino free kick on the hour. It had been four brief years since the exuberance of Brazil's finest hour as Pelé, Gerson and Tostao blessed the world with their football, leaving so many 'spellbound by the combination of football that most of us had never seen before',[86] as Graham Hunter recalled. Two other members of the forward line from Mexico, Jairzinho and Rivellino, had survived to the 1974 squad. The joyful ethic of their play had, however, been lost. This version was a very different Brazilian team. Coach Mario

84   Winner, David, *Brilliant Orange* (London: Bloomsbury, 2000)
85   https://www.marca.com/en/football/international-football/2020/03/22/5e7780902
     68e3e48638b459a.html
86   Hunter, Graham – Interview with the author

Zagallo had been a World Cup winner in 1958 and 1962 as a player and was coach of the fabulous team that entranced the world in Mexico.

More influenced by the disappointment of 1966, when referees stood and watched as players formed disorderly lines to queue up and kick Pelé out of the World Cup, than the joy and majesty of 1970, Zagallo feared another overly physical tournament as the World Cup returned to Europe. His team eschewed joy and enthusiasm, instead grasping at physicality and caution, determined not to be muscled off their throne. The caution was years out of date, though, and ill-suited to 1974.

Brazil had struggled through their group games playing out goalless draws that could have produced even worse results against both Yugoslavia and then Scotland, seeking solace in defence and seemingly intent on shooting from long distance, enveloped by caution and concern of getting caught on the counter-attack if they committed forwards. Scotland in particular took Brazil close. The Scots had already defeated Zaire, albeit by an unconvincing 2-0 margin that would eventually come back to haunt them, when they faced Brazil who had, even less convincingly, drawn 0-0 with Yugoslavia.

The game, in Frankfurt's Waldstadion, could have gone either way. 'Brazil played in a way I didn't recognise, and I didn't like,' Graham Hunter recalled. 'And we should have beaten them.'[87] It's not an unreasonable assessment, but Zagallo's team escaped with another goalless draw. Only a 3-0 victory against Zaire saw the champions progress, with Scotland having only beaten the Africans 2-0. Had Willie Ormond's team scored just one more against Zaire, it would have been the Scots, rather than Brazil, in the runners-up spot and qualifying.

Four days after the opening games, the Netherlands and Brazil both played their second fixtures. Both were expected

87   Hunter, Graham – Interview with the author

to win. The champions were pitted against a much-changed Argentine team, as Vladislao Cap shuffled his pack following the demolition inflicted by the Dutch. Games between the two South American football powerhouses are never anything but ferociously contested, however, and Brazil came through with a narrow 2-1 win thanks to goals from 1970 heroes Rivellino and Jairzinho, either side of an equaliser from Brindisi. If the Dutch could overcome an East German team now looking uninterested and politically sated following the epic defeat of their neighbours, the final fixture of the group would be a *de facto* semi-final.

Before that game though, astonishingly, Michels left his squad and flew back to Spain to coach Barcelona in the final of the Copa del Generalísimo against Real Madrid at the Estadio Vicente Calderon. It had been part of the agreement when the Catalan club gave consent to their manager taking up the role with the national team. Cruyff was naturally unavailable, but with Spain not involved in the World Cup, Real Madrid were at full strength and triumphed 4-0. On his return to Germany, Michels made the fairly easy decision to send out the same team that meted out the comprehensive defeat of Argentina to face East Germany. The world waited for another performance from the team that had lit up the tournament through sun and rain a few days earlier. This time, they would deliver a victory of an entirely different nature.

As with so many games across the tournament, the rain came down as the teams lined up, and hardly relented throughout the game. It would be the waves of Dutch attacks, however, that washed East German aspirations down the drain. Just seven minutes in, following a short corner from the right and cross into the box, an initial header was blocked on the line, before a brief scramble resulted in Neeskens sliding in to guide the ball home. From that point, the game was practically over. The East Germans struggled with paltry results, as the

Oranje barely extended themselves beyond second-gear. A Martin Hoffmann shot from distance that Jongbloed comfortably collected was the best of their efforts ahead of the break. Fifteen minutes into the second period, Cruyff and Jansen combined to allow Rensenbrink to guide the ball inside the far post from the edge of the area. The victory set up the clash of champions against pretenders, the footballing royalty, albeit in an unfamiliar guise, against the anarchic new order, reactionaries against revolutionaries, South America against Europe. It was a game for the ages.

It should also have been Total Football against *Jogo Bonito*, a contest of artists each competing to paint the brightest picture with elegant strokes of footballing creativity on a green canvas. Sadly, it was none of those. The Dutch delivered their style, but Zagallo's Brazil were sulking, snarling streetfighters. Some called their style pragmatic. Others called it brutal. Graham Hunter went further. 'They were like ... thugs!'[88] Even the colours were different. The Dutch wore an all-white strip, those stripes on the sleeve highlighted in the inevitable Oranje, and socks of the same hue. Brazil wore two-toned blue shirts and shorts. The canary yellow kit was at least saved from the ignominy of being besmirched by such an un-Brazilian display.

Wherever they were as they watched, the souls of the 'Pearl', Gerson and Tostao would surely have been troubled. At least one hero from 1970 recognised the Dutch as the new heirs to the beautiful game. Carlos Alberto, the man who lifted the Jules Rimet Trophy in the Estadio Azteca, conceded, 'The only team I've seen that did things differently was Holland at the 1974 World Cup in Germany. Since then everything looks more or less the same to me ... their "carousel" style of play was amazing to watch and marvellous for the game.'[89]

88   Hunter, Graham – Interview with the author
89   Alberto, Carlos, *World Soccer – 50th Anniversary edition*, 2010

When the game kicked off, it took less than 40 seconds for Brazil to signal their intent. Neeskens was tumbled to the turf as he skipped past Rivellino, back defending on the edge of his own area. It wouldn't be the last such occasion. Pelé would later lament the approach, and that the free-flowing ethos of 1970 had been discarded. 'We have suddenly become too defensive-minded … Perhaps it is only an uncharacteristic phase that will pass in due course. I hope so at least.'[90] It would, but for now this was an entirely different challenge for the Dutch, but one they were ready to take on.

Two minutes later, it was Jairzinho's turn to halt Neeskens with a trip. The two survivors of the glory days of 1970 had sadly set the tone for the game. A clumsy punch by Leao following a corner from Cruyff was sent back to the kicker, who then had to nimbly jump out of the way of a lunging two-footed challenge by Ze Maria. It was the sort of tackle often labelled as a leg-breaker, and had it made contact with the Dutchman's shins, the consequences could have been catastrophic.

By this time, the nature of the game had been set, and the Dutch weren't slow in getting their counter punches in to show they would not be bullied. Had they been primed to fight fire with fire? Jan-Hermen de Bruijn had no doubts. 'Yes. That is what the players all said. They knew that they had to be equally physical to survive. Ajax had done that several times before [in European games] and everybody was up to it. Feyenoord too by the way. For them it was their natural game. Van Hanegem and Jansen dictated that. Dutch training was also very physical. Always Ajax/Feyenoord rivalry.'[91] Rep had certainly made his intentions clear after Rivellino's persistent niggling by using his elbow, unseen by the officials. 'Today Rivellino is my friend,' he said. 'But if we played that game

---

90   Rensenbrink's injury looks like putting him out of the final, *The Times* – 5 July 1974.

91   De Bruijn, Jan-Hermen – Interview with the author

today, there would be six red cards.'[92] Some think the total would have been higher, including Jan-Hermen de Bruijn. 'Holland was also extremely aggressive. It was a total miracle there was just one red card. In modern times there would have been ten.'[93]

The first goal nearly came after five minutes when a poor defensive header dropped to Cruyff near the penalty spot, but his instant shot was tipped around the post by a diving Leao. Then Van Hanegem volleyed over. All of the football was coming from the Dutch as the crowd, massively in favour of the European team, roared them on. With ten minutes on the clock, and a goal kick about to be taken by Leao, West German referee Kurt Tschenscher signalled for him to wait. The official held the game in stasis for some 60 seconds, before signalling Leao to continue. Few fans watching across the world would have known the reason for the hiatus. Following the death of Argentine president, Juan Peron, FIFA had decreed that all of the games that day should halt at the tenth minute – significant apparently for Peron's ten years in power – as a mark of respect. To do so in Argentina's game against East Germany would have been understandable, but to copy the tribute across all games that day left more than a few people perplexed. The fact that the following tournament was scheduled for Argentina, with Peron being a significant factor in that decision, may have offered at least some explanation.

The political climate in Argentina would be a significant factor four years later. Peron's wife and vice president, Isabel Martinez de Peron, had assumed the presidency, becoming the first female president in the Americas. Familial connections, however, were hardly sufficient credentials for accession and, with the country in crisis and the economy devastated, she was swept from office by a *coup d'état* headed by General

92   https://www.theguardian.com/football/2001/apr/10/sport.comment1
93   De Bruijn, Jan-Hermen – Interview with the author

Commander of the Army Jorge Rafael Videla on 24 March 1976. The regime's harsh repression of dissent would create a backdrop of inhibition and fear for the 1978 World Cup. Raphael Honigstein considered that in Germany, 'There was a very oppressive atmosphere because of what happened in 1972 at the Olympics … stringent security measures and the players felt uncomfortable … being watched by armed police. It just made it a very joyless affair.'[94] The Argentina World Cup would surpass that by some measure.

It would be easy to say that the stoppage disturbed the rhythm of the game, but there hadn't been much rhythm anyway. Both before and after, the Dutch probed intelligently, while the Brazilian build-up was ponderous in comparison with shots from distance hardly causing Jongbloed a passing concern. A pass to Paulo Cesar on the edge of the Dutch box on 25 minutes was their best opportunity, but the midfielder fired wide. It inspired the South American fans to chant for their team, but responses from the Oranje-clad section of the crowd quickly quelled their ardour.

Given the nature of the game, it was a surprise when the first yellow card went to a Dutch player. Chasing forward on to a through ball, full-back Suurbier missed out and a late challenge trying to block a clearance provoked the sanction. Brazilian defender Luís Pereira's complaints and gesticulations saw him added seconds later. Soon after, Neeskens elegantly slipped his marker to charge clear down the right flank. Cruyff was running to support in the centre, until an off-the-ball tug halted his progress. Krol's rapid retribution in conceding a free kick was akin to retaliation. Paulo Cezar's foul on Cruyff seconds later was not.

Towards the break, with the game still goalless, the physical battle was ratcheted up. Krol's robust challenge on

94   Raphael Honigstein – Interview with the author

Ze Maria brought a rolling response from the Brazilian that failed to impress the referee, vindicated by the player's apparent miraculous recovery. There certainly seemed little wrong with him a few short minutes later. Graham Hunter recalled the events. 'There's a long ball from Wim Jansen to Cruyff ... who's playing high wide left, and a Brazil player ... rugby tackles him. Now, it turns out it was Ze Maria. He's just been caught on the turn, Cruyff's away, and he begins to stumble. If he stumbles and doesn't touch Cruyff, Cruyff is free. But as he goes down ... it's a perfect rugby tackle.'[95] The yellow card was inevitable.

From the resultant free kick, the ball was headed clear as, unseen by officials, a Dutch player suffered another off-the-ball incident. Neeskens lay still, felled by a blow to the head as play continued and only a late block by Rijsbergen prevented Jairzinho giving Brazil the most unwarranted of leads. Minutes of attention passed before Neeskens recovered sufficiently to continue. The perpetrator went unidentified and unpunished. Graham Hunter again, 'That was emblematic to me of what was going on. This beautiful team in white was playing the way I'd seen that amazing Brazil team play four years earlier.'[96]

Fouls were now becoming the customary way of breaking down Dutch attacks. Jansen and Cruyff combined to set the Feyenoord midfielder free and closing in on the Brazilian back line. A ball played past Marinho Peres took him out of the game, but the defender's body-check on the Dutch player did precisely the same thing to him. Another yellow card. At the break, the game remained scoreless. Brazil looked like a team who had only scored six goals in the tournament so far, three of those coming against Zaire, and yet the best chances had probably fallen to them. It was something that the Dutch players were well aware of, as Cruyff related. 'I'd already

95   Hunter, Graham – Interview with the author
96   Hunter, Graham – Interview with the author

declared that we were looking forward to playing Brazil, and in the second half we showed why. We'd been lucky not to concede a few times early in the first half, and after we'd scared ourselves stupid the team rallied to play the best football we could.'[97]

The opening minutes of the second period had been deceptively quiet but, when Van Hanegem played a quick free kick to Neeskens, advancing into the Brazilian half, all that would change. Playing a ball wide to the right to Cruyff, he then scampered into the area. The return was perfectly placed for Neeskens to stretch out a right foot and guide the ball over Leao and into the net. The Dutch were ahead and their celebrating fans sang out, confident that this Brazil side had little chance of a comeback. The players were becoming accustomed to the vociferous backing. It had followed them around Germany. Rensenbrink remembered the lift it gave to the team. 'It felt like every game was a home game. There must have been 20,000 Dutch supporters at every match.'[98] The Dutch were free-flowing, the Brazilians hesitant and increasingly petulant. On 65 minutes the killer blow was struck.

Neat interplay with Rep set Krol running free down the left. The cross met up perfectly with Cruyff's dart into the box, and a side-foot finish did the rest. It was a goal 'of glorious nature',[99] Graham Hunter enthused. Beaming Dutch smiles. Angry Brazilian glares. The game was done – but not quite the drama. A mere handful of seconds later Rensenbrink played off a pass, immediately reaching his hand down to the back of his right thigh. It was the classic tell-tale sign of a hamstring injury. He limped off the pitch and, with the final just four days away, he was surely hobbling out of the tournament as well. Theo de Jong came on as

97   Cruyff, Johan, *My Turn* (London: Macmillan, 2016)
98   Football's Greatest International Teams, Sky Sports, 2010
99   Hunter, Graham – Interview with the author

his replacement. Would the 26-year-old also be inheriting Rensenbrink's place in Munich?

Brazil were now forced to gamble, and attack – at last. There was always the danger of being caught on the break, though, by the quicksilver Dutch forwards. Time ebbed away and emotions turned from frustration, through desperation, then to anger. A body-check brought Rep to the floor. Another one did the same to Cruyff. An elbow by Marinho Chagas felled Rep. Neeskens leapt to avoid Rivellino's knee-high challenge and, as the ball ran loose, the Brazilian stamped across the loose ball and down Jansen's leg before flooring Neeskens at the second attempt. Surely, this was only going to end up one way. With five minutes remaining, the seemingly inevitable happened.

This type of incident is often described as being a 'bad tackle' or 'poor challenge', when such terms are mere euphemisms for what is simply bordering on assault. On 85 minutes, Neeskens gathered possession and advanced towards the Brazil box. Luis Pereira, already cautioned in the first period, ran across and kicked him, taking his legs away. Simply put, there was no attempt to play the ball whatsoever. As the Dutch player lay injured, the referee produced a straight red card. Almost instinctively, Rivellino began to protest against the decision, but it was pointless and he knew it. Pereira was ushered from the field but, such was his ensuing rage, he seemed intent on inviting the entire stadium to fight with him. Michels sent Israel on to replace the battered Neeskens and with Brazilian tempers at least now held a little in check, the Dutch played out the remaining minutes intent on avoiding further injuries. In their first tournament appearance for 36 years, they had reached the World Cup Final.

In a neat piece of symmetry, the other group had followed a similar pattern, with the final game between West Germany and Poland serving as a semi-final. On a pitch that was surely unfit for play by any reasonable measure, but compelled into action by television schedules, the Polish pattern of play was compromised more than the Germans' tactics. The scrappiest of one-goal victories meant that the hosts would also reach the final. The scene was set for one of the classic games in the history of international football.

Before the showdown however, another battle would be played out. German tabloid newspaper *Bild* ran a story headlined 'Cruyff, Sekt, nackte Mädchen und ein kühles Bad' (Cruyff, Champagne, naked girls and a cool bath) alleging that one of their reporters had infiltrated the Dutch camp and seen 'wild parties' going on there, particularly involving the Dutch captain, on the eve of the game against Brazil. Understandably, Michels denied all of the allegations in a press conference and any player interviewed followed the same party line, claiming it was some kind of dastardly German plot to unsettle the squad. The oft-repeated rebuttal largely became common currency. Photographs were apparently in the newspaper's possession, but the fact that they were never released only further diminished the story's credibility, painting the Dutch squad as innocent victims. Perhaps that wasn't the case though. 'It's now accepted that the *Bild* story was not only accurate but it was a very mild reflection of the lack of discipline that had overtaken the Dutch squad,'[100] David Winner suggested. Whatever the case, it clearly had an effect on the players, particularly the captain, Jan-Hermen de Bruijn said: 'Cruyff was almost 24 hours in *pijnde* [trouble] with his wife three days before the final.'[101]

Whatever the truth or otherwise of such allegations, few would contest that there was now, not only a growing conviction amongst the Dutch that they would win the trophy

---

100 https://www.the42.ie/holland-1974-world-cup-tragedy-1488354-Mar2016/
101 De Bruijn, Jan-Hermen – Interview with the author

– 'We knew that we were better,'[102] Cruyff simply stated later – but also an arrogance that they could do it, in precisely the manner that they chose, and possessed a determination to do so. David Winner summed up the perception of the mood in the camp. 'They thought they were going to win easily and the Germans prepared very thoroughly and the Dutch didn't. They felt that the hard game for them was beating Brazil in the semis and so they took their foot off the gas and didn't keep focus and weren't as sharp as they should've been.'[103] They were the best team in the tournament, an eclectic collection of talents brought together and coaxed into outlandishly devastating football by Michels's tactics. Perhaps the problem was that they knew it to be so. It was the fatal flaw in their make-up. The freedom they had to express themselves, the iron-clad conviction that their way of play was without doubt the best and that this was their time, would all conspire against them. 'That's part of the tragedy – that they did it to themselves to some degree. They underestimated the event and the task and the opponents,'[104] David Winner reflected.

On the day of the final, Rensenbrink was amazingly passed fit to play by the Dutch medical team. Later, rumours would abound that although not truly fit, he needed to play in the final to fulfil a boot contract. It seemed a shallow accusation, and Rensenbrink would later try to dispel it, declaring that there was such a deal but the amount involved, a few thousand guilders, was hardly the reason he wanted to play. This was, after all, the World Cup Final, and he wanted to win.

For some members of the Dutch squad, there was also another reason why they should beat the Germans; why they needed to. The Second World War had ended less than 30 years previously, and many scars were still raw. Van Hanegem had

102 Cruyff, Johann, Football's Greatest International Teams, Sky Sports 2010
103 https://www.the42.ie/holland-1974-world-cup-tragedy-1488354-Mar2016/
104 https://www.the42.ie/holland-1974-world-cup-tragedy-1488354-Mar2016/

lost his father and two brothers in a German bombing raid. It was a pain he carried. In a magazine interview later, he spoke of his dislike for Germans. The interviewer asked him to explain. 'Well, they've got the wrong ancestors of course,' answered Van Hanegem. The Dutch word *fout*, meaning 'wrong', also has the specific meaning 'wrong in war'. 'That's not their fault,' said the journalist who was playing devil's advocate. 'Maybe not,' Van Hanegem replied, 'but the fact remains.'[105]

Despite the Germans being at home and reigning European champions, it was the Netherlands who were many pundits' favourites. Even those most loquacious of companions, taxi drivers, were somewhat subdued. One remarked to *Times* journalist Geoffrey Green that expectations were low. 'Holland, I fear, will win,'[106] he told the scribe. Green didn't disagree.

It was an understandable assessment. In comparison to the thrusting form of the Dutch, the hosts' progress to the final had been stuttering and unconvincing. A fortunate win against the underestimated Poles, when water polo would have been more suitable than football, only reinforced the view – whilst Dutch confidence was topped up to the level labelled as 'Swaggering Arrogance'. Raphael Honigstein considered that the German performances were a pale shadow of those that had delivered the European Championship two years earlier. 'This Germany team, who had probably played the best football ever seen from a West German team in 1972, never really got fully going.'[107]

There were also rumours of dissent in the German camp, with Beckenbauer's influence undermining that of coach Helmut Schoen. Accusations of a similar nature were almost *de rigueur* for the Dutch with regard to Cruyff's influence over the coach. For such things to happen with the Germans, however, would hardly have helped their cause and, at a press

---

105 Kuper, Simon, *Football Against the Enemy* (London: Orion, 1994)
106 Rensenbrink's injury looks like putting him out of the final, *The Times*, 5 July 1974
107 Honigstein, Raphael – Interview with the author

conference, whilst the coach was happy to concede that he consulted with his captain, he was keen to emphasise that he was the man in charge. Beckenbauer confirmed the coach's words. 'I am his representative on the field and the reason I tried to ginger up our team while we were losing to East Germany was because I felt we had let down both Helmut and ourselves.'[108] It seemed to put the matter to rest, although Raphael Honigstein believes there were certainly things amiss in the German camp. 'There were disciplinary issues. Beckenbauer was going to see a girlfriend at night. They couldn't really agree on a formation and Schoen, I think, was losing control of the dressing-room.'[109]

On the day of the final, as the teams lined up in the tunnel ahead of kick-off, the Germans sought to balance things out a little by trying to gain a psychological advantage. Bernd Holzenbein explained: 'We planned to look them in the eye, to show we were as big as they were. They had the feeling they were invincible – you could see it in their eyes. Their attitude to us was, "How many goals do you want to lose by today boys?"'[110]

With Rensenbrink confirmed as a starter, the Dutch team was the same as had played against Brazil. The bench was manned by Schrijvers, Israel, De Jong, Keizer and Rene van de Kerkhof, who had apparently been earmarked to play if Rensenbrink hadn't made the cut. The stage was set. How could the Dutch lose? What could possibly go wrong? Even the German players felt overawed by their opponents. Holzenbein again: 'While we waited to go on to the pitch, I tried to look them in the eye, but I couldn't do it. They made us feel small.'[111]

108 Rensenbrink's injury looks like putting him out of the final, *The Times,* 4 July 1974
109 Honigstein, Raphael – Interview with the author
110 Winner, David, *Brilliant Orange* (London: Bloomsbury, 2000)
111 Winner, David, *Brilliant Orange* (London: Bloomsbury, 2000)

In a foretaste of what would happen four years later when Argentine shenanigans held up the start of the 1978 final, English referee Jack Taylor was compelled to do the same for the game in Munich's Olympiastadion. Taylor's appointment had more than a shade of controversy around it. Scottish referee Bob Davidson, who had earlier officiated the Argentina v Netherlands game, was convinced that the honour of taking control of the final had been granted to him. Part of the officiating team that travelled with FIFA as the group were moved from Frankfurt to Munich by train, he related that, 'I was sitting having a meal in the dining car when Ken Aston [leader of the World Cup referees' commission] hit me on the shoulder, gave me a thumbs-up sign and said "Congratulations, you're refereeing the final on Sunday."'[112] Sadly for Davidson, it transpired that the unofficial announcement was either in error, or that minds were changed at a later date, with Taylor getting the gig. The Englishman's handling of his two games, Bulgaria v Uruguay and West Germany v Argentina in the second group stage, had apparently held sway with the commission.

It was therefore the Englishman, not the Scotsman, who noticed that the corner flags had been removed so that the tournament's closing ceremony, which took place before the final, could be completed unhampered by something as trivial as the necessary pitch markings for the biggest game in world football. Despite the reputation for German efficiency, someone had forgotten to replace them after the collection of dancers and performers had vacated the pitch.

Fortunately, a similar occasion, early in Taylor's refereeing career, had ensured that checking such things were part of his pre-game ritual. 'As a local referee I remember doing a game where a guy came up to me and said, "You've got to restart." I

<hr />

112 Angry Scottish referee walks out, *The Times*, 5 July 1974

asked why and he said, "There's no corner flags." It's something I never forgot and so when you come to a World Cup Final in Germany, such an efficient nation who never make mistakes, and there's no corner flags you can't believe it. There's millions of people watching and here I am, this one little guy, coming all the way around the pitch sticking corner flags in.'[113] Once all was sorted, he could begin the game. It wouldn't be long however, before Taylor would need to intervene once more.

The game would be one of the most talked about major finals in the history of football, and little wonder. Author and journalist Rob Smyth described it as, 'one of the most interesting, layered games imaginable – even before it started. The historical context, the emergence of the Netherlands team, the Ajax/Bayern rivalry, the fact West Germany were on the way down from 1972 yet under such huge pressure to win as hosts: a scriptwriter would kill for this stuff.'[114] The old adage suggests that 'history is always written by the winners.' In this game though, that seems not to be the case, with the accepted narrative emanating from a Dutch perspective. In order to provide a little balance, therefore, the views of Raphael Honigstein were sought to offer a German point of view.

Van Hanegem and Cruyff kicked off, and the ball went back to Krol, then Rijsbergen, Haan and Suurbier. All the Dutch players were taking an early touch. From Suurbier back to Haan, who swapped passes with Rijsbergen. Now Cruyff was in the back line, inevitably becoming involved, orchestrating, guiding, prompting. The ball was moved on to Rijsbergen, then Krol, before Neeskens joined the party. Finally, the ball found its way to Cruyff again. Even in these early moments it was clear that Schoen had allotted the unenviable task of man-marking the Dutch captain to Berti Vogts. Many years later,

---

113 Which matches have been delayed by crossbars, corner flags and kitmen? *The Guardian*, 16 May 2012
114 Smyth, Rob – Interview with the author

in an interview with Graham Hunter, Cruyff would describe Vogts as his 'toughest rival. You'd beat him, run past him, you'd stop to think for a second, and he'd be back, snapping and snarling at your ankles again. He's like a little aggressive dog.'[115] It was a disparaging description, but one that carried the greatest of respect for an honoured opponent.

The stalwart Borussia Monchengladbach defender would dutifully fulfil his remit throughout the game. In this first minute of Dutch play, however, despite his dogged adherence to the task, he was burnt by Cruyff's sudden acceleration, as he mercurially transformed sedate possession into scintillating, scything attack. When he collected the ball, the only Dutch player behind the No.14 was goalkeeper Jongbloed. Vogts was left trailing as Cruyff drove forward, and on towards the box in full flight, swaying and swerving. Closing from the right to try and cover, Uli Hoeness jabbed out a foot. It sent Cruyff tumbling to the floor. Perfectly placed, probably no more than three metres away from the incident and with a clear view, Taylor had no doubts. If Hoeness's reactions were less than perfect, Honigstein offered a reason. 'Hoeness didn't sleep all night because of nerves.'[116]

The penalty was awarded and German complaints that the challenge took place outside of the area were brief and quickly dismissed. Later Beckenbauer confirmed that he had also said to Taylor, 'You are an Englishman,'[117] before walking away. He conceded that it was intended to suggest an inbuilt bias against the Germans following the World Cups in 1966 and 1970 and two wars. Taylor was a widely experienced official, but some contend that the comment struck home, and affected the official's judgement of an incident in the game some 20 minutes later. Neeskens smashed the ball down the middle as

115 Hunter, Graham – Interview with the author
116 Honigstein, Raphael – Interview with the author
117 Jack Taylor Obituary, *The Telegraph* – 27 July 2012

Sepp Maier threw himself to his right. Less than two minutes had passed when the German goalkeeper fished the ball out of his net. He was the first German to touch the ball since kick-off. 'No team has ever made so perfect a start to a major final.'[118] Graham Hunter recalled the moment as he sat watching the game in his Aberdeen living room. After that coruscating, cascading move opened the scoring, he said to his mother, 'Even the great England team of 1966 could never come back from that!'[119] Or so it seemed.

As Oscar Wilde wrote, 'Quando dio vuole castigarci, ci manda quello che desideriamo'[120] ('When the gods wish to punish us, they answer our prayers.') Later Johnny Rep would lament, 'It would have been much better if West Germany had scored first.'[121] They didn't, though. Van Hanegem was also a little unsettled by the early goal, 'I remember thinking, that could be a bit of a problem.'[122] Was this the moment that actually cost the Dutch the final? Already massively confident, were any thoughts of caution dismissed?

Understandably, the Germans were stunned and off balance, but instead of driving on for what may well have been the killer second goal, the Dutch stood back, convinced of their supremacy. They reflected, admiring themselves in the mirror, transfixed by their own beauty. They were in the lead, in their pomp, and spent the next minutes as if considering options from a menu of delicious alternatives by which to pick apart their prey. 'They're Germans. They're not our friends, so let us humiliate them in front of their own fans,'[123] Van Hanegem recalls thinking.

118 Winner, David, *Brilliant Orange* (London: Bloomsbury, 2000)
119 Hunter, Graham – Interview with the author
120 Wilde, Oscar, *An Ideal Husband*, 1899
121 Winner, David, *Brilliant Orange* (London: Bloomsbury, 2000)
122 Van Hanegem, Wim, Football's Greatest International Teams, Sky Sports, 2010
123 Van Hanegem, Wim, Football's Greatest International Teams, Sky Sports, 2010

Cruyff was aware of the emotions. Recalling that same interview with him, Graham Hunter explained how the Dutch captain articulated his thoughts at the time. 'He spoke about the fact that, for some reason, collectively, without expressing it, it was in Dutch nature, still not having shaken off the world war, the invasion or the occupation, but also this sense of neighbours chafing against each other, particularly the economic and sometimes arrogant powerhouse neighbour, Germany, and a need to outstrip them. The two nations over the years have been nose-to-nose in so many ways. Cruyff expressed that it came to them all, that they wanted to humiliate West Germany, and that they abandoned playing the way that they would have played normally.'[124]

They wove intricate patterns with their passing, movement and control, producing beautiful images, Dutch Masters of another age, but with as much artistry at their command. It was designed to humiliate, and live up to the impression offered to Holzenbein in the tunnel. 'We are so much better than you. The game is won.' Like some high-rolling gambler revealing his hand full of aces, they placed their cards on the table, face up, inviting the Germans to 'read 'em and weep'. *De Telegraaf* journalist Jaap de Groot summed up the mood. 'OK, we're going to teach them a lesson.'[125]

Vogts was booked in the fourth minute as he floundered around, increasingly frustrated by chasing the elusive Cruyff. 'We wanted to make fun of the Germans. We didn't think about it, but we did it, passing the ball around and around,'[126] Rep recalled. 'I didn't mind if we only won 1-0, as long as we humiliated them,'[127] Van Hanegem conceded. For 20 minutes, the Dutch were lords of all they surveyed. They passed the

124 Hunter, Graham – Interview with the author
125 Football's Greatest International Teams, Sky Sports, 2010
126 Winner, David, *Brilliant Orange* (London: Bloomsbury, 2000)
127 Winner, David, *Brilliant Orange* (London: Bloomsbury, 2000)

ball. They controlled the game. It was men against boys. The Germans were led a merry dance and Cruyff was the conductor of the Dutch orchestra. Whoever pays the piper calls the tune and Dutch guilders were the currency of choice.

Self-indulgence and success are rarely easy bedfellows, though. 'I think we played a little too confident,'[128] Cruyff accepted. 'We forgot to score the second goal,'[129] Rep conceded. At this stage, the Dutch were performing well, while the Germans had struggled to reach the final. The issue with *Bild* only angered the Dutch players more. It was wonderful to watch, but also dangerous, as Jan-Hermen de Bruijn recalled. 'They became more annoyed than careful ... Holland forgot that ... Germans are most dangerous when underestimated. Holland scored without the Germans touching the ball and then came the feelings of superiority, all over the team. They played so much better than the Germans, it was so easy.'[130]

There was something particularly Dutch about this, so let someone on the inside explain the emotions. 'You really must be a Dutchman to understand this ... and arrogance was a part of it,' said Jan-Hermen de Bruijn. 'Many things happened in the run-up to the final. First of all, Holland started to think they could win the World Cup and that they were much better than West Germany. Against Uruguay, and I don't need to explain to you, that Dutch people, at that time, were not in love with German supporters, and there was a lot of rivalry. Already, at the end of the first week, there was a Saturday night that in Hamburg, West Germany lost 1-0 against the DDR; the Sparwasser game. On the next day, Holland went to Dortmund for the game against Bulgaria, again 30,000 people came again, and they were teasing the Germans, all over the

128 Football's Greatest International Teams, Sky Sports, 2010
129 Winner, David, *Brilliant Orange* (London: Bloomsbury, 2000)
130 De Bruijn, Jan-Hermen – Interview with the author

place. "Sparwasser" means "spare water" so every Dutchman would ask every German he came across, if he could have, or drink, a glass of spare water.'[131]

Midway through the first period, the Germans came more into the game. Like a boxer floored by a devastating punch, they were both surprised and relieved as their foe stood off performing the footballing equivalent of 'Ali Shuffles', throwing shapes and shadow boxing, rather than delivering the knockout blow. 'The story in Germany,' Honigstein recalled, 'is that the Dutch tried to humiliate Germany, doing tricks, doing keepy-uppies, doing back-heels and the Germans thought, "Oh no. This is not going to happen," and they got back into it.'[132]

Now, with heads cleared, they could start counter-punching. It was a dangerous time for the Dutch, as Rob Smyth identified. 'West Germany were mentally stronger. The Netherlands were a superior team and in better form. I'm not sure many teams in history could have come back from the complete humiliation of being 1-0 down, in their own World Cup Final, against their biggest rivals, before they had even touched the ball. I'm not saying the Netherlands were mentally weak – they weren't, and they were far tougher physically than many people remember. It's just that the Germans – especially the spine of Maier, Beckenbauer and Muller – were a little bit stronger and a bit more ruthless.'[133] Raphael Honigstein saw merit in the assessment. 'The Dutch are beautiful to look at, but maybe lack that professionalism to get over the line, and I guess 1974 is the perfect example. If the German team takes the lead in the first minute, that is the end. They wouldn't be doing the stuff that the Dutch did.'[134]

131 De Bruijn, Jan-Hermen – Interview with the author
132 Honigstein, Raphael – Interview with the author
133 Smyth, Rob – Interview with the author
134 Honigstein, Raphael – Interview with the author

On 25 minutes, a surging run by Holzenbein caused alarm in the Dutch defence. Haan was beaten, leaving Jansen as the only covering player as the German drove on into the penalty area. The Feyenoord midfielder lunged into a challenge but, video recordings seem to suggest, missed contact with both ball and German leg. Holzenbein hit the turf, though, and Taylor faced another big decision. Did Beckenbauer's earlier comment weigh on his mind? Was this an example of the 'ruthlessness' Rob Smyth referred to? Regardless, Taylor pointed to the spot and the Germans had a penalty.

The incident led to a German word being taken into the Dutch language. *Schwalbe* literally translates as 'swallow', but is perhaps better understood as 'swallow dive' and is commonly used for someone who falls to the floor without being touched. In the Netherlands it has acquired more sinister overtones. 'Everything that is foul, that is untrue and unsporting is easily called "*schwalbe*" in Dutch football.'[135] To see a lead lost in a World Cup Final to a perceived injustice would infuriate the most placid of souls, but in everything there is a need for perspective. Germans tend to view diving in the penalty area with a more sanguine approach, in general, not just this specific occasion but, as Raphael Honigstein acknowledged, 'Holzenbein has always been very tongue in cheek about it. I think the Germans are aware that the Dutch see it as a dive.'[136] Four years later, Holzenbein would be accused of another *schwalbe* incident when playing against the Dutch.

Cruyff was incandescent at the perceived injustice. At half-time, he would still be protesting to Taylor as the teams walked from the pitch, earning a yellow card. Three years later, in a television documentary, Taylor conceded that the decision was an error. As honourable as the admission was, it mattered little on that July day in 1974. Breitner stroked

135 De Bruijn, Jan-Hermen – Interview with the author
136 Honigstein, Raphael – Interview with the author

home the penalty, as Jongbloed barely moved. The Dutch lead had vanished.

Amazingly, the Germans were now in the ascendancy. Vogts broke clear and nearly scored, but Jongbloed denied him with an outstanding reflex, one-handed save. A chipped free kick from Beckenbauer was gratefully tipped over the bar by Jongbloed, and Rijsbergen cleared a Hoeness effort from near the line. Cruyff dropped deeper, seeking greater involvement. It came, but the further from goal his possession, the less effective his input as an attacking force. The Germans seemed quicker to the ball now, with the Dutch shaken a little from their self-assurance, but they fought back. Cruyff was almost clear, as he closed in on Maier, drawing the goalkeeper to him, before slipping a pass to Rep. The shot was weak, though, and directly at Maier. The chance was gone, but the Dutch had weathered the brief storm, and regained a measure of control as the game headed towards the break. Then disaster struck.

Two minutes before half-time, a pass released Rainer Bonhof down the German right flank. As he approached the area, Haan advanced to close him down. For once, however, the midfielder's defensive naivety betrayed him, and the German skipped past an impotent challenge. In the middle, Rijsbergen was drawn towards goal, to cut out any potential cross, but the move left the dangerous Gerd Muller in space. Seizing the opportunity, Bonhof pulled the pass back towards the striker as Krol tried to cover the danger. Muller's first touch looked poor, diverting the ball away from goal, but it also wrong-footed Krol, creating a small space. It was all that the master marksman required.

Muller pivoted and drove the ball home. Jongbloed could only wave the ball on its way into the net. It was a dagger to the heart of Total Football. The Bayern Munich forward was playing at his club's home ground in his 62nd international for West Germany. The goal was his 68th for his country. In his last international game Gerd Muller delivered the World Cup. The role of pantomime villains apparently came easy to the Germans. In *Danish Dynamite*, Rob Smyth, Lars Eriksen and Mike Gibbons say of the Germans, 'They were the bête noire of the beautiful team – Hungary 1954, Holland 1974, France 1982.'[137]

For so much of the tournament, the Netherlands plan had worked so well. Haan had been competent and composed, but at the last, when the big question was asked, his understandable lack of experience as a defender had proven so costly. Conjecture about such things is always a folly, but there's an irresistible urge to consider whether, had Hulshoff been fit and available, would the Dutch have conceded both, or indeed either, of those goals? In that vital period of the latter part of the first half, after Neeskens had scored, when Germany first equalised, then took the lead, would the presence of the absent libero have made their task more difficult? It surely would. Would it have changed the dynamic of the game? Probably, but how far?

'Very small details always make the difference,' Jan-Hermen de Bruijn suggested. 'In final stages all teams in all the tournaments are extremely good. The exception is Brazil in 70 who were two classes above the rest. Being just one class better as Holland was in 74 is not enough to win if several details run against you.'[138] Arie Haan was a superb player and in the 1978 World Cup, his distance shooting would embarrass both Maier and the Italian goalkeeper Dino Zoff. He would, however, surely never claim to be a sustainable replacement for the colossal presence of Hulshoff. In a game against as canny a performer as Gerd Muller, any defensive frailty was always likely to be exposed. On that July day, it was.

137 Smyth, Rob, Eriksen, Lars & Gibbons, Mike, *Danish Dynamite* (London: Bloomsbury 2014)
138 De Bruijn, Jan-Hermen – Interview with the author

At the break, Michels removed the clearly unfit Rensenbrink, sending on Van de Kerkhof. The Germans had hardly been expansive, certainly not as expansive as the Dutch, but they had been efficient. When under pressure they hadn't conceded, they had been solid and resolute and, when the chances arose, they had struck back effectively. Schoen's decision to play the businesslike Wolfgang Overath, rather than the ebulliently talented Gunter Netzer, was winning the day. It's surely not a selection decision that Michels would have made had the squads been reversed. Perhaps the difference between the two players was less pronounced than has been widely perceived, however. 'Netzer was very inconsistent,' Raphael Honigstein suggested. 'Overath would give you more solid performances. Overath was a skilful player but perhaps with fewer highs and fewer lows than Netzer.'[139]

Could the Dutch fight back in the second period? Early on the Germans pressed forward, as much to keep the ball as far as possible from their goal, as to attack, but it brought chances and Bonhof should surely have done better with a free header from a corner. Eventually though, as the half progressed, they sank further and further back as the Dutch flowed forwards. Persistent Oranje waves broke on the rocks of Beckenbauer and Bayern Munich team-mate Schwarzenbeck at the centre of the German defence.

A poor punch from Maier required Breitner to head clear from under his own crossbar, and a Haan diving header from a Cruyff free kick was saved by the goalkeeper as the pressure grew. A Neeskens far-post volley threatened to cut Maier in half, but the ball was scrambled away. Whenever the Dutch penetrated, Maier was in unbeatable mood. 'We missed too many chances. Sepp Maier played the game of

139 Honigstein, Raphael – Interview with the author

his life in the German goal,'[140] Cruyff lamented. Perhaps understandably, Raphael Honigstein offers a different narrative. 'It's a bit of a cliché to say that the Dutch killed Germany in the game and Sepp Maier was keeping them alive, but it's not borne out by watching the game. It was quite even in the second half as I recall.'[141] Whatever the case, the Dutch continued to press. Rep went close following a low cross from Suurbier, after Rijsbergen was removed and replaced by De Jong. Often Jansen was left as the lone sentinel to watch the back door as the Dutch piled forward again and again.

As time ticked on, though, the colour seemed to metaphorically drain from the players in Oranje, and they uncharacteristically resorted to launching high balls into the German box. This wasn't Total Football and their players were ill-suited to the tactic. Had this been at Michels's behest? Had he deserted the Total Football faith? Talented artists were turning into artisans, portrait masters into painters and decorators, and sculptors into clay modellers. Walloping whitewash crudely covered the fine lines of artistry. When a goal was required, the approach that had taken them so far was almost neglected.

If Muller's goal had plunged a blade into the heart of Total Football, it bled to death in the dying minutes of the game. 'In the midst of World Cup failure, they had inexplicably become like all the others. Out of ideas, they were reduced to imitation. It seemed a sin. They were revolutionaries,'[142] David Winner lamented.

Legend has it that, on the way to the final, the regular tape that the Dutch listened to in transit to games had been lost. Instead, the David Bowie song, 'Sorrow' was played. It now

140 Cruyff, Johan, *My Turn* (London: Macmillan, 2016)
141 Honigstein, Raphael – Interview with the author
142 https://www.the42.ie/holland-1974-world-cup-tragedy-1488354-Mar2016/

seemed somehow prophetic. It was a sadness that also found a home in the heart of a young French boy, who would grow up to be a legend in English football. A young Eric Cantona recalled that, 'As an eight-year-old, I watched the 1974 World Cup Final between West Germany and Holland and I was supporting the Dutch. I cried my eyes out when they lost. I was very sad.'[143]

The game ended. To the Germans the prize. To the Oranje mere admiration. 'But as the full-time whistle sounded, the Dutch drew two major conclusions: the Germans had cheated and Holland had done well – the World Cup had been a resounding success with just a minor blip at the end. And those two misguided conclusions ensured the country is still trying to get over the trauma,'[144] David Winner explained. Consolation in defeat? With apologies to Don McLean for the amendment, the words of a song referring to a fellow countryman and artist seem appropriate. 'This world [cup] was never meant for one as beautiful as you.'[145] There's a phrase in *Danish Dynamite* about Denmark's 1986 World Cup team that seems apposite. It was written to describe Denmark, but fits equally well here. 'The fact that their story had a bittersweet tang and a doomed innocence only accentuates their alternative appeal. The best stories in life are the ones where those involved don't get the girl, the happy ending or even the Jules Rimet Trophy.'[146]

It would be wrong to say that a football ethos died that day in July 1974, but certainly a little of the romance did. Is being the Beautiful Bridesmaid fulfilling though? Surely not. 'Cruyff said afterwards "We were very successful in a

143 Eric Cantona's Perfect XI: who broke the King's heart? *FourFourTwo* – 2 March 2016

144 https://www.the42.ie/holland-1974-world-cup-tragedy-1488354-Mar2016/

145 McLean, Don – Vincent from *American Pie,* 1971

146 Smyth, Rob, Eriksin, Lars & Gibbons, Mike, *Danish Dynamite* (London: Bloomsbury 2014)

way because we were acclaimed for our style and everybody said we were the best team. But it deflected attention away from the failure. Over the years it became an excuse. The Dutch thing became beautiful losing.'"[147] Their style certainly became their legacy. The home of *Catenaccio* was no different, as Alex Frosio explained. 'The impact was huge. Everybody wanted to be like that Dutch team; young, wild and free ... some tried or at least [were] inspired, Torino in 1976, Perugia in 1978.'[148] It was clear that Italian football recognised the insurrection of the new paradigm as well. Frosio continued, 'It was a revolution for another reason. They lost two finals, true, but they are unforgettable. I think it's the only team you can say a lot [about] – line-ups included – though they won nothing. And winning is usually crucial in football. [It] marks the difference between glory and oblivion.'[149]

There were few recriminations, especially back in the Netherlands. 'It was a shame we lost, but the public's enthusiasm for us was enormous,'[150] Rensenbrink recalled. The team was feted for their achievements, and perhaps the style that Cruyff alluded to as well. 'We lost the final, but everyone was talking about the Dutch side,'[151] Krol explained. The Germans won the trophy, but the Dutch won people's hearts. Rep remembers the events after the game, and when returning home. 'We drank a lot. And we hadn't been allowed to exchange shirts after the match, so I exchanged my jacket with Paul Breitner. The next day we flew home and went to see the Queen and the parliament. So, I met the Queen in Paul Breitner's light blue jacket.'[152]

147 https://www.the42.ie/holland-1974-world-cup-tragedy-1488354-Mar2016/
148 Frosio, Alex – Interview with the author
149 Frosio, Alex – Interview with the author
150 Football's Greatest International Teams, Sky Sports, 2010
151 Football's Greatest International Teams, Sky Sports, 2010
152 https://www.theguardian.com/football/2001/apr/10/sport.comment1

But there was more to it than that. There was a deep sense of loss as well, as *De Nijmeegse Stadskrant* journalist Erik Janssen explained. 'A national trauma was born. It was the zenith of the Dutch–German football rivalry.'[153] The game became known as 'The Lost Final', and its consequences seeped deep into the Dutch understanding of the world, informing their outlook. 'We should have won. The Germans cheated. It was never a penalty. Holzenbein dived. Of course, he did. I saw it. *Schwalbe*! You saw it, didn't you? How could we have lost?' Disappointment grew over the years and festered into resentment. To despise the Germans was almost part of the culture. If the Dutch felt cheated, should football have felt the same? 'If Holland had won the world title in 1974, it would have been the crowning of the work of something very, very special,'[154] Jan-Hermen de Bruijn explained.

Understandably, in Germany events were viewed very differently as Raphael Honigstein described. 'The story in Germany is not about this mythical Dutch team. Of course people appreciated them at the time – and they appreciate them now. But in Germany it is about Germany winning and it isn't one that's seen as a travesty of sport, that the Dutch were denied by this very dour Germany side. Germany feel they had the best side in the World Cup and they won it. That's it. The Dutch were very good, but not good enough, and that's where it stops. People celebrated, but we sort of shrugged it off. Yeah, we won again, and that was it. It didn't have this mass outpouring of euphoria and nationalistic fervour. It was very much a time when it was a bit embarrassing to be waving German flags. So, it was almost a quiet triumph.'[155] Why wouldn't Germans think that way? When he moved to

153 Janssen, Erik – https://dutchreview.com/culture/history/dutch-german-football-rivalry/

154 De Bruijn, Jan-Hermen – Interview with the author

155 Honigstein, Raphael – Interview with the author

England, a different perspective loomed into view for Raphael Honigstein. 'It's only when I came to London that I found out about this different narrative, about this wonderful Dutch team and Germany cruelly denying them.'[156]

As the bright Oranje flame of Dutch Total Football burnt so brightly before consuming itself in the 1974 World Cup Final, in Kerkrade, a town in the Netherlands, virtually lying up against the German border, an amateur footballer watched on television. Little did he know that, four years later, wearing the famous colours of his country, he would score the goal that gave the Netherlands renewed hope of laying to rest the ghost of the numbing defeat to his German neighbours. To reach that point, Dick Nanninga would go from a part-time footballer and full-time construction site worker, to being the robust and rugged embodiment of a muscular iconoclast among a different squad of Dutch artists; the man who gave hope of redemption to his country.

156 Honigstein, Raphael – Interview with the author

PART 4

The 1976 European Championship

Qualification

The defeat in the 1974 final was the last game of Rinus Michels's first spell in charge of the Netherlands. Over the coming years, he would return three times. In November 1984, he took temporary charge for two games after Kees Rijvers had been ousted. He returned on a more permanent basis in March 1986, and would lead the team to its greatest triumph at the 1988 European Championship. Finally, his swansong would be in September 1990, replacing Leo Beenhakker, following the Dutch elimination in the 1990 World Cup – to West Germany, who else?

After the 1974 World Cup, Michels returned to Barcelona, and the KNVB looked to Ajax for his replacement. Although, as Jan-Hermen De Bruijn explains, other than Michels it may not have mattered who was appointed as coach. 'Every year the influence of Cruyff was growing in the national team. He was in almost every front the leader, and it really didn't matter much who was the coach, although Michels had a big influence in '74 of course, but at the same time, Cruyff had too. Without Michels, he was the king of the national team.[157]'

The most experienced coach in the world would have had problems dealing with such a situation, but that was hardly the criterion the KNVB seemed to focus on. Instead, they appointed someone who, Jan-Hermen de Bruijn said, was regarded as a 'small-town coach'.[158] To many, the choice of George Knobel was a surprise. His experience of three years with amateur club VV Baronie, and then as coach of MVV Maastricht for four seasons, finishing in mid-table positions in the Eredivisie, had somehow led him to be appointed as the man with the unenviable task of picking up the baton from Stefan Kovacs when the Romanian left Ajax after their third European Cup triumph to take over the French national team.

157 De Bruijn, Jan-Hermen – Interview with the author
158 De Bruijn, Jan-Hermen – Interview with the author

By the measures of both Michels and Kovacs, Knobel was hardly a roaring success, or even a success at all, with the Amsterdam club in his single season there, before being shown the door. A third-place finish in the Eredivisie, ten points adrift of Feyenoord, and defeat in the KNVB Cup to PSV Eindhoven in the semi-final made the domestic season a disappointment for a club used to glory and silverware. UEFA Super Cup success against AC Milan brought a little compensation, with a six-goal home win overturning a single-goal defeat at the San Siro. By that time, though, the club had already endured their biggest disappointment.

Granted a bye in the first round of their European Cup defence, Ajax faced CSKA Sofia in pursuit of their fourth successive title. The first leg was played at Olympisch Stadion in Amsterdam on 24 October 1973 and, although many of the names on the Ajax team-sheets across both games were familiar, the outcome was not. The first leg was a rough-and-tumble affair, with both teams overindulging in physical excesses and CSKA's goalkeeper Stoyan Yordanov ending up with a broken arm. Perhaps it was straying away from their gilded ambitions of Total Football that drew the sting from Ajax's football, but when Jan Mulder gave the champions an early lead, it seemed that the formbook was playing out. Later, Johnny Rep had the chance to double the lead from 12 yards, but the opportunity was squandered and Ajax had only the slenderest of margins for the return game in Sofia two days after Bonfire Night. There would be plenty of fireworks in the Bulgarian capital.

Knobel sent out an unchanged team for the return leg, and despite having just the single-goal lead, would surely have maintained a decent level of confidence. After all, only 12 months earlier, the Dutch club had visited the same stadium and ran out 1-3 winners. The holders played out the first period without much concern, and even offered some threat up front, but the Bulgarians were both resolute at the back and boisterous in attack. The game was still in the balance when, halfway through the second period, skipper Piet Keizer was dispossessed on the edge of the Ajax penalty area. A quick cross found the defence out of position as Marashliev efficiently headed past Stuy to bring the aggregate scores level. The spectre of Rep's missed penalty in the first leg was now looming large.

There was no more score before the end of normal time and, as the game went into an extra 30 minutes, home coach Manol Manolov removed midfielder Tsvetan Atanasov, replacing him with the forward Stefan Mihaylov. It would be a portentous decision. With a mere five minutes remaining, it would be the fresh Mihaylov ramming the ball past Stuy for the winning goal. It was the only strike he would ever record in Europe's premier club competition, and it eliminated the tournament's reigning champions.

The European Cup, that had resided in the Amsterdam club's trophy cabinet for three years, would now be removed. After a period of dominance unknown since the formative years of the competition and Real Madrid's early monopoly, it wouldn't return to the Dutch capital for more than two decades. It's been argued that although so many familiar names were in the team that lost to CSKA, Knobel had been compelled to take over an ageing squad, now denied the services of Cruyff and soon to lose Neeskens. On top of that, Hulshoff, hampered by that knee problem, was no longer the colossus he had been.

Such mitigation founders when confronted with the statistics. The average age of the Ajax team that lost out to CSKA was a shade less than 26.50 years, and no player had yet reached their 30th birthday. Suurbier and Keizer were the 'elder statemen' of the group, both aged 29, and Hulshoff remained an outstanding defender. Despite this loss and the fairly ordinary season with Ajax, Knobel was given the opportunity to take over the team that Michels had taken so close to glory in Germany, and lead them to the European Championship in Yugoslavia, assuming qualification could be achieved.

If Knobel had considered taking over from Kovacs at Ajax had been difficult, succeeding Michels with such an independently minded group of players in the national squad was of an entirely different order. The situation was certainly not helped by the fact that Cruyff felt the new manager was part of the reason he had lost the captaincy at Ajax. Reports suggest that, on the first day of the club's pre-season training camp at De Lutte, the captaincy issue had been raised by the new coach. At the end of a team meeting, he had suggested, 'There's one last thing. The captaincy. We'll have to decide who's the captain.'[159] Cruyff had assumed that he would merely continue from the previous season, and felt there was no need to raise the issue at all. The announcement, and its consequences, didn't so much rock the Ajax boat, but fatally hole and capsize it, scuttled by its skipper.

Knobel always insisted that he hadn't been intent on causing issues or seeking to exert his authority, but was merely following club tradition as had been explained to him. 'Every year the captain of Ajax was chosen by the players without the presence of the coach. It was the custom for many years. The assistant coach, Bobby Haarms, told me that every year it was the same system. I wasn't even in the room when they voted. When the meeting was finished, I heard the results and that was it.'[160] At the time, Knobel apparently felt that the issue was done and dusted. It was far from the case, however, and Cruyff would hardly have warmed to the new national manager's appointment. The

159 Winner, David, *Brilliant Orange* (London: Bloomsbury, 2000)
160 Winner, David, *Brilliant Orange* (London: Bloomsbury, 2000)

power dynamic between Knobel and Cruyff would lead to explosions in the squad later.

Arie Haan also had issues with Knobel. When the coach arrived at Ajax, he had, perhaps unwisely whether it was true or not, given an interview criticising much of the squad's behaviour with regard to drinking and alleged womanising. Haan had taken exception to the comments and a rift had quickly developed, with rumours circulating that the midfielder had been keen to get the coach out of the club. Was it true? Had there been a rift? Well, when Knobel took over the national team, Haan, who had played every minute of every game during the 1974 World Cup finals, and would feature strongly in the 1978 tournament, was never selected, and would be absent from the Oranje for almost two years.

Sometimes, plucking unheralded managers from relative obscurity can pay dividends; the appointment of Kovacs at Ajax, for example. Such serendipity is hardly a regular occurrence, however, and certainly not something that should be adopted as *modus operandi*. Knobel's sole season with Ajax had painted an accurate picture of his ability dealing with top players with big personalities. In Jan-Hermen de Bruijn's judgement, 'He was fairly OK as a coach, but not as a "big-city" coach. He was a failure with Ajax, for the same reasons he was a failure later on for the national team ... He never had the personality to put his mark on the events.'[161] An inability to take charge is clearly something in the demerit column for anyone charged with leading a squad of players with such strident personalities, but the Oranje's must influential player had no problem with it. 'Cruyff liked this. It gave him the opportunity to be the man in charge,'[162] De Bruijn added. It was always a position Cruyff enjoyed.

161 De Bruijn, Jan-Hermen – Interview with the author
162 De Bruijn, Jan-Hermen – Interview with the author

Things were hardly all sweetness and light in Knobel's relations with the head honchos at the KNVB either, and even his eventual departure was tinged with controversy after he had tried to end his contract on a number of occasions. Although it had been agreed that he would leave after the European Championship, the news was leaked out, reportedly by the members of the KNVB, at the most inappropriate time. It seemed the fortunes of the team were pushed into second place behind a long-brewing animosity between Knobel and some of the powerbrokers at the KNVB. This was the Netherlands, though. Going into a tournament without an upset simply wasn't the way to do things.

There was another issue, too, and probably one that any new Netherlands manager would have faced, with the possible exception of Kovacs had he chosen Oranje, rather than *Les Bleus*. Johnny Rep summed up the general feeling of at least the more senior players in the squad. 'Knobel was a really nice person but he was not respected by the players. I think he had too much respect for us.'[163]

It was a far from perfect scenario for the new man, and qualification hardly looked to be an easy task either. The Dutch were drawn into a group with Italy, Poland and Finland. Despite failing to qualify from the group stages behind Poland and Argentina in the 1974 World Cup finals, the *Azzurri* would finish in fourth place at the World Cup in 1978, and were building a strong team towards that tournament. If one puts aside the Dutch tale of trials and tribulations, the Poles had probably been the unluckiest team in the 1974 World Cup. Their exit after losing on the waterlogged pitch against West Germany robbed football of what looked to be a potentially mouthwatering final against the Dutch. They would be strong rivals and qualification would be tough, with just one team

163 Winner, David – *Brilliant Orange* (London: Bloomsbury, 2000)

advancing from the group. The sole makeweights in the section appeared to be the Finns. Even topping that group, though, would only lead to a two-legged play-off against another group winner to secure one of the four places in the semi-final and final mini-tournament in Yugoslavia. Getting to Germany two years earlier looked a doddle in comparison, and how close to failure had the Dutch come then? An old foe from those times would again provide a barrier to progress.

Knobel's reign began with a friendly fixture in Sweden on 4 September 1974. It was the only chance for the new coach to see his players in action before the qualifying fixtures began. Unsurprisingly perhaps, he selected a highly recognisable starting XI, and fed in three untried options as replacements. The first change followed an injury to Rep, with Peter Ressel making his debut. After the break, FC Twente's Rene Notten won his second cap, replacing Van Hanegem, and later NEC Nijmegen's Jan Peters replaced Neeskens. The first two would only win a further five caps between them, but Peters would go on to star for the Oranje, winning 31 caps, and famously score both goals that defeated England at Wembley in 1977. The Dutch won the game 1-5, with a brace from Neeskens, and one each for Cruyff, Haan and Rensenbrink. Bigger tests awaited, though.

Three weeks later, Knobel took his team back to Scandinavia to face Finland in a European Championship qualifier. A 3-1 victory, after falling behind to a Timo Rahja goal, secured the points. Two goals by Cruyff and a Neeskens penalty overcame the early setback. A single-goal victory at home to Switzerland with a more experimental side followed in October before a key qualifying game at home to Italy. The Finns had already lost to Poland before playing the Dutch and, before Fulvio Bernardini's team turned up at Rotterdam's Stadion de Kuip, Poland won the return game 3-0 in Poznan. The Italians had yet to kick a ball in anger, and the Poles had four points, the Dutch two. The encounter on 20 November was a big game for both countries.

If Knobel had wanted a positive start to the game he was disappointed. On five minutes, a cross from the left found Roberto Boninsegna in space around the penalty spot. The man who had opened the scoring in the World Cup Final of 1970 chanced his arm, flicking a header towards goal, but would have been as surprised as anyone when the ball squirmed past Jongbloed at the near post. The *Azzurri* – actually, the *Bianchi* on this occasion as they had changed strip due to a perceived colour clash with the home team – celebrated, and Dutch heads sank.

Giving the Italians a goal start was a never a good idea, but Ajax's victories in the European Cup, twice overcoming Serie A teams in finals, had dispelled any predating myth of inferiority. Plus, despite having the estimable and experienced Dino Zoff in goal, the back line of Francesco Rocca, Moreno Roggi, Andrea Orlandini and Francesco Morini was hardly of classic Italian vintage, mustering only 15 caps between them. There was still plenty in the game for the Dutch.

In typical fashion, as the Dutch pressed, the visitors settled back to defend with a number of robust tackles. Rep in particular was left hobbling after one such challenge. Midway through the first period, though, the Oranje equalised as Rensenbrink stretched to divert a cross past Zoff. It was their only success of the half, however, as the Italians defended resolutely, frustrating the home team. A booking for Van Hanegem after 40 minutes illustrated the Dutch irritation. At the break the scores remained level. As the game resumed, the struggling Rep was removed and PSV Eindhoven's Willy van de Kerkhof replaced him, making his second appearance in Oranje.

The change hardly disrupted the pattern of the game, with the Dutch in charge and pressing forward. Just past the hour mark, they took the lead. A free kick floated in by Suurbier was partially cleared, but when the ball was nodded back into the area, another flick sent it towards goal, and Cruyff was alert to prod it past Zoff from close range. Italian appeals for offside were brief and unconvincing. Despite the slenderness of the lead, there was only one team going to win the game now and, ten minutes from time, a classic raid from full-back by Suurbier opened the door for the third goal. Driving forwards, he exchanged an exquisite wall pass with Neeskens, collecting the ball again as he powered into the area. Zoff was compelled to advance and narrow the angle, but Suurbier merely squared the ball for Cruyff to tap into the unguarded net.

Three friendly games followed in the following year, as Knobel considered his options. A 1-0 defeat in Belgium saw seven Dutch debutants. Cruyff was absent, otherwise he may well have tried to raise the matter of the German penalty back in Munich with Jack Taylor, who refereed the game in Antwerp. The following month, another much-changed side held world champions West Germany to a 1-1 draw in Frankfurt. Van Hanegem's goal just after the restart equalised Herbert Wimmer's early opener. The trio was completed a couple of weeks later in Belgrade, as Yugoslavia beat a team containing three more debutants and the same number of players winning their second caps. The games gave Knobel food for thought. Which of the players that Michels took to Germany should be retained? Were any of the new players demanding inclusion? He had the summer to contemplate, as the Oranje would play no more games that season. In September, though, the qualifying schedule resumed.

On 3 September, the Finns visited Nijmegen for the return fixture. Knobel had decided to mix and match his players. The tried-and-trusted Suurbier, Krol, Jansen and Van Henegem combined with debutant Harry Lubse of PSV Eindhoven and centre-back partnership of Adrie van Kraay and Niels

Overweg. Only two players from Ajax and Feyenoord were selected, with five coming from PSV, including Jan van Beveren in goal. By this time, Johnny Rep, who didn't play, had moved to Valencia in Spain as the break-up of the great Ajax team continued apace. The following year he would move on to France's Ligue 1 and Bastia on the island of Corsica.

It was a risky selection, but a 4-1 result was enough for Knobel to claim justification for his decisions. Earlier, Italy and Poland had played out a goalless draw in Rome, before the Italians travelled to Helsinki and won 1-0, thanks to a Giorgio Chinaglia penalty. The Poles were emerging as the Netherlands' main opponents to top the group and when, the week following the victory over the Finns, the Dutch travelled to the Stadion Slaski in Chorzów, the result looked disastrous.

Both Cruyff and Neeskens were allegedly granted special privileges, additional days' break from training – both officially and unofficially. The original premise had been to allow extra travelling time from Catalunya. Things had moved beyond that, though. Jan-Hermen de Bruijn confirmed that the general perception was that Cruyff was 'always taking liberties'[164] and, inevitably, others within the squad, especially those not connected with Ajax, past or present, began to resent the inequality. One rumour suggested that Cruyff had even used one of these free days to take his wife, Danny, shoe-shopping in Milan, rather than attend training. Knobel felt hamstrung to rein in Cruyff's misdemeanours, however, as, on the field, he was producing the performances that kept the team winning. Ahead of the game in Poland, Jan-Herman de Bruijn reported that Cruyff was 'also late on to the training field.'[165] But this time the result would go against the Dutch.

Cruyff, Neeskens and Rene van de Kerkhof had been brought back to form the forward line, but there was still

164 De Bruijn, Jan-Hermen – Interview with the author
165 De Bruijn, Jan-Hermen – interview with the author

a lack of experience at the heart of the Dutch back line and the Poles exploited it ruthlessly, galloping into a four-goal lead before a late consolation from Van de Kerkhof offered a crumb of comfort. Later the same month, a draw in Italy for the Finns only emphasised the importance of the Oranje's next game. Topping the group now seemed to be between the teams who had finished second and third in West Germany at the 1974 World Cup. On 15 October, the Poles would visit the Olympisch Stadion. Before that, though, there was just time for another of those internal rumpuses within the Dutch squad, with Cruyff inevitably at its heart.

PSV Eindhoven were becoming the dominant force in Dutch club football. They had won the Eredivisie title in 1974/75, and would retain it the following season. As a consequence, the club's representation in the national squad was growing, but many of their players felt like second-class citizens, with the Ajax–Feyenoord axis holding sway. Goalkeeper Jan van Beveren had carried a grievance since 1974, when Michels and the goalkeeper fell out ahead of the World Cup squad selection. The new scenario was hardly designed to heal such wounds. Despite the enhanced presence of PSV players in both squad and team, the influence of Cruyff hardly seemed to wane. It was an underlying current, just waiting for a trigger to set off a wave of disruption.

With the Polish game around the corner, the players gathered for a training session and, when Cruyff and Neeskens appeared, Van Beveren's team-mate Willy van den Kuylen is reported to have remarked, 'Here come the Kings of Spain.' Whether the two Barcelona players were supposed to hear or not, word of the comment reached Cruyff. Retribution was swift. Knobel was apparently issued with a curt 'them or me' option. There would be no debate, as Jan-Hermen de Bruijn confirmed. 'The national coach, and almost all of the

players picked [Cruyff].'[166] Van Beveren and Van der Kuylen –
depending on which version you read – were either sent home
or walked out of the squad, no longer prepared to tolerate
Cruyff's all-consuming power. Whichever version you think
more feasible, the cause and effect are hardly in question. Some
reports have suggested that the Van de Kerkhof twins were
also primed to follow their PSV club-mates out of the door in
solidarity, but Van Beveren talked them out of it.

Jan van Beveren, the outstanding Dutch goalkeeper of the
1970s, would again be denied the chance to play in a major
tournament by squad politics. Despite being largely the innocent
victim in both cases, Dutch public opinion inevitably favoured
Cruyff, and Van Beveren's leaving the squad was seen as some
kind of desertion from the national team. It later turned into
an official retirement from international football, albeit with an
aborted return in 1977 that lasted for merely one game.

Despite Cruyff's absence from the 1978 World Cup,
there was little chance of Van Beveren returning to the team
again, even if the coach had been minded to try and persuade
him to do so, and his sole involvement with the tournament
looked to be as a pundit working for Dutch TV. Such was the
groundswell of bad feeling towards him, however, that the
broadcaster received a number of threats made against him
and his family and it was decided to abandon the idea. It was
sufficient for the goalkeeper to decide to leave the Netherlands
as soon as possible.

There were two years left on his contract with PSV,
which he duly honoured. By 1980, little had happened to
change his mind. In fact, a further dispute, this time with
coach Kees Rijvers, only cemented the decision. Offers of a
contract extension were shunned and, despite approaches from
a number of top European clubs, Ven Beveren decided on a

166 De Bruijn, Jan-Hermen – interview with the author

clean break for himself and his family, moving to the USA and joining NASL club Fort Lauderdale Strikers.

Former Newcastle United midfielder, and now ESPN and SiriusXM football commentator Ray Hudson, was with the Strikers at the time. Hudson had played with Gordon Banks at the club earlier, and saw many similarities in Van Beveren's approach. He recalled that after Banks retired, his position had been taken by popular USA international Arnie Mausser, but when former Netherlands international Cor van der Hart was appointed as head coach at the club, he brought in Van Beveren.

Initially there had been resentment from the fans as he displaced the popular Mausser, but the goalkeeper's performances quickly made him a hero there. Hudson recalls two saves in particular. First, whilst playing at Giants Stadium against the New York Cosmos, Giorgio Chinaglia hit a shot which Van Beveren had covered, but a huge deflection diverted the ball by 'about 45 degrees.'[167] Van Beveren managed to change direction and make the save. Hudson recalled his astonishment at the agility. 'It was one of those saves, like time stood still. My God, what a save!'[168] The second occurred as the team progressed to the Soccer Bowl and were playing Edmonton Drillers. Dutch forward Jan Goossens hit a ferocious volley from about ten yards, heading for the top corner, 'where only the spiders live'[169] as Hudson explained. 'But the Big Grasshopper, as I called him, got to it. It was an even more jaw-dropping save.'[170] Given Hudson had shared a dressing-room with Banks, his esteem of Van Beveren is clear when he describes him as, 'the best goalkeeper I played with in my career, magnificent, stupendous.'[171]

---

167 Hudson, Ray – Interview with the author
168 Hudson, Ray – Interview with the author
169 Hudson, Ray – Interview with the author
170 Hudson, Ray – Interview with the author
171 Hudson, Ray – Interview with the author

Asked if Van Beveren ever spoke about missing out on the big tournaments for the national team, Hudson recalls the reflective tone that Van Beveren adopted. 'Sad, hurt, and not a little bitter, although equally he didn't talk about it much.'[172] The history was later related to Hudson by coach Van der Hart who, despite being an Ajax man himself, relayed how the issue was caused by 'the Ajax players, the Ajax group'[173] at the time. It was then that Hudson appreciated why Van Beveren's body language always seemed different when he played against any of the Dutch players in the NASL at the time, including Cruyff, Neeskens and Krol. 'Whatever it was with Michels and Cruyff, people talk about Michels, but I got the sense that … whenever Cruyff's name was brought up that it was … some looks and some emotions … and Jan was definitely in that corner. You always got the feeling with Jan that there was something that stuck with him about not going to those World Cups.'[174] It feels like a sad story, with all parties losing out. How different would football history have been had Van Beveren played another 50 or so times for the Netherlands, as he surely should have done?

Changes for the game against Poland were now inevitable. Another PSV player was added when Kees Krijgh was brought in to partner club colleague Van Kraay in the centre of the defence. Other changes suggested that the old order was still in power. Aside from the two PSV defenders, if you include Rep, Cruyff and Neeskens as still part of the Ajax camp in the squad, the only other player selected who was not from either Ajax or Feyenoord, was FC Twente's midfielder Frans Thijssen, winning his third cap. For all their injured indignation, it appeared there was merit in the stances of Van Beveren and

172 Hudson, Ray – Interview with the author
173 Hudson, Ray – Interview with the author
174 Hudson, Ray – Interview with the author

Van den Kuylen. Cruyff had won out. Now the Oranje had to do the same.

It was left for Cruyff to justify the situation, and he did so in typical fashion as Jan-Hermen de Bruijn related. 'That was one of the games that Cruyff then protected Knobel … because Holland then played one of the best games that they'd ever played … and Cruyff was magnificent in the extreme.'[175] The game certainly started with the Dutch meaning business. Cruyff looked particularly inspired and Jan Tomaszewski in the Polish goal was repeatedly called into action inside the first dozen minutes or so. Approaching the quarter-hour mark, the Dutch broke through. Suurbier attacked down the right flank, crossing low into the box and a diving header by Neeskens beat Tomaszewski. It was a vital goal, but the Poles nearly struck back when a cross to Henryk Kasperczak found the Stal Mielec midfielder in space inside the box. He headed back across the goal, but the returning Piet Schrijvers calmly watched as the effort drifted wide of the far post.

The defeat in Poland had damaged the Dutch goal difference and, with the final group standings likely to be close, a one-goal victory was hardly sufficient for the Dutch. A Cruyff shot seemed to be scuffed, and easy for Tomaszewski to collect, but a bobble caused him to fumble. The ball rolled free towards Neeskens following up, but Wladyslaw Zmuda swept the ball clear. The Poles were dangerous on the break, but the Dutch kept the visitors' back line busy and the coach, Kazimierz Gorski, would have been happy to get his team into the break only trailing by the one goal.

That relief would turn to disappointment three minutes into the second period. Neeskens crossed and the diminutive Ruud Geels somehow found space and headed home. Two goals were good, but three would be better. A corner from the

175 De Bruijn, Jan-Hermen – Interview with the author

left brought a header on the Polish goal, but the ball was cleared from the line. Cruyff danced past and deceived two defenders before cutting inside to open up space ten yards from goal, but the shot was tame and Tomaszewski smothered the effort. The third goal was surely coming, though. Just before the hour, Cruyff crossed towards Neeskens. His Barcelona team-mate calmly headed down towards Thijssen, who controlled before firing powerfully home from just inside the box.

More chances came at both ends. Schrijvers saved well from a powerful free kick. Then Cruyff got a foot to a cross but, fortunately for the goalkeeper, the ball was diverted straight into Tomaszewski's grateful arms. A Polish corner saw a header strike the woodwork, and more headers went close at both ends. At the final whistle, though, a three-goal win was more than useful. The remaining two games would see Poland entertain Italy, and the Dutch visit Rome. The Oranje topped the table with eight points, the Poles had seven, and the Italians just four. Theoretically, any of the three countries could end up winning the section. Realistically, it was surely between Poland and the Netherlands.

Cruyff's display and the Dutch performance had only served to underscore the captain's influence in the squad and over Knobel. Around this time, with Cruyff's prompting, Knobel, who was by now constantly threatening to resign, forbade officials of the KNVB to stay in the same hotel as the squad. Knobel's relationship with the KNVB was hardly cordial, but the move had Cruyff's fingerprints all over it.

Ten days after losing in Amsterdam, Poland played out another goalless draw against Italy, completing their programme. It meant the Italians could no longer progress and any result other than a defeat in Rome would mean the Netherlands topping the group. If they lost, however, goal difference would decide the issue. Ahead of the final game of the group, the Polish goal difference was +4, and the Dutch

+7, and having scored more goals. It meant that anything other than a defeat by four goals or more would be sufficient for Knobel to take his team into the play-offs for their first European Championship.

By now, the Italian team looked very different to that defeated in Amsterdam earlier and, with little other than pride to play for, when the game in Rome ended with a 1-0 victory for the hosts, both teams would have left the field satisfied. The Netherlands would now face an old, regular and somewhat bitter foe in the play-offs, Belgium.

Although, what was in effect a quarter-final was scheduled to be decided by home and away legs, on 25 April, a Dutch team now strongly resembling the selections of Michels, crushed the Belgians 5-0 in Rotterdam, rendering the return leg redundant. There would be no controversies over goals ruled out for offside this time. Apart from Schrijvers in goal, Adrie van Kraay in the centre of defence and Willy van de Kerkhof stepping in for the absent Van Hanegem, it was the team that kicked off the World Cup Final almost two years earlier, and they played like it as well. A now fully-fit Rensenbrink hit a hat-trick, with Rijsbergen and Neeskens adding the other goals.

Just past the quarter-hour mark, an indirect free kick was awarded to the Dutch on the edge of the Belgium penalty area. Swiss referee Jean Dubach took an age to persuade the white wall of defenders to retreat sufficiently as Cruyff stood over the ball, primed to tap it to Neeskens stationed beside him. Eventually, Dubach seemed to concede that ten yards would be impossible to achieve and settled for the eight or nine he had got. The whistle went, and Cruyff feigned to tap the ball to his right as Neeskens shaped to power in for the shot. It was sufficient to make the defenders crack from the wall and rush towards Neeskens to charge down the shot. Cruyff then made the pass. Instead of Neeskens collecting, however, the ball ran to an unnoticed Rijsbergen, who ran from deep and rifled low past Christian Piot to put the home team ahead. It was the only goal that the Feyenoord defender would score in his 28-cap career.

The second goal, and the first of Rensenbrink's strikes against the country where he played his club football, came on 28 minutes. A corner from the left flank was swung in by Cruyff and Rensenbrink ran forward into space to head home comfortably. A two-goal lead was a more than promising start, but there was more to come after the break. Approaching the hour mark, the ball was shuttled forward down the left flank, then inside to find the Anderlecht striker on the edge of the area. He skipped inside a defender, rounded Piot, and rolled the ball home. Even at this stage, still with more than 30 minutes to play, the matter of qualification was surely settled, but the Dutch left little to chance.

Inside the last ten minutes, a clever chip over the line of advancing defenders found Van de Kerkhof springing the offside trap and closing in on Piot. As the goalkeeper advanced, the PSV midfielder lifted the ball over him and towards the empty net. A Belgian hand on the line tipped it over the bar. The hand, however, belonged to a defender, not the goalkeeper. The resulting penalty kick was obvious. The reliable Neeskens placed the ball on the spot. A dozen photographers crowded behind the goal, and the Barcelona midfielder delivered, driving low into the right-hand corner. A minute or so later, Rensenbrink headed home a cross from the left to complete the rout, and his personal hat-trick. More than 48,000 fans left the De Kuip that evening convinced that both the task of qualifying was completed, and that their team would travel to Yugoslavia with a real chance of redeeming the disappointments of Munich two years earlier.

A month later, with the same team, apart from Van Hanegem returning for Jansen, an early Belgian goal from

Roger van Gool was cancelled out by strikes from Cruyff and Rep. After failing to reach the finals of a major competition for almost four decades, the Dutch had now reached two in as many years. This was their chance to collect a trophy if the lessons had been learnt from 1974. Avoid distractions, concentrate on football and don't become over-confident. It sounds simple, doesn't it? The problem is that keeping things simple was similar to how Cruyff described 'playing simple football'. For the Dutch, it was 'the hardest thing there is'.

As Jan-Hermen de Bruijn pointed out, 'In short, in the run-up to the European Championship, there was much wrong in the relationship between coach and officials, and in the team where Cruyff was very, very dominant, although he was producing the goods [on the pitch].'[176]

The tournament

Aside from the hosts and the Netherlands, the other teams to qualify for the finals were Czechoslovakia and, inevitably, the world champions West Germany. The Dutch were drawn to play against the Czechs, and Knobel later insisted that he had reservations about the outcome even before the team travelled to Yugoslavia, saying that all the players seemed to have on their minds was a chance to beat the Germans and gain revenge for 1974. No one was thinking about playing Czechoslovakia first. Had he tried to counsel the players to be more disciplined in their approach? 'I tried to warn them, but most of them were in their late 20s, almost 30. They weren't children any more. They had had a lot of success, made a lot of money. They had their own opinions about things. You can't do anything about it because arrogance is part of the Dutch character.[177]

176 De Bruijn, Jan-Hermen – Interview with the author
177 Winner, David, *Brilliant Orange* (London: Bloomsbury, 2000)

It may well have been true – there was certainly no lack of self-belief among members of the Dutch squad, especially the more senior and influential ones. Perhaps, however, there's a measure of the coach seeking to deflect blame for what happened. The relationship with elements within the squad was already less than ideal, and with so many strong characters among the players respect for the coach was at a low level and discord was almost inevitable. Van Hanegem was never one to hide his views, and ahead of the Czechoslovakia game, the seemingly inevitable happened.

The players weren't aware at the time but, during a conversation between Knobel and KNVB chairman, Jacques Hogewoning, the coach's resignation had been accepted, although it was agreed that the decision would not be announced until the team returned to the Netherlands. There was plenty of politics to play out. Hints about the story were leaked to reporters of two newspapers, *Algemeen Dagblad* and *De Telegraaf*, although the identity of the sources is less than clear. Neither reporter was keen to publish the story, being aware of the potential harm it could inflict on the team's chances. It's reported, however, that unnamed officials of the KNVB then conspired to ensure that the news broke. They told each reporter that they should publish, because their rivals were about to do so, otherwise, they'd miss the 'scoop'. Lex Muller of *Algemeen Dagblad* recalled the events. 'They told Jan [de Deugd, reporter at *De Telegraaf*], that *Algemeen Dagblad* was about to print the story, and they told me that I had to publish because *De Telegraaf* knew everything. It was unbelievable. I remember that afternoon very well. They asked me to come along to their hotel and they told me everything. It was not one KNVB official; it was several, and they were all very keen to tell me all the details and make sure I published the story.'[178]

178 Winner, David, *Brilliant Orange* (London: Bloomsbury, 2000)

195

The breaking news in the first editions was sufficient to cause an overnight rush of reporters to converge on the Dutch headquarters at Samobar, some 27km (17 miles) outside of Zagreb. It was hardly an ideal way to prepare for the semi-final of a major tournament. Were the KNVB prepared to sacrifice the team's chances of success merely to defame Knobel? Strangely, the wider Dutch perception was that however much the coach was tarnished, it would hardly have adversely affected the team for the upcoming game. 'You must realise,' Jan-Hermen de Bruijn explained. 'It is almost impossible to say, because it sounds too arrogant, how strong, and how much stronger Holland was compared to all the other teams at that moment. They just thought that they could do all those things, because games like the game against Czechoslovakia were, in effect, too simple to spoil.'[179]

If the KNVB couldn't scupper Dutch aspirations perhaps the players could. The day would hardly get better, as Van Hanegem recalled. 'There was a bad atmosphere between Knobel and the players, and before the game there were big problems between him and the people from the KNVB. They spent the whole evening before the game talking.'[180] The distrust between Knobel and the Feyenoord midfielder was hardly a secret, and certainly not something that the typically forthright and honest player sought to hide. In the tense atmosphere, it would take little to ignite the feud into open warfare. Van Hanegem continued, 'The players thought: maybe he's out. I didn't like him. Knobel was not honest with the players, he was not straight about many things. I told him "You're not a straight guy" and that made him angry. He said I couldn't play, so I was a substitute.'[181]

179 De Bruijn, Jan-Hermen – Interview with the author
180 Winner, David, *Brilliant Orange* (London: Bloomsbury, 2000)
181 Winner, David, *Brilliant Orange* (London: Bloomsbury, 2000)

Whether you take the player's description at face value or not, when the team was announced, it was Willy van de Kerkhof wearing the No.10 shirt that most expected to be given to Van Hanegem. Knobel deployed Suurbier, Rijsbergen, Van Kraay and Krol in defence. Neeskens and Jansen joined Van de Kerkhof in midfield, with Rep, Cruyff and Rensenbrink as the front three. It was one of those 'on paper' scenarios when the Dutch were strongly favoured to win.

The Czechs had headed their group narrowly from England, a 2-1 victory in Bratislava on 30 October over Don Revie's team being the pivotal result. Scheduled for the previous day, the game had been abandoned due to heavy fog, and England lost their way in the replayed game after going ahead with a Mick Channon goal. Victory over the Soviet Union in the play-offs confirmed the Czechs' place in Yugoslavia. Their team may not have contained many household names to fans in western Europe, but this tournament would earn them acclaim. They were hardly a team to be considered a mere stepping-stone on the way to an anticipated final. That wasn't how the game was perceived in the Netherlands however, as Jan-Hermen de Bruijn explained. 'Nobody in Holland even mentioned the game. They were absolutely, totally convinced that they would win against [Czechoslovakia] ... every player they had was so much below the level of [the Dutch players] that they were not discussing it.'[182]

The game was scheduled for the evening of 16 June at the Stadion Maksimir in Zagreb, and on a windswept Balkan evening, with rain lashing down, another self-inflicted Dutch disaster had already been set in train. Throw in controversial Welsh referee Clive Thomas and the stage was set. The rain and driving wind should have offered a note of caution that this perhaps wasn't the day when beautiful football would step

---

182 De Bruijn, Jan-Hermen – Interview with the author

confidently forward. It may also have been the reason that the referee's attempts to demonstrate a kinship with elegant football was betrayed by a maladroit attempt to juggle the ball while the teams warmed up. Although a second attempt in front of Cruyff as the Dutch skipper waited to kick off, may have benefited from the Ballon d'Or winner's presence. Had the game turned out differently, so many of the events feeding into the Dutch preparation may well have evaporated into the ether as mere trivialities, background noises playing off-stage as the Oranje strode to success. That wasn't to be the case, however. Jan-Hermen de Bruijn remarked that even worse for the Oranje was, 'something that hardly ever happens, Cruyff really had a poor day … because he was tired, he had a knee injury, which was aggravated in the first moment of the game.'[183]

Not only was the game considered to be a 'disaster'[184] in itself by Cruyff, as he recalled in *My Turn*, it also fed into growing doubts the Dutch captain was having about whether he should continue his international career up to the next World Cup. Later games would change his mood, and it was an entirely different set of circumstances that caused his omission. That was for another day, however. There were plenty more trials and tribulations for the Oranje to come, but the game against Czechoslovakia had to be dealt with first.

Knobel's comments suggested that the Dutch players were expecting the game to provide a comfortable win. It was anything but. Knobel's opposite number Vaclav Jezek was experienced and had seen Dutch football up front and centre. After spending five years coaching Sparta Prague in his homeland, he'd moved to the Netherlands, taking over ADO Den Haag from 1969 to 1972 and steering them to a highly laudable third place in the Eredivisie in 1970/71. Qualification

183 De Bruijn, Jan-Hermen – Interview with the author
184 Cruyff, Johan, *My Turn* (London: Macmillan, 2016)

for European competition in that and the following term was rewarded with the appointment to lead the national team.

Jezek's experience of Dutch football had taught him that to stand off this Oranje team would be to invite trouble, so he insisted that his players hustle and harry when the Dutch were in possession to knock them off their comfortable, flowing rhythm. Even overzealous challenges contributed to the cause and, as Jan-Hermen de Bruijn insisted, the Dutch players 'were irritated by the way the Czechoslovakian players were kicking their legs, more than kicking the ball.'[185] Regardless, the ploy worked like a charm and when the towering libero Anton Ondrus headed powerfully home from a free kick inside 20 minutes, it was no more than the Czechs deserved.

The Dutch huffed and puffed but seemed bereft of any fluidity. Cruyff's downcast demeanour spread through the team like a virus, and the Oranje's play deteriorated accordingly. Fifteen or so minutes later, Van Hanegem made his belated entry as an injury to Rijsbergen forced his withdrawal. The defender had been injured minutes earlier, heroically preventing a second Czech goal.

Adding a midfielder for a defender hardly changed the flow of the game, however, and at the break the Dutch were still both labouring for any rhythm, and a goal behind. It had been a game dominated by the sodden condition of the pitch, rather than greatly by any of the 22 players attempting to gain an advantage for their team as they slipped and slid. Unusually for Thomas, no cautions had been administered to either side. That would change as the game progressed and the referee eased his way towards his more comfortable position as the centre of attention.

The second period began much as the first one had ended. Scrappy play by both teams hardly enhanced the spectacle

185 De Bruijn, Jan-Hermen – Interview with the author

but, after five minutes, a clumsy challenge and then a show of dissent earned Jaroslav Pollak a yellow card. Thomas's book was open. Ten minutes later, the Dukla Banska Bystrica player demonstrated a lack of appreciation for the Welshman's reputation. Before that, though, Willy van de Kerkhof was the first Dutch player cautioned when a high and late attempt to block a clearance by Ondrus drew the justified caution. Almost from the restart, a long ball down the Czech right flank was intercepted by Neeskens, who drove forward in typical fashion. It's difficult to ascribe anything other than a measure of malicious intent in the lunging challenge that Pollak deployed to curtail the Barcelona player's run. If there was an attempt to play the ball it was minimal, mistimed and well away from its target. The red card surprised no one, despite the obligatory protests.

Had the Dutch been searching for a break to bring them back into the game, perhaps this was it. Understandably, for the next dozen minutes, the Czechs dropped deep to protect their lead, only sporadically venturing forwards. Knobel sent on Ruud Geels for the ineffective Rep, and Neeskens dropped into the back line alongside Van Kraay to initiate attacks, while Suurbier and Krol moved down the flanks. An interception by Neeskens that looked to have hit his hand led to the equaliser. Thomas saw no offence. The ball was switched out to the right flank and Geels sought to deliver a cross. It was poorly directed and arrowed towards Ondrus. As he shaped to hook clear, though, the ball skewed from his foot and flew past startled goalkeeper Ivo Viktor. It was the most fortunate, and largely undeserved, of equalisers. Surely now the Dutch would go on and win the game.

Three minutes later the one-man advantage disappeared as Thomas levelled up the team numbers by showing a straight red card to Neeskens. The challenge was clumsy and ill-timed for sure but, had Pollak not already been dismissed, it's difficult not to think that a yellow card would have been deemed appropriate. Seconds later, Cruyff was shown a yellow for dissent as the Dutch discipline looked like falling from a cliff ... Maybe the incessant rain tempered their ardour, though, and the remaining minutes were played out without further goals – or cards. Extra time would be required.

The first 15-minute period did little to dispel growing convictions that only a penalty shoot-out would decide the issue. Fatigue and the continuing deterioration of the pitch mitigated against coordinated play. The winner seemed likely to be the team least compromised by the conditions, rather than the one with the best players.

In the second period, it was the Dutch pressing more, but with barely six minutes remaining another sally forward by Cruyff was brought to an abrupt halt as Panenka upended him. The Dutch paused in anticipation of the clear free kick, but Thomas remained silent and the Czechs swept forward. The ball came out to the right and substitute Vesely Frantisek crossed to the far post for Zdenek Nehoda to head home. Writing in *The Guardian*, Rob Smyth related that when the referee was interviewed as part of a Dutch TV documentary in 2010, he conceded he had made an error. 'Thomas accepts it was a foul on Cruyff. "I apologise," he says. "It was the wrong decision." This does not vindicate Holland's behaviour; these mistakes happen all the time, and Holland would not have played at the 1974 World Cup without a serious refereeing error.'[186]

If some of the Dutch players were prepared to forgive and forget, at least one carries an indelible memory. Wim Van Hanegem can carry a grudge and deliver a barb with the same studied precision as he kept possession and delivered a pinpoint pass. In the same documentary, he offered his response to

186 The Joy of Six: European Championship controversies, *The Guardian*, 22 June 2012

Thomas's acceptance of his error. 'He needn't take 32 years to do that [acknowledge his mistake],' Van Hanegem fumed. 'That strikes me as a little long. [Narrator: it was the first time in 32 years he'd seen the images.] 'I can't imagine that, don't try to convince me of that. He's just incredibly vain, when you see that little man walk, so pedantic, an annoying little fella, always saying, "Come here." You don't think he has [those images]? You don't think he has that? That he sends Neeskens off? That he calls Cruyff over to give him a yellow card? He had it enlarged. He was the first to have one of those [holds hands far apart] plasma screens, believe me, to watch that. That's the sort of little man he is.'[187]

The Dutch protested furiously, and Van Hanegem was dismissed, for dissent said Thomas in *Brilliant Orange*. 'As I'm walking back to the halfway line, Van Hanegem says to me: "No goal – very bad decision." So, I said to him: "Do not say that again."' It was hardly the end of the matter as Thomas explains. 'I showed him the yellow card. He continued to disagree with my decision. I said: "I'm going to the halfway line, if you step one foot over that line, I will show you the red card." He did that, so I sent him off."'[188]

Van Hanegem's take is different. 'I protested about the bad foul on Cruyff, but that wasn't the problem. The problem was that Clive Thomas told me take the kick-off. I said: "Why? I'm, a midfield player. Ruud Geels is the striker – he should take the kick-off." Thomas said: "Come over here."'[189] Video of the incident does suggest something along these lines as Thomas points to a spot in front of him. Van Hanegem doesn't comply and eventually the inevitable red card is flourished.

187 The Joy of Six: European Championship controversies, *The Guardian,* 22 June 2012
188 Winner, David, *Brilliant Orange* (London: Bloomsbury, 2000)
189 Winner, David, *Brilliant Orange* (London: Bloomsbury, 2000)

A couple of minutes later, with the Dutch now in disarray, a through ball allowed Vesely to skip round Schrijvers and score the third goal. 'The players just gave up. They didn't feel it anymore,'[190] Jan-Hermen de Bruijn said dismally. David Winner said it had been a 'calamitous'[191] performance. A few days later, a team bereft of Rep, plus the suspended Van Hanegem and Neeskens, the latter of whom was on a flight with Cruyff bound for Barcelona the same evening as the Czechoslovakia game, restored a modicum of respect, defeating Yugoslavia in the third-place play-off. Also absent was Knobel, who left the coaching to his assistants.

The recriminations were already under way by then, and there was plenty of blame to go around. The players had let themselves down with ill discipline, and again had fallen prey to that Dutch arrogance. Knobel had hardly been inspirational, a divisive figure in the camp where he should have been leading and uniting. The KNVB had politicked against their own coach, regardless of the potential damage to the hopes of the country, and discord among the squad had hardly helped. All that of course was before drawing a focus on the appalling weather, Cruyff's struggle against injury and the refereeing style of Clive Thomas. The next World Cup was only two years away. The talismanic Cruyff was minded to opt out, Knobel was already history and Total Football was in intensive care. The 1978 World Cup was surely already in the bag!

---

190 De Bruijn, Jan-Hermen – Interview with the author
191 Winner, David, *Brilliant Orange* (London: Bloomsbury, 2000)

PART 5

The 1978 World Cup

Qualification

George Knobel had been a controversial appointment as head coach of the Oranje. At the end of the abortive campaign in Yugoslavia, KNVB, coach and players were all relieved that the unhappy relationship had been terminated. The coach returned to club football and the KNVB returned to the drawing board. The next appointment had to be right. The 1978 World Cup would, in all probability, be the last chance for this generation of players to deliver on the big stage. Strangely, or perhaps not so strangely given the Dutch penchant for changing horses in midstream, the post of head coach to the Netherlands would become a little like a game of pass the parcel. The problem was that, when the music stopped, it wasn't always clear into whose lap the parcel had been deposited.

Jan Zwartkruis had enjoyed a fairly unspectacular playing career as a defender with Amersfoort-based club HBC. In the 1950s he became a captain in the Royal Netherlands Air Force, taking control of coaching for the military football team in 1962. At that time, there was still conscription into the armed forces in the Netherlands and the military team became a breeding ground for many burgeoning Dutch talents. The list of players that broke through under the wing of the Air Force captain featured many future internationals, including Rob Rensenbrink, Barry Hulshoff, Jan van Beveren, Jan Mulder, Henk Houwaart and Willy van der Kuylen.

In 1962, the KNVB appointed Zwartkruis as an assistant to Elek Schwartz and, from that point, he very much became a consistent figure in the background of the KNVB, including being a part of Knobel's team of coaches in Yugoslavia. Although shaded from public glare, the quiet effectiveness of Zwartkruis suggested him as the sort of solid and dependable insider who could pick up the team from the disappointment of the European Championship and point them along the road to the 1978 World Cup, before handing over the role to a more permanent appointment. It was therefore to Zwartkruis that the KNVB turned to replace Knobel, albeit initially on a temporary basis. Unwilling to lose out on his military pension, Zwartkruis was reluctant to leave the Air Force, and was instead in effect loaned out to the KNVB.

The original appointment was for two games, although that was quickly extended. Taking control in September 1976, Zwartkruis gradually restored discipline and a sense of purpose to a squad who looked as if they had lost their way. Initially, his attempt to instil a 'Special Forces' type of discipline caused friction, but Zwartkruis was experienced enough to appreciate how slightly toning down his approach could produce the results required. Players were allowed a little more freedom to play a more natural game, whilst still within the tactical plan of the coach. He was rewarded with trust and respect.

With no time for adjustment or consideration, the new coach was plunged in at the deep end with the first game of the 1978 World Cup qualifying tournament. The finals in Argentina would include 16 teams, a minimum of nine of them – the tenth depending on an intercontinental play-off against a team from the CONMEBOL federation – would come from UEFA, with the first of those places allocated to West Germany as defending champions. Thirty-one other countries would compete for the remaining places. The Netherlands were placed into Group Four, alongside Belgium, Northern Ireland and Iceland. Only the group winners would progress.

The Belgians had already visited Reykjavík, and come away with a scrappy 1-0 victory thanks to a 73rd-minute goal from Franky van der Elst three days earlier, when the Dutch began their campaign in the same stadium on 8 September. If there were any doubts that Zwartkruis was his own man, rather than someone merely prepared to offer a steady hand on the tiller until his tenure expired, they were quickly dismissed by the new coach's first selection. Cruyff was unavailable, having undergone an operation to relieve a long-standing injury back in Barcelona, but there would be other changes as well.

In goal, Zwartkruis gave Anderlecht goalkeeper Jan Ruiter his first cap. Ruiter had been with the Belgian club for five years, since moving from FC Volendam in 1971. A fortnight shy of his 30th birthday, it hardly looked like the beginning of a long career on the international stage and, although he would keep a clean sheet in the game, this would be Ruiter's only game for the Oranje. In front of him, the coach went for a back three of Krol, promoted to the captaincy in the absence of Cruyff, Rijsbergen and Van Kraay. Zwartkruis also brought Ajax's Arie Haan back into the fold, after he had been exiled by Knobel. He would partner Jansen in the centre of midfield. Further forward, the Van de Kerkhof brothers would be linked with Geels, Rensenbrink and another player brought back in from the cold, Van der Kuylen.

Iceland in September hardly holds out the promise of sunshine, and the game was played on a partly frozen pitch hardly conducive to flowing football. A goal by Geels, cleverly turning to volley home after a clipped free kick over the defensive wall had deceived the defence, was sufficient for the points. The temporary coach had started his tenure with a win – the next game would prove far more troublesome.

On 13 October, the Dutch welcomed Northern Ireland to the Stadion de Kuip. Over the years, the fortunes of the team from the six counties of the north had waxed and waned in tune with the passing of some outstanding talents. The team that turned up in Rotterdam was probably one of the better ones, with Pat Jennings, Jimmy Nicholl, Pat Rice, Allan Hunter, Sammy McIlroy and a certain George Best among its number. Best had turned 30 earlier that year and was making his first international appearance for three years, drawn back into the fold by new coach Danny Blanchflower for his first game in charge.

Zwartkruis brought Eddy Treytel back in goal, behind the same back three. Haan and Jansen were joined by the 'Kings of Spain' returning from Barcelona, and Geels, Rensenbrink and Willy van der Kerkhof completed the line-up. It was a strong Dutch team and many expected a comfortable home win. Things started badly, though.

Best had recently left Los Angeles Aztecs and now moved to Division Two club Fulham, joining Rodney Marsh and Bobby Moore. Few doubted that this was a career in decline, but one moment in this match would serve as a reminder of a great talent that should have shone so much brighter. Early in the game, cutting in from the left wing to the right, Best beat one man, then another, then a third. Finally, faced by Cruyff, he played the ball through the Dutch captain's legs, collecting it the other side, and raising a clenched fist to the crowd in triumph.

With only four minutes played, McIlroy skipped past Van de Kerkhof on the left and crossed for Chris McGrath to head back across goal, beating Treytel on his far post. The marking was shabby and it was a poor goal to concede. For much of the next 60 minutes, the Dutch dominated possession and position but, with Jennings in fine form, the men in green kept the home side at bay with spirited defence.

On the hour mark, Zwartkruis removed Geels and sent on Van der Kuijlen to join his Kings of Spain. A few minutes later, the coach was reaping a royal reward as a powerful drive from Krol flew past Jennings into the top corner to level the game. When Cruyff scored again, at the second attempt, just two minutes later from a Van de Kerkhof shot, the job looked done. The spirited Irish fire had been doused. Well, not quite. Inside the last two minutes, a driven cross from the left was fumbled out by Treytel, and Blackpool's Derek Spence crashed the ball home. The following month, Belgium defeated Northern Ireland 2-0 in Antwerp. The year ended with the Dutch trailing their neighbours. They'd have to wait until March of the following year to try to close the gap. The Irish would have to wait for more than a year for their revenge, but when that chance finally arrived, they took it with some vigour.

Ahead of the visit to Belgium, the Netherlands faced a friendly at Wembley in February 1977. It was perhaps the only time the outcome of an international football match was influenced by a post-modernist sculptor. Legend has it that before the game with England, the sculptor Jeroen Henneman, together with his friend Jan Mulder, who Ajax had purchased to replace Cruyff, visited Zwartkruis and Cruyff, pleading the case for young AZ Alkmaar forward Jan Peters to play. So compelling was the argument, apparently, that the coach and captain acceded. Peters played, scored twice and the Oranje won 2-0. It was an ideal boost ahead of the visit to Belgium the following month; the perfect tonic, after drawing against the Irish.

The Netherlands visit to Antwerp on 26 March was a crucial fixture, and there's no evidence of artists of any description influencing the line-up. The draw at home to Northern Ireland had put a solid dent into Dutch aspirations. Lose again, and the Belgians would be disappearing away over the hill on the way to Argentina. Even a draw may only put a temporary hold on their progress.

Zwartkruis had reverted to a back four against England. Suurbier returned to the right flank and, with Krol now establishing himself in the centre of the defence alongside Rijsbergen, Alkmaar's Hugo Hovenkamp was drafted in to defend the left making his debut. The clean sheet against Don Revie's men was sufficient for the coach to leave the same four in place for the Belgium game. Cruyff had the captain's armband alongside Barcelona club-mate Neeskens, with Kees Kist, Rensenbrink, Rep and Willy van de Kerkhof completing the XI. It was a team that spoke of experience and one accustomed to winning key games.

On the opposite side, Belgian coach Guy Thys had gone with a much less experienced team. Goalkeeper and captain Christian Piot was winning his 40th cap, but the remaining ten players could only muster 65 between them, with only three in double figures, and the highest at a mere 13. In this particular battle between youth and experience, it was the older hands that held sway.

Just before the 20th minute, a cross to the far post saw Rep head powerfully on goal. The ball bounced directly in front of Piot and up towards the goalkeeper. Hardly a straightforward save, but he would still have been disappointed to fumble the ball over the line and gift the visitors the lead. The Dutch continued to be the dominant force, and when the second goal came, midway through the second period, it virtually closed out the victory. A lobbed through ball by Rep allowed his captain to run clear of a Belgian defence forlornly appealing for offside. A neat lob over Piot completed the task, and the Oranje were home and dry. Returning to his line after the goal, Piot sportingly patted Cruyff on the head as they passed, acknowledging the skill deployed.

The two away victories had been very much in the style of the Dutch at their height. Had Zwartkruis managed to re-install the team's belief? Cruyff later admitted that he was now rethinking his decision not to go to the World Cup. 'I started seriously wondering whether I should take the opportunity to go to Argentina the following summer with such a strong team.'[192] Some may consider this a classic case of Dutch hubris. After all, qualification hadn't even been achieved yet, but the win had certainly now put the Dutch in the driving seat. That serene feeling was about to be disrupted, though. Zwartkruis's four-game reign was now completed. Talk at the time suggested that any potential extended term

192 Cruyff, Johan, *My Turn* (London: Macmillan, 2016)

with the national team would cause problems with the coach's Ministry of Defence contract, and adversely affect his pension entitlements. The problems didn't seem insurmountable, more of the inconvenient type. Especially as staying on as an assistant didn't cause similar issues.

The KNVB had decided that, despite the run of success – only the draw against Northern Ireland had prevented a perfect sequence of games – Zwartkruis would be demoted within the international set-up, although still retained as a coach. In a move that had so many similarities to the scenario before the 1974 tournament, the association appointed a man whose club success at the turn of the decade had done so much to set the pattern for the Oranje's play. The new head coach, and the man to lead the Netherlands into the World Cup, would be Ernst Happel. It was not the end of the story for Zwartkruis. Unlike Fadrhonc, he would 'not go gentle into that good night',[193] and with good reason.

At the time, the decision to appoint Happel made perfect sense. At Feyenoord, not only had he developed some of the players who would travel to South America, he had also taken the European Cup to Rotterdam. His success in Belgium with Bruges rounded out his CV nicely. Perhaps some at the KNVB even saw him as Michels 2.0, an updated version of the master coach who had taken the Oranje so close in 1974. He was certainly perceived as one of the game's natural winners, and his hard-headed approach to organisation, together with experience of coaching Feyenoord, suggested giving him control of a squad now heading in the right direction again thanks to Zwartkruis was the ideal solution for the World Cup.

---

193 Thomas, Dylan, Do not go gentle into that good night, from *In Country Sleep, And Other Poems* (London: Dent, 1952)

Zwartkruis had considered Happel to be a 'genius'[194] of a coach, but that was an admiration granted given the benefit of distance. Working together would be a different matter. There wasn't an easy symbiotic relationship between Happel and Zwartkruis. They were not exactly polar opposites tactically, but certainly had a different perspective on the best way to play. Few would dispute that the Austrian considered defensive organisation as a key element to success, although this emphasis was never allowed to crowd out attacking intent. A proactive approach when out of possession, including harrying opposition players, if necessary in twos and threes, to prevent play developing was something that Michels had used to great effect in 1974. Happel also favoured the high-pressing defensive line, facilitating an effective offside trap. Zwartkruis may have seen things from a different angle, but that was hardly seen as a problem. The quality both shared was a natural ability to deliver the best outcome from a group of players. It was important, as much of the day-to-day operations of the team remained with Zwartkruis for a while longer.

Very much as with Michels's situation with Barcelona, Happel was still under contract with Bruges in Belgium, who were on their way to retaining the domestic league title and contesting a European Cup Final against Liverpool to be played on 10 May, around three weeks before the World Cup began. In effect, Happel was almost coach *in absentia* and would not be scheduled to take full control of the squad until the World Cup began. In the interim, Zwartkruis was *de facto* still leading the Oranje. Was it a strange scenario? Of course, it was. Remember, however, this was the Netherlands national team. If things weren't strange, they weren't normal.

The next qualifying game was at home to Iceland on the last day of August. With Van Beveren in goal, another

---

194 Bongers, Michael & Bremer, Rene, *Kapitein van Oranje* (Netherlands: Belluci, 2008)

parallel situation with 1974 was forming. Once more, the PSV goalkeeper – widely acknowledged as not only the best Dutch exponent in that position, but also one of the top half-dozen across Europe – would play a role in getting the Oranje to a World Cup, but miss out on the tournament itself. It was almost two years since his last cap away to Poland, before he and Van den Kuylen had left the training camp ahead of the 1976 European Championship qualifying home game against the same opponents. Zwartkruis used his long-standing relationship with Van Beveren – dating back to the time when he had coached him in the military team during national service – to persuade him to return to the international fold.

In *Voetbal International*, former Oranje goalkeeper Jan Ruiter explained the caoch's dilemma. 'Zwartkruis tried not to bother about the hierarchy that had arisen under his predecessors George Knobel and Rinus Michels, but was also put under pressure by Johan Cruyff.'[195] The coach was trying to square the circle, and please both parties by selecting Van Beveren for squads, but leave him on the bench, doubtless hoping that time would heal the rift and allow him to reintegrate the country's outstanding goalkeeper back into the national team. It was a ploy doomed to failure.

Inevitably Van Beveren became frustrated at not playing, and approached the coach. Zwartkruis was faced with the same dilemma that Knobel had been forced to deal with. 'Jan, I'm just being manipulated,'[196] Zwartkruis reportedly conceded, confessing both the situation and his impotence to resolve it. Unsurprisingly, Van Beveren decided the unequal fight simply wasn't worth the effort and announced his final retirement from international football. At 30 he was at his peak, and 32

195 In the name of Orange: from the forgotten goalkeeper to Krul, *Voetbal International* (www.vi.nl)
196 In the name of Orange: from the forgotten goalkeeper to Krul, *Voetbal International* (www.vi.nl)

international appearances was a scandalously low number of caps. The loss to the Oranje was even recognised amongst his peers. Echoing the thoughts of Ray Hudson expressed years later, Jan Ruiter spoke for many with clear frustration, 'If Van Beveren had played in '74 or '78, we would certainly have become world champions once.'[197]

In front of Van Beveren in what would be his last international game was the back four of Suurbier, Krol, Rijsbergen and Hovenkamp. Jansen, Willy van de Kerkhof and Van Hanegem formed the midfield three, with Rep, Geels and the other Van de Kerkhof twin up front. Both Neeskens and Cruyff were absent. Few knew it at the time, but the totemic No.14 and captain of the Netherlands would only play twice more in Oranje.

To all intents and purposes, the game was settled inside the first 25 minutes. By then, Van Hanegem, Geels and Rep had the Dutch beyond the reach of any but the most outlandish Icelandic aspirations. Sigurvinson scored a second-half penalty, but Geels restored the three-goal margin in the final minute. Three days later, the Belgians went one better, defeating Iceland 4-0 in Brussels. The next game for the Dutch would be a visit to Belfast in October. Before that, however, an event that took place well away from any football pitch would compromise Dutch hopes of success in Argentina.

On 17 September, Johan Cruyff was sitting at home in his Barcelona apartment watching a basketball game on television when the doorbell rang. Opening the door to what he thought was a courier, the captain of Barcelona and the Netherlands was confronted by a gunman. It was an attempted kidnap. Fortunately, the commotion raised the alarm with neighbours and the plan was foiled, but not before Cruyff, his wife and children had been subjected to a terrifying ordeal, including

197 In the name of Orange: from the forgotten goalkeeper to Krul, *Voetbal International* (www.vi.nl)

him being tied up. Conversely, the assailant's attempts to tie Cruyff to a piece of furniture gave his wife the chance to escape and raise the alarm. It had been an understandably traumatic and emotional episode, and one that convinced Cruyff that flying to South America for a football tournament would come a very distant second to being at home to protect his family. 'Anyone who would leave his family behind in those circumstances would be out of his mind,'[198] he later explained.

From then, both Cruyff and his family had heavy police protection, and although it offered some sense of security, any connection with normality was shattered. In *My Turn*, Cruyff remarked that the police strongly advised him not to publicise what had happened, as it 'might put ideas into the heads of other lunatics.'[199] It meant that although Cruyff could make clear that he was not going to travel to South America if the Dutch qualified, he could not give the reason why. Such a stance inevitably had two effects. Firstly, people came to their own conclusions about the reasons for his absence and, secondly, efforts began to change his mind.

Understandably, Cruyff was both angry and frustrated when 'accusations that Danny [Cruyff's wife] was the evil genius behind [his] refusal to play in Argentina'[200] began to circulate and he was unable to put scurrilous talk to bed by revealing the facts of the matter. 'I kept quiet about all this for decades, but the rumours and accusations continued to be dragged out regularly. It was like our family was constantly receiving a slap in the face.'[201]

Even when Happel, clearly unaware of the true reason for his withdrawal, telephoned Cruyff to try and persuade him to go to the tournament, the player kept his counsel, but

198 Cruyff, Johan, *My Turn* (London: Macmillan, 2016)
199 Cruyff, Johan, *My Turn* (London: Macmillan, 2016)
200 Cruyff, Johan, *My Turn* (London: Macmillan, 2016)
201 Cruyff, Johan, *My Turn* (London: Macmillan, 2016)

was adamant that his mind was made up. 'I told Happel that I wasn't in the right physical or mental state to play in such an important tournament. I don't think he was convinced, because a World Cup is on a different level. A great sportsman like Happel felt that to miss such an opportunity wasn't right, but I couldn't give him the whole story.'[202]

For so many people in the Netherlands, travelling to a World Cup finals, and having the opportunity to lay the ghost of 1974 to rest without Cruyff was borderline unthinkable. How different would it have been if Cruyff had played? Jan-Hermen de Bruijn has no doubts. 'All the difference in the world, because in the moments until he retired Cruyff was, perhaps with Beckenbauer, the best player in the world still.'[203]

Not being even vaguely aware of the real reason for his absence, there was an understandable groundswell of opinion that his mind could be changed. Championed by parts of the media, the 'Pull Cruyff Over the Line' campaign gathered rapid momentum and the national team's captain recalled that he received, 'postbags full of requests from Dutch fans pleading with [him] to go with the Oranje and begging [him] to change [his] mind.'[204] Only much later would everyone understand that it was never a feasible option, he said. 'After nearly 30 years, once all the children had left home, I decided to reveal the truth. And that was that. That was that for good.'[205]

The decision was clearly understandable, honourable and the only one that a dedicated family man could have made. For all that, though, there were inevitable regrets expressed by Cruyff. 'When the Netherlands reached the final again, the BBC invited me to be a pundit for the game. I had a hard time in the studio there [watching the Dutch lose again]. You

202 Cruyff, Johan, *My Turn* (London: Macmillan, 2016)
203 De Bruijn, Jan-Hermen – Interview with the author
204 Cruyff, Johan, *My Turn* (London: Macmillan, 2016)
205 Cruyff, Johan, *My Turn* (London: Macmillan, 2016)

watch a game like that and the thought runs through your head that if you'd been there your career might have ended with a world title. If only I'd done this, if only I'd done that. It doesn't happen to me very often, but it really took hold of me that time. A feeling of what I could have achieved had I been there, but knowing full well that I would have had to leave my family behind to achieve it. And I couldn't have done that.'[206]

Under the strange amalgam of Happel and Zwartkruis as coaches, the Netherlands played their next game, a friendly against the Soviet Union on 5 October at the Stadion de Kuip. Jongbloed returned in goal to add his name to the list of goalkeepers playing ahead of the finals, and in contention for a place to Argentina should the Netherlands get there. The now regular-looking back four stayed in place but, ahead of them, things looked less experienced. Ajax's Tschen La Ling made his debut, albeit only for 55 minutes, before he was replaced by Van der Kuylen. Jan Peters gained his 12th cap and Kist his 14th. Just past the hour mark, Ernie Brandts, another debutant, entered the game. There was more action from the bench than in the goalmouths, as the game ended in a tepid 0-0 draw.

Before the visit to Belfast in mid-October, the Dutch had seven points, Belgium six and Northern Ireland three. All three had two games to play. Iceland had completed their programme, having two points from their win over the Irish in Reykjavík, and were out of contention. Following the draw in Rotterdam, and despite other results experienced by Blanchflower's team, the Dutch would hardly have been expecting an easy ride at Windsor Park. They were not disappointed. Two changes had already been made before the sole goal of the game arrived. Dusbaba replaced Rijsbergen, just after half-time, and then Van der Kuylen came on for

206 Cruyff, Johan, *My Turn* (London: Macmillan, 2016)

Cruyff inside the last 20 minutes. Just when it appeared that a draw would frustrate Dutch hopes, with 15 minutes to play, a mix-up saw the ball reach Willy van de Kerkhof, five metres or so from goal, with just Jennings to beat. A gentle prod completed the job and the Dutch scampered away with two valuable points.

The result ruled the Irish out of qualification, and two weeks later the deciding game was played out in Amsterdam. In simple terms, Belgium would need to beat the Dutch and then go on to Belfast and win again to pip the Oranje for qualification. Any other combination of results would see the Netherlands progress to Argentina. With the attainable requirement of just a draw needed to qualify, the Dutch decided to complicate matters for themselves again. Happel had been taking a largely watching brief, despite his appointment being known, although officially not in effect unless, or until, qualification had been secured. He was still in the full employ of Bruges.

For whatever reason, however, Happel let it be known that he wanted to lead the Dutch team against Belgium. It was hardly a diplomatic move. With the Austrian working for a Belgian club, and seeking to coach a team playing against Belgium, a rumpus was inevitable. Sure enough, the Belgian FA sent a letter to their Dutch equivalents describing any such move as unethical, with the clear implication of a potential conflict of interests, as three of his Bruges players would be representing Belgium, including the captain, Raoul Lambert. It was a difficult argument to counter, and the KNVB conceded the point. Happel would have to wait. Another problem was around the corner, though.

The controversy had pointed out to Zwartkruis the tenuous nature of his position, and he tendered his resignation. Ahead of the crucial qualifying game, from having in effect two coaches, the Dutch were now left with none. With uncharacteristic vigour, the KNVB moved swiftly to smooth out Zwartkruis's ruffled feathers, and persuaded him to stay, but what had they offered him as an inducement to withdraw his threat? Some reports suggest he had been granted equal status with Happel, despite there being a significant and hierarchical difference in their respective titles. It was a 'sticking-plaster' solution and, as with such remedies, when it came time to rip off that plaster, it wouldn't be painless.

It was hardly a game for experimentation and with the issue of coaching authority hanging over the game like a rain-filled cloud ready to break, a solid-looking team was selected. Jongbloed was in goal behind a back four of Suurbier, Krol, Dusbaba – standing in for the injured Rijsbergen – and Hovenkamp. The three-man midfield comprised Jansen, Neeskens and Willy van de Kerkhof, with twin Rene in the forward line, alongside skipper Cruyff and Rensenbrink. It would be the captain's final game in Oranje.

Such games are rarely a feast of football and, when Rene van de Kerkhof put the Dutch ahead with just a few minutes played, it proved to be the only goal of the game. The Oranje would be in Argentina, but without their captain, and three-times European Footballer of the Year. They would, however, have one more coach than the normal quota. In an attempt to square the circle, the KNVB had reportedly given Zwartkruis the title of Head Coach, and Happel that of Supervisor, although some reports put the titles the other way around. It's something that only highlights perhaps how meaningless they were – certainly in respect of each other. The problem being that there was no agreed definition of what each of those meant.

Preparation

With the Belgium game being the last of 1977, it wouldn't be until February 1978, just four months ahead of the tournament, that planning could commence in any real way.

A game against Israel at the National Stadium in Ramat Gan brought a 2-1 victory in a match that seemed more designed to shake off the dust and rust of a winter than as part of any substantial experimentation. Only La Ling, winning his second cap, and FC Den Haag forward Henk van Leeuwen, on his debut, were newcomers. Neither would make the final cut for Argentina. The remaining players were now established regulars or internationally experienced. The goals came from an early Rensenbrink penalty and a second-half winner from La Ling, after Yitzhak Peretz had equalised for the Israelis.

The second friendly came two months later with a visit to Tunisia. This time the selection offered opportunities to a number of less established players, as well as a switch to a 3-4-3 formation. Suurbier, Krol and Van Kraay were the back three, although Rijsbergen would replace Krol at half-time. In midfield, Willy van de Kerkhof and Jansen had two debutants outside of them on the flanks in the FC Twente pair of Piet Wildschut and Arnold Muhren. The former would be included in the final squad for South America whilst the latter would miss out. A decade later, though, he would be part of a successful Dutch team at a major tournament. Johan Boscamp, then with Belgian club RWD Molenbeek, made his debut coming on as a second-half substitute for Van de Kerkhof, and would also travel to South America to win his only other cap.

The forwards were Van Leeuwen, winning his second cap, and two JC Roda forwards, Dick Nanninga and Pierre Vermeulen. The game finished with a 4-0 win for the Dutch and the two JC Roda forwards shared three of the goals, the other going to Van Leeuwen. Vermeulen would miss out on the trip to Argentina, but Dick Nanninga was in the travelling party.

Born in the early days of 1949, Dirk Nanninga, commonly known as Dick, came late to the professional game, joining JC Roda for the 1974/75 season. Despite Total Football still being the dominant *lingua franca* of the Dutch game, Nanninga was cut from an entirely different cloth. The presence of a forward such as Nanninga would have felt like an irritating stone in the shoe to the Dutch team of 1974.

He did, however, have something in common with the greatest of Dutch stars, Johan Cruyff. Nanninga was also sponsored by Puma and, along with the Van de Kerkhof twins, followed their former captain's lead from four years earlier and in Argentina wore shirts with two stripes down the sleeves, rather than the Adidas trademark of three. As far as Nanninga was concerned, that is where any similarity began and ended. Strangely, the issue wasn't deemed to be so important to the twins when they played for PSV. The club's shirts were supplied by Adidas.

During his eight years with Roda, Nanninga deployed his robust approach and fearless attitude, eschewing potential and repeated physical costs, to intimidate opposing defenders and goalkeepers. To some, it may have been very much the antithesis of the Dutch approach to football at the time, but 107 goals in 225 league games illustrated that the old adage of there being more than one way to skin a cat still held true, and when he left the club in 1982 for a brief sojourn with Hong Kong-based team, Seiko, his haul made him Roda's all-time top goalscorer. It's a distinction that endures at the time of writing.

Nanninga joined Roda a couple of seasons after they had achieved promotion to the Eredivisie by winning the second tier Eerste Divisie title, and for much of his time with the club, Roda were a journeyman outfit, usually safe, and often in the top ten of the league, but hardly troubling the top end of the table. They did achieve qualification to the European Cup Winners' Cup at the end of the 1975/76 season, courtesy of losing in the final of the KNVB Cup to PSV Eindhoven, who took a European Cup spot instead, as winners of the league.

The forward's play was particularly respected by long-time Roda manager Bert Jacobs, who took charge of the club in the same year as Nanninga arrived, and would lead Roda for the next six seasons, before moving first to Willem II in Tilburg and then to Seiko in Hong Kong, where he signed Nanninga.

Nanninga hadn't made his debut for Roda until he was 24, and his international chance came a little under ten months short of his 30th birthday. In typically robust style, though, he grabbed the opportunity, netting his brace against the Africans. It was clearly enough to convince Happel that he had his 'wild card' player for the tournament. There would be one other game for the Dutch ahead of the trip to South America, but Nanninga missed the match against the manager's native Austria in Vienna. Before that an early training camp had been arranged for 8 May. Things did not go particularly well.

It seemed a strangely early date to call a camp with the potential of so many players being absent due to club commitments, and so it transpired. Originally 26 players had been selected to attend, but only 16 arrived to be greeted by Zwartkruis. Also absent was Happel. Some of the absentees had perfectly reasonable reasons for their absence, others less so. Happel, for example, had the European Cup Final to play against Liverpool two days later. For the moment he was still contracted to Bruges, and the chance to add another European Cup success to his CV would not be something to cast easily aside, even had his contract allowed such careless abandon. The final was lost and Happel would have to wait a further five years to become the first manager to win the trophy with two different clubs, when SV Hamburg defeated Juventus in 1983.

A number of other players would also be required for the second leg of the UEFA Cup Final on 9 May, when French club Bastia lost 3-0 to PSV Eindhoven following a goalless draw in Corsica. As well as losing the Eindhoven contingent, Johnny Rep was now playing for Bastia, following a short period in

Spain with Valencia. A KNVB Cup Final played on 5 May featuring AZ Alkmaar and Ajax was hardly helpful, and it wasn't surprising that Alkmaar decided that their players would be better served resting after the game, rather than turning up at a training camp. Neeskens called in from Catalunya and said he would be unable to attend as Barcelona had organised a series of medical examinations around that date.

Over in Belgium, there was understandably scant concern for the Netherlands' World Cup campaign. Only five days earlier, Anderlecht had beaten Austria Vienna 4-0 to win the European Cup Winners' Cup, with club captain Rensenbrink notching two goals. They were not overly keen on sending both their skipper and Haan, who had by now moved to the Belgian capital from Ajax, to a training camp. Instead, they let it be known that they would be retaining their players for friendly games that had been scheduled before notice of the camp had been received.

Understandably, Zwartkruis had considered calling the camp off and sending the players back home, but Ruud Krol, who had inherited the captain's armband following Cruyff's retirement from international football, insisted on proceeding, convincing the coach that having 16 players was far better than having none, and time was getting short. Even the opportunity to have some of the players together in the same place would have benefits. Any discords could be worked on and, if players were needed to fit into new slots, here was the chance to work on some tactical options. It all seemed logical and the camp went ahead. As ever though, complications waited around the corner.

The president of Ajax contacted the KNVB demanding that the club be paid compensation for sending six of its players to the camp, and having to cancel potentially lucrative friendly games, whilst Anderlecht had been allowed to simply deny the request for their players. Had Krol been duplicitous, knowing that his encouragement to press ahead with the camp would provoke such a reaction from the club? There's little evidence to suggest any devious involvement, but the whole sorry episode provoked a public backlash, with journalists pointing fingers at the coach and slapdash organisation as the cause. The opening day of the 1978 World Cup was less than a month away.

The footballing world in Europe, and especially in the Netherlands, in 1978 was very different from that in the months ahead of the 1974 World Cup. Rep wasn't the only player to have left Ajax, following Cruyff and Neeskens through the exit door in search of pastures new. The team that won the club's third European Cup had largely drifted apart. Goalkeeper Heinz Stuy moved to FC Amsterdam in 1976, replacing Jongbloed who would move to JC Roda the following year.

Wim Suurbier moved to Bundesliga club Schalke in October 1977, but his time in Germany was brief, only encompassing a dozen league games before he crossed the Atlantic to join NASL club Los Angeles Aztecs. Barry Hulshoff left to join MVV Maastricht in 1977, playing there for a couple of seasons before being compelled to retire, serving some of that time with George Knobel as his coach. He would return to coach Ajax towards the end of the next decade, taking them to the 1987/88 UEFA Cup Winners' Cup Final, losing to Belgian club KV Mechelen. His central defensive partner, Horst Blankenburg left at the same time, returning to his native Germany with SV Hamburg. Did he ever regret not accepting the apparent invitation to take up Dutch nationality and play in the 1974 World Cup? It's an interesting issue to consider. He never did reach the international stage with West Germany.

Arie Haan had left for Anderlecht the season after the triumph over Juventus, joining Rensenbrink in the Belgian capital. Both players would feature in Argentina. Gerrie

Muhren, who had opted out of the 1974 tournament for family reasons, moved to Spain in 1977, joining La Liga club Real Betis in Seville. That just left Piet Keizer, who retired after the 1974 World Cup, and one other. Ruud Krol was the sole survivor, although the addition of Piet Schrijvers and Ruud Geels to the Ajax roster from Michels's 1974 squad boosted their international prestige, but only Schrijvers would make the cut for Argentina. Of the 22 players selected just three came from Ajax. Krol and Shrijvers would play a prominent part in the tournament, but the third member, midfielder Dick Schoenaker, who had yet to win his first cap, would only feature briefly as a substitute. Even in Catalunya, the fortunes of the former Ajax duo, Cruyff and Neeskens were hardly flourishing. After the success of 1975, they had failed to win the La Liga title again. Michels left Barcelona and briefly returned to Ajax in 1975, without any significant arrest of the club's decline, before going back to Barcelona the following year. By now though, the magic had apparently faded.

Much the same was true of the fortunes of Feyenoord. Together with Ajax, they had dominated Dutch domestic and continental club football in the run up to the 1974 World Cup. But the Eredivisie league table at the end of the 1977/78 season was a telling indication of the new balance of power in the Netherlands. Feyenoord were down in 14th position, and although Ajax finished as runners-up, the new powerhouse, somewhat fittingly considering their tie-up with the Philips electrical organisation – PSV stands for Philips Sport Vereniging (Philips Sports Union) – were PSV Eindhoven.

Former international midfielder Kees Rijvers had joined the club as coach in 1972, after six years with FC Twente. It heralded a sustained period of success. The KNVB Cup was won in 1973/74 with a thumping 6-0 victory over NAC Breda in the final, after defeating Ajax in the last four. Both of the

Van de Kerkhof twins scored, with Van der Kuylen netting a brace and Swedish striker Ralf Edstrom adding a goal.

The triumph set a trend for the period up to the next World Cup. The Eredivisie title was won the following season, making PSV the top Dutch club for the first time in a dozen years. Feyenoord and Ajax were trailing in second and third. The wait for the next league success would be much shorter. The title was retained with the erstwhile big two again slotting in behind. For good measure, another KNVB Cup triumph was added, defeating a JC Roda team featuring Nanninga. Again, Edstrom was to the fore, scoring the winning goal in extra time.

Following a fallow 1976/77, PSV returned to the top of the league, winning the Eredivisie title in 1977/78, a clear four points ahead of Ajax. The UEFA Cup success against Bastia was the club's first continental triumph. Rijvers would leave PSV in 1981 to take over the Dutch national team, succeeding Zwartkruis, but with the 1978 World Cup around the corner, his work with PSV would be recognised with six of the club's players making up the largest contribution to the squad from a single club.

The big issue was that without Cruyff, the Oranje would either have to find someone who could replace him, without altering the established system of play overmuch, or settle on different tactics. Happel's inclination may have been for the latter. On a number of occasions before the tournament, he emphasised the importance of having a 'team' rather than a few 'stars'. The problem was that this was the Dutch national team, and so many players in the squad considered themselves as stars. Happel would have a problem instilling his collective ethic into a group of players who, for so long, had been used to being led by Cruyff, the brightest star in the Dutch firmament.

Zwartkruis advocated a different approach. After 1974, Rensenbrink had developed into the leader of the Anderlecht team, with his role evolving from being the left-sided attacker to a more fluid position, not that different to the way Cruyff operated for the Oranje. Although he was not suggesting that the gap between the ability and leadership qualities of the two players was small, Zwartkruis considered it not to be so large that a mere adjustment to the existing pattern of play, with Rensenbrink operating in a similar way, could be the solution. The team and tactics could be organised around the Anderlecht player.

Happel, as ever, was wise enough to listen, but hardly convinced. The bigger task would be to convince Rensenbrink of the scheme's merits. Playing ability is one thing, but leadership an entirely different matter. Cruyff had the simple belief that he was destined to be the leader of whatever group he was part of. No one had to ask or persuade him to lead, that was his role.

When he was ousted from the captaincy of Ajax in that ill-fated election, many considered that his subsequent departure for Catalunya was a fit of pique, sulking because he felt people didn't love him anymore. Instead, should it be viewed as annoyance at the error of others; their failure to recognise that his talents and ability could best produce the outcomes they desired if he was allowed to deploy them to the maximum effect – as a leader? Whatever the case, to be the fulcrum of a team there needs to be an inherent belief that it's a role a player is utterly convinced he can perform. That may not have been the situation with Rensenbrink.

It wasn't that Rensenbrink lacked confidence, far from it. From 12 yards, he was both cool and deadly effective in the battle of wits with goalkeepers, as David Winner attested to. 'The phenomenally cool Rob Rensenbrink … missed only two in his whole career and scored four in the 1978 World Cup. Rensenbrink actually enjoyed penalties, and when he was at Anderlecht practised taking them for ten to 15 minutes at the end of every training session. His method was to tell the goalkeeper in advance which of the four corners of the goal he was going to put the ball, and then beat them there anyway.'[207] Confidence and leadership quality are hardly the same thing, though.

Jan Mulder played alongside Rensenbrink for a season at Anderlecht and was adamant that 'Robbie Rensenbrink was as good as Cruyff,'[208] but added the caveat that, 'Only in his mind he was not.'[209] Why was that? Mulder suggested an answer. 'Rensenbrink was one of the all-time great players, but he had complexes with Cruyff in the national team; he was always in Cruyff's shadow because of his character.'[210] It's not an unusual situation, even amongst a star-studded cast such as the Oranje were in the years leading up to Cruyff's retirement. Cruyff was a dominating personality, and it's unlikely that Rensenbrink was the only player who deferred to him. 'I never argued with Cruyff [about my position]. For me it was no problem,'[211] Rensenbrink explained. 'We had success in every game. But I didn't play really at the level I did in Belgium. I played much better in '78 because Cruyff wasn't on top of me, but also because I was four years older.'[212] Even outside of Cruyff's shadow, and four years older, Rensenbrink was not sold on Zwartkruis's idea.

It may well have been a wise decision. Everything flowed through Cruyff, and to expect the other players in the squad to accept anyone as the 'new Cruyff' would not only be a huge leap of faith, it would be very many huge leaps, and there was no certainty that others would be minded to jump. At that point, the idea lost force. If the player at the centre

207 Winner, David, *Brilliant Orange* (London: Bloomsbury, 2000)
208 Winner, David, *Brilliant Orange* (London: Bloomsbury, 2000)
209 Winner, David, *Brilliant Orange* (London: Bloomsbury, 2000)
210 Winner, David, *Brilliant Orange* (London: Bloomsbury, 2000)
211 Winner, David, *Brilliant Orange* (London: Bloomsbury, 2000)
212 Winner, David, *Brilliant Orange* (London: Bloomsbury, 2000)

wasn't convinced, there was little chance that anyone else would be.

Another option was Van Hanegem, but even in his younger days – by the time of the tournament he was 34 – he never possessed that burst of speed that Cruyff had. At their best, the Dutch play was like the hypnotic stare of a cobra, swaying gently from side to side, lulling its prey into a somnambulistic state before striking with devastating speed. Van Hanegem could play alongside Cruyff, he had the artistry to hypnotise, but he was a constrictor, not a venom-laden killer.

There was one more official game before the World Cup. The Dutch would travel to Happel's home country on 20 May to take on Austria in Vienna. No one knew it at the time, but it would be a dress rehearsal for a more serious encounter 25 days later. In this game neither Austrian coach Helmut Senekowitsch, nor Happel felt very much like experimenting. The only new name on the Dutch team-sheet was PSV's Jan Poortvliet. Very much in the way that Wim Rijsbergen went from debutant to playing in a World Cup Final in a little over a month in 1974, Poortvliet would enjoy a similarly meteoric rise in 1978.

The other significant selection was Van Hanegem. Did this mean that the AZ67 Alkmaar midfielder – he had left Feyenoord in 1976 – would have a key role in Argentina? It wasn't to be. It became common currency that Van Hanegem opted out of the squad as Happel had refused to guarantee his selection in the team. It's a rumour the player is keen to dispel. 'People think the problem was that I was second choice for Argentina, but that's not true. Happel told me he planned to leave me out for the first game with Iran because that wasn't so important, but wanted me to play against Scotland and all the other games. The real problem was money.'[213]

213 Winner, David, *Brilliant Orange* (London: Bloomsbury, 2000)

In 1974, all of the players' earnings from commercial activities had gone into a single pot to be shared equally amongst the entire squad and backroom staff. In 1978, however, some of the senior players had decided to opt out of any similar scheme, keeping their own earnings for themselves. Van Hanegem says he was outraged. 'Everyone from one to twenty-two is important. Everyone should get the same, including the man who cleans the boots because if he's not there, I must clean my own. I went to Happel and I said I was not happy with some players, and if we were away for three or four weeks, maybe we would have a lot of problems. Happel and I talked for one and a half hours with him trying to persuade me. But my feelings said no, and when I say no, I mean no.'[214] The Oranje would have no Cruyff and no Van Hanegem in Argentina.

Happel arranged two last-minute friendly matches against Bruges. It may seem strange for the coach of an international team to play friendlies against the club he had just left, but the existing links with the club may simply have made it the easiest way to arrange games. Plus, there was the added bonus of Happel knowing how the Oranje's opponents would play. The only complication may have been remembering which dugout he should sit in ... No matter how 'friendly' a friendly game is, there is always the chance of an unfortunate injury ruling someone out of the tournament. All went well, though, and, after the second match, the squad list was submitted to FIFA.

Four years earlier, Michels had numbered his squad alphabetically, with the exception of Cruyff. Happel cared little for such an orderly approach. Some of the players who had featured under Michels four years earlier opted to retain the same numbers, whilst others wanted their club or 'lucky' numbers. The remainder filled in the gaps. The squad

214 Winner, David, *Brilliant Orange* (London: Bloomsbury, 2000)

contained 12 players who had been selected by Michels four years earlier. No other squad in the tournament could match that experience. They also had the largest number of non-domestic-based players with six of the squad earning their living in countries other than the Netherlands.

Three goalkeepers were chosen but, once again, the outstanding Dutch shot-stopper Jan van Beveren was absent. As with the 1974 tournament, and indeed the European Championship of 1976, he had contributed in the qualification tournament, but never had the honour of representing his country in a major tournament. It seemed a perverse sort of ill fortune. In 1978 he should surely have been on the plane to South America.

Happel's goalkeepers were Schrijvers, Jongbloed and Pim Doesburg of Sparta Rotterdam. Doesburg seemed to fit into the mould of Jongbloed four years earlier, perhaps without the advocacy of Cruyff. Now 34, he had a mere two caps to his name, both dating back more than a decade. His debut had come under Georg Kessler during a friendly against Belgium in Antwerp in April 1967, when conceding the only goal of the game. In the following month he replaced starting goalkeeper Tonny van Leeuwen in a European Championship qualifying game against Hungary in Budapest. When he joined the action, the Dutch were already two goals down, and he kept a clean sheet for the remainder of the game … The difference with the experience of Jongbloed, however, would be that while the left-field selection of 1974 played every minute of every game in the tournament, Doesburg would sit out every minute of every game in 1978.

Five goalkeepers had played in the previous year or so. Doesburg hadn't been one of them, but it seemed that as the choices were rotated, other that Schrijvers and Jongbloed, none had made solid claims for a place in the squad. The other option could have been Jan Ruiter of Anderlecht. He had a measure of tournament experience, being part of Knobel's squad for the European Championship in 1976, but as with Doesburg, he hadn't played international football since 1976. His first and last cap had come in Zwartkruis's first game as temporary manager, the 1-0 victory in Iceland.

Playing in Belgian football may not have been to his advantage. With Happel at Bruges, he would certainly have seen much of Ruiter's play. Perhaps that was the problem … Whilst age is considered much less of a factor with goalkeepers, the fact that Happel's three nominated keepers were Schrijvers at 31, Jongbloed at 37 and Doesburg at 34, probably says as much about the dearth of young up and coming goalkeepers in the Netherlands as it does about the ability of three that would travel to South America.

As well as skipper Krol, the defenders comprised Poortvliet, Van Kraay, Hovenkamp, Rijsbergen, Suurbier, and another player with a single cap behind him, Ernie Brandts of PSV. He made his debut on the international stage in the goalless draw against the Soviet Union in October 1977, but hadn't featured since. It was a mix of the experienced in Krol, Suurbier, Rijsbergen, and, to some extent, Van Kraay, who had made 11 appearances for the Oranje, balanced out against much younger blood. Poortvliet, Brandts and Hovenkamp could only muster ten caps between them. The situation was then complicated by Hovenkamp's late withdrawal from the squad due to injury. With the squad details already submitted it was too late to nominate a replacement. The Netherlands would travel to Argentina with 21 players in their squad. That 'young blood' in the back line now looked even younger – Brandts and Poortvliet were both 22 – and inexperienced. Both would feature in the tournament.

In midfield there was a block of experienced internationals; many who had played in West Germany and Yugoslavia had case-hardened tournament experience. Jansen, Haan, the Van de Kerkhof twins and Neeskens gave the Dutch midfield an impressive look. The solidity of Jansen and the dynamism of Haan and Neeskens would be invaluable in the heat of South America. The twins would add no small amount of creativity, but without Cruyff and Van Hanegem there was still a lament for what the squad could have looked like. The midfield was completed by Piet Wildschut of FC Twente who had made his debut even later than Poortvliet, during the friendly against Tunisia. The group was completed by the uncapped Ajax player Dick Schoenaker and Johan Boskamp. The Molenbeek player had also made his first appearance against Tunisia, coming on as a substitute for Willy van de Kerkhof after 65 minutes, and would perform the same service for Neeskens after ten minutes in the game against Scotland in the World Cup. They would be the only two caps in his career.

Although such definitions can be a little liquid at times, with either of the Van de Kerkhof brothers sometimes used as forwards, there were four players widely recognised as fitting into that category. Rep and Rensenbrink were well established and Nanninga had made his mark with his brace against Tunisia. The final member of the quartet was PSV's Harry Lubse. The 26-year-old had made his debut three years previously, scoring in a 4-1 victory over Finland in a European Championship qualifying game. He wouldn't feature in the tournament, or afterwards. That cap would be his only one.

Perhaps the unluckiest player to miss out on selection was Ajax forward Ruud Geels. Finishing as the Eredivisie top scorer across the previous four seasons, averaging more than 30 goals per term, he looked to be the sort of striker any team would want with them on the big occasion, especially in tournaments where goals were at a premium. Across an international career spanning seven years, he had accumulated only 20 caps, and in eight of those he had appeared as a substitute, and in three more, when he had started, he had been taken off. Despite that apparent failure to convince a variety of coaches of his worth for a regular starting – and finishing – berth, he had still scored 11 goals. In the qualifying games for this World Cup, he played four times, delivering three goals, but it was still deemed to be insufficient to earn a seat on the plane to Argentina.

Arguably, the squad was more functional than flair-driven, when compared to that of four years earlier. Shorn of Cruyff and Van Hanegem, that was inevitable, but it may also have suited Happel's more physical approach to the game, and how he saw the team playing. There was, however, plenty of potential flexibility from back to front. Krol's versatility allowed different systems to be deployed in defence. He had evolved into an outstanding libero, organising and pushing forward with possession. It meant a back four with him alongside a stopper centre-back such as Rijsbergen was an attractive proposition for the coach. Equally, those two could fit into a back three, with Van Kraay slotting in alongside. There was also the option of putting Krol in his old position of left-back and having Rijsbergen and Van Kraay in the centre. Or even shifting Rijsberben out to the full-back role he played until Michels converted him in 1974 … The vastly experienced Suurbier, and the younger Brandts and Poortvliet offered other options. Midfielders such as Wildschut, Haan and Jansen could also drop back to fill holes as required.

Haan was almost any manager's dream option. Having played in 1974 as a libero, where the Dutch only conceded three goals in the tournament, he had demonstrated his ability to fit into almost any role as required. He was equally happy in a holding midfield role, or further forward probing for openings for others, and his distance shooting would become a key feature of the Dutch progress in Argentina.

The squad was ready. It had hardly been a smooth ride through qualification to squad announcement. Across the months, the Oranje had, at various times, had one or two coaches in charge, and for a short time, none at all. Two of the country's most creative players had decided not to travel. To paraphrase Oscar Wilde, 'To lose one … may be regarded as a misfortune; to lose both looks like carelessness.'[215] Then they had lost an experienced defender, too late to have him replaced. Hovencamp's name remained on the squad list, even though he didn't travel. There was one final hurdle to trip over. In a number of press conferences, Happel had been pressed to explain how his team would play. How would he arrange things to compensate for the loss of Cruyff, not to mention Van Hanegem? After batting the questions back a number of times, the coach eventually gave in and declared that he would work with a back three and five men in midfield. The media pounced.

Over a number of years, England managers approaching a major tournament are teased and taunted with the question. 'Do you think England are going to win it?' It's the classic 'Have you stopped beating your wife?' type of question. Answer in the affirmative, and the hapless manager is a hostage to fortune, primed to be hung out to dry when elimination follows. Reply in the negative and it's even worse. The manager has no belief in the squad, what are England even going there for? Happel was caught on the horns of a similar dilemma. After giving an answer to the question, he was slated for betraying the team's secrets before a ball had been kicked.

Was he naïve? There's surely a massive question mark against any such assertion. Few international managers would face an opponent and know nothing of their style and tactics. Even if that most unusual of cases did apply, it would surely only take a few minutes of watching a game to detect the answer, and adjust your own tactics accordingly. Perhaps it was

215 Wilde, Oscar, *The Importance of Being Earnest* (St James's Theatre, London, 1895)

just time to kick the table over. If the press had been assisted by the KNVB to cause problems before the 1976 European Championship, this time they seemed capable of doing so without any outside assistance. By this stage a situation that had been brewing away for a while was coming to the boil.

Four years previously, ten minutes into that epically violent encounter with Brazil, the referee had called a temporary halt to the game to honour the passing of Argentinian president Juan Peron. What felt like an irrelevant minor irritant at the time, later heralded a much larger and hugely relevant issue when the Dutch were preparing for the 1978 World Cup in Argentina.

The accession of the president's third wife and vice-president, Isabel Martinez de Peron, to take control of the country had hardly been successful. The first female president in South America was ill-suited to the inherited role, and Argentina spiralled into turmoil. With the economy overtaken by rampant inflation and on the brink of civil war, on 24 March 1976, Senora Martinez de Peron was swept from office by a military coup. After years of growing social unrest, economic decay and conflict between right-wing paramilitaries and left-wing guerrillas, the majority of ordinary Argentines had initially welcomed the military, hoping for a return to order, stability and a better life. Two years later, though, any aspiration that the coup would lead to more enlightened times for the country had been crushed under the jackboot of a violently oppressive regime.

Freedoms were trampled underfoot and anyone defined as an enemy of the state, perhaps more objectively described as a dissenter against the regime, was identified and became prey to imprisonment, torture or admittance into the legions of the 'disappeared'. The World Cup was heading to a country seen by so many across the world – other than those sponsoring it as a perceived bulwark against communism – as a pariah.

Should the tournament go ahead? FIFA, unsurprisingly, did little. Perhaps cynically deciding that a World Cup held in a country under military control would be more orderly than with a potentially chaotic democracy in charge, they held their nose and counted the money.

Videla had little or no interest in football, but recognised that the success of the tournament, especially if the hosts won, would be a global boon to his regime, with the sweet smell of success at least temporarily masking the fetid stench of murder, torture and abuse of human rights. Money that the country could ill-afford was lavished on stadiums, infrastructure and facilities that would present the grotesque mask of a smiling face of Argentina to the world as a forward-thinking, safe and happy country.

Videla even tried to have the logo for the tournament changed. Stylised from the characteristic pose of Peron, it symbolically featured two raised, cupped hands in the colours of the Argentina flag, holding a ball. Any connection with the old regime that may deflect glory from the military was to be avoided and Videla ordered that FIFA be informed that the country wished to change the logo. The request was denied. FIFA made it clear that it was too late to change it as many sponsorship contracts and commercial agreements were already in place. Not even fear of a military junta could prise FIFA's fingers from their pot of loot.

Videla's influence was also deployed to give his players the best chance of success. Any number of other teams would later feel that Argentina's natural advantage of playing at home had been stretched and distorted beyond all reason as the tournament progressed. Before that could happen, however, there were major doubts as to whether some teams would even turn up.

FIFA's apparent acceptance of the situation only inflamed passions elsewhere. Europe, in particular, was still in the throes of a growing political awareness among the young and restless, eager and infatuated with idealism to make the world a better place. Amnesty International spoke for many with the slogan, 'Yes to Football, No to Torture!' The movement would also gain traction in the Netherlands.

After qualification for the World Cup had been achieved, letters had begun to arrive at the KNVB headquarters from Latin American unions asking whether the players were aware of the situation in Argentina. They were hardly requiring a 'Yes/No' response. An 'If not, why not?' would have been more appropriate. For the most part the letters were simply ignored; certainly none received replies.

How bad was the situation in Argentina? The documentary film, *A Dirty Game* offered troubling answers. 'Early surveys reported 30,000 prisoners, torture and systematic terror. Within the junta some described such numbers as overinflated, suggesting the real total would be no more than 7,000.'[216] The statement seemed to carry the implication that a figure of that sort was entirely reasonable. It hardly served to cool the ardour of the protests. As pressure began to mount, with newspapers detailing some of the atrocities committed, the KNVB decided to dispatch the team doctor Dr Frits Kessel to Argentina on a fact-finding mission. To some, it may sound like a naïve exercise, or one that was merely designed to offer a laminate of concern to pacify noises off stage. Although the situation in Argentina was anything but normal, the doctor could hardly come back and say anything over than that the country seemed to be orderly. Invitations to speak to dissidents, and examine prison cells or torture rooms were not on his itinerary.

On 14 January 1978, members of the KNVB had attended the World Cup draw ceremony at the General San Martin Cultural Centre in Buenos Aires. The proceedings ended

216 Verdenius, Jaap & Mastenbroek, Kay, *A Dirty Game* (2002 - https://www. themoviedb.org/movie/536232-a-dirty-game?language=en-US)

with the Dutch placed into a group alongside Iran, Peru and Scotland, with their opening game scheduled to be against the Iranians on 3 June. In the same month as the great and good of football associations from around the globe gathered in Buenos Aires, no less than 41 corpses of 'disappeared' people were washed ashore on the beaches of Uruguay. 'The football executives decided to look the other way. But when the officials of the Association are back in Holland an unpleasant surprise awaits them.'[217]

On 27 January, two Dutch comedians got together to launch a campaign aimed at ensuring the Dutch did not go to the World Cup. Following a conversation with a friend working for Amnesty International, Freek de Jonge had been convinced that he should join the cause. The following day, he met comedy partner Bram Vermeulen, and they decided on a plan to develop a protest movement in the Netherlands, aimed at convincing the Oranje not to travel to Argentina. They were hardly a lone voice in the wilderness. Across Europe other movements were springing up with similar causes in mind. In France, *Le Monde* had taken the lead in October 1977, with the first call to boycott the World Cup, and organisations such as the famous COBA[218] movement developed and carried on the fight, forcing questions such as 'Will the World Cup, planned for June 1978 in Argentina, take place amongst concentration camps?'[219] into the public's attention.

Vermeulen and De Jonge's campaign gained momentum among the politically active young in the Netherlands, but official endorsement was more difficult to achieve. Only Felix Rottenberg, chairman of the Young Socialists, was keen to offer support. Whilst the government offered sympathetic nods

217 Verdenius, Jaap & Mastenbroek, Kay, *A Dirty Game* (2002 - https://www. themoviedb.org/movie/536232-a-dirty-game?language=en-US)
218 http://papelitos.com.ar/nota/el-boicot-al-mundial?z_language=en
219 Verdenius, Jaap & Mastenbroek, Kay, *A Dirty Game* (2002 - https://www. themoviedb.org/movie/536232-a-dirty-game?language=en-US)

towards the cause, they emphasised that the matter was purely an issue for the KNVB to decide and that it would be wrong for the government to intervene. A stance perhaps summarised by the phrase that, 'Our opinion was that in this situation the responsibility was not ours, the Football Association was fully and solely responsible.'[220] It wasn't quite the Pontius Pilate approach of washing their hands of responsibility, but it was getting there. As any decision would have political costs, passing the buck looked the most expedient option.

Some politicians did take a stand, albeit whilst also emphasising the personal, rather than political, nature of the decision. Gerard Wallis de Vries, State Secretary for Culture, Recreation and Social Work, of the People's Party for Freedom and Democracy, decided not to go to Argentina for the tournament, claiming, 'My decision not to go was my personal decision, I didn't do it to demonstrate.'[221] The lack of any vocal opposition among the government to his stance made it plain to him, however, that many of his colleagues were of the same view. He added, 'You can conclude that my views were shared by the rest of the government. There was little sympathy for the fact that we were going to participate in a show over there.'[222] What that says, or indeed doesn't say, about any government or organisation is probably best left open to personal opinion.

Some organisations felt that the comedians had stepped beyond their bounds. It was certainly the stance of the KNVB at a meeting with Vermeulen and De Jonge. Karel Jansen, a representative of the Players' Union, summed up the feeling. 'We thought they were a nuisance on the eve of the World

220 Verdenius, Jaap & Mastenbroek, Kay, *A Dirty Game* (2002 - https://www.themoviedb.org/movie/536232-a-dirty-game?language=en-US)

221 Verdenius, Jaap & Mastenbroek, Kay, *A Dirty Game* (2002 - https://www.themoviedb.org/movie/536232-a-dirty-game?language=en-US)

222 Verdenius, Jaap & Mastenbroek, Kay, *A Dirty Game* (2002 - https://www.themoviedb.org/movie/536232-a-dirty-game?language=en-US)

Cup.'[223] On 3 February members of the campaign met with a number of MPs, after which a government letter was sent to the KNVB, but it was a tepid response, hardly likely to convince anyone to change opinions on the matter. The Young Socialists passed a motion supporting the proposed boycott, but that also carried no real effect.

Although the Netherlands of the time was a very progressive country, and most Dutch people would have considered the situation in Argentina as abhorrent, the campaign failed to gain committed support among the political left or the unions. Later, Felix Rottenberg lamented the failure of the campaign, but recognised its inherent weakness. 'It was, of course, a middle-class campaign. The better classes. They were not in regular contact with football players. They were no threat to the players.'[224] Jan Mulder was the only player who supported the campaign and he was no longer in serious contention for a place in the squad.

In March, the KNVB met the government to discuss how things should proceed, but had declared beforehand that a boycott was not on the table. Jacques Hogewoning later explained the KNVB position … 'I think our standpoint is right when we say: Let's take Argentina as a starting point for a discussion about our future behaviour.'[225] If they were hoping for approval from the government, it wasn't forthcoming, but neither was an instruction not to go. The government would not intervene. Rather than a ball, it was a tin can that was kicked down the road. When the squad flew out to South America, a planned demonstration in the airport's departure lounge was stymied when the group entered by an alternative

223 Verdenius, Jaap & Mastenbroek, Kay, *A Dirty Game* (2002 - https://www. themoviedb.org/movie/536232-a-dirty-game?language=en-US)

224 Verdenius, Jaap & Mastenbroek, Kay, *A Dirty Game* (2002 - https://www. themoviedb.org/movie/536232-a-dirty-game?language=en-US)

225 Verdenius, Jaap & Mastenbroek, Kay, *A Dirty Game* (2002 - https://www. themoviedb.org/movie/536232-a-dirty-game?language=en-US)

entrance. The boycott had failed in one sense, but it was now impossible for anyone to pretend they had no knowledge of the issues in Argentina.

The travelling squad were placed in an invidious position. The government offered advice to keep away from areas where political activity was likely or where demonstrations took place. Understandably, many tried to distance themselves from the politics. Johan Neeskens argued that, 'You should never mix sport with politics, otherwise you can't play any match. Everywhere in the world shit is going on.'[226] Jan Poortvliet was one of the younger members of the squad, but took a similar line. 'We didn't pay attention to human rights. Or what was going on there, but I didn't do any research into the situation there.' Interestingly though, when he was asked whether the KNVB had informed the players about the nature of the Argentinian government, the defender replied, 'Absolutely not.'[227]

Was that done with the best of intentions? Was the stance along the lines of the less the players knew of the situation, the less they would be concerned by it? Perhaps. Yet again though, as in 1974 and 1976, the Dutch were hardly going into a major tournament with a clear focus, bereft of distractions. These things were surely not coincidences. How badly would they be affected?

The tournament

Once in South America the Dutch were quickly moved on to their camp in the Andes mountains, far away from any urban centres. According to Poortvliet, it was an ideal situation, well away from distractions. 'From the moment we arrived

226 Verdenius, Jaap & Mastenbroek, Kay, *A Dirty Game* (2002 - https://www.themoviedb.org/movie/536232-a-dirty-game?language=en-US)
227 Verdenius, Jaap & Mastenbroek, Kay, *A Dirty Game* (2002 - https://www.themoviedb.org/movie/536232-a-dirty-game?language=en-US)

in Argentina, we were isolated. From the airport to our resort in the mountains. There we could eat, exercise, drink, watch TV and play cards. That was all we did for the first couple of weeks. Totally isolated.'[228] Others found the camp much more difficult, though. Rep in particular had problems. 'It was far away from home and people didn't have the money to go. We spent three weeks in a training camp in the Andes. Nobody there. We went crazy.'[229]

Acknowledging the isolation felt by the group, Dr Kessel also understood it provided something of a security blanket, protecting the Dutch from a harsh reality that would become clearer much later. 'Most of the time we didn't know what was going on around us. We got some days' old newspapers. You just didn't know. You heard everything much later.'[230] Four years earlier in West Germany, understanding the newspapers would have been less of an issue. Although that also had its drawbacks, Jan-Hermen de Bruijn explained. 'In the last phase of 1974, the aggression of German press played a role. In 1978 nobody could read Spanish.'[231] Given Neeskens had spent four years in Barcelona by this time, and that Rep had spent a season with Valencia, that may not have been completely accurate.

If the squad were shielded from the trauma of the country hosting them, that was less the case within the camp itself. The simmering conflict between Zwartkruis and Happel could only be kept on a low heat for so long. Eventually it was bound to warm up. Perhaps it had been Zwartkruis's reluctance to give up his position with the military that had persuaded the KNVB that a full-time, fully committed coach was required

228 Verdenius, Jaap & Mastenbroek, Kay, *A Dirty Game* (2002 - https://www. themoviedb.org/movie/536232-a-dirty-game?language=en-US)

229 Williams, Richard, *The Guardian*, https://www.theguardian.com/football/2001/ apr/10/sport.comment1

230 Verdenius, Jaap & Mastenbroek, Kay, *A Dirty Game* (2002 - https://www. themoviedb.org/movie/536232-a-dirty-game?language=en-US

231 De Bruijn, Jan-Hermen – Interview with the author

to give the Oranje the best opportunity in Argentina, or maybe they just saw Happel as a better coach. The uneasy relationship between the two was hardly entirely satisfactory to either man but, so long as Zwartkruis was prepared to tolerate his No.2 role, there was at least the semblance of a working relationship. It wouldn't last until the end of the tournament, however. Even before a ball had been kicked, the cracks were beginning to show.

Happel's disclosure of the tactics the team was likely to use did not go down well with Zwartkruis. It seemed like hubris, if not mere folly, and certainly offered no advantage to the team. The growing tension was then ratcheted up when, during press conferences ahead of the opening game, Happel would state and reiterate his perceived need to expunge any 'Cruyff Complex' from the squad. The Austrian felt that the former captain was still casting a long shadow, and that any doubts among the players that they would be unable to perform at the highest level without him needed to be cleared from their minds. To Zwartkruis it appeared to be a clumsily veiled message to him that his friendship with Cruyff, and whatever influence was bequeathed because of it, would not be allowed to stand in the way of the new coach's methods. Did Zwartkruis provide a conduit for Cruyff to influence the players? There appears little clear evidence to support such a theory, but sometimes perception can be more persuasive than evidence.

Perhaps Happel felt a little like an outsider. It was something that Zwartkruis believed could be the case, and that there may have been an element of resentment. 'I always talked with the boys,' he said, describing his comfortable relationship with the squad. 'When Happel was around he looked angry. He thought I had to stay away and talk less, unbelievable.'[232] Zwartkruis

---

232 Bongers, Michael & Bremer René, *Kapitein van Oranje* (Netherlands: Belluci, 2008)

was convinced that such an approach only led to the coach sacrificing any hope of achieving a beneficial relationship with the players on the altar of exerting his control. The air of authority and sense of awe for his achievements, that Happel had brought with him when he was first appointed was, for Zwartkruis, beginning to be exposed as a paper-thin veneer. 'The whole tournament was a horror,' he said. 'I was opposed from all sides and there was no cooperation with Ernst Happel. He was a jerk.'[233] With Argentine political problems locked outside, and particularly Dutch ones inside, it would have been a blessed relief when the tournament started. The Dutch schedule suggested that they would have a comfortable start against bottom seeds Iran, and then face trickier encounters against Peru and Scotland.

Qualification from the CONMEBOL federation had been hugely simplified by Argentina hosting the competition. With only three places, plus a potential fourth depending on a play-off against a UEFA group runner-up, allocated to the federation, the prospect of Brazil, Argentina and Uruguay hogging the spots was diluted. Qualification was decided via two group stages. Firstly, three groups, each of three teams, would play to produce winners. These three teams would then play in a further group at neutral venues, with the top two qualifying as of right, and the third-place team going into the play-off.

The Peruvians topped their group, winning their home games and drawing away against Chile and Ecuador. In the second phase, they lost to Brazil and beat Bolivia to claim second place behind Brazil and book their ticket to Argentina. It was only the second time since 1930 that Peru had reached the finals, losing out to eventual champions Brazil in the quarter-finals of 1970. It's a record every bit as lamentable

233 Bongers, Michael & Bremer René, *Kapitein van Oranje* (Netherlands: Belluci, 2008)

as the Dutch before 1974. This was a classic Peruvian squad, containing the talents of Hector Chumpitaz, Teofilo Cubillas and Juan Carlos Oblitas amongst many others, and they would give the Dutch all the trouble they could handle in the group game. Later in the tournament, there was more than a whiff of scandal when they conceded a cascade of goals against the hosts to set Argentina on the way to the final.

Scotland had also come through what looked like a difficult qualifying group, facing European champions Czechoslovakia and a domestic encounter with Wales. The bright spot had been the opening victory against the Czechs at Hampden Park, where a 2-0 success put them on the way. The journey was completed with another 2-0 win, this time against Wales.

Despite it being a 'home' fixture for Wales, crowd trouble during a match against Yugoslavia the previous year had meant that Cardiff's Ninian Park could not be used, although no such sanction was applied against Scotland following the Wembley pitch invasion a few months before the Wales match. Apparently opting for financial reward over home advantage, the Welsh FA had then decided that rather than play the game at Wrexham's smaller Racecourse Ground, it should be moved to Anfield, where they were clearly hoping for a large chunk of Welsh support. It was a naïve move. A full house did accrue, but for that night Liverpool was part of Scotland as the Tartan Army temporarily annexed Merseyside.

It was the sort of game many would have expected. A domestic squabble – Wales still had memories of Scotland manager Ally MacLeod's disparaging remarks about their team – masquerading as a World Cup game. Chances were about as rare as any considered play, and with just under 15 minutes left, a draw seemed increasingly inevitable. With a home game to come against Wales, the Czechs were waiting to cash in.

Then, in the 78th minute, Asa Hartford hurled a long throw into the Wales area, heads and arms went up in a tangle and a hand was seen to flick on the ball – but whose hand? The Welsh players had little doubt, and assumed a free kick would be awarded to them. French referee Robert Wurtz, however, took a different view and awarded a penalty. The Welsh team was incandescent, with goalkeeper Dai Davies proclaiming that it was Jordan who handled the ball. Unsurprisingly, Scots take a different view, and despite replays appearing to show Jordan's blue-shirted arm reaching up to the ball, the striker maintains that it was a correct decision.

Whatever the case, Don Masson stepped up to convert the chance and a Kenny Dalglish goal five minutes before time stamped the passports. After the game, MacLeod was uncharacteristically phlegmatic. 'All I know is that a hand punched the ball, and it's up to the referee to make the decision,' he shrugged. 'I think we should have had a penalty earlier. You lose some, you win some. I am just glad to have reached the finals.'[234]

This was the Scotland of Ally MacLeod, celebrations before flying out, pumping confidence and belief in his team. Before heading to Argentina he had reportedly been asked what he was going to do when he returned from the World Cup. 'Go out and retain it,'[235] he replied. Hubris was never far away from the skirl of the bagpipes at the time, but any team containing the likes of Dalglish and Souness of European champions Liverpool, Burns, Robertson and Gemmill of English champions Nottingham Forest, plus luminaries from Manchester United, Derby County, Aberdeen and Rangers were equipped to give anyone, including the Dutch, a more than decent game.

234 World Cup Moments: Ally's Tartan Army die in their boots, *The Irish Times,* 31 May 2018
235 Hunter, Graham – Interview with the author

All of the Oranje's first-phase games would be played at the Estadio Mundialista Malvinas in Mendoza, located in a region of foothills and high plains on the eastern side of the Andes, towards the border with Chile, 1,000km (620 miles) or so from Buenos Aires. The stadium was new, only being opened on 14 May. On 3 June at 16.45 local time, the Dutch began their journey in search of the title that had slipped through their fingers four years earlier.

Ahead of the tournament, many had thought that Schrijvers would start in goal, if only because Jongbloed had been troubled by a sprained ankle.[236] If Cruyff had been Jongbloed's main advocate for the starting position in 1974, that argument was mute now, unless one believed that the former captain really did have a line of influence through Zwartkruis. Despite that, it was Jongbloed who played in the key qualifier against Belgium, and then in the last two of the official friendlies building up to the tournament. It seems entirely logical, therefore, that the JC Roda goalkeeper was chosen to keep goal against Iran, despite approaching his 38th birthday. It made him the oldest player across any of the 16 squads competing at the tournament.

The back line was comprised of three defenders, much as Happel had suggested to the press would be the case. Suurbier, Rijsbergen and Krol provided a widely experienced line-up of veterans from 1974. Had Hovenkamp not been forced to withdraw with injury, the opportunity to play him on the left, with Suurbier defending the right flank and Rijsbergen in alongside Krol in the middle, may have been a tempting prospect, but with the AZ Alkmaar man unavailable, and Poortvliet excluded from consideration as he had not recovered sufficiently from a knee problem,[237] the coach went with the back three. Following this game, for the remaining two

236 Netherlands will not risk the injured Poortvliet, *The Times*, 2 June 1978
237 Netherlands will not risk the injured Poortvliet, *The Times*, 2 June 1978

fixtures in this initial phase, regardless of information given to the press, the Oranje would play with a back four.

In midfield, Happel's predictions were already looking less than accurate, although with positions very flexible among the Oranje, others may suggest to the contrary. Jansen, Neeskens, Haan and Willy van de Kerkhof looked to provide a solid midfield, not bereft of creativity, but certainly with a leaning towards Happel's natural tendency to be both competitive and combative. Zwartkruis's approach of having Rensenbrink as some version of a 'new Cruyff' was shelved, with the Anderlecht striker on the left of a front three. The other flank was occupied by PSV's Rene van de Kerkhof, with Rep in the middle. With the fluid nature of the Dutch play, it was always likely that one of Rensenbrink or the Van de Kerkhof twins would drop into midfield on occasions, with perhaps Rep then drifting wide to take up the space created, but a 3-4-3 formation looked the likeliest.

Perhaps the only contentious issue was that Nanninga's efforts, and goals in the warm-up games may have been sufficient to earn him a starting place, especially against Iran, who were expected to be the makeweights of the group. His inclusion may well have meant a move to the right for Rep, with one of the twins missing out. On 70 minutes this assumption was given weight when Happel made that precise change with the robust JC Roda striker replacing Rene van de Kerkhof on the field, and Rep doing so in the formation.

The starting selection meant that the back and front of the team were players who Michels had used in the 1974 final, although Rene van de Kerkhof had only appeared after the struggling Rensenbrink had succumbed to the inevitable at half-time. The only player not to have featured was the other Van de Kerkhof twin in midfield. Cruyff and Van Hanegem were the only two players from the starting XI in the final four years previously not to begin the campaign in Argentina.

Despite the change in the balance of power in Dutch club football, and Happel's repeatedly stated conviction to remove the 'Cruyff Complex', it hardly looked like a revolution.

The Iranians had played more qualifying games, 12 in total, to get to the tournament than any other competing nation and, understandably, they weren't merely there to make the numbers up, regardless of what supporters of other teams may have thought. They were an unknown quantity. Graham Hunter wasn't alone when he summed up most British fans' attitude towards Iran. 'Clearly, nobody had even seen Iran play, most of us had never heard about them much.'[238] It was a fairly widespread opinion outside of Britain as well and, as the game started, the Dutch were clearly expecting to win and set off at a pace to ensure that was the case.

To no one's surprise the team in orange dominated both possession and position, but the Iranians tackled with vigour and tried to counter-attack when the opportunity arose. A Rensenbrink header from a free kick, comfortably caught by Nasser Hejazi, was the nearest to a breakthrough inside the first half a dozen minutes. Iran were organised and well drilled at the back as their record of only conceding three goals in their qualifying games showed. They even threatened on rare occasions and on another day a break from Hossein Faraki could have easily led to a goal. Worryingly for the Dutch, the three-man back line looked anything but solid when called upon to defend. If the unfancied Iranians could cause a few fleeting moments of concern, a more accomplished team would surely take more tangible rewards. It was something for the coaches to note.

For most of the first period, though, the Iran emphasis was very much on their defence, as they stuck rigidly to their 4-4-2 formation, paying avid attention to their defensive

238 Hunter, Graham – Interview with the author

duties. The biggest threat seemed to come from aerial attacks, with balls crossed into the box where the Dutch appeared to have a physical edge. As the game approached half-time, still without any score, Happel may have been thinking of sending on his battering-ram of a forward Nanninga in the second period. He would be ideally suited to exposing the frailty. Before any such switch could be made, though, the Dutch scored.

Intercepting a careless pass, Rene van de Kerkhof drove into the box from the right flank. Cleverly drawing Nasrullah Abdollahi towards him, he then slipped the ball outside of the defender. A clumsy challenge by the off-balance Abdollahi felled the forward, and Mexican referee Alfonso Gonzalez Archundia had no hesitation in pointing to the spot. It was a clear trip, with the ball well away and, with five minutes to go until half-time, it was a prime opportunity for the Dutch to open their account. Displaying that famed ice-cool demeanour from 12 yards, Rensenbrink stroked the ball into the right corner of Hejazi's goal, as the goalkeeper tumbled in the other direction. Van de Kerkhof's fall had caused him to damage his wrist and, for the remainder of the tournament, he would be compelled to wear a lightweight protective cast on the joint. The Dutch authorities ensured that the protection was approved by FIFA first, but a controversy around it would still erupt ahead of the final.

Strange to say perhaps, but in the dressing-room, the coaches of both teams would have cause for a measure of satisfaction. The Dutch were clearly in control and, so long as their defence was vigilant, there was little danger of an Iranian comeback. Plus, with the dam now breached, other goals should follow. Heshmat Mohajerani would surely also have been boosted by his team's first-half performance against the losing finalists of 1974. For much of the first 45 minutes, aside from danger emanating from crosses, they had largely kept the Dutch at arm's length, and it had taken a tired pass, and a mistimed tackle, after 40 minutes of solid defence, to break them down. Would they look to attack more in search of an equaliser in the second period and risk getting caught out again, or maintain their same approach, ensuring any defeat would not be of embarrassing proportions? The Dutch were probably hoping for the former. In reality, anything but the latter was hardly likely.

The efforts of the first half, chasing down possession and seemingly endless defending, would demand a price to be paid in terms of fatigue, both physically and mentally. The continued pressing applied by the Dutch was beyond what the Iranian players were used to and despite organised and largely disciplined play, as time went on gaps began to appear more consistently. Just past the hour mark, Rene van de Kerkhof's excellent cross from the right found Rensenbrink running in to head home from just inside the six-yard line. It was game over. Dutch confidence grew as Iran tired.

With 20 minutes to play, Happel was showing no mercy to the Iranians. The game was safe, and Rene van de Kerkhof was taken off, with Nanninga given his chance and Rep now pushed out towards the right. The move to the role he had played for so much of his career seemed to energise the Bastia forward. Eight minutes later, Rep scythed through the white-shirted ranks, beating one man, skipping past another weak challenge and driving towards goal, swerving past two more defenders before being upended inside the box. It was a second penalty, and the Iranian complaints were probably more driven by frustration than conviction, as witnessed by Andranik Eskandarian knocking the ball from the referee's hands, and being fortunate only to receive a yellow card.

Even if the defenders were worn down by fatigue, it was still a pulsating piece of play by Rep, drawing echoes of the dynamism of 1974 Oranje vintage. This team still had plenty to offer. Rensenbrink sauntered up to the ball and fired high to Hejazi's left, as the goalkeeper dived low to his right. If his desire had been to get as far away from the ball as possible, he couldn't have achieved it much more efficiently. A hat-trick for Rensenbrink.

The Iranians were falling apart. A high ball looked to be dropping into the waiting hands of the goalkeeper, but Hejazi contrived to miss the ball totally and only a rapid turn and recovering dive to flip it behind for a corner prevented Rensenbrink netting a fourth as he closed in.

The Iranians would doubtless have been reasonably satisfied with their performance, coming out of their most difficult fixture with a defeat, but their heads held high. The Dutch had played through the tough first period where their opponents' enthusiasm and organisation had made finding the opening goal difficult. Once in front, though, they were always going to win. The only question was by how many. Three seemed plenty. One of their key players had begun the tournament with a hat-trick, and aside from the damage to Van de Kerkhof's wrist, there were no injuries to be concerned about. The defence hadn't conceded either, but that may well have been more due to the paucity of attacks against them than to any efficiency of performance. Consideration of the backline would occupy Happel before the next game, as the Oranje contingent returned to their splendid isolation in the foothills to contemplate their future.

In the group's other game, Scotland had taken an early lead against Peru, and then missed a penalty before conceding three goals. In the words of Graham Hunter, Scotland were 'pumped by Peru. We were taught a lesson.'[239] For a number of reasons, the Peruvians would become one of the most talked

---

239 Hunter, Graham – Interview with the author

about teams in the tournament. The South Americans were next in line to face the Oranje.

In 1974, the Dutch had won the opening game of their group before playing the team that would finish second, a draw giving them every chance to qualify in the final game. They seemed set on a similar path in Argentina. The win over Iran, and Peru's victory against the Scots put them both in a strong position. A win for either would guarantee progress and, regardless of the result in the other game, even a draw would mean that merely avoiding defeat in the final match would be sufficient.

The Peru victory over Scotland was probably a bigger shock for fans in Britain than it had been for followers of South American football. The team that had impressed so much in 1970, were considered to be superior to that of 1978. As Graham Hunter recalled, there was a consensus that Peru were 'Good in 1970 but, eight years on, probably past it ... Peru weren't Argentina, Uruguay or Brazil.'[240] It's an opinion that journalist Norman Fox of *The Times* would not have disputed. 'Peru are indisputably more organised and a better team than Zaire [who Scotland beat by only two goals in 1974] but the situation is similar. They offer Scotland an ideal test, not being among the strongest of competing countries here but at their best, competent enough to make the Scots work for their goals.'[241] He also added later in the same article that Peru were an 'aging side with a suspiciously weak defence.'[242]

It's certainly true that Peru weren't as strong as Argentina or Brazil – as results later in the tournament would indicate – but they had qualified ahead of Uruguay, and although 34-year-old Chumpitaz was the elder statesman among a group of experienced players, a number of his team-mates

240 Hunter, Graham – Interview with the author
241 Scotland's first step could decide their fate, *The Times*, 2 June 1978
242 Scotland's first step could decide their fate, *The Times*, 2 June 1978

were much younger, still in their mid-twenties, and hadn't played in Mexico eight years previously. There's no logical corollary in being unaware of a team's form and considering that as a valid reason to label them as weak. A draw against the Netherlands, with a final game to come against Iran, would probably suit Peru more than it would the Dutch, who would still have to face Scotland.

When Happel's team was announced, it caused more than a few surprises. Rep had been dropped to the bench, with the young Poortvliet brought into a new line-up at the back. The idea of a back three had been discarded. The apparent leak that Happel had given to the press, and been castigated for doing so, had been half right for the opening game against Iran, but now bore no resemblance to the team that would start the second game. Had the Austrian merely fed the press a line, or had his thinking genuinely been changed by events or other persuasion?

Whatever the cause, Suurbier was now deployed on the right flank, with Rijsbergen and Krol in the centre and the youngster on the left. There were also changes in midfield, with Jansen alongside Neeskens and Willy van de Kerkhof. Rensenbrink was on one flank of the forward line, with Rene van de Kerkhof on the other. In the middle, promoted from midfield into what looked remarkably like the role previously the sole domain of a certain Johan Cruyff, was Arie Haan, who had played throughout the previous World Cup as a libero and the opening game of this one as a central midfielder. It's probably worth mentioning that with the term 'ageing' in relation to the Peru team gaining common currency, the average age of their starting XI in this game was a shade over 27. The average age of their Dutch opponents was more than 29, with Jongbloed being comfortably the oldest player on either side.

If the game against Iran had served as some kind of echo of the opening game against Uruguay in 1974 when the

Austrian coach Ernst Happel who led Feyenoord to European Cup glory and coached the Dutch in the 1978 World Cup.

European Cup 1970 – Feyenoord become the first Dutch club to win the European Cup after beating Celtic 2-1 in the final.

*European Cup
1973 – Final
– Chaired by
Ajax players
wearing Juventus
shirts, coach
Ștefan Kovács
holds the trophy
aloft as the club
celebrate their
third successive
triumph.*

*Barry Hulshoff
– The titanic
Ajax defender
who missed out
on selection for
the 1974 World
Cup due to a knee
injury.*

World Cup 1974 – Second Phase – Johan Cruyff balletically eludes the challenge of Argentine goalkeeper Daniel Carnevali, before opening the scoring in a 4-0 victory.

World Cup 1974 – Second Phase – Referee Kurt Tschenscher dismisses Brazil defender Luis Pereira (2), as Dutch midfielder Neeskens lies injured on the floor.

World Cup 1974 – Final – Johan Cruyff is tumbled to the ground by Uli Hoeness. Neeskens scored from the penalty and the Dutch were ahead before a German player had touched the ball.

World Cup 1974 – Final – Dejected Dutch players leave the field after losing 2-1 to hosts West Germany.

World Cup 1978 – Final – Dutch substitute Dick Nanninga (18) wheels away in triumph after heading the Dutch equaliser inside the final ten minutes.

World Cup 1978 – Final – Inches from glory. In the last minute of the game, with the scores at 1-1, Rob Rensenbrink steers the ball past Argentine goalkeeper Ubaldo Fillol, but it strikes the post and is cleared.

*World Cup 1978 – Final –
Dejected Dutch players leave
the field after losing 3-1 to hosts
Argentina.*

European Championships 1988 – Final – From an 'impossible' angle, Marco van Basten volleys the second Dutch goal against the Soviet Union.

European Championships 1988 – Rinus Michels celebrates after coaching the Dutch to success. Earlier he had guided Ajax to European Cup victory and led the Dutch squad in the 1974 World Cup.

World Cup 2010 – Final – English referee Howard Webb dismisses Dutch defender John Heitinga in extra time. The Dutch would lose 1-0 to Spain.

Dutch laboured to a win, the game against Peru certainly had similarities to the encounter with Sweden four years earlier.

The Netherlands returned to Mendoza in the late afternoon of 7 June to play Peru. Whether Happel's selection had been influenced by calculations about the probable number of points needed to progress, or merely to enhance his team's performance, dropping Rep to the bench was hardly likely to ensure a more dynamic forward line, although the return to a more traditional back four certainly added solidity to the defence. Expecting Haan, for all his estimable quality, to fill the huge gap left by Cruyff would be folly, and perhaps Happel didn't even see it that way, merely using the player's skills to offer different problems to the opposition defence. But he was no Cruyff, as Martin Tyler concluded. 'The Netherlands' lacklustre performance against Peru gave more evidence towards providing the answer to the most asked question in these World Cup finals: How can the Dutch cope without Johan Cruyff? Not very well it seems.'[243]

The attacking edge certainly seemed to be fairly blunt. In the opening 45 minutes the only effort worthy of note for the Dutch came from a long-distance free kick from Rensenbrink that Peruvian goalkeeper Ramon Quiroga unconvincingly coaxed around the post for a corner. Suurbier had hit in a shot from similar distance earlier, but Quiroga had merely waved it on its way over the bar. A run down the right by Rene van de Kerkhof was brought unceremoniously to an end by Toribio Diaz. Whether because of the after-effects of that challenge or a tactical switch, the PSV man did not appear after the break, his place going to Rep.

The change seemed to have given more spark to the Dutch, and Rijsbergen exchanged a couple of passes advancing from the back, before drawing his shot just wide of Quiroga's

243 Dutch cutting edge blunted without Cruyff, *The Times*, 7 June 2002

post ... The shot was scuffed and, had it been on target, the goalkeeper would surely not have been troubled. At least it offered some momentum going forward. Peru seemed more than content to sit back and defend, relying on their speedy wingers Munante and Oblitas to chase down punted clearances and trouble the Dutch defence. It offered the Netherlands more time and space in the Peru half and, inevitably, more chances followed. With around 20 minutes to play, a bout of head tennis ended with Rensenbrink firing in a shot, with his favoured left foot, after teeing himself up, that Quiroga plunged on to save.

As play moved upfield, the figure of Neeskens lying by the penalty spot suggested he had been injured in the passage of play. After a couple of minutes, he was carried from the field by Quiroga, to be replaced by Nanninga, with another shuffle of formation required.

Late on, a lofted ball into the box saw Nanninga climb high in a challenge with Quiroga. The Dutch striker clearly got to the ball first, but headed it over the bar. The goalkeeper fell in a heap on the floor and a few Peruvians initially went to remonstrate with the Dutch player, but thought twice about it when the muscular striker stood his ground. Quiroga rolled around for a while but was eventually coaxed back to his feet. It was the last meaningful action, and the game drifted away to a goalless, thrill-less, draw.

In the group's other game, Scotland struggled to a draw with Iran, as Ally MacLeod's Tartan Army of a team took on the guise of a bedraggled rabble. Before the start of that day's games, a draw seemed to favour Peru, having Iran to play in the last game. After the hapless performance by the Scots, however, the Oranje's task of overcoming a team that looked to be coming apart at the seams, appeared just as simple. Reporters on the ground appeared to concur with such assessments. One such account, in *The Times*, described

Scotland as the 'most discredited'[244] team, before going on to say that, 'Scotland … came here badly prepared and, unless the Dutch take leave of their senses in Mendoza on Sunday will have no reason for annoyance at being dismissed.'[245] Things in football are rarely what they seem, though, particularly if the Dutch or the Scots are involved, and especially so if both are.

In contrast to 1974, when Michels started with the same 11 players across the entire tournament, barring a single change for the goalless draw with Sweden, Happel seemed unable to leave things alone. The result of the Peru game and Scotland's tepid 1-1 draw with Iran meant that the Oranje only needed to avoid defeat by three clear goals or more to progress, but Happel decided to tweak his line-up again. The gamble of pushing Haan further forward was discarded and Rep returned to the team. The unfortunate Haan wasn't even granted a place among the substitutes. Early in the game, unless the move had been compelled by injury, that decision would look like an error. The bench comprised Schrijvers, Brandt, Wildschut, Boscamp and Nanninga. Before the break Happel needed to dip into his reserves to replace two injured players.

There were, of course, still lingering hopes for Scotland, with some diehard fans talking up the positive aspects of just needing a three-goal margin of victory over the Dutch to qualify. After all, or so the argument went, where the Scots had struggled against the same opponents, the Dutch had only achieved a less-than-convincing victory over Iran, and a draw against Peru. Many others were talking of the need to lock such people up for their own safety. Stealing a line from Bob Dylan however, 'When you ain't got nothing, you've got nothing to lose,'[246] seemed to be the new mantra of Scotland.

244 Dutch may well go canny against discredited Scots, *The Times*, 9 June 1978
245 Dutch may well go canny against discredited Scots, *The Times*, 9 June 1978
246 Dylan, Bob, Like a Rolling Stone, *Highway 61 Revisited* (Columbia 1965)

In his previous competitive game, Liverpool's combative midfielder Graeme Souness had created the winning goal in the European Cup Final for Kenny Dalglish with an astute pass against Happel's Bruges at Wembley. Could he do the same in the dark blue of Scotland for his Anfield team-mate? In a reshaped Scotland midfield, now featuring the energetic promptings of Hartford, the tireless Archie Gemmill alongside the experienced Bruce Rioch and now Souness – who was the only one of the Scots mouthing the words of 'God Save the Queen' as the anthems were played ahead of kick-off – beleaguered Scotland manager Ally MacLeod rolled the dice to find out.

The only other change was that both teams switched strips. The Scots had played both of their previous games in dark blue shirts and shorts, while the Dutch had worn all orange. Whether it was deemed that the contrast in colours was insufficient to offer clarity to anyone viewing in black and white is unclear, but the Scots turned up in white shorts, and the Dutch had shirts of the same colour.

In Mendoza, on 11 June 1978, the teams met for a pulsating game, probably the best of the tournament up to that point, where both teams would leave the field with a measure of satisfaction. Regardless of the final scoreline, both coaches would be seen to have won, but also lost. When the game got under way, it quickly became apparent that the Scottish midfield were both more combative and mobile than had been the case in the earlier games. If the Dutch had been convinced by reports of Scotland being in disarray and uninterested, they were quickly disavowed of such thoughts.

Perhaps now freed from the burden of expectation, Scotland tore into the Dutch with a vigour that would surely have brought better results had it been deployed against Peru and Iran. With barely four minutes gone, Scotland's spirit was illustrated by Hartford driving forward through a couple of challenges before dragging his shot wide of the near post. It served as a notice of intent, and one that the Dutch should have heeded.

Barely a minute later, a quickly taken free kick released Souness to drive down the right wing before checking to consider his options. The Dutch defence had been drawn like moths to a light by the towering presence of Joe Jordan and, as the striker looked to occupy the far post, space was emptied in front of him. Advancing from midfield, and seeing the gap, Rioch raced into the area. Souness spotted the run and flighted a perfect cross to coincide with his team-mate's arrival in the box. Unmarked, he leapt and thudded a header goalward. The ball crashed against the bar, before bouncing to safety, with Jongbloed transfixed and motionless. A slow start by perhaps an over-confident Dutch team had gifted momentum to the Scots, and they struggled to win it back against a growing tide of threats to their goal.

Like a boxer stunned by an early punch, the Dutch sought time to clear their heads with a counter-attack … Rene van de Kerkhof cut into the box from the right, but his cross was cleared. Less than a minute later, a clearance from a short corner saw Scotland have the ball in the net. As the Dutch defence advanced, seeking to catch the Scottish strikers offside, Tom Forsyth, either showing a striker's instinct or a defender's naivety, stood stationery as the Dutch and Scottish players rushed past him out of the area. Forsyth, as confirmed by film of the incident, was onside and put the ball neatly into the net off the left-hand post. As he turned, the linesman's flag went up, apparently not against him, but to ping his colleague Stuart Kennedy who, out of picture way out on the right flank, had dawdled in getting back. A long way out from the action, there was little chance of Kennedy affecting play, and in modern times the goal would surely have stood. The fact that Jongbloed took the free kick from the spot where

Forsyth received the ball suggests that the Dutch may have been fortunate. Echoes of Verheyen?

Much as Ralf Edstrom had troubled Rijsbergen with his muscular play for Sweden in 1974, Jordan was creating similar problems, offering a reliable target for long balls from the Scottish defence, and establishing possession in the Netherlands half of the field. The Dutch remained second best and, still inside the first ten minutes, the Scots could easily have been ahead. Things hardly promised to get better when Neeskens was forced from the field following a challenge with Gemmill. It looked a similar problem to the one he had sustained against Peru. Had his selection been a gamble? If it had, the discomfort etched on to the Barcelona midfielder's face as he was stretchered off exposed any folly involved.

At almost any time over the previous decade, the sight of a player named Johan wearing the No.14 shirt trotting on to the pitch would have been one of great comfort. Unfortunately, this Johan was Boscamp, rather than Cruyff. It would surely have been the bravest of decisions to ask for that shirt number, and it may have been that it was merely allocated to him. Regardless, it would have been a heavy burden to carry. Although a more than decent midfielder, who had won the Belgian title with RWD Molenbeek in 1975, this would be his second and final cap following a 35-minute debut from the bench in the pre-tournament friendly against Tunisia. With his team being dominated in midfield, and having lost his most dynamic player in that area, having Haan to call on would surely have been preferable. Things weren't going well for Happel and his team, but fortune was about to smile on them.

Depending on your point of view, the Dutch offside plan had operated effectively so far, but a dozen minutes in, Alan Rough, sporting a nifty blue cap precariously balanced on his perm, punted a long ball downfield. Krol slightly misjudged the flight of the ball and his attempt at a headed clearance merely served to flick the ball towards the Dutch goal. As the ball ran on, short of the sanctity of Jongbloed's area, Rijsbergen chased back to cover, with Dalglish close on his heels. As the defender neared the ball, the Liverpool striker jabbed his foot out to lift it over the advancing Jongbloed and into the net, tumbling Rijsbergen to the floor at the same time.

It took referee Erich Linemayr, an Austrian compatriot of Happel's, the briefest of hesitations to decide that Dalglish had fouled Rijsbergen in his attempt to get to the ball and the goal was chalked off. It looked like the right decision but, on another day, given Rioch's header, Forsyth's effort ruled out for offside, and this incident, that three-clear-goal advantage the Scots required could already have been in the bag inside the first quarter of an hour, and the Oranje had hardly threatened at the other end at all. Minutes later, interplay between Gemmill and Rioch saw Dalglish striding forward through a defence that now appeared to have all the holding power of a colander, but he dragged his shot wide.

To say the Oranje's performance was off colour would be an understatement and nothing to do with the shirts they were wearing. In contrast, who were these vibrant players pretending to be the deflated players of Scotland, who had been 'pumped' by Peru and struggled to gain a draw against Iran? For all their chances, though, Scotland had no tangible advantage, and the Dutch hadn't been forced to pay the price for their slovenly opening. With the first half of the opening period approaching, not scoring began to look costly, as the Dutch took on a more familiar look. A shot across Rough's goal from Rensenbrink heralded a change as the game headed towards a period of almost parity. Given the various estimations of the teams before the game, even that state was a compliment to the Scots and a criticism of the Dutch, but at least the Oranje were carrying a threat now.

Approaching the half-hour mark, Krol stepped elegantly forward to intercept a pass in the centre circle. With the Scottish back line exposed, he strode forward before releasing an incisive pass that split the defence, setting Rensenbrink in hot pursuit of the ball. Chasing out from his goal, though, Rough reached the ball first. Instead of hacking clear, he slid on to the ball, clasping it securely to his body. The problem was that he was at least five yards outside his area. In the modern game, a red card would have been inevitable. This time, the only sanction was the need to defend a free kick with his team back in position and organised. It came to naught. A few minutes later, another Scottish error would be more severely punished.

Before that, Rijsbergen was felled by a heavy challenge from Joe Jordan. The defender received treatment before continuing. As he hobbled back into position it was clear that further recovery was hoped for, rather than actual. There would be a price to pay for such aspiration. Seconds later, Rough played the ball out to Kennedy, who exchanged passes with Souness before looking to turn inside and play the ball back to Rough. Pouncing on the chance, the alert Willy van de Kerkhof bundled him out of possession. The ball ran free to Rep who galloped clear into the penalty area. As he was about to shoot, Kennedy lunged in with a challenge. 'What a good tackle that was,' declared David Coleman commentating for the BBC, as Rep sat on his haunches. Linemayr disagreed, pointing to the penalty spot. The Scots protested, but the only thing the arguments achieved was the award of a yellow card for Gemmill. Although Rough guessed the right way to dive, Rensenbrink's penalty was too accurate and powerful. The Netherlands were ahead. It was the 1,000th goal in World Cup history.

There were still problems to deal with. Happel had already used one of his permitted two substitutions when Neeskens was replaced. Now Rijsbergen was clearly struggling with the effects of Jordan's challenge. He was loath to make the change before the break so that he then had time to consider options, and hesitated. The delay would be punished. With a minute to play before half-time, a cross from Souness to the far post saw Jordan head the ball back across goal. The struggling Rijsbergen was unable to track Dalglish's run into the box and the Scot volleyed home the equaliser.

The horse had bolted, but Happel now decided it was time to lock the stable door. Wildschut came on for Rijsbergen, to take up a wide midfield position, with the defence switching to a back three. At the break there were no further goals. The scoreline favoured the Dutch, but the momentum favoured the Scots. Half of the game had passed, and still the Scots needed a minimum of three more goals to qualify. A minute or so after the restart, their task suddenly looked highly achievable.

A corner from the right was played short by Dalglish who then received the ball and clipped a cross to the far post, from where it was headed down towards Souness on the six-yard line. He was surely about to score when bundled over by Willy van de Kerkhof. This time it was the turn of the Dutch players to complain to no avail. Linemayr stood ramrod straight on the spot. Don Masson had missed a penalty against Peru, but wasn't in the team now anyway. Archie Gemmill stepped up and, showing no nerves, hit low and hard to Jongbloed's left to put the Scots ahead.

Two more were now needed for a resurrection to rival that of Lazarus. There was little doubt that Gemmill believed it was possible. The ball had hardly hit the net by the time he had turned and run back towards the centre circle, brushing aside the congratulations of his team-mates as he urged them to get into position for the restart. It was now one of those games when a pundit sagely declares that, 'The next goal is big.' On this occasion it was. In more ways than one.

Just ten minutes later, Kennedy played a ball down the right to Dalglish. He tried to cut inside but was tackled and the ball ran loose to Gemmill. Collecting possession, he danced past Jansen and jagged into the penalty area. He then cut back outside of Krol's impetuous challenge, and skipped past Poortvliet, leaving the third Dutchman on the floor trailing in his wake. With only Jongbloed to beat for one of the World Cup's most memorable goals, he clipped the ball left-footed over the goalkeeper's dive and walked into the World Cup Hall of Fame. 'A brilliant individual goal,' bellowed Coleman. Who could argue?

Strangely, despite how well Scotland had played when the required three-goal margin of victory looked impossible, now, when they were in touching distance of it, perhaps their nerve failed them. When there was no pressure, they played with elan and flair. Now though, as Graham Hunter explained, 'At the point we're 3-1 up, we were acting and behaving as if that's enough when ... we needed another clear goal.'[247]

Should the manager have thrown on fresh legs to drive home the advantage? It's easy to be wise after the event of course but, in *The Times* the following day, Norman Fox thought so. 'Even in yesterday's game [MacLeod] did not grasp the opportunity to punish the Dutch when they were 3-1 down and looking agitated. At the time, Souness, who had not played a full game for three weeks, was beginning to suffer from the enormous amount of energy he put into the first hour. Mr MacLeod's curious reluctance to use Derek Johnstone was never more absurd than at that point. The Dutch defence looked uneasy against the power of the bigger Scots and Johnstone's fresh strength could have completed the upset. Souness had done his work.'[248]

247 Hunter, Graham – Interview with the author
248 MacLeod's most effective combination a cause for even greater Scottish anger, *The Times*, 12 June 1978

Perhaps, but the momentum was all with Scotland and changing anything risked blowing that. Imagine the outcry against MacLeod if he had removed Souness and the game had drifted away. The real problem may have been that, as the light at the end of the dark tunnel came into sight, instead of inspiring its brightness dazzled the Scottish players and their manager. After having nothing to lose, suddenly there was so much to lose. Just seconds after the goal, a Dutch free kick into the Scotland area saw Kennedy stoop to head an interception. The ball slipped just past the post. So close to an own goal.

The goal had the reverse effect on the Dutch. There seemed little way that their rejigged defence could hold out now if they merely sat back. They'd conceded three times in 24 minutes of playing time and there was still around the same amount to play. Perhaps attack may be their best form of defence. There were 20 minutes remaining when Ruud Krol elegantly strode forward, the ball at his feet. Rep came short and exchanged passes with his captain, before accelerating past Krol once more. Shirt hanging loose, Krol moved the ball on to Rep. Fatigue may have been setting in, but as Rep advanced towards the area, no Scot closed him down. It was clear the striker was lining up to shoot. Graham Hunter tells the famous tale about MacLeod's shout from the bench at that moment. 'Aye, go on, [...] shoot. Shoot!'[249] At the last second, Gemmill flung himself in with a forlorn effort to block. Too late. From 30 yards, the ball flew past Rough and into the top corner. Rep later admitted, 'I just shut my eyes and hit out.'[250]

As Rep jogged back towards his relieved and celebrating team-mates, he passed Hartford and Gemmill who almost in synchrony looked to the heavens, blowing out their cheeks. There was still plenty of time on the clock, but the Scottish fervour and emotional reserves had been emptied. To all intents

249 Hunter, Graham – Interview with the author
250 Scotland's 1978 rollercoaster, *The Guardian*, 29 March 2018

and purposes, the game was over … The fates had permitted the Scots a glance at what could have been before dashing it cruelly away. The time between Gemmill's moment of immortality and Rep's riposte had been a mere three minutes. It was all the time that Scotland were allowed to dream. There was just time for a robust challenge on Suurbier to reduce him to the status of hobbling passenger for the final seconds of the game as Scottish frustration turned to petulance. The game ended in a 3-2 win, but a Pyrrhic victory has probably rarely felt more like a defeat. The Netherlands had joined Zaire in the exclusive club of countries that Scotland had beaten in World Cup finals.

The Oranje had escaped, but what now? Rijsbergen was out of the tournament and that late challenge on Suurbier also ruled him out of the remaining games, and Neeskens would miss the next game at the very least. The three group performances hardly promised much prospect of success in the second phase. The squad was battered and bruised and optimism was low. Some people blamed the condition of the pitch in Mendoza for the inconsistent displays. Others placed the responsibility elsewhere. Things would need to change, and they would. The Oranje could always be relied on for a revolution.

On the day before the game against Scotland, Argentina faced Italy in a game that would decide who topped Group One. The referee of the game would describe it as, 'The most important game in the first round, especially for Argentina.'[251] Both teams had already assured themselves of qualification but, especially for the hosts, winning the group was important, as it would keep them in Buenos Aires and playing at River Plate's home ground, the Estadio Monumental. It was a highly-charged game, and one that required the strongest of officials.

---

251 A chat with Abraham Klein, *These Football Times* podcast, 27 January 2020

The referee appointed was the Israeli, Abraham Klein, who as Rob Smyth said in *The Guardian*, 'was generally accepted as the world's best in the 1970s and early 1980s.'[252] The vastly experienced Klein would later describe it as the most difficult game of his career.[253]

Klein later explained to the author that ahead of the game, he had watched Argentina play against both France and Hungary, noticing 'The passion of the crowd ... all the generals ... they tried to influence all the referees in Argentina.'[254] The pressure may have worked. Hungary had two players sent off, and France conceded a controversial penalty. Argentina won both games 2-1. This game would be different. When Klein waved away a couple of Argentine penalty appeals just before the break, the crowd erupted in anger. 'Players were diving in the area ... tried to influence me all the time ... it was very difficult,'[255] he recalled.

The Italians won 1-0 and Argentina were compelled to travel to Rosario for the second phase. Klein recalled the atmosphere at full-time. 'I remember that after the game, they came to my dressing-room and said, "Don't go out because people are outside and waiting [for] you." I told them look, I go outside, I am not afraid.'[256] He wasn't, and his performance in the game would be widely acclaimed. Three examples came in the British press.

'He looked the beast in the eye and did not blink. There was nothing more impressive in this World Cup,' Brian Glanville is quoted as remarking in Smyth's *Guardian* article, 'than the way he stood between his linesmen at half-time in

252 The Forgotten Story of Abraham Klein, the 'master of the whistle', *The Guardian*, 22 March 2012
253 The Forgotten Story of Abraham Klein, the 'master of the whistle', *The Guardian*, 22 March 2012
254 A chat with Abraham Klein, *These Football Times* podcast, 27 January 2020
255 A chat with Abraham Klein, *These Football Times* podcast, 27 January 2020
256 A chat with Abraham Klein, *These Football Times* podcast, 27 January 2020

the Argentina–Italy game, scorning the banshee whistling of the incensed crowd.'[257]

The comments were echoed in the same article by David Lacey … 'Italy produced a marvellously balanced and co-ordinated performance to beat Argentina, and much of the credit for creating the circumstances in which they were allowed to do so must go to Abraham Klein, of Israel, whose firm, fair refereeing was precisely what the situation demanded.'[258]

In the *Mirror*, Frank McGhee said, 'He didn't make a single wrong decision in the whole 90 minutes of a marvellous match … My most abiding memory of the match is the way both teams queued up at the end to shake hands with Klein. They knew, we knew, he had done most to make it a match to remember.'[259]

FIFA appeared to agree, as Klein recalled. 'I feel in that game that I did my job, and later they assigned me West Germany in the second round against Austria.'[260] Some were less impressed, however. The performance marked Klein's card with the Argentine regime. His honesty and commitment was laudable. 'When I'm on the pitch, only two things are important to me: being fair to both teams and making my decisions bravely. I think all referees are fair, but not all of them are brave, probably.'[261] It may well have cost him a place in the middle of the World Cup Final, however, and the Netherlands would have cause to regret that outcome. 'Abraham Klein from Israel, who was unwaveringly insistent on applying the laws

257 The Forgotten Story of Abraham Klein, the 'master of the whistle', *The Guardian*, 22 March 2012

258 The Forgotten Story of Abraham Klein, the 'master of the whistle', *The Guardian*, 22 March 2012.

259 The Forgotten Story of Abraham Klein, the 'master of the whistle', *The Guardian*, 22 March 2012

260 A chat with Abraham Klein, *These Football Times* podcast, 27 January 2020.

261 Kuper, Simon, *Ajax, The Dutch, The War* (London: Orion 2003)

as they were written – with the resultant hail of abuse from the home country when they lost, and widespread acclaim in Europe. Ironically, his brave, conspicuous performance robbed Klein of his rightful claim to the final,'[262] wrote David Miller in his book *The Argentina Story*.

With Peru's victory over Iran taking them to the top of the group, the Netherlands were compelled to leave their isolation in Mendoza for a move to Cordoba. They were placed into Group A of the second phase, alongside Italy, Austria and old foes West Germany. It wasn't the only change in the Oranje camp.

Four years earlier, under Fadrhonc, the Dutch had come so close to missing out on the 1974 World Cup. Only that highly dubious offside decision against Belgium had nudged them over the line. It had hardly been a convincing campaign and, together with a palpable lack of player confidence in the coach, it was sufficient to convince the KNVB that a change was required if the team were to deliver on their full potential. At the time, it could have been considered as folly to bring in a new coach, albeit one known to many of the players, at such a late stage. Michels confounded such opinion, however, and so nearly delivered the greatest footballing prize of all.

Ahead of the 1978 tournament, the KNVB had been emboldened to try a similar ploy. Along with Michels, Happel had been the main architect of Dutch club success around the turn of the decade, both domestically and in continental competition. His success in Belgium with Bruges rounded out his CV nicely. With Zwartkruis still retaining commitments to his military career, appointing the Austrian seemed logical and based on the experience of what Michels had achieved in seemingly similar circumstances. Although perhaps not

---

262 Miller, David, *The Argentina Story* (London: Frederick Warne and Company, 1978)

recognised as such at the time, however, there were a number of significant differences.

In 1974, Michels could call on a large contingent of players who had worked with him at club level, and enjoyed success as his methods proved their worth. There was, therefore, an established relationship of trust and belief that the coach could draw on. Plus, he had the perfect lieutenant in Cruyff. If Michels was God, Cruyff was the Pope, God's vicar on Earth ensuring all of his flock were guided along the path of righteousness. In sharp contrast, Fadrhonc's stock was at a particularly low level at the time, with many players, Cruyff in particular, feeling that he simply wasn't up to the job, and some players weren't particularly reticent about venting their opinion.

In 1978, the situation was very different. Although Happel had been appointed in the year before the tournament, in reality it was Zwartkruis that coached the team to qualification, with the Austrian still consumed by concerns at Bruges. Rather than crawling over the line, as Fadrhonc had done four years earlier, Zwartkruis had achieved qualification with a relative swagger, winning five and drawing one of their six fixtures. When Happel officially took charge, after all matters in Belgium had been resolved, it was a popular and trusted coach being usurped, rather than one who few of the players had confidence in. Though Zwartkruis could enforce discipline at times – given his military background how could it be different – his overall ethos was more in line with that of Michels than Happel, and he was respected for that.

But there was more. Unlike Michels four years earlier, when Happel assumed command, there were hardly any of his former players to call on. Only Jansen and Rijsbergen were Feyenoord players, and the latter hadn't spent that much time working under the Austrian. It may have been another reason why Happel was so keen to persuade Van Hanegem to join the squad. Instead of being there as support to 'the best coach in my life',[263] however, as David Winner related, the man who could have lent considerable to support Happel, 'sat out the tournament on a beach in Spain.'[264]

It meant that after the Oranje had struggled and stuttered before crossing the finishing line to progress into the second phase, with just a single win to their credit there was precious little support for Happel in the squad, whilst Zwartkruis remained popular. Part of Happel's characteristic demeanour was a gruff and fairly uncompromising presence. It was something Zwartkruis saw as treating the players 'as footballers, rather than as human beings.'[265] Being uncompromising and authoritarian is fine when your team is winning and performing well; in other circumstances, it merely serves to alienate and, when you look for support, that warm blanket of reassurance isn't there.

Even before leaving Mendoza there was a clear and palpable discord between Happel and many others in the group, not least some players. His approach and tactics found few friends and results were only reinforcing the problem. Two days before the first game of the second phase, ironically against Happel's native Austria, the quiet coup was attempted. In a land where the military had felt compelled to sweep a failing civilian authority from power for the good of the country, here was a Dutch military man doing the same to someone who had been chosen to lead the Oranje. If the whole world was aware of Videla's coup, until 2008, when Zwartkruis released his memoir, *Kapitein van Oranje*, very few knew of this very Dutch type of coup other than members of the squad and officials of the KNVB.

---

263 Winner, David, *Brilliant Orange* (London: Bloomsbury, 2000)
264 Winner, David, *Brilliant Orange* (London: Bloomsbury, 2000)
265 Bongers, Michael & Bremer René, *Kapitein van Oranje* (Netherlands: Belluci, 2008)

Interpretation of events long passed and only related in a book some 30 years later can be a difficult circle to square. Some have suggested that, in a Cordoba hotel lobby, Jan Zwartkruis made a push for power. In *Kapitein van Oranje*, he recalled his pitch to the KNVB officials: 'Now it's over, I take it upon myself. If you're in, you must also do the same and not run away from what is a difficult moment.'[266] Was he seeking total control of the squad, usurping Happel, or was it merely that he had some ideas that he wanted to convince Happel of and was looking for support should it be needed?

If some have suggested the former, others are convinced that the latter was the case, Jan-Hermen de Bruijn being among them. 'Zwartkruis's role was always more important than it looked, but Happel always was the number one coach, very clear. But, after the game against Scotland ... it was Zwartkruis who suggested that changes were needed, and not one or two changes, but that there should have been much more emphasis on PSV players, who were in top form. Happel also saw that the three games in the first round were all not very good, and agreed on every suggestion. So, they changed the team in every way that Zwartkruis suggested ... Happel was a very clever man ... and was always listening to good advice.'[267] It seems a far more plausible analysis.

Whether any of the players were aware of Zwartkruis's intentions is unknown. It seems quite likely to have been the case, however; Zwartkruis clearly had good relations with at least the senior members of the group, and captain Ruud Krol served as an able lieutenant, ensuring that an air of calmness was maintained. 'Happel saw the storm coming,'[268] Zwartkruis said, adding weight to the analysis that the coach was aware

---

266 Bongers, Michael & Bremer René, *Kapitein van Oranje* (Netherlands: Belluci, 2008)

267 De Bruijn, Jan-Hermen – Interview with the author

268 Bongers, Michael & Bremer René, *Kapitein van Oranje* (Netherlands: Belluci, 2008)

of the problems, and readily agreed to the suggested changes. In training the day before the Austria game, although both men stood side by side at times throughout the session, it was Zwartkruis conducting the training and Happel's quiet acquiescence spoke volumes. This was a coach who had just guided a team to the European Cup Final. Had he truly been usurped, would he have tolerated the situation and stayed in the Dutch camp?

To the outside world, nothing had changed. In fact, so discreetly was the situation handled that Happel was given the credit for the team's success. His coaching career certainly didn't seem to be harmed. He was even awarded the inaugural Sepp Herberger Award as European Coach of the Year for his season with Bruges and the Netherlands national team. After leaving the Oranje at the end of the tournament, with Zwartkruis officially appointed as coach of the team, Happel returned to club football, having already made it clear to the KNVB that he wasn't interested in carrying on in the post after the tournament. The Austrian 'didn't rate the job of national coach too much', as Jan-Hermen de Bruijn recalled. 'He thought it was a job for lazy people!'[269]

He spent a brief time with Belgian second-tier club Harelbeke, before joining Standard Liège in 1979, winning the Belgian Cup in 1980/81, defeating Lokeren 4-0 in the final. It was the club's first success in the tournament for 14 years, and was followed up with a Belgian Super Cup win. Happel then moved on to West Germany in 1981 to join SV Hamburg, where he would achieve more glory. A Bundesliga title in his first season took the club into the European Cup, and victory over Juventus in the final made Happel the first coach to win Europe's premier competition with two different clubs, following on from his success with Feyenoord 12 years earlier.

269 De Bruijn, Jan-Hermen – Interview with the author

The league title was retained the following year, with another Sepp Herberger Award coming his way. In 1986/87, success in the DFB-Pokal completed the set of German trophies, before he returned to his native Austria taking over at Swarovski Tirol, where he delivered the domestic double in the 1988/89 season, and then retained the league title the following year. He was given charge of the Austrian national team in 1992, but died in November of the same year after just nine games in charge.

Taking into account his earlier success with Feyenoord, it's difficult to paint a portrait of Happel as anything other than an outstandingly successful coach. In 2013, *World Soccer* organised a vote to establish the greatest manager of all time. Sir Alex Ferguson came out on top, perhaps betraying a little British bias – despite its global label, it is an English language magazine – with Michels in second and Happel ninth. Six years later, *France Football* conducted a similar exercise. This time Michels topped the table, with Happel again ninth. Jan Zwartkruis wasn't mentioned in either listing.

Perhaps as has been suggested, the lack of appreciation for the important role performed under Happel was an itch that irritated Zwartkruis for many years, and one that he was keen to eventually scratch when he released his memoirs in 2008. By this time, however, the story was 30 years old. Happel had passed away 16 years earlier and Zwartkruis was past his 80th birthday. He was adamant that, 'This story should be told.'[270] Jumping back to Cordoba on 14 June 1978 at the Estadio Chateau Carreras, that story was about to unfold.

Group A had often described in the press as the 'European Group' and, but for the inclusion of Poland, Group B perfectly fitted the profile of being the 'South American Group' comprising Argentina, Brazil and Peru. The group

270 Bongers, Michael & Bremer René, *Kapitein van Oranje* (Netherlands: Belluci, 2008)

looked anything but an easy task for the Dutch. Italy had already defeated the Argentinians in the game where Klein's insistence on balanced refereeing had allowed the *Azzurri* to prosper. The Germans, as no Dutch player needed reminding, were the reigning champions, and Austria had topped their group, ahead of Brazil. They would be the Oranje's next opponents.

Writing in *The Times* on the day before the game, Norman Fox used an article headlined with a warning about facing the 'originally underestimated Austrians', to describe how the Dutch had been 'vehemently criticised' after losing to Scotland.[271] Should the Austrians even have been 'underestimated' though? In Hans Krankl they had European football's Golden Boot winner, who had notched 41 goals in just 38 league games the previous term. Nevertheless, to many it was the Oranje's first opponents that looked to be the weakest team, and one that they needed not only to beat but, given that topping this group was a passport to the final, by as wide a margin as possible.

When the team was announced, although changes for the injured players were inevitable, others were less predictable. Perhaps the most striking change was that of the goalkeeper. Jongbloed could hardly have been blamed for the misdemeanours of his team further forward, but when Schrijvers was announced as the goalkeeper for the Austria game, with Doesburg, rather than the displaced former No.1 on the bench, initial thoughts were of an injury to the veteran, but these were dispelled. Zwartkruis's plans were being played out, and he had long considered that Happel's decision to play Jongbloed had been far too influenced by reputation rather than reality. The veteran was not his idea of the ideal goalkeeper.

---

271 Danger ahead for Germans and Dutch in second stage, *The Times*, 13 June 1978

In his four games in sole charge before Happel had been appointed, Zwartkruis had selected three different keepers – none of them being Jongbloed. Now he believed that the rationale for picking Jongbloed in 1974, to play as the sweeper-keeper in a formation that encouraged the defence to play a high line, was no longer valid. The team were playing a different style. As such, his simple deduction was that Schrijvers was the better goalkeeper, and therefore should play. Happel seemed content to go along with the logic.

Of the outfield players, the absence of Suurbier, Rijsbergen and Neeskens would mean a substantial amount of experience was missing but, if the temptation was to replace it with as much like-for-like options as possible, it was largely resisted. The return of Arie Haan into midfield made perfect sense, but with the apparent reversion to a 3-5-2 formation – as Happel had leaked to the press would be the case weeks ago – the door was opened for some fresh faces, younger legs and burgeoning ambitions.

PSV central defender Ernie Brandts was selected for his second cap. His first had come as a second-half replacement for Krol in the goalless friendly against the Soviet Union the previous year. He slotted in alongside Krol and Poortvliet, forming a back line with 62 caps between them. It sounds like an experienced trio. Krol, however, had 56 of those. Across the middle of the pitch, the Van de Kerkhof twins, Haan and Jansen were joined by Piet Wildschut, who would patrol in front of the back three, with Rep and Rensenbrink forming the forward pairing.

If the coaches had agreed to a quiet revolution behind the scenes, its consequences were now being played out in the team selection and tactics. The opening game of the tournament against Iran had seen nine players retained from the team who had contested the final four years earlier. That number was now reduced to five. Although the baby-faced Wildschut was a year younger, the biggest gamble was the selection of Brandts, who had only played a single season with PSV, after joining them from mid-ranking second-tier club, De Graafschap. It was a gamble to trust in the youth of the squad, but one that would pay handsome dividends.

The cool damp weather in Cordoba, together with what looked like a much more consistent playing surface, seemed very much to Dutch tastes, and in the early minutes the Oranje shirts buzzed around the pitch energetically, denying the Austrians time to construct any serious forward movements, and grabbing firm control of the game. The rewards came quickly. On six minutes, Jansen was upended out on the right flank as he bamboozled Gerhard Breitenberger before being crudely halted by the same player. Krol flighted the free kick towards the far post and Brandts ran in, unmarked, to head powerfully past Friedl Koncilia in the Austrian goal. It surely wasn't the way that the coaches had hoped for the youngster to justify his inclusion, but they were happy enough to take it. There isn't any video of the reaction on the Dutch bench, but they must have been nodding contentedly. It was the ideal start, and there was more, much more, to come.

It may have been the influx of young players. It may have been the change of tactics, or perhaps even the inspiration offered by Zwartkruis. Whatever the cause, this was an entirely different Dutch team. Further invigorated by the goal, they tore into the Austrians with enthusiasm and conviction, stealing possession and intercepting passes time and again. On nine minutes, Wildschut intercepted a pass, glided past Bruno Pezzey and drove on towards the box. He drifted inside of Erich Obermayer and was ready to fire on goal, when the sweeper jabbed out a leg to bring him crashing to the floor. For a brief moment, there were shades of Cruyff. 'Suddenly the Dutch are starting to play like we know they really can play,' said Jack Charlton, sitting alongside Hugh Johns, commentating for ITV. 'If they go on like this, they could win this game comfortably.' It was hardly the most insightful of comments, but was true nonetheless. From the free kick Koncilia was forced to plunge to his right and turn the ball around the post as Rensenbrink's shot arrowed towards the bottom corner.

For the next 15 minutes or so the Austrians concentrated on not conceding again, and gradually played their way into the game. As the clock approached the half-hour mark, though, the players in Oranje began to threaten again. Twice, Rene van de Kerkhof had chances from the right-hand side of the penalty area, but they came to naught. One goal is hardly ever enough, and only a timely intervention by Krol prevented Krankl from tapping into an empty net after Schrijvers had gone absent without leave from his goal.

In midfield, Wildschut was looking to the manner born. Covering at the back and striding forwards with the ball, gliding past players and drawing defenders out of position. It was the sort of energising play that had been missing in the Oranje's earlier games. The dynamism it produced was always going to cause problems for the Austrians.

The second goal came ten minutes before the break, when Jansen collected a pass and slipped a cross into the area. It was headed back out towards him by a defender. Collecting and controlling, he drove past Herbert Prohaska – the Austrians' most creative player having been forced back to defend – before a body-check halted his progress and Scottish referee John Gordon pointed unhesitatingly to the spot. Rensenbrink fired high to the goalkeeper's left.

The Austrians were in trouble now, and within a minute their fate was sealed. A long throw-out from Schrijvers found Rensenbrink marauding in space on the Dutch left, as the Austrians funnelled back. Curling an exquisite pass around the forlornly lunging Obermayer, the ball landed perfectly with Rep running forward centrally in support. A slight error in control was a minor inconvenience and, as Koncilia rushed to challenge him, Rep coolly lifted the ball over him and into the unguarded net. Strauss may have been Austrian, but it was the Dutch waltzing their way to victory, and the Danube would have been feeling very blue indeed.

Before the break, there was even an opportunity for Schrijvers to show a passable imitation of Jongbloed, hurtling 20 yards from his area to control with his chest and then volley clear, before producing a diving save to thwart a long-range effort from Josef Hickersberger. Another Dutch chance arrived when the left flank of the Austrian defence was breached again, but Jansen's cross eluded Rensenbrink.

When the referee ended the half, the Dutch walked from the field with the game in their pockets. It had been far and away their best performance of the tournament so far, and Austria had conceded more goals in 45 minutes than in their entire qualification campaign. The second half did not improve for the country of Happel's birth, despite there being a false dawn when Pezzey, overlapping down the left, crossed to the far post to find Krankl closing in unmarked. With his reputation he should surely have scored. Instead he headed tamely wide. The miss would be expensive; less than a minute later the Dutch were four ahead.

Schrijvers hit the resulting goal kick long, finding Rensenbrink in space. His first touch took him clear. His second eluded a desperate challenge from Obermayer, drawing Koncilia towards him, and his third squared the ball across the box for Rep to tap into an empty net. 'That was so simple,' Hugh Johns told his audience. And it was. It was almost like a declaration in cricket when Happel removed Rene van de Kerkhof half a dozen minutes later, sending on 25-year-old Ajax midfielder Dick Schoenaker for his debut. As he left the pitch it was difficult to discern whether Van de Kerkhof's limp was due to an injury, or merely the sort of affected stance a player often assumes when being substituted.

On 66 minutes the reason for Brandts being replaced by Van Kraay became more obvious. Stretching for a ball he appeared to suffer a muscle strain, and hobbled around for a minute or so before limping off. Given his performance, there would have been huge relief in the Dutch camp when he, as with Van de Kerkhof, was deemed fit for the next game. Perhaps it was a ploy designed to break up the play, but the Dutch looked to be suddenly picking up injuries with alarming regularity. Rep trudged over to the bench for treatment, before resuming. As he trotted back on, Wim Jansen lay flat out after suffering an apparent knock on the head. The stretcher was called on to remove him and, with both substitutes already used, the Dutch were down to ten men. For most of the game it had seemed like there were a couple more orange shirts on the pitch anyway, such was their dominance. Perhaps now the balance was a little more even. The numerical advantage was short-lived, however, as Jansen returned after a few minutes.

The Dutch seemed sated by their four goals, and comfortably kept Austria at arm's length without overextending themselves. But with ten minutes remaining, sweeper Obermayer ventured forward unmarked to receive a cross into the Dutch penalty area, and lofted the ball over Schrijvers to reduce the arrears. It was a wake-up call for the Oranje who had been playing in second gear since the fourth goal, and had now been punished for their complacency.

Two minutes later, a long ball from defence found Rensenbrink wide on the left, with Rep and Willy van de Kerkhof in support. Drawing the last two defenders towards him, the Anderlecht player cleverly created a huge space around the penalty spot that was quickly filled by Van de Kerkhof and the ball. A simple finish put the Oranje four clear again. In the dying minutes, Rep nearly added a sixth when coming close to intercepting a back pass from Obermayer, but Koncilia spared his team-mate's blushes.

At the end of the game it had not only been a crushing defeat for Austria, but a ringing endorsement of the changes in personnel and tactics by the Dutch. Four years earlier, in the opening game of the second phase, the Oranje had torn Argentina asunder, declaring to the world that they were real contenders to win the tournament. In Cordoba, against Austria, this Oranje team had done pretty much the same thing. A headline in *The Times* the following day brooked little dissent, declaring that, 'Dutch give five-goal warning to the world'.[272]

In 1974, it had been an irresistibly ebullient and mercurial Cruyff motivating his team. This time, despite Rep scoring twice, it was the elegant Ruud Krol beating out the rhythm, playing the libero role with calm assurance when under pressure, and inspiring forward play when in possession. *Gazzetta dello Sport* journalist Alex Frosio's father Pierluigi played a similar role for Serie A club Perugia at the time. The following season, he would be a key part of the team that staggeringly completed a Serie A league season unbeaten under coach Ilario Castagner's own version of Total Football. Frosio recalls, 'When I was a kid, I don't remember much of my father's playing football. One of the few things I remember is a movie we watched together, and it was all about Krol playing football. Krol was transformed in a kind of "libero" that inspired my father.'[273]

At the same time as the Netherlands were igniting their campaign, over in Buenos Aires, Italy and West Germany were playing out a goalless draw that added extra lustre to the two points accrued from the Dutch demolition of Austria. The Oranje were now in an ideal position in the group, and their

272 Dutch give five-goal warning to the world, *The Times*, 15 June 1978
273 Frosio, Alex, *Gazzetta dello Sport* – Interview with the author

four-goal margin set a high bar for others to clear when they faced Austria. Four days later they returned to Cordoba to play West Germany. It was an encounter that had always caused the Dutch problems in the past. Since the end of the First World War, they had faced the Germans 16 times, winning only three matches and, since their last victory in 1956, they had drawn one and lost four of the five games, including the defeat in Munich four years earlier. If any games were guaranteed to define the Dutch psyche, it was those against the Germans. After the success against Austria, their old foe was waiting.

If the West German team of 1974 had been efficient rather than enthralling, this tournament's team under the ageing Helmut Schoen, who would retire when German interest in this World Cup came to an end, were dour by comparison. Playing a back four and a five-man midfield, with Dieter Muller as the lone striker, the tactics were unadventurous and the outlook often cynical. Stars like Beckenbauer and Gerd Muller were gone, but four survivors from the victory in Munich faced the Dutch again. In goal, Sepp Maier now moving towards the veteran stage of his career at 34, was defending the proud record of not conceding a goal in a World Cup tournament for almost seven and a half hours; in fact 449 minutes, comprising four clean sheets in this tournament, plus 89 minutes in the final of 1974.

The other players looking to repeat the results from 1974 were Berti Vogts, Rainer Bonhof and Bernd Holzenbein, the latter forever marked down in the debit column of the Dutch following his *schwalbe* plunge to the turf that led to Breitner's equaliser from the penalty spot. Fate has a strange way of moving in circles and the words 'Holzenbein' and '*schwalbe*' would again figure prominently in the Dutch lexicon used to describe this game.

Zwartkruis and Happel would have been pleased to see that any minor knocks from the Austria game had cleared up sufficiently for an unchanged team to be selected, with Krol, Haan, Jansen, Rep and Rene van de Kerkhof offered a chance for revenge from Munich. Schrijvers had also been on the bench in Munich. There was one other survivor from the game in back in 1974. Referee Ramon Barreto of Uruguay had run the line in Munich, but had now traded in his flag for a whistle and cards – which would come into play farcically, late in the game. Four years earlier, the Oranje had scored inside two minutes, and then failed to secure the victory. What was it about fate and circles again?

Rensenbrink had already fired the first shot of the game high and wide of Maier's goal when Holzenbein was felled on the edge of the Netherlands penalty area. Rainer Bonhof meticulously placed the ball before retreating eight yards or so. Charging in, he drove the ball powerfully towards the side of the goal unprotected by the wall. Schrijvers dived to block, but could only parry the ball forward and Rudiger Abramczyk stooped to head the rebound home as two defenders stood transfixed, unable to intervene. The Dutch were behind and, a few short minutes later, their frustration came to the surface as Willy van de Kerkhof followed through with a late challenge on the goalscorer and was booked. Only three minutes were on the clock. The goal was tardy by comparison to 1974, but early enough to ruffle Dutch feathers. The simmering, deep and long-standing resentment the Dutch felt for their opponents needed only the briefest of flames to come to the boil again.

In 1974, the early Dutch goal had led to a period of dominance by the team with the advantage, strutting and with an arrogance that demanded a display of their superiority. Four years later, the team in front sank back into sullen defence as the players in orange took firm control of the game. Confidence is the more attractive twin of arrogance, and it was this acceptable sibling urging the Dutch forward with a resolute refusal to bend the knee. The Germans carried a threat on the break, but with the midfield line offering reinforcements to the defence more often than in support of Muller, they conceded the balance of possession. With a strong wind at their backs, and seeking to restrict the Dutch to efforts from distance, they settled into a comfortable retreat.

Haan fired in a long-range shot that flew well wide – he would do much better later – and a Rensenbrink header from a free kick compelled Maier to throw himself to his left to turn the ball round the post. With six or seven white shirts dropping to the edge of, or into, the Germany penalty area, the Dutch forwards were often stifled by the weight of numbers as they pressed forward. Over-committing nearly cost a second goal when a Vogts header put Muller clear against Schrijvers, but he hooked it well over the bar. The offside flag offered the FC Cologne player a fig leaf to hide his embarrassment. The next goal would come at the other end.

Just past the midway point of the first half, Willy van de Kerkhof hit a shot from distance that threatened the corner flag more than Maier's goal. The next Dutch effort would be much more dangerous. After exchanging passes with both the Van de Kerkhof twins, Haan unleashed a shot from around 35 yards. Firing the ball into the teeth of the wind may have caused it to swerve, bewildering Maier into misreading its flight. Alternatively, perhaps he knew he was beaten, but the goalkeeper merely leaned in its general direction as the ball ripped into the net. The scores were level. This time it was the Dutch who had struck back after falling behind to an early goal.

The strike put an extra yard into the pace of the Dutch, and a period of confident possession ended with Rep heading wide from an opening seven yards or so out. With the Germans having dropped into an unadventurous period of play, they were finding it difficult to cast off their self-imposed lethargy in attack. Their problem was that, after the results from the first games, a draw would be far more valuable to the Dutch, who had two points already in their pockets. In the remaining minutes of the half, play became more even as the Germans pushed further forward. It brought no tangible reward for either side, and at half-time the players returned to the dressing-rooms level at 1-1.

The second half started with the Germans eager to press forward, keenly aware that another draw may not further their cause greatly. As they pressed, however, the Dutch looked to spring their counter-attacks against a denuded defence. Ten minutes after the restart, neat interplay with Rensenbrink saw Rep galloping clear of Rolf Russmann on the right, with just Manfred Kaltz separating the Flying Dutchman from goal. The SV Hamburg defender, who would later enjoy European Cup success under Happel, had justifiably earned an uncompromising reputation however, and a body-check on Rep brought his run to a juddering halt. The Dutchman sprang to his feet, indignation written over his face, but Kaltz rolled around on the floor long enough for the referee's ire to lessen, before struggling to his feet and escaping without even a cautionary word. With the wind at his back, Haan chanced his arm from 35 yards or so, but the shot cannoned into the wall and away.

Another break saw Poortvliet charging forward and causing chaos. Rene van de Kerkhof crossed from the left, but the ball just evaded Rensenbrink on the far post. Then Rep had the ball in a four-man break, against the same number of white shirts, but the Bastia forward dawdled before shooting and the chance was gone. The Germans were struggling to find anything effective going forwards, with the Oranje bossing the game. 'The Dutch are controlling the game, they don't look in any trouble at all and we're just sitting here waiting for them to score,' remarked Jack Charlton. But, just as in Munich, they didn't.

With the Dutch in total control and, despite having the greater need, the Germans had hardly produced a threat worthy of the name. On 70 minutes, a rare sortie forward saw a free kick conceded midway into the Netherlands half. As the Dutch were disputing the award, the Germans took advantage of the lapse of concentration. Quickly taking the free kick, the ball found its way out to the left, from where Beer crossed, and Muller dashed between three defenders to head the ball past Schrijvers. It was a classic sucker-punch goal. The Germans celebrated like they couldn't believe their luck. The Oranje were 2-1 down to West Germany in a World Cup again. Four years ago, they failed to retrieve the situation. Could they do so now, or had the fates dealt cruelly with them again?

Within two minutes the answer was nearly given. Rep cut inside from the left, slipped past a defender and fired in a shot that beat Maier for both power and direction via a slight deflection. The ball crashed against the crossbar, before ballooning high into the air. The Germans had a reprieve. Now West Germany sank back again. Much as after their first goal, defence was now their priority. The Dutch pressed, but rapid counter-attack was an ever-present danger and, when Abramczyk appeared in space with a dozen minutes to play, the chance to kill off the game was squandered as his shot was skewed wide. Another chance arrived as Beer volleyed on goal, but Schrijvers punched clear. The Netherlands were forced to walk a tightrope, needing to score, but knowing that another goal conceded would close out the game. With ten minutes left, Nanninga was summoned from the bench to replace Wildschut. The remaining time to the final whistle would be filled with drama.

First, a misdirected cross by Beer eluded Schrijvers and the ball bounced on top of the crossbar before drifting clear. A booming long ball into the Germany area from Krol was nodded towards Nanninga, who volleyed in from the edge of the box. Maier fell to the ground to parry and then gather. The storm was gathering. Then came the goal.

Poortvliet gained possession around 25 yards out as Nanninga dashed towards the right of the area, drawing defenders with him. The move created space for Rene van de Kerkhof on the left. Poortvliet slipped the ball to his PSV team-mate. Here was the chance. Coolly gaining possession, Van de Kerkhof had the composure to fake a shot, causing a sprawling challenge to forlornly slip away, before checking back on to his right foot. Maier charged forward to narrow the angle, but the curled shot was well clear of the dive and the desperate figure of Russmann could only punch the ball into the net, flying like some superhero without a cape – or hope.

Eyes wide in exaltation, Van de Kerkhof turned and ran in celebration, arms aloft, before being engulfed by his team-mates. Whereas the colour had drained from the Dutch in 1974, in this World Cup, Oranje shone brightly. As much as the German goal had been undeserved, this one had merit written all over it. The drama wasn't finished yet, though.

Could the Dutch score again? Nanninga headed back across goal, but Maier just got to the ball ahead of Haan. A free kick on the edge of the Germany area saw Krol hammer the ball against the post, but the referee hadn't given permission for the restart, and the kick was retaken. Haan's shot was blocked. The Germans had profited from a quickly taken free kick earlier. Had the ball hit the back of the net from Krol, what would the referee have called?

With three minutes left, after Holzenbein had recovered from blocking Haan's free kick, he became involved in a ruckus with Nanninga, reportedly falling to the floor without much contact. Another *schwalbe*? If you were Dutch, you thought so. It brought a yellow card for the substitute. Seconds later it was followed by a red. Nanninga takes up the story following the yellow card. 'As the ref was walking away, someone else said,

"Stupid ref!" and he thought it was me, and he sent me off. I'd only been on the pitch for seven minutes.'[274] Protestations of innocence fell on deaf ears, and after around five minutes of fevered debate Nanninga trudged from the field.

Despite the late reduction in their numbers, the Dutch saw out the remaining few minutes, and in the other game, the Italians overcame the Austrians with a single goal from Paolo Rossi. It meant Austria were out of contention, having lost both of their games. Both the Italians and Dutch had three points, but Happel's team had a far superior goal difference. West Germany had two points and had the Austrians to play in their final game, whilst the Dutch and Italians would confront each other. Unless West Germany defeated Austria by a substantial margin – a minimum of five would be required – a draw against Italy would be sufficient to take the Netherlands to their second successive World Cup Final.

There was further good news ahead of the Italy game as both Suurbier and Neeskens were deemed fit enough to return to training. The defender may well have been resigned to sitting out the game anyway, with the back three of Brandts, Krol and Poortvliet looking to be a tight unit. With Neeskens fit again, despite his excellent performances in the last two games, Wildschut's place was surely in peril.

Surprisingly, the Germans lost out to their neighbours with a Hans Krankl goal, his second of the game, on 87 minutes securing victory and restoring a little pride for Helmut Senekowitsch's team. Meanwhile, at the iconic Estadio Monumental in Buenos Aires, the Dutch and Italians were engaged in what was, to all intents and purposes, a World Cup semi-final.

The Italians had been effective in their games to date. Topping a group that included Argentina as well as France

---

274 Donald, Michael, *Goal!* (London: Hamlyn, 2017)

was no mean feat, and the victory over the hosts was highly commendable, especially given the raucous atmosphere. The goalless draw with West Germany in their opening game of the second phase was the only time they hadn't been victorious, and Enzo Bearzot's team had the sort of skinflint defence that made Scrooge look like an overly generous, gregarious life and soul of the party, insisting on buying all the drinks for his friends. The midfield was constructive and destructive in equal measures and in attack they had the Old Lady of Turin's favourite son Roberto Bettega and Vicenza's Paolo Rossi. In fact, the inclusion of Antonello Cuccureddu, replacing Mauro Bellugi, meant that nine players from the Juventus team who had overcome Ajax on penalties in the last eight of the European Cup a few months previously would line up against the Dutch. A more positive spin was that Happel's Bruges had then eliminated Juve in the semi-final.

As had been expected, Neeskens was brought back into the starting XI with Wildschut somewhat harshly relegated to the bench. The option of having the experienced and hugely committed Neeskens in midfield was, understandably, just too much of a temptation to resist, especially against such an accomplished team as the Italians. In what was later shown to be a highly significant factor, Jongbloed was on the bench to cover for Schrijvers.

In another strange circle of fate, the Dutch would again wear white against a team in blue, just as they had in the surrogate semi-final against Brazil four years earlier. In contrast to the Brazilians, Italian physicality would be more measured. The *Azzurri* had been successful so far, but with a typically guarded mode of play. Only a victory would do for them in this game, though. Any inclination to stay within a strict *testado* of defence would have to be tempered by the requirement to win.

As the teams lined up in the early afternoon sunshine of 21 June, both knew that the next 90 minutes would decide who would return to the same stadium four days later to contest the World Cup Final. Later that day, the final game of Group B would be played out in Rosario between Argentina and Peru. The result would decide whether it would be the hosts or Brazil reaching the final. The game would provoke much comment and discussion, but that was for the future. For now, the focus of the footballing world was on the Argentine capital, and the game that could take the Oranje to their second successive World Cup Final.

The opening minutes suggested that Bearzot's players had full appreciation of the situation. It was the team in blue taking the early initiative, drawing Schrijvers into action on a couple of occasions, although without any real threat of scoring. Rossi's header from a right-wing corner was probably the closest, but with the bulky Schrijvers rapidly closing on the diminutive forward, he distractedly headed over. A scuffed left-footed shot from Rensenbrink that bobbled and bounced towards Zoff was all the Dutch offered in reply. Approaching ten minutes, the first real opening came as Cabrini burst forward into space on the Italian left, but he blazed his shot high over the bar from just inside the penalty area. Seconds later, Causio stole possession following a Dutch throw-in, but was unable to exploit the chance as a challenge saw the ball run into the welcoming arms of Schrijvers.

Unusually for the Dutch, their midfield was being outplayed by the opposition. As a consequence, chances for Van de Kerkhof, Rep and Rensenbrink were few and fleeting. A long cross from the left nearly produced a goal against the run of play. Rensenbrink was left in unforgivable amounts of space, and his header back across goal defeated Zoff by a wide margin, but did the same to the crossbar by much less.

It seemed as if Bearzot had instructed his team to exploit the space on the flanks exposed by the three-man Dutch back line. Time and again, a ball into space there drew the defence out of position and caused problems. Even when Krol, Brandts or Poortvliet drifted wide to cut out the danger, they were compelled to give possession away via a throw-in or corner. Risking a back pass to Schrijvers from a wide position was fraught with danger unless the goalkeeper was alert. Just past the quarter-hour mark, a Brandts attempt at such a pass came close to conceding, but the goalkeeper plunged to just beat Bettega to the ball.

The ploy was now creating a worrying amount of chances for the Italians. Another raid saw the Dutch defence drawn away, before a pass released Romeo Benetti. He pulled his pass across the Dutch goal, eliminating Schrijvers from the equation, but a galloping Franco Causio couldn't make contact and the ball drifted wide. Whilst the Italians threatened, the Dutch attack seemed impotent in comparison. Rep was almost as anonymous as Rene van de Kerkhof, as Gentile's tender care suffocated him with tight marking.

On 19 minutes, Brandts upended Bettega as another ball down the left flank caused problems. The defender received a ticking-off from Spanish referee Angel Franco Martinez, but greater retribution would soon follow. Neat interplay found Bettega chasing a through ball and closing on Schrijvers, who charged forward to cut down the angle. In a desperate late lunge, Brandts got to the ball first, but only succeeded in diverting it past Schrijvers and into the net for an own goal. Even worse was to follow. His momentum carried him forward into a collision with the goalkeeper. Bettega celebrated his peripheral part in the goal as Schrijvers lay injured. As *The Times* reported, 'Italy had the final in their grasp, and for 20 minutes were, by such a wide margin, the better team, that there was no suggestion that they would fail to return to this elegant stadium on Sunday [for the final].'[275] It was a testing time for the Oranje.

Before the game could restart, Schrijvers was stretchered from the pitch, with Jongbloed summoned to take his place. It would be difficult to argue that the lead was not fully merited. The Dutch were on the back foot and within a couple of minutes of entering the fray, Jongbloed was called on to save a close-range effort from Rossi after a rare error from Krol, and then a volley from the edge of the box as Benetti fired a shot in. Concede again, and it could have been curtains for Dutch hopes. So far in the tournament, Italy had specialised in winning games by a single-goal margin. If the Dutch had fallen two behind, there would have been a mountain to climb – and there are precious few mountains in the Netherlands for the Dutch to have practised on.

A series of niggling fouls betrayed the Dutch frustration – or was it the sign of a determination to fight back – as the remaining period of the half progressed. With the single-goal lead safely pocketed, the constant breaking up of any rhythm in the game neatly served Italian purposes. Much as with the game against West Germany, though, conceding the goal injected a little life into the Dutch as the midfield managed to get a foothold in the game and began to press forward as the Italians settled back into a comfortably familiar pattern, caution to the fore, but dangerous on the break. By the end of the half the Oranje had cleared their heads and were well into the game. Either due to their pressing, Italian acquiescence, or a combination of both, despite the Italian lead, the outcome was back in the balance.

The second period began with the Dutch displaying a determination to assert themselves. Both physically and through attacking intent, they shaded the first few minutes.

275 Netherlands again find their strength and inventiveness when it matters most, *The Times*, 21 June 1978

Neeskens was encouraged to play further forward and quickly took advantage with a header from a free kick, touched over the bar by Zoff. The corner was cleared, but Dutch recycling of possession brought another corner on the opposite side ... Zoff collected under heavy pressure, but seconds later the Dutch were pressing again. A half clearance fell to Brandts, up supporting the attack. He controlled then fired in a shot that left Zoff flailing at thin air as the ball zipped past him into the net. After conceding the own goal, there was clearly an enhanced elation for the defender as, 'He somersaulted and leapt to celebrate his freedom from recrimination,'[276] reported *The Times*.

If Happel and Zwartkruis had ordered a rapid start to the second half, they had their reward. Bearzot had brought on the more defensively minded Claudio Sala for Causio at half-time, with the intention of solidifying the Italian back line. It hardly worked as the *Azzurri* sacrificed the initiative.

There's a thin line between enthusiasm and being out of control, and Haan crossed it minutes later, fouling Tardelli and collecting a yellow card. Again, though, as a message of intent it was delivered with gusto. Rossi had the ball in the net, but the offside decision was expeditious and clearly correct. Tempers frayed as tackles flew in from both sides. Cabrini and Tardelli entered the referee's book. With the scoreline now favouring the Dutch, the Italians were compelled to come forward again, but fell foul of the Happel offside trap with frustrating regularity.

Twenty minutes in, Happel removed the largely ineffective Rep, sending on Van Kraay to play in front of the Dutch defence, in effect making the formation into a 3-5-2, with Rensenbrink and Van de Kerkhof seeking progress on the flanks and looking for support from midfield. Perhaps the

---

276 Netherlands again find their strength and inventiveness when it matters most, *The Times*, 21 June 1978

more obvious move would have seen the introduction of Wildschut, who had played the role twice already. Instead, the coach went for the extra height, physicality and defensive nous of the PSV central defender. It had the desired effect.

Italy pressed, but their cutting edge of the first period had now been blunted and, as time drifted away, concentration at the back was inevitably compromised by the increasingly urgent need to score. Ten minutes after Van Kraay's arrival, a harmless ball into the middle of the pitch brought a petulant foul by Gentile on Rensenbrink. Given the position of the play, it was needless and would prove to be expensive in the extreme.

Krol collected the ball and rolled a short pass off to Haan. The midfielder's howitzer against West Germany had that 'once in a lifetime' look about it. It's not the sort of thing you try in successive matches, in a World Cup, against goalkeepers of the experience of Sepp Maier and Dino Zoff. Not that is unless your name is Arie Haan. This one was probably closer, just the 30 yards or so from goal, but the result was the same.

If Archie Gemmill's slaloming goal had given him a ticket to the pantheon of World Cup goalscorers, those two efforts by Haan had surely done the same, and were enough to inspire the imagination of any young football-mad boy. Rob Smyth was precisely that. 'My recollection is of Arie Haan's two ludicrous goals. I have a precise, if fuzzy memory of one of the goals, Italy I think, being illustrated in a Christmas annual when I was very young, so Haan's name was one of the first to evoke the glamour and mystique of the World Cup. And to stimulate the imagination: I probably didn't see the goal, illustrations aside, until YouTube came along when I was in my 30s.'[277] Dino Zoff didn't see much of the goal either. For Graham Hunter, it was something that stuck in his mind as

---

277 Smyth, Rob – Interview with the author

well. 'The way the Dutch struck the ball was branded into my memory.'[278]

Needing two goals with less than 15 minutes to play, it was all up for Italy. Bearzot played his last card, throwing on Francesco Graziani for Benetti. If he was looking for an ace, it turned out to be the two of diamonds. As the hopes drained away from the Italians, the Dutch nearly scored again with Haan and Neeskens combining to create the sort of Total Football chance that would have made Michels purr with satisfaction.

A game that began with Italy dominating, thrusting and looking in control, ended with the Dutch coolly playing out time with the victory locked down and chained with a double padlock. Afterwards, Bearzot would decry the Dutch performance for 'using tactics of systematic violence,'[279] explaining that, 'For all of the first half, we had to submit to unacceptable aggression on their part. On this excessive aggression they evidently prepared a second half that was a direct manhunt.' Without doubt the game had a physical side to it, but to paint the defeat as being the result of any kind of Dutch violence conjured up the image of someone eating grapes of the sourest kind. Perhaps the comments were more for domestic consumption.

In successive games, this Dutch team had fought back from being behind – twice in the game against West Germany, when the team of 1974 had failed to do so on its big day. If this shade of Oranje may have lacked a little in innovation and flair compared to their predecessors – and which team didn't – perhaps they had made up for it in determination and will to win. The Oranje had an unenviable reputation of losing games they should have won. Had they now flipped that coin on its head, and learned how to win games they should have lost?

278 Hunter, Graham – Interview with the author
279 Dutch are accused of violence by Italy, *The Times*, 22 June 1978

In the Netherlands, it was beginning to look that way. 'They had more or less been outplayed by Italy, but still managed to win, 2-1,'[280] recalled Jan-Hermen de Bruijn. Perhaps that was the key; the one to open the door to World Cup glory. The team that everyone had admired four years ago would play in the biggest game in world football once again, and so many football fans outside of Argentina would want them to succeed. Within that country, though, and perhaps Italy, the attitude was quite different.

In any tournament it is understood that the hosts have an advantage. In Argentina, however, there was barely a legitimate loophole – and some outside of legitimacy as well – that the organisers didn't jump through to give the home nation every chance of winning the tournament. In the second-phase group, for example, whereas all the matches in Group A were played simultaneously, in Group B things were different. The same thing had happened in the initial group stages, again the hosts were given the advantage of playing after the other group game. Each time Argentina took to the field, they had the advantage of knowing what kind of result they needed. Although perhaps a mere marginal advantage in the earlier games, by the time the concluding group game was about to be started at 19.15 local time on 21 June, that advantage had assumed massive proportions.

Brazil and Argentina had drawn their group encounter, but Brazil had triumphed in their other two games, defeating Poland 3-1 and Peru 3-0. Argentina had also overcome the Poles, but only by 2-0. It meant that, ahead of the final fixture, Brazil topped the group with five points and a goal difference of +5. Argentina, with a game against Peru to come, were second on three points, with a goal difference of +2. Poland had completed their programme and were on two points. Peru were sitting rock bottom without a point. In simple terms, Argentina needed to beat Peru by four clear goals to qualify for the final. The hosts knew precisely what they needed to do, and it's difficult not to assume that it wasn't exactly what the organisers had planned for them.

The junta had invited former USA Secretary of State Henry Kissinger to attend the game. The Americans had been a supporter of the dictatorship, seeing it as a bulwark against the intrusion of left-wing governments in South America, and weren't reluctant to let people know. As Doctor Peter Watson, Teaching Fellow in the Department of Spanish, Portuguese and Latin American Studies at the University of Leeds, referring to press statements by the American, told the author, 'Kissinger gives clear praise for the organisation of the tournament in the interview that he gives.'[281] It's not difficult to appreciate, therefore, what sort of outcome to the game that he would consider appropriate, but how far did he, and the junta, go to make that happen? In response to that, Dr Watson's revelation that 'Kissinger and Videla actually go into the Peru dressing-room before the game,'[282] suggests that the answer may be 'quite a way'. Peru had topped their initial group ahead of the Netherlands and Scotland, playing outstanding football, and some even thought they were dark horses for the title itself. Given how the game ended, therefore, a six-goal victory for Argentina, more than a few people detected a whiff of chicanery.

The Peruvians clearly had nothing to play for, and it has been suggested that they merely capitulated against the hosts and a ferociously partisan crowd. Dr Watson related that,

281 Watson, Doctor Peter, Teaching Fellow in the Department of Spanish, Portuguese and Latin American Studies, University of Leeds – *These Football Times* podcast with the author
282 Watson, Doctor Peter, Teaching Fellow in the Department of Spanish, Portuguese and Latin American Studies, University of Leeds – *These Football Times* podcast with the author

'The great Hector Chumpitaz said, "You know we got as far as we ever thought we could do. We were really tired. We weren't used to playing this amount of games in a row with this amount hanging on it."'[283] It's a logical case, but others suggest something far different. There were rumours of grain shipments being transferred to Peru as some kind of payment, but with little evidence to back up the assertions at the time, although of late, any doubts around that seem to have been dispelled. In 2012, *The Guardian* reported that, 'A million tonnes of free grain were shipped from Argentina to Peru shortly before the game and a $50m credit line was unfrozen between the Argentine and Peruvian central banks.'[284]

Years later, the *Daily Mail* reported a story that seemed to throw back the curtain screening the events and expose them to the glare of public scrutiny. The article revealed that, 'Former Peruvian Senator Genaro Ledesma has confirmed the shock result was agreed before the match by the dictatorships of the two countries. Mr Ledesma, 80, made the accusations to Buenos Aires judge Noberto Oyarbide, who last week issued an order of arrest against former Peruvian military president Francisco Bermudez. He is accused of illegally sending 13 Peruvian citizens to Argentina as part of the so-called Condor Plan, through which Latin American dictatorships in the 1970s cooperated in the repression of political dissidents. Once inside Argentina, the prisoners were tortured by the brutal military regime and forced to sign false confessions. Mr Ledesma, an opposition leader at the time, claims Argentinian dictator Jorge Videla only accepted the political prisoners on condition that Peru deliberately lost the World Cup match – and by enough goals to ensure Argentina progressed to the

283 Watson, Doctor Peter, Teaching Fellow in the Department of Spanish, Portuguese and Latin American Studies, University of Leeds – *These Football Times* podcast with the author
284 Salvation army: part two, *The Guardian*, 4 June 2006

final. He said in court, "Videla needed to win the World Cup to cleanse Argentina's bad image around the world. So, he only accepted the group if Peru allowed the Argentine national team to triumph.'"[285]

In the Netherlands, the story was reported by *De Volkskrant* with understandable reaction. FIFA stated that they would investigate the matter, but there will be little surprise to discover that nothing came out. It's not the only evidence of something being seriously awry with the game and its result. There were concerns in Argentina as well. Interviewed on *A Dirty Game*, the Argentine sport journalist, Ezequiel Fernandez said, 'I've talked with players from Peru and Argentina and I'm convinced the match was fixed. But most players were not aware of the match-fixing. The deal was made higher up. The junta not only wanted to show they could organise the tournament and that all Argentines lived in peace and harmony, they also wanted to become champions.'[286]

Peru defender Rodolfo Manzo played in the game, and joined Argentine club Velez Sarsfield the following season. Dr Watson asserted that, 'He admits that ... several players were paid off.'[287] Manzo also later denied it in a television interview. The truth in such matters is always difficult to isolate among the plethora of information and misinformation, accusations and denial, claims and counter-claims. Suffice to say that at least some element of a dark cloud hung over the outcome of that game, and shrouded Argentina's path to the final to play the Dutch.

285 We fixed it! Peru senator claims 1978 World Cup game against Argentina was rigged, *Daily Mail*, 9 February 2012

286 Fernandez, Ezequiel, Argentine sport journalist, Verdenius, Jaap & Mastenbroek, Kay, *A Dirty Game* (2002 - https://www.themoviedb.org/movie/536232-a-dirty-game?language=en-US)

287 Watson, Doctor Peter, Teaching Fellow in the Department of Spanish, Portuguese and Latin American Studies, University of Leeds – *These Football Times* podcast with the author, 2020

There were four days between the victory that took the hosts into the final and the denouement taking place back at the Estadio Monumental on 25 June 1978. Very little of that time was wasted. The popular Argentine sports magazine *El Gráfico* carried a letter from Ruud Krol extolling the virtues of Argentina and how the soldiers on the streets were loved by the people, who often placed flowers into the barrels of their rifles as a mark of respect and affection. The problem was that Krol knew nothing of any such letter, let alone had written one. The propaganda war was swinging into action.

Behind the scenes as well, things would take a turn against the Dutch. In *The Guardian*, Rob Smyth recalled that, 'After another excellent performance in the second group-stage match between – of all teams – Austria and West Germany, [Abraham Klein] seemed a certainty for the final. Pelé thought it; Jack Taylor thought it; even educated fleas thought it.'[288] The Israeli certainly received plenty of positive vibes about the matter. 'And then everyone told me that I am a candidate to referee the final in Argentina,'[289] Klein said. It wouldn't be the case. The honesty and integrity he had shown, and been widely lauded for when the hosts lost to Italy, would count against him.

The Guardian article went on to explain that the final went to Sergio Gonella, 'Reportedly on the casting vote of another Italian, Dr Artemio Franchi, the chairman of the referees' committee. Klein's consolation prize was the third-place play-off between Brazil and Italy. Clive Thomas, the Welshman who also referreed at the tournament, called the decision an 'utter disgrace.'[290] In his book, *The Complete Book of the World*

288 The Forgotten Story of … Abraham Klein, the 'master of the whistle', *The Guardian*, 22 May 2012

289 A chat with Abraham Klein, *These Football Times* podcast with the author, 27 January 2020

290 The Forgotten Story of … Abraham Klein, the 'master of the whistle', *The Guardian*, 22 May 2012

Cup, Cris Freddi also described it as 'disgraceful.'[291] 'To tell you the truth I was very disappointed,' Klein admitted. 'I think at that time I was fit to referee the final. But only one man can referee the final, and if I look back I am still happy with what I had in my life, in my refereeing life.'[292] Klein is certain he would have had no problem being impartial, despite him having spent a year living in the Netherlands at Apeldoorn.

There are a couple of theories for Klein's rejection. One is that Argentina protested about his links with Holland. It sounds good, but at that stage nobody knew of his year in Apeldoorn. 'Nobody knew because nobody asked me,' he says. 'Nobody at the Argentinian government or FIFA knows about it, so this cannot be true.'[293]

More likely is that he was punished for his performance in the Italy game; that Argentina bullied FIFA into picking another referee. 'Maybe this was the reason,' Klein said. Either way, there is a startling lack of bitterness. 'Some of the journalists were told that some of the members of the referees' committee wanted me, but I cannot tell you one wrong thing about the referees' committee or the FIFA president. They support me throughout my career. You cannot find many referees from small countries who had the games that I had. I refereed Brazil seven times, Italy seven times. They gave me the best games in the world. Maybe Gonella was better than me.'[294] The Italian's performance in the final quickly give the lie to that modest and self-effacing assessment from Klein.

Quoted in *Brilliant Orange*, Ruud Krol certainly believed that it was Argentine pressure that saw Gonella given the

291 The Forgotten Story of ... Abraham Klein, the 'master of the whistle', *The Guardian*, 22 May 2012

292 The Forgotten Story of ... Abraham Klein, the 'master of the whistle', *The Guardian,* 22 May 2012

293 The Forgotten Story of ... Abraham Klein, the 'master of the whistle', *The Guardian*, 22 May 2012

294 The Forgotten Story of ... Abraham Klein, the 'master of the whistle', *The Guardian,* 22 May 2012

honour of officiating in the final. 'There was already a discussion before the game about the referee because FIFA wanted Klein, the Israeli, for the final. But Argentina had lost against Italy, when Klein was the referee, so they wanted Gonella.'[295] Without rancour, Klein doesn't dispute the assessment. 'I understood later that Videla was against me because they lost, the only game that they lost. How they influenced the other members of FIFA, I don't know.'[296] Was it true that the decision had been swayed by Argentine pressure? There seems plenty of evidence to suggest that it was the case. The problem now was, if Gonella knew the highlight of his career had been gifted to him by the hosts, would there be a debt to pay?

Was the historic link between Argentina and Italy also a factor? Italian migration to South America in search of a better life was a significant phenomenon around the turn of the 20th century, one later reversed as the *Oriundi* recruits – South American-born players of Italian ancestry – were taken back to Italy. It meant that Italianised names such Tarantini and Bertoni were not unusual participants in the Argentine national team.

It should be stated that Gonella was an experienced official. Two years earlier, he had officiated the European Championship final, when Czechoslovakia defeated West Germany on penalties, as well as 175 games in Serie A. Big games, and the attendant pressures that inevitably accompanied them, were nothing new to him. The final took place a few weeks after his 45th birthday, and he retired afterwards, taking up a two-year post as president of the AIA (Italian Referees' Association), and joining the UEFA Arbitration Commission. Criticism of referees can usually be understood via partisan

295 Winner, David, *Brilliant Orange* (London: Bloomsbury, 2000)
296 A chat with Abraham Klein, *These Football Times* podcast with the author, 27 January 2020

focus, but it's also fair to say that there was an amount of criticism for Gonella's performance. In *The Times* for example, Norman Fox described him as a 'lenient, sometimes bemused referee.'[297] Other comments would later focus less on matters of competence, and more on those of impartiality. In a BBC blog, Jonathan Stevenson asserted that, 'Gonella failed to exercise any control as the tackles went flying in and the 50-50 decisions seemed to mostly fall in favour of Argentina.'[298]

At the end of the day, there was little the Dutch could do about the selection of the referee. Instead, Happel and Zwartkruis concentrated their minds on selecting the best options for their line-up. The Dutch team for the final would include seven players from the final four years earlier, eight if you include Rene van de Kerkhof who came on at half-time. It was a team that had matured and grown into the tournament, progressing as they went and for many, despite being pitted against the hosts, were favoured to win. For example, Norman Fox in *The Times* asserted that 'The Netherlands, I think, can take the trophy back to Europe.'[299] Schrijvers's injury had deprived him of the chance to play in the final, with Jongbloed, who a little over four years previously had an international career spanning precisely five minutes, as a substitute at the end of a friendly, playing in his second such game. Krol had Brandts and Poortvliet alongside him who, aside from the first half of the game against Italy, had looked a solid unit.

In midfield Jansen, Haan, Neeskens and Willy van de Kerkhof would battle out for mastery of the game with Rene van de Kerkhof, Rep and Rensenbrink looking to score the goals. Schrijvers's injury prevented him even making the

297 Fox, Norman, Argentina keep a date with destiny by scoring dramatically in extra time, *The Times*, 25 June 1978
298 https://www.bbc.co.uk/blogs/jonathanstevenson/2010/05/the_story_of_the_1978_world_cu.html
299 Three compelling reasons for Dutch seeing it that Europe prevails, *The Times*, 23 June 1978

bench and Doesburg moved up to understudy Jongbloed. The unlucky Suurbier and Rijsbergen, who had both lost their places following injury, offered experience if required, with Van Kraay and the robust Nanninga completing the 16.

Even on the day of the game, there were still three more ploys to be played out in the farrago of schemes destined to tilt things in favour of the hosts. Skipper Krol recalled the eventful coach journey to the stadium. 'We were in a hotel outside Buenos Aires and they took us a very long way round to the stadium. The bus stopped in a village and people were banging on the windows, really banging and shouting "Argentina! Argentina! Argentina!" We couldn't go backwards or forwards. We were trapped. For 20 minutes we stood in a village like this and some players were really frightened because the crowd was really banging and pushing on the windows of the bus.'[300] There are some that suggest this was an accidental misdirection by the driver and the arrival in the village with the fans was merely coincidental. It seems a difficult case to sustain, and if the intention was to unsettle the Dutch before entering what was understandably, and not unreasonably, a bear-pit of an atmosphere at the stadium, it was effective.

The stadium itself offered no sanctuary. There were '500 Dutch people and 80,000 Argentines,'[301] according to Nanninga's recollection. The 500 may well have been an exaggeration. Rep also recalled the way the number of fans at the Oranje's games had changed since their time in Mendoza. 'In the first game, against Iran in Mendoza, there were 5,000 people – not many Dutch. No atmosphere. We played very badly. Against Scotland, 10,000. Again, no atmosphere. Against Austria in Cordoba, maybe 15,000. Against West Germany, maybe 20,000. That was the difference. Later, when we played against Italy in the River Plate stadium in the semi-

300 Winner, David, *Brilliant Orange* (London: Bloomsbury, 2000)
301 Donald, Michael, *Goal!* (London: Hamlyn, 2017)

final, there were 80,000 – mostly Italians. Then there were 80,000 for the final, of course – but that was terrible, too. Argentina had to win. It was bizarre. Not a normal situation. There was some fear, too. A lot of people said that if we won the game, there would be a big problem afterwards.'[302]

As the Dutch left the dressing-room for the pitch, they found that they were on their own. Where were the Argentines? Two minutes, passed, three, then four. The Dutch stood there as the crowd bayed. The inaction of the match officials hardly placated Dutch concerns about any potential impartiality. Five minutes passed with the Dutch team waiting, isolated, with vitriolic abuse flooding down from the crowds in waves, and surrounded by military personnel. Finally, Daniel Passarella led out the Argentine team. But there was more to follow.

Passarella began to complain about the cast on Rene van de Kerkhof's wrist, demanding that he should be banned from the game. As similar casts had been worn for each game since the injury had been sustained against Iran in the Netherlands' opening game of the tournament, it was surely not a genuine concern, but it led to further delay. A strong referee would have called a halt to such obvious shenanigans, but this game didn't have one. 'Gonella lost control of the match even before it started, with the kick-off delayed by over 10 minutes by Argentinian gamesmanship,'[303] suggested Klein.

Eventually, Dutch patience was exhausted. "'OK, enough is enough," Krol decided. "If he cannot play, we are going off." Within two minutes we were playing ... They were trying to unnerve us."'[304] His resolution persuaded all concerned that pantomime time was over, and a game of football broke out. The hosts had played their full hand of cards designed to

---

302 https://www.theguardian.com/football/2001/apr/10/sport.comment1

303 The Forgotten Story of ... Abraham Klein, the 'master of the whistle', *The Guardian*, 22 May 2012

304 Winner, David, *Brilliant Orange* (London: Bloomsbury, 2000)

disrupt the Dutch. Perhaps less intentionally, the Argentines had also inflamed the temper of their opponents and, as was shown in 1974 against an over-physical Brazil team, when required to do so, the Dutch were more than capable of looking after themselves physically.

Inside the first couple of minutes, Poortvliet charged into a challenge on Daniel Bertoni, quickly followed by a Haan foul on Osvaldo Ardiles. It led to Americo Gallego squaring up to the Oranje shirt nearest to him. When that turned out to be Neeskens, he seemed to quickly think better of it. The scene was set for a niggly opening five minutes, with fouls committed every 20 seconds or so, and Gonella whistling as ineffectively as a sparrow trying to scare away a fox. The game was quickly getting beyond the referee.

Then came the first real chance. Haan was fouled out on the Dutch left flank. From his free kick, Rep arrived late to head powerfully down and past Ubaldo Fillol in the Argentina goal, but the ball flew inches the wrong side of the post. It was a golden opportunity, but perhaps, as had been the case four years earlier, scoring early may not have been the best of ideas. The Dutch had gained a measure of control with studied possession and rotating movement, but any flow of the game was consistently disrupted by free kicks.

Each team considered the other the main culprits. Dutch physicality in the challenge produced roars of disapproval from the packed terraces and howls of protests from the Argentina players. At the same time, the off-the-ball elbows, cynical trips and shirt-pulling indulged in by the Argentines frustrated the Dutch. It was not only a contrast of footballing styles. It was also a contrast of what was deemed acceptable as part of the game. A European referee would have been thought to be more sympathetic to the mode of play he was used to officiating, but it was hardly the case as the elegantly unconvincing dives of the Argentines seemed to induce a

Pavlovian response of whistle to mouth and blow. What's Spanish for *schwalbe*?

Approaching the quarter-hour mark, there was nothing overly theatrical in Bertoni's fall as Krol's trip brought his thrusting run to a halt. Gonella's first yellow card was shown. It was fully merited. Bertoni's unseen elbow into the stomach of Neeskens should have brought at least a similar sanction, but although Gonella was looking straight at the incident and had the card in his hand, he merely listed the Dutch captain's name in his book. From the free kick, Passarella drove a shot low past the wall to Jongbloed's right, but the goalkeeper smothered comfortably. Stop-start staccato action remained a feature of the game, but gradually the Argentines played themselves into at least an arguable equality, and when Passarella fired over coming late on to a cross from the right, they delivered their first serious threat on Jongbloed's goal. The first quarter of the game had been completed.

Suddenly, the chances were arriving. A control and volley by Rep at the other end brought a flying save from Fillol. It may have been 'one for the cameras' but he touched the ball over the bar effectively. A few minutes later, collecting the ball after a header from Neeskens was much less trying for the goalkeeper. With 15 minutes to the break, a pass found Bertoni in space. The offside flag stayed down, but he screwed his shot wide. FIFA were persisting with the exercise of having referees run the line. It's arguably not the best option when the man in question fulfils a different function for most of his professional life and is then switched to a role requiring entirely different reflexes.

Five minutes later, Jongbloed tipped a looping header from Passarella over the bar for a corner, but a goal was on the way ... A throw-in gave the ball to Ardiles. Evading three challenges, he played the ball forward to Leopoldo Luque who squared to Mario Kempes on the edge of the box. Cleverly using his body to shield the ball from his marker, he took it in his stride, advanced and stroked home past Jongbloed.

In so tight a game, the first goal was always going to be important, and its arrival so close to the half-time break was even more significant. The Argentines only needed to hold out for around six minutes before walking off to huge acclaim. Those six minutes were eventful, though. First, Ardiles became an unlikely first Argentine to find his name noted in Gonella's book for a foul on Rene van de Kerkhof, then Galvan escaped similar punishment for a deliberate handball, blocking a pass that threatened to break the home team's back line.

In the final minute, the Dutch came so close to an equaliser. A cross from Willy van de Kerkhof was headed back across goal to find Rensenbrink closing in unmarked a mere few yards out. Any contact would surely bring the scores level. Instinctively, and out of desperation, Fillol jabbed out a leg. The ball struck it, finding the only place in the entire half of the goal that would deny the Dutch. The ball was scrambled away. As saves go it wasn't athletic or aesthetic, but it was vital. Seconds later the whistle for half-time signalled a huge roar. Despite having most of the game, and the best chances, the Dutch were compelled to sit in their dressing-room contemplating the unpalatable prospect of losing successive World Cup Finals.

The second period began with the Dutch pressing forwards. A period of possession ended with Haan forcing in a shot that was diverted for a corner. The pattern was set for much of the next 30 minutes or so. Oranje shirts pressed forwards, striped ones defended, looking to hit on the break. Cast back four years and it could have been another time and place. On that occasion, all Dutch efforts had been in vain. Would it be different this time?

A long ball found Luque raiding, but he was hustled out of possession. Another goal for Argentina now would surely end

Dutch apsirations. Luque on the break again, but this time Jongbloed advanced to hack clear. Haan hit a shot from long range that Fillol could only parry, but he recovered before Rene van de Kerkhof could profit from the error. Inside the first ten minutes and the game was opening up. Then we moved from drama to vaudeville as Gallego offered up what must have been one of the most embarrassing dives in World Cup history. Even the commentators laughed. Points for *schwalbe*? 6.0.

Ten minutes after the break, nothing had changed. Happel spoke with Zwartkruis and Nanninga was sent to warm up. Seconds later, Luque just failed to force the ball past Jongbloed. The Dutch tightrope walk was getting increasingly precarious. As another Argentine handball preventing a through pass went unpunished by anything other than a free kick, Happel made his move. Off came Rep, and on went Nanninga. The card missing from Michels's hand four years earlier, having a big target man up front, was now being played by Happel. The elegant swordplay of Rep's rapier was placed back into its scabbard, and out came the claymore. There were 30 minutes to play.

If anything, the change blunted the Dutch forward play initially as Passarella and his fellow defenders found the much less mobile, if more muscular, Nanninga an easier option to mark than the elusive Rep. The situation may have convinced Argentina coach Cesar Luis Menotti to make a change of his own. With less than 25 minutes to play, and more than half an eye on keeping things tight, he removed the creative Ardiles, sending on the more defensive-minded Omar Larrosa.

Bringing on Nanninga hadn't worked, so Happel doubled down on the tactic. Wim Suurbier was sent on for Jansen. He dropped into the back line alongside Poortvliet and Krol, whilst Brandts was sent forward to support Nanninga. In 1974, Michels's team had forsaken their Total Football instincts in a forlorn pursuit of hoisting balls forwards with no real target man to aim for. Happel's ploy at least had that vital ingredient – in fact it now had two of them. Could the Dutch find the right ball in the time remaining, as the Argentine crowd tried to sing their team home?

Inside the final ten minutes, Argentina sank further back, willing the hands of the clock to speed up. As they conceded space, it gave more opportunity for accurate crosses. Nanninga was becoming a factor as positioning rather than pace, power rather than poise and punch rather than precision became the order of the day. Willy van de Kerkhof dropped further back, assuming the role of a mortar, to launch the ball long. From a throw-in, Tarantini sought to lash the ball downfield, but sliced dreadfully. Nanninga recalled the passage of play that led to the equaliser. 'The goal came from the left from Poortvliet to Arie Haan, and Haan passed it to the midfielder. He played it to the right to [Rene] van de Kerkhof and I was in the centre when the ball came.'[305] The cross arrived among a posse of Argentine defenders, but such moments were meat and drink to a player who had feasted on crosses throughout his career. Arriving with a run, he climbed above the defence and powerfully headed past Fillol, who had little time to react. Dutch jubilation. Argentine heads in hands. Whither now the momentum?

It lay with those in Oranje. Van de Kerkhof was free again down the right. A shimmy inside a defender, but this time, with Nanninga waiting, the cross was diverted behind for a corner by Tarantini. If the Dutch had the momentum, the Argentines had the frustration. Another break saw Neeskens peeling off for a return ball before being floored by an Argentine forearm. Video evidence suggested Passarella was the assailant, but he cleverly slipped away from the scene of the crime. The referee may have been watching the ball, but the linesman should

305 Donald, Michael, *Goal!* (London: Hamlyn, 2017)

surely have seen the assault. The Barcelona midfielder was down for a few minutes as time ticked on. Surely extra time would be needed. Unless there was one last chance ...

Ten seconds of added time were registering on the clock as Krol stood over a free kick deep in the Netherlands half of the field. Isolating his target, he fired the ball long and high. Unaccountably, the Argentine back line, perhaps transfixed by the moment, missed the flight of the ball. On it went, bouncing inside the area as Rensenbrink closed in from the left. Suddenly, there was just Fillol to beat. The angle was tight, but the Dutch forward got to the ball and prodded it past Fillol. Was this the moment? The agonising defeat of 1974. The disaster of 1976. Now was the chance for redemption. Fillol's desperate star jump was forlorn. The ball passed him unimpeded.

'It is this close,' says Ruud Krol, holding his thumb and forefinger about a millimetre apart. 'No, more like this.' The gap is down to a couple of microns. 'If it goes in, it's finished.'[306] Two nations held their breath. This is the Netherlands. This is the Oranje. These things never seem to work out in the big games, on the big day.

Rob Smyth recalled the moment. 'I'm surprised more isn't made of the freakish bounce when Rob Rensenbrink hit the post in injury-time in the final. It's hard to be certain because of the TV angle, but it looks like it is going in until it kicks like a "leg break" and hits the near post. It feels like one of the ultimate what ifs, yet people don't talk about it that often – it's never on those lists of 10/25/50/100 great or iconic World Cup moments, yet it should be in the top ten every time.'[307] The dull clump of the ball striking the post is the death knell of Dutch hopes. The ball is hacked clear. The chance is gone. Fate maliciously scuttles away with its prize.

306 Winner, David, *Brilliant Orange* (London: Bloomsbury, 2000)
307 Smyth, Rob – Interview with the author

In extra time, Dutch legs, wearied by the intense pursuit of an equaliser, were unable to cope with a renewed and now rejuvenated Argentina, as two more home goals saw them lift the trophy. The Dutch were relegated to bridesmaids once more. Had Rensenbrink's effort found the net, Nanninga's goal would have been lauded as the one that threw the lifeline. Instead, it was merely relegated to being a footnote of history. It's a lament that was redolent in the forward's memory. 'In extra time they made it 2-1, and then 3-1, and it was done – you know you can't do anything anymore to win the final. The whistle blew and we went in. We had lost. We went back into the changing-room and the first thing I did was roll a cigarette and light it up. We had a few drinks that night though.'[308]

For the Dutch, there was still a sense of achievement, even more so with odds stacked so highly against them. Jan-Hermen de Bruijn explains: 'In the final, they played partly the best football of the tournament, because they felt free and without any pressure to perform because, already, they had outperformed the expectations. We were surprise finalists who were not supposed to be in the final.'[309] The Dutch failed to attend the press conference after the game, and didn't collect their medals. Belles of the ball perhaps, but always in the kitchen at parties.

There's an intense sense of fatalism about the Dutch and this frozen scenario. It's almost a need to explain away the importance of the moment, to diminish it with mitigation. Jan-Hermen de Bruijn again: 'Everybody knows, and it is a part of our history that we could have won the World Cup after Rensenbrink hit the post, but many people still think that Gonella would have played on, even up to today, to give Argentina a chance to equalise.'[310] It's a conspiracy

---

308 Donald, Michael, *Goal!* (London: Hamlyn, 2017)
309 De Bruijn, Jan-Hermen – Interview with the author
310 De Bruijn, Jan-Hermen – Interview with the author

theory hardly bereft of support, as David Winner illustrated in *Brilliant Orange*. 'There are many in Holland who believe that if Rensenbrink's shot had gone in, the Dutch would still have been denied victory somehow. Sergio Gonella ... would have played enough time to award Argentina a penalty. Or Rensenbrink's goal would have simply been disallowed. Or there would have been a pitch invasion or something worse.'[311] The latter comment is something that Poortvliet takes as some compensation for the defeat.

'If you'd have won, you wouldn't have survived. I didn't care.'[312] It seems a little out of character that Nanninga, all muscular endeavour and physicality, owned a flower shop. Few players get to experience a World Cup, let alone appear in a final and score. He was one of those few, but he maintained a reasoned balance between what it meant, and what it could have meant. 'We flew home the next day and I went back to work in the flower shop the day after. The neighbours had decorated the shop because we had got second place but I just went back to work ... OK, it was a goal in a World Cup Final, but it's still just a goal. I was a labourer's son ... I still am. My greatest achievement is my kids and my grandchildren.'[313] There's little doubt that Dick Nanninga knew which flower smelt the sweeter.

Rensenbrink offers a slightly different view ... 'We had shots and chances in the first half; it could have been 2-0 to us before half-time ... I think "if only" thoughts of course.' And the last-minute chance that hit the post? Rensenbrink considered it less of a chance than many others suggest. 'But it was not a chance. I did well to hit the post. The ball was almost on the goal-line. I had no space to do anything. I

311 Winner, David, *Brilliant Orange* (London: Bloomsbury, 2000)
312 Verdenius, Jaap & Mastenbroek, Kay, *A Dirty Game* (2002 - https://www. themoviedb.org/movie/536232-a-dirty-game?language=en-US
313 Donald, Michael, *Goal!* (London: Hamlyn, 2017)

had no chance to control the ball and come inside. There was a defender in front of me. I had to shoot first time. The goalkeeper left a very narrow opening. Sometimes I think it would have been better for me to miss completely. Then people wouldn't ask about it. If it was a big chance, I would still suffer from it, but really it was impossible to score.'[314] Rensenbrink was known as *Het Slangenmens* (The Snake Man) because of his ability to wriggle out of even the tightest situations. In this passage, was he seeking to use that legendary skill to work his way free of an inescapable regret? In January 2020, Rensenbrink passed away. But for those 'couple of microns' suggested by Krol, he would have been remembered as the man who took the World Cup to the Netherlands, perhaps even surpassing Cruyff in the affections of Dutch football fans, a legend of Oranje.

Even outside of the Netherlands, some think that the Dutch were never going to be allowed to win, perhaps easing the pain of loss. Rob Smyth suggested that, 'The climate in Argentina, with the junta and everything else, made it incredibly difficult for any other team to win that World Cup. The Netherlands still came bloody close, and Lord knows how much added time would have been played had Rensenbrink scored. It feels like Argentina were always going to win that World Cup. In that sense I think the Netherlands were unfortunate. Their two World Cups as a great side coincided with two hosts who, for different reasons, were incredibly difficult to beat.'[315]

Poetry asserts that, ''Tis better to have loved and lost than never to have loved at all.'[316] Perhaps the emotions at play here speak against such eloquence. If you never had a real chance of winning, then losing is less a reason for lamentation. If you were never in love, the pain of separation is more bearable, or

314 Winner, David, *Brilliant Orange* (London: Bloomsbury, 2000)
315 Smyth, Rob – Interview with the author
316 Lord Tennyson, *Alfred, In Memoriam A.H.H.* (London: Moxon, 1850)

perhaps less unbearable. If you were never truly near to being the bride, then the role of bridesmaid can be considered a joy, rather than a curse. The only problem is the difficulty of convincing yourself of that version of reality, no matter how hard you try.

There's an irony about the Oranje at the 1978 World Cup. Perhaps the least regarded of the three teams that contested the major tournaments of 1974, 1976 and 1978, they came the closest to winning the big prize. Jan-Hermen de Bruijn asserts that the best chances for Oranje glory lay in other tournaments. 'They would and should and easily could have won in 1974 and 1976.'[317] It's a familiar mantra, but perhaps you had to be part of the Oranje in Argentina to fully appreciate the squad and its achievements. Zwartkruis was very much on the inside in Argentina, and the apparent lack of respect for that team clearly rankled. 'Everyone is always talking about the Oranje of '74 and '88, but skip 1978.'[318] Why is that? Is it linked to the downturn in the fortunes of previously continentally dominant Dutch clubs perhaps? 'In Holland … 1978 arouses much less feeling. There the golden age of Dutch football seems to be already over by then,'[319] said Jan-Hermen de Bruijn.

So were the 1978 vintage of Oranje, the most 'beautiful losers' to borrow Cruyff's sad epitaph? Bram Vermeulen believes it to be so. 'Losing made things, politically, a lot easier for them. They had everybody's sympathy. Everyone saw Argentina cheating. The Dutch were moral winners.'[320] Perhaps there should be another word at the end of that line – 'again'. For many, despite going closer to victory than in 1974, the team of 1978 dwells in the shadow of the one of four

317 De Bruijn, Jan-Hermen – Interview with the author
318 Bongers, Michael & Bremer René, *Kapitein van Oranje* (Netherlands: Belluci, 2008)
319 De Bruijn, Jan-Hermen – Interview with the author
320 Verdenius, Jaap & Mastenbroek, Kay, *A Dirty Game* (2002 - https://www. themoviedb.org/movie/536232-a-dirty-game?language=en-US)

years earlier. Jan-Willem Bult offers a reason why. 'The 1978 team was without Cruyff and Van Hanegem, the two aces of Amsterdam and Rotterdam, and participating in Argentina under dictatorship was always debated to be controversial. The team also lost to Scotland 3-2 and drew against Peru 0-0 and West Germany 2-2, which was not as impressive as the road to the final in 1974. So, there is not much reference to that team that played far away in the shadow of the 1974 team.'[321]

321 Bult, Jan-Willem – Interview with the author

PART 6

Tomorrow and tomorrow and tomorrow

BEAUTIFUL BRIDESMAIDS DRESSED IN ORANJE

Tomorrow: 1980–88

'Holland is only a small country, so to expect us to challenge the big countries at every tournament is a lot to ask,' former Netherlands midfielder Ronald de Boer told BBC Sport.

'Once in a while you get a great group of players but in between you always have periods in which you can't expect us to always challenge with the big boys like Italy, France and Germany, who have much greater resources.'[322] The history of Dutch football certainly lent evidence to De Boer's assertion. Qualifying for two World Cups, in 1934 and 1938, missing out for more than three decades, followed by two successive World Cup Finals. If history was anything to go by, it would be a while before the Dutch flame ignited again.

As Henry Ford once said, though, 'History is more or less bunk. It is tradition. We don't want tradition. We want to live in the present and the only history that is worth a tinker's dam is the history we make today.'[323] Had the 1978 World Cup campaign been a success or a failure? It was hard to decide. Were the Oranje an unfancied squad who had overperformed, or a team that struggled to find form early on, but prospered as they progressed, turning in their best performance in the final and should have returned to Europe with the trophy? Whichever the case, it was time to look to the future.

Happel's contract was completed and he left to return to club football, as Zwartkruis resumed the role he occupied before the Austrian was co-opted. The relationship with Happel had been strained at times, and now the former military man could put his own battleplans into action. If one writes off the 1976 European Championship loss to Czechoslovakia as one of those occasions when anything that can go wrong does go wrong, Zwartkruis had a hugely talented and experienced squad at his disposal. Some of the older players had seen their

322 http://news.bbc.co.uk/sport2/hi/football/euro_2008/netherlands/7415457.stm
323 1916 interview with reporter Charles N. Wheeler – *The Chicago Tribune*

best days, but there was still the nucleus of the team that had played in successive World Cup Finals, now complemented by the new generation who had burst through in Argentina. The 1980 European Championship offered a chance of instant redemption, and the Dutch were, as was now becoming the norm, one of the favoured teams. The first task was to qualify.

It was a task immediately front and centre for Zwartkruis. The qualifying group also contained Poland, East Germany, Iceland and Switzerland, with only the winners progressing to the finals in Italy. September, October and November 1978 saw three qualifiers played in quick succession – first at home in Nijmegan to Iceland, before visiting Bern and then entertaining East Germany at the Stadion de Kuip.

A team looking similar to the one that played out the end of the tournament in Argentina started the campaign against Iceland. The only new face was Roda JC wide man Adrie Koster. With club-mate Nanninga in the central striker role, the logic of playing a winger used to feeding the strengths of the big man was obvious. It was only the second time that the forward had started a game for the Oranje; the first being his debut in the warm-up game against Tunisia earlier in the year. He would be an inconsistent starter from then on, more often than not joining from the bench. If Koster's career for the national team was tied to that of Nanninga, it's perhaps little surprise that he only earned three caps.

A three-goal victory kicked the campaign off nicely, as first Krol netted, and then Rensenbrink scored twice. The new Zwartkruis reign was up and running. Further encouragement followed on 11 October when a broadly similar team journeyed to Switzerland and returned with 3-1 victory. Five weeks later, the seal was set on the year's competitive fixtures, with another three goals, this time without reply, against East Germany in Rotterdam. Zwartkruis was looking like the real deal, and his team were responding perfectly. There was still one more game to play before the turn of the year, with a visit to Dusseldorf on 20 December for a friendly against West Germany. Both coaches experimented a little, but a 3-1 defeat deflated any early Dutch Christmas celebrations.

The new year started with a friendly against Italy – and another defeat. Zwartkruis selected a team based around PSV and Alkmaar players, with only three of the 12 who took part coming from other clubs. The team was also light on star names; Krol being the obvious example. The *Azzurri* took full toll and the swagger from the early days of Zwartkruis's sole coaching tenure was looking more like a hesitant walk. A 3-0 victory over Switzerland at home was counterbalanced by a 2-0 defeat in Poland and, after playing Argentina in a 0-0 draw to celebrate 75 years of FIFA, the next two qualifiers, away to Iceland and home to Poland, were assuming vital importance. Goals from John Metgod and Willy van de Kerkhof, together with a brace from Nanninga, were enough to overpower the Icelanders, but after a 1-0 friendly win over Belgium, a draw against the Poles put qualification into severe doubt, although it also made it impossible for Poland to advance. The final game of the group would be played a month later in Leipzig. Both the Netherlands and East Germany had 11 points, with the Dutch having a far superior goal difference. It meant that only a win for the East Germans would see them qualify, and the Dutch miss out.

It was a crucial game for the team and the coach, but the players Zwartkruis selected were startlingly inexperienced. The starting XI had 183 caps between them, but 134 of them were shared between Schrijvers, Krol and Rene van de Kerkhof. Of the others, seven weren't even into double figures. Approaching half-time, two goals down and with both teams down to ten men, the selection looked to have been suicidal. A header by Frans Thijssen cut the arrears, and offered a little hope as the teams headed for the dressing-room, but it was Rene van de

Kerkhof who transformed the game in the second period. First, a scintillating run down the right and cross left Ruud Geels with a simple finish and then an interception and pass set the PSV player clear. He slipped past the goalkeeper and scored to take the victory and the group top spot. The game was dubbed as the Miracle of Leipzig. Zwartkruis had his redemption, and took his team to the finals.

Perhaps looking to repeat the trick of 1978 when a number of younger players, Poortvliet, Brandts and Wildschut for example, energised a jaded-looking Oranje, and emboldened by the success in Leipzig, Zwartkruis selected a young squad. Only four players were over 30, and two of them, Haan and Nanninga, were only 31. Almost half the squad had less than ten caps, and three had yet to make their debuts. It looked an even bigger gamble than the team selected for Leipzig. This time, however, Zwartkruis's luck was out. Jan-Hermen de Bruijn declared that it backfired terribly, turning into 'the most horrible European Championships I had ever seen.'[324]

Grouped with West Germany, Czechoslovakia and Greece, the tournament got off to a shaky start as a largely unrecognisable team were saved by a Kees Kist penalty that gave them a 1-0 victory over Greece. In the next game, against their old nemesis West Germany, the Dutch were three goals astray just past the hour mark, and late strikes by Krol and Willy van de Kerkhof were too little, too late, to turn the tide. A sorry performance in the competition was completed with a 1-1 draw against Czechoslovakia and the Dutch were eliminated. It felt like the end of an era, and it was. After a decade of prominence, decline had set in. It had taken 36 years for the Oranje to qualify for another World Cup after 1938. After 1978, it would take another dozen before they did

---

324 De Bruijn, Jan-Hermen – Interview with the author

so again. Ten years after the loss in Argentina, they did taste glory, but there was a fallow period first.

In 1981 after struggling in the World Cup qualifying tournament, Zwartkruis was dismissed and former PSV coach, Kees Rijvers took control. Transferring domestic success on to the international stage though is never simply a given, even when you have a body of players to call on that you have coached successfully at club level. Rijvers's tenure would be short and largely unsuccessful. He failed to qualify for the 1982 World Cup in Spain, with the Oranje finishing fourth of the five teams in the qualifying group. Although two places were available, perennial opponents Belgium, and the France team of Platini and the first incarnation of the *Carré Magique* were too strong. The Dutch finished two points behind the former and one adrift of France. At the time, France were coached by Michel Hidalgo, who had taken over from Stefan Kovacs in 1976.

Two years later, the Dutch again missed out on a major tournament, this time the European Championship to be held in France, albeit in the most extraordinary of circumstances. With only a single qualifying place available, Rijvers's team were pitted against Spain, the Republic of Ireland, Iceland and Malta. Although there were a few stumbles along the way – the Netherlands drawing in Iceland, Spain drawing in Dublin – once both of the big teams had won their home games against the other the issue was decided on goal difference. The final two fixtures saw first the Dutch, then the Spanish, entertain Malta across four days in December 1983.

Ahead of these games, both teams had 11 points. The Dutch had a goal difference of +11, much superior to the Spanish, who were on +5. On 17 December, 58,000 fans in the De Kuip saw the Netherlands add a further five goals to the total, boosting their level to +16. It meant that Spain were now required to beat Malta by a minimum of 11 goals to snatch the qualifying place away from the Oranje. Despite the Maltese having lost six of their seven group fixtures before the game in Seville's Estadio Benito Villamarín – they had beaten Iceland 2-1 in the group's opening fixture – Spain had laboured to victory in Ta'Qali, actually trailing 2-1 for a dozen minutes or so, until Carrasco equalised and then Gordillo scored the winner inside the final five minutes.

A crowd of substantially less than 20,000 in the stadium illustrated the confidence, or perhaps lack of it, swirling around the Spanish fans that they could achieve such an unlikely triumph. Before the game, Malta goalkeeper John Bonello had reportedly declared that Spain couldn't even score 11 goals against a team of children. Had it been mere bravado? Perhaps, but when Senor squandered a second-minute penalty, maybe the assessment hadn't been far off the mark.

Spain did go ahead with a quarter of an hour played when Santillana scored, but a decidedly cold and wet blanket was dropped over any growing Spanish enthusiasm, when 21-year-old Maltese central defender Michael Degiorgio equalised ten minutes later. By the break, the home team were back in front but they still needed a further nine goals. What looked unlikely before kick-off was now entering the realms of fantasy.

Just a minute after the restart Hipolito Rincon added a fourth goal, but it was a small step on a long journey, and Spain wouldn't score again for a further ten minutes, when the same player added a fifth. Then, in the space of the next eight minutes, hope returned as a further three goals were added. Maceda netted twice and Rincon completed his hat-trick. Suddenly even the most extraordinary things looked possible. After 63 minutes, though, Spain stopped scoring, as suddenly as they had started. With 15 minutes to play, they still needed four more goals, and hopes were dwindling again. Three goals in rapid succession reignited them. On 75 minutes, Santillana scored his fourth goal, 9-1. Rincon joined him on four goals three minutes later, 10-1. Athletic Bilbao midfielder Manuel Sarabia scored a minute later. With ten minutes still to play, Spain needed just one more goal. How expensive was Senor's missed penalty looking now? Fortunately for the Alaves player, he redeemed the mistake and scored the all-important 12th goal with five minutes to go.

Spain had recorded an historic victory, but one that hardly felt satisfactory outside of the Iberian peninsula, and particularly in the Netherlands. The scheduling had not only conspired to tell the Spanish what they needed to do – the result squared the goal difference off at +16, but having scored 24 goals, against the Dutch total of 22, they qualified – but also compelled a largely unprofessional team to play two games in different countries across a four-day period.

Rijvers would survive a mere two further games. A six-goal victory over Denmark with a largely experimental side offered hope but, when the qualifying tournament for the 1986 World Cup began with a 2-1 home defeat to Hungary, his position was compromised. Returning to his old post after three years in the Bundesliga with FC Cologne, Michels briefly took charge of the team for a couple of away qualifying games before being compelled to step down after being diagnosed with a heart condition that would need surgery. The results had hardly helped. A 1-0 loss to Austria was followed by a scrappy 1-0 victory in Nicosia, thanks to a goal inside the final five minutes from Feyenoord's Peter Houtman. In February 1985, Leo Beenhakker was appointed on a caretaker basis to try to resurrect the 1986 World Cup qualifying campaign, before Michels could resume his duties towards the end of the year, by which time, Beenhakker had found much more lucrative employment.

The Rotterdam-born coach had enjoyed domestic success with Ajax, winning the Eredivisie title in 1979/80, before moving to Real Zaragoza in Spain. He joined the Oranje after a short period back in the Netherlands, coaching Volendam. For the remainder of the season, he would share both jobs. The situation hardly panned out well for either team, especially when Volendam, ironically nicknamed *Het Andere Oranje* (the Other Orange), were relegated at the end of the season.

When Beenhakker took up the reins, the Dutch were already struggling, with just two points; Austria had four, but the table was topped by the Hungarians on six. There were seven UEFA qualifying groups, and the winners, plus the four best runners-up, would qualify automatically. The next best second-place teams would face each other in a play-off, whilst the runner-up with the worst record would play off in an inter-confederation game against a team from Oceania.

Having already lost twice in their three games, Beenhakker's task was to win each of the remaining fixtures. They were unlikely to catch Hungary, having already lost at home to the Magyars, but second place still offered a chance of qualification. In his first game, the Dutch skittled Cyprus 7-1, but successive victories for Hungary, at home to Cyprus and then away to Austria, guaranteed them top spot. The Dutch now needed to finish second ahead of Austria, garnering as many points as possible and hope to qualify directly from there, or via a play-off place.

On the first day of May, the Oranje entertained Austria in Rotterdam. A win would give their aspirations a boost, but a disappointing 1-1 draw provided quite the reverse. A week later, Austria completed their programme, scoring four times against Cyprus to take their tally to seven points. The Dutch were on five, but with a much better goal difference, and a game to play. A win would see them pass Austria. The problem facing them was that their remaining game was away in Budapest against a Hungary team who had won all of their five matches so far.

The team who travelled to Hungary contained only Willy van de Kerkhof from the 1974 and 1978 vintage of Oranje. He would be substituted in this game, and play only twice more before leaving the international arena. The old guard were exiting the international stage. Aside from Van de Kerkhof's 61 caps, Beenhakker's team looked short on experience for such a task. Skipper Ben Wijnstekers had played 33 times, and fellow Feyenoord defender Michel van de Korput 21, but none of the remaining players could muster 20 caps. The nascent talents of Frank Rijkaard, Ronald Koeman and Marco van Basten were deployed, though, and a wonderfully skilful solo goal from half-time substitute Rob de Wit, in only his second outing for the Oranje, delivered an impressive victory.

When all the calculations and comparisons had been made, the early losses counted against the Oranje. A play-off offered their only salvation. As fate would have it, as so often seems to have been the way, the qualification play-off would be against their neighbours Belgium. The first leg would take place at Anderlecht's ground in Brussels on 16 October, with the return in Rotterdam in the middle of November. For many reasons, these games would mark a turning point for Dutch football.

Compared to the turmoil that the Dutch were experiencing, as was their custom, Belgian football was decidedly on the up. They had been runners-up to West Germany in the 1980 European Championship, qualified for the World Cup in Spain in 1982, and narrowly came up short for a semi-final spot in the 1984 European Championship. Under the sage leadership of the wise old head Guy Thys, players such as Franky Vercauteren, Jan Ceulemans, plus the emerging Enzo Scifo, had sprinkled enough stardust over the Red Devils to give them hope of automatic qualification before a shock 2-0 defeat in Albania dropped them into second position, and a play-off against the Dutch.

The game in Brussels would mark the return to international action of Eric Gerets, following a two-year ban for a match-fixing scandal at the end of the 1981/82 season. Just three minutes in, though, it was an expulsion, not a return that swung the game dramatically in favour of the home team. A marauding run forward by Gerets was brought to a halt by what Italian referee Pietro D'Elia deemed to be an illegal challenge. As Franky Vercauteren picked up the ball and shaped to take a quick free kick, Wim Kieft closed him down, and tapped the ball away to prevent it. The Belgian then made a kind of kicking out motion stamping towards Kieft's shins. The Dutch forward appeared to swing an arm in retaliation; perhaps a push more than a punch, but Vercauteren went down holding his face as if felled by Mike Tyson. Dutch defender Adri van Tiggelen was understandably angry, but also understood. 'I didn't really like that mentality. I prefer clarity: just hand out a tap or a kick. But in retrospect you can only say that Franky was the smartest of them all.'[325] The fall was enough to convince D'Elia, who instantly produced the red card. For the remaining 86 minutes, the Dutch were a man down.

The remonstrations of skipper Ben Wijnstekers, complete with a repeat of Vercauteren's action, cut little ice with D'Elia. Later, Vercauteren would admit that incident wasn't one that he was particularly proud of and, in the return leg, he would be barracked mercilessly by the Dutch crowd. Any belated regret, be it affected or sincere, would be of little comfort to the Dutch. The matter was hardly helped when the same player put the home team ahead after 20 minutes, cutting in from the right flank and firing across Hans van Breukelen into the far corner of the net. It was enough to win the game and, with Kieft suspended and joined by Marco van Basten, who

325 https://www.nieuwsblad.be/cnt/dmf20151120_01980928

329

received his second yellow card of the qualification process in the latter stages of the game, all of the advantages seemed to lie with the Belgians.

The night of 20 November in Rotterdam was bitterly cold and a much-changed Dutch team set about turning things around. If the pitch was cold and icy, there was plenty of heat in the action. It wasn't a night for beautiful flowing football; on such a treacherous surface, direct balls would surely pay the best dividends. It was a time for gloves, tracksuit bottoms and tights, but the temperature of the game was undiminished. Although the Dutch had plenty of the ball, it was the more direct play of the visitors that created the best chances of the first period. A long raking ball put Ceulemans clear, running into the area, but he lashed over wildly with a left-foot shot as he fought for balance around eight metres from goal. Then Vercauteren nearly added to his burgeoning reputation in the Netherlands as the villain of the piece. Profiting from a bouncing ball that had the Dutch defenders struggling to turn, he fired just wide of Van Breukelen's post from the edge of the area. An opportunity from a cross came Ruud Gullit's way, but the ball bounced before reaching the welcoming arms of Jean-Marie Pfaff.

At the break, needing a win, Beenhakker rolled the dice. John van Loen of Utrecht was just 20, uncapped, and hardly had an explosive goalscoring record – perhaps not the man many would have turned to in such a situation. He was tall and rangy, and sending him on to replace defender Michel van de Korput was clearly a positive, if not borderline desperate, move by Beenhakker. The fates were not about to reward the coach's decision.

As the game restarted, Guy Thys decided to respond to the threat of the extra Dutch forward, replacing Franky Van der Elst with Anderlecht centre-back Georges Grun, as the anticipated aerial assault began. The experienced Grun was an accomplished defender, and knew his task. He tenaciously stuck to the young Utrecht forward, denying him space with which to work and won most of the aerial duels. Any that he failed to deal with were gobbled up by Pfaff, or punched clear by the goalkeeper.

The first 15 minutes of the second period passed without undue concern for Belgium as Dutch concerns rose. 'Cometh the hour, cometh the man,' as the saying goes or, in this case, cometh the Houtman. On the 60-minute mark, an error by Gerets saw Rob de Wit scamper down the left before crossing high to the far post where Houtman rose to nod past Pfaff and square the scores on aggregate. A dozen minutes later, all composure in the Belgian defence seemed to disintegrate. Gullit crossed from the right, but the ball was deflected by a Belgian leg. Already committed to coming for the cross, Pfaff could only flap at the ball, diverting high rather than away. It dropped to De Wit who controlled and then fired home from a tight angle. 'The Netherlands are on the way to Mexico,' shouted the Dutch television commentator. But there was still almost 20 minutes to play, and another twist of fate to come.

The first ten minutes passed. Beenhakker switched Gullit into a sweeper role as an extra precaution, as Thys now threw Grun forward. 'They had to come, the Belgians. We were leading 2-0 and had the qualification. Belgium started to play all or nothing. Thanks to Hans van Breukelen we had already escaped a few times, but the pressure continued,'[326] Van Tiggelen recalled. One goal, one away goal, would change everything. Van Breukelen denied the visitors time and again. Aside from those dozen minutes, Belgium had largely been in control, but now the qualification that their play had probably deserved, was slipping away. Every save from Van Breukelen was heralded like a goal, and now there

326 https://www.nieuwsblad.be/cnt/dmf20151120_01980928

was only five minutes separating the Dutch from another journey across the Atlantic.

Shirts were never going to be exchanged at the end of the game, but boots were very much on the other foot as minutes ticked away. Now it was Van Loen, playing as a defender to keep tabs on Grun, but at the vital moment, much as he had done when defending against the young forward, the Anderlecht defender was too powerful for him as Gerets hoisted a ball towards the far post. A year or so later, Van Tiggelen would join Anderlecht and become a team-mate of Grun, and the Dutch defender takes up the story: 'And then Georges Grun turned up for the goal. Coach Beenhakker wanted me to take care of the second post. There I was when Georges was central for the goal – a metre or two away – so competed with John van Loen. I still see it in front of me, that duel. But I was powerless and Hans was too.'[327] The header was powerful and from only a couple of metres' range, Van Breukelen had no time to react. 'And the whole of the Netherlands knew [...] that it was over, yes. How could we recover from that sledgehammer blow? We only had five minutes to score twice, against a team that was overflowing with energy. Being so close to qualifying made it so hard,'[328] Van Tiggelen added sadly.

The game finished 2-1. The late goal had put Belgium through on away goals. They would justify their qualification, finishing in fourth place in Mexico, but for the Dutch, there were just recriminations and criticism. Beenhakker was slated for his half-time decision and Van Loen also came in for harsh treatment. Surely unfair on a player making his debut, but he would not play for the Oranje again for more than three years. For Beenhakker, the blame should very much be targeted at the players, as he made clear after the game. It was almost a

327 https://www.nieuwsblad.be/cnt/dmf20151120_01980928
328 https://www.nieuwsblad.be/cnt/dmf20151120_01980928

stream of consciousness rant, rage induced, and often bereft of coherence.

'They sat there at half-time like golden roosters. Nobody was tired, out of breath or had anything wrong. On such a field. Apparently, everyone had spared themselves. How can you have nothing on such a field, how is that possible? That was the disillusionment for me, that lack of sense of reality: up or down under everyone, there was no such thing ... Netherlands–Belgium, NO yellow cards, with a 2-0 lead, in such a match, NO yellow cards. You can only make this generation stronger, more mature, more strong-willed, by letting them play. Against the stronger, against the arrived. And we, anyone who has anything to do with football, should STOP PROTECTING today's players. Is there anything easier than forming the young so-called talents together? Yes, I would like to do that for a while.'[329] Unsurprisingly, Beenhakker didn't hang around for long, quickly exiting Zeist for the coach's job at Real Madrid. In March 1986, a recovered Michels would return.

The coach was already in the employ of the KNVB, as technical director, and whilst the team were falling short, Michels was already at work in the background remedying the problems he perceived as holding back Dutch football. Jan-Willem Bult explains: 'The legacy of the '74 team, Total Football [was being] institutionalised by the KNVB. Michels [...] wrote the *Zeister Visie* (Vision from Zeist). Zeist is the place in the centre of the Netherlands where is the HQ of KNVB. The *Zeister Visie* is the basis of the education of coaches in the Netherlands. It refers to the time that footballers grew up on the streets, playing football on small and uneven areas that made them develop their tactical skills. For instance, Cruyff did that as a kid on the streets and small grass fields of Amsterdam Beton Dorp. The generation of Gullit, Rijkaard,

329 https://www.vi.nl/nieuws/de-donkere-oranje-dagen-van-de-jaren-tachtig-en-de-woede-van-beenhakker

Davids on the famous Balboa Plein (Square) in Amsterdam West. The *Zeister Visie* says that children don't grow up on the streets anymore so the football training has to simulate that. Many training forms are with limited space and time and the general Dutch formation is 4-3-3. Cruyff even started to build football pitches in neighbourhoods [Cruyff Courts] to bring back that street football feeling. So even today the echoes of the Seventies dominate the football culture in the Netherlands.'[330]

The football that had led to the success, or near-successes of 1974 and 1978, would not be lost to future generations. Writer on Dutch football, Michael Statham, illiustrated the importance. 'The Netherlands sides of the Seventies were absolutely key in facilitating the identity of the Dutch on the footballing map. They inspired generations that followed, and gave the Netherlands a unique flavour of playing style and tactics. The Dutch will always look back on the players in the team at the time with fond memories, and the current crop of internationals are never pressured by this past.'[331]

Jan-Hermen de Bruijn highlighted how it had been a fallow time for the fortunes of the Oranje, 'The only generation that really failed, in the eyes of the Dutch, is the one from the early eighties, characterised by Ben Wijnstekers of Feyenoord, who was the right-back and captain for many years. They never impressed.'[332] In the same period that the Oranje had laboured to qualify, and fell short, Dutch clubs were finding it increasingly difficult to make any meaningful impact in European competition. In 1981, Alkmaar lost out to Bobby Robson's Ipswich Town in the final of the UEFA Cup. It would take another six years before a Dutch club returned to a European final. The fortunes of Dutch clubs and the

---

330 Bult, Jan-Willem – Interview with the author
331 Statham, Michael – Interview with the author
332 Bult, Jan-Willem – Interview with the author

national team were again seen to be inextricably tied together. In 1987, Ajax defeated Locomotive Leipzig to win the Cup Winners' Cup, and the following year PSV Eindhoven took Dutch football back to the top of the tree, defeating Benfica on penalties to return the European Cup to the Netherlands. Their pre-eminence in Dutch club football was also rewarded with a domestic double and, in 1988, under the coaching of Barry Hulshoff, Ajax reached the UEFA Cup Final, only to lose out to Belgian club KV Mechelen. With a renaissance of club success and Michels back in charge of the national team, was it time for the Oranje flame to burn brightly again?

... and tomorrow ... 1988

Michels returned to the fold for a series of four friendly games ahead of the qualification tournament for the 1988 European Championship that began in October of that year. It opened with a visit to East Germany, followed by a home game against Scotland, and then away fixtures in West Germany and Czechoslovakia. They were hardly designed to give a confidence-boosting canter through a few easy games, and it certainly didn't pan out that way.

In the first game, a young-looking Dutch side overcame a much more experienced home team in Leipzig, thanks to a strike by Van Basten, but things would slide downhill from there. In April, with Alex Ferguson temporarily in charge, Scotland visited Eindhoven's Philips Sportpark, and only 14,500 fans turned out to watch a turgid goalless draw. In fairness to Michels, it was a much-changed side, with four new caps wearing Oranje for the first time. Danny Blind of Sparta Rotterdam was joined by Ajax's John van't Schip and John Bosman in the starting XI, with Fortuna Sittard's Wilbert Suvrijn joining the action from the bench later.

Games against West Germany may sometimes be labelled as 'friendlies' but for the Dutch, that hardly ever translates into reality. With the qualifying process approaching, the tournament itself to be held in West Germany – scene of the 'lost final' – and the fact that *die Mannschaft* was now being coached by Franz Beckenbauer who had lifted the World Cup back in 1974, any existing tensions would only have been drawn tighter. Nevertheless, both coaches persisted in playing experimental sides, with copious use of substitutes. The 3-1 defeat for the Dutch would still have stung. A single-goal reverse in Prague on 10 September suggested anything but the team being ready to launch into qualifying the following month with any kind of confidence. As this was the Dutch, that was probably no bad thing.

The Netherlands were in a five-team group with old rivals Poland and Hungary, supplemented by Greece and Cyprus. Their first task, a visit to Hungary, also appeared likely to be the most daunting, especially as they had topped their World Cup qualifying group two years earlier, compelling the Dutch to face that traumatic play-off against Belgium.

After using the four games earlier in the year to cement his ideas, rather than being overconcerned about results, Michels now had a developing team. Hans van Breukelen was established as the number-one goalkeeper, and for the game in Budapest's Nepstadion, he played behind a back four of Ronald Koeman as sweeper, alongside the Ajax pair of Sonny Silooy and Ronald Spelbos, with Adri van Tiggelen, who had now moved to Anderlecht. The midfield comprised Gullit, Rijkaard, Van't Schip and Jan Wouters, with Simon Tahamata and Van Basten up front. Just past the hour mark, a pass saw Gullit driving into the area, rounding goalkeeper Szendrei Jozsef, and squaring the ball for Van Basten to hit the winning goal. The players' celebrations and those on the terraces by the Dutch fans suggested how important the win was, although Michels merely stood watching implacably, hands behind his back. There was still plenty of work to do.

A goalless draw at home to Poland the following month emphasised the point and when a 2-0 victory in Cyprus was followed by a 1-1 draw at home with Greece, with Van Basten equalising an early Greek strike, that win in Hungary felt less like the confident early steps on a strong run to qualification, and more like the only result keeping the Dutch in with a chance of progress. Fortunately, their rivals were also tripping over their own feet. The Dutch had six points from four games, the Hungarians just two from three matches and Poland three from two. Unexpectedly, the table was topped by Greece with seven points from their four games.

On many other occasions, such setbacks would mean the Dutch would be struggling to catch up but, even now, they needed to step up the pace. Fortunately, that's what happened. Victories at home to Hungary and then away in Poland, combined with a 3-0 reverse for Greece in Cyprus, pushed the Oranje to the top of the group. On 28 October, Cyprus visited the Stadion de Kuip for what looked like a run-of-the-mill victory for the Netherlands, who only needed a point from their last two fixtures to be guaranteed qualification. It turned out to be anything but, and despite scoring eight goals, the game would, for a period, enter the record books as a 0-3 defeat.

A first-minute goal by Bosman suggested an easy victory, but a couple of minutes later, events took a dramatic turn. A smoke bomb was hurled from the terraces behind the Cypriot goal. Some reports say that the missile struck visiting goalkeeper Andreas Charitou on the head, but video of the incident suggests that it passed him, and then exploded in front of him, rendering him temporarily deaf and affecting the sight in his right eye. Play was held up for a long period whilst the stricken Cypriot received treatment with press photographers hovering like vultures around him. After receiving treatment on the pitch, it was decided that he could not continue and was replaced by Giorgos Pantziaras. As Charitou was leaving the field, however, the other Cypriot players followed him and refused to restart the game.

When appointed to officiate the fixture, Luxembourg referee Roger Philippi may, not unreasonably, have been expecting a fairly uncontroversial game. But all such hopes were lost in the smoke that enveloped the fallen Cypriot goalkeeper. It was only his second international match, having refereed Switzerland v Malta the previous year. Now he was faced with a situation that the vast majority of officials are fortunate enough never to have to deal with across an entire career. After consulting with UEFA officials about whether to abandon the game, it was decided to try to persuade the Cypriots to continue. It took more than 30 minutes but eventually they did return and, in the very abnormal atmosphere, the Dutch scored another seven goals, with Bosman netting four of them to add to his first-minute strike.

A UEFA investigation initially decided that the Netherlands should be punished for not controlling their fans and Cyprus were awarded a 3-0 win. Suddenly, what had seemed like a stroll to qualification for the Dutch was thrown into the air. Greece had nine points, the Dutch had ten. The final fixture for Michels's team was away to the Greeks. A home win would see them heading to West Germany with the Dutch missing out on qualification again. It may have been that the Oranje would have been good enough to go to Greece and secure at least a draw, but when the KNVB lodged an appeal against the verdict the decision was overturned. Instead, the fixture would be replayed in December, albeit behind closed doors.

Understandably, the Greeks were furious, considering that the Dutch had got off scot-free and merely given another chance to play the game. It seemed a not unreasonable conclusion, but perhaps, just for once, fortune had favoured the Dutch. The game was played on a frozen pitch at Stadion

De Meer, Amsterdam on 9 December. As was to be expected, the Dutch were still far superior to their opponents, and were two goals clear, thanks to a brace by Bosman, when Cypriot frustration rose to the surface. Despite the six-week gap from the initial game, Charitou was not deemed fit enough to play, and Pantziaras again deputised. Just past the hour mark, what seemed a blatant penalty was duly confirmed by Czechoslovakian referee Ivan Gregr. Despite Gullit being tumbled by two defenders, Pantziaras was furious at the decision and, after being beaten by Koeman's spot kick, refused to retrieve the ball from the net, and prevented his team-mates from doing so as well.

With the teams lined up for the restart, Gregr called for Pantziaras to send the ball back upfield. He refused. The referee then was compelled to run the 50 metres or so to act as a ball boy, pausing to administer a yellow card to the recalcitrant goalkeeper as he passed. The game ended with Bosman confirming his hat-trick, and the Dutch qualified. Although no fans had been allowed to watch the game, England coach Bobby Robson was in attendance. The Dutch would visit Wembley for a friendly in March, and would later be placed into England's European Championship group. Despite the ghostly atmosphere surrounding the game in a deserted stadium, Robson was clearly impressed by what he had seen, believing that, '… the Netherlands, who had been unbeaten in the qualifying competition so far [were] threatening to refresh glorious memories of their predecessors some 15 years ago. They will present a serious threat in the finals and particularly since, with some 30,000 fans behind them, every game will seem like a home game.'[333]

The Oranje then travelled to Rhodes and the Diagoras Stadium with its limited capacity of around 3,500, with

333 Protest of Cyprus goalkeeper falls on deaf ears, *The Times*, 10 December 1987

qualification already assured. A 3-0 win was the icing on the cake. Since the World Cup in 1978, the Netherlands had only qualified for a single major tournament, the tepid challenge for the 1980 European Championship. Now they had another chance. That 1980 performance stood alongside the shattering disappointment of 1976 in the same competition. History might well be bunk, but European Championships had never been a happy hunting ground for the Oranje, even when they managed to negotiate the qualification process. It was time to prove Mr Ford correct, and debunk that history.

Marco van Basten had moved to Milan in September of 1987, as Ajax cashed in on their outrageously talented centre-forward. The striker's footsteps would later be followed by Gullit and Rijkaard as the Dutch trio brought success back to the San Siro. The Oranje would have a price to pay, albeit in a different kind of currency to the one paid out by the *Rossoneri*. A series of niggling ankle injuries threatened to derail Michels's hopes of having Van Basten lead the line for his team in West Germany, and although John Bosman had shown himself to be a reliable goalscorer in the qualification tournament, Van Basten was probably the best striker in Europe at the time. If he couldn't play, he would be sorely missed.

Ahead of the tournament, Michels had three friendlies to get his squad into shape, the first at Wembley in March 1988. By now the draw for the tournament groups had taken place, and Robson's visit to Amsterdam had been given added importance, with England and the Netherlands drawn in the same group, alongside the Soviet Union and the Republic of Ireland. Often in such circumstances, teams are reluctant to play pre-tournament games, in case they unwittingly hand an advantage to their opponents. England skipper Bryan Robson was surprised the game went ahead as scheduled. 'I suppose it will work out when the whistle blows but, once we were drawn with the Dutch, it seemed strange to let the game go ahead.'[334] Hindsight is a wonderful thing, but not one granted to the people who decided to press ahead with the fixture. In a foretaste of what would happen a few months later in Germany, Wembley experienced one of the most one-sided 2-2 draws ever seen at the old stadium, as Robson's team escaped after being a goal up in 13 minutes, and 2-1 down after 26.

Michels then put out a fairly experimental team at home to Bulgaria. A goal from Jan Wouters looked to have secured the win, but two strikes from the East Europeans inside the final ten minutes turned the tables. Finally, on the first day of June, less than two weeks ahead of the opening game, a more recognisable team, although still bereft of Van Basten, as had been the case against England and Bulgaria, overcame Romania in front of 12,500 fans at the Olympisch Stadion, with goals from Bosman and Kieft.

PSV were now coached by Guus Hiddink and were the dominant domestic force in the Netherlands. They had topped the Eredivisie in 1986/87 and 1987/88, and would do so again the following term. Their KNVB Cup success in 1988 would be repeated in the following two seasons ánd, when they defeated Benfica on penalties on 25 May, they joined Ajax and Feyenoord as the only Dutch clubs to ascend the heights of European club football. That the victory was achieved at the Neckarstadion, Stuttgart, just a couple of weeks ahead of the European Championship beginning in the same country added a little extra piquancy to the victory.

With all but four of the 16 players that comprised the squad for the final being Dutch, it was expected that the PSV contingent would form a substantial part of Michels's squad. When the announcement came, six places were allocated to players from the Eindhoven club and, despite trailing in second place by nine points behind the champions, Ajax contributed

---

334 Robson expects an evening of style and flair, *The Times*, 23 March 1988

five. The Amsterdam club had been runners-up in the Cup Winners' Cup competition. It could be argued that the next highest contributors were AC Milan, with Van Basten, Gullit and Rijkaard, although the latter would not officially become a *Rossoneri* player until after the tournament following a loan spell with Real Zaragoza.

With 20 places available, Michels selected two goalkeepers, seven defenders, seven in midfield and four forwards. The flexibility offered by players such as Rijkaard and Gullit meant that such definitions were at times elastic, and shown to be so as the tournament progressed. PSV's Hans van Breukelen was the undisputed number-one choice as goalkeeper. This time the Dutch had managed to get their top goalkeeper into the squad for a major tournament. To many, it seemed the crucial advantage when balancing out the squads that lost out in successive World Cup Finals against the one that would compete for the European crown in 1988. Jan-Hermen de Bruijn was very much of that opnion, 'In general, individual qualities of 1974 was better than 1988. But 1988 was much better than 1978. The big difference was the goalkeeper. Van Breukelen [was] superior to Jongbloed and Schrijvers.'[335] Few would dispute that assessment. The worry was that if he was injured during the tournament, his back-up was Feyenoord's Joop Hiele. He had a mere four caps, the last being the pre-tournament defeat to Bulgaria. Previous to that he had played once in each of 1980, 1986 and 1987. It wasn't quite a Jongbloed moment, but had Hiele been called on to deputise, as happened with Schrijvers ahead of the 1978 final, there may have been eerie echoes.

Very much as in 1974, and unlike Happel in 1978, Michels kept faith with the same defence throughout the tournament. His first-choice back four would be Ronald Koeman as

335 De Bruijn, Jan-Hermen – Interview with the author

sweeper accompanied by Berry van Aerle, both from PSV, Van Tiggelen and Rijkaard. Aside from Van Aerle with only six caps, it was an experienced back line, and could call on Wilbert Suvrijn, Sjaak Troost and Wim Koevermans as cover. Despite playing as the organiser of PSV's defence, Koeman had rattled in 21 goals in the domestic season, making him the country's third-top marksman.

Across midfield, Gerald Vanenburg, Jan Wouters and Arnold Muhren would play in every game, with the latter now a veteran at 37, although having only 17 caps before the tournament began. John van't Schip would play in the first game, but after that his place would be taken by Erwin Koeman. Ajax's Aron Winter and Hendrie Kruzen of Den Bosch also made the trip, but didn't play. The forwards were Bosman, who had top-scored in the qualifying tournament, Kieft, Dutch football's top scorer for the season, skipper Gullit and Van Basten. Some saw the selection of the Milan striker as a gamble given his injury-ravaged season in Serie A, but surely leaving him out would have been a bigger one.

Aside from Muhren, many key members in the squad were approaching their peak years. Koeman, Rijkaard, Kieft and Gullit were all 25, Van Basten and Bosman two years younger. It's not widely known, but before the tournament, there were rumours that the Dutch came close to losing their coach. Michels was apparently considering taking up a post with PSV as their technical director, but the KNVB enforced his contract, and he was compelled to start the European Championship with the Dutch team.[336]

After England had fallen to an early goal from Ireland's Ray Houghton in the group's afternoon fixture, the Dutch began their programme with a game against the Soviet Union. For Michels there may have been an element of looking in the

---

336 nrc.nl/nieuws/1990/04/02/de-ondergang-van-thijs-libregts-carriere-van-bondscoachgehinderd-6926891-a616134

mirror when glancing across at the other bench. Coaching the Soviets was the legendary figure of Valeriy Lobanovskyi. If Michels was regarded as the Professor, people saw Lobanovskyi as the Scientist. Both were considered pioneers of coaching techniques, and examples of how success could be achieved.

Very much in the mould of Michels in 1970, the Soviet Union coach had built his national team with a strong nucleus from the club side he had developed. Lobanovskyi's strategies had been established with the Dynamo Kiev side during a long association with the club. Going into the tournament, he was in charge of both the national team and his home-town club. More than half of his squad for the European Championship were Kiev players, and the tactics of the national team were based on the success he had enjoyed at club level. 'Under him, Kyiv have been champions seven times, claimed the cup on five occasions and lifted the Cup Winners' Cup in 1975,'[337] *The Times* reported, confirming the coach's pedigeee.

A former engineering student at Kiev Polytechnic Institute, Lobanovskyi earned the Scientist nickname for instilling a robust collective structure to his teams, coupled with an adherence to his tactics. In *Inverting the Pyramid*, Jonathan Wilson described the approach as being, 'meticulously planned, with the team's preparation divided into three levels. Players were to have individual technical coaching so as to equip them better to fulfil the tasks Lobanovskyi set them during a game; specific tactics and tasks for each player were drawn up according to the opponents; and a strategy was devised for a competition as a whole, placing each game in context by acknowledging that it is impossible for a side to maintain maximal levels over a protracted period.'[338] The game-plan was wonderfully aided by the use of two pacey forwards in Igor Belanov and Oleh Protasov. Hitting high balls into space

337 Spartan life for Soviet side built for the 21ˢᵗ Century, *The Times*, 23 June 1988
338 Wilson, Jonathan, *Inverting the Pyramid* (London: Orion, 2014)

over the opposition back line allowed the front men to find space consistently, and drive the defences deeper to counteract the threat.

His players were committed to following the coach's plans, and almost in awe of his presence, as former Kiev and Soviet Union international Sergei Baltacha confirmed. 'Lobanovskyi was everything for Dynamo Kiev and Russian football. Ukraine cannot reach that level now. At that time a lot of people knew the city of Kiev because of Dynamo and because of Lobanovskyi and the players that played for him. He was the best coach I've ever seen. He was a coach who brought a scientific background to football in the early 1970s and, when I joined Kiev in 1976, we had a background of doctors and scientists, the kind of thing that not even now many countries have. He was very tactical, too. We played the kind of pressing game like Barcelona do now. It was a new era for football. As a person he was very demanding and was an example for us because he was a top professional.'[339]

Two years earlier, at the 1986 World Cup, the Soviet Union were only eliminated in controversial fashion by Belgium after extra time, and coming into the European Championship, many pundits considered them as dark horses for the title. In the game against the Dutch, they were to establish their credentials … Michels had resisted the temptation to throw Van Basten into the fray from the start, clearly still less than totally convinced of his fitness. Instead, Gullit was partnered by Bosman, although the Dutch skipper often dropped back into midfield, linking up with Van't Schip, Muhren, Wouters and Vanenburg to overwhelm the outnumbered Soviet quartet.

Early on, the Dutch appeared to be the more accomplished team. Gullit dominated the midfield, and in defence, Rijkaard exerted comfortable control of the Soviet Union forward line,

339 https://www.bbc.com/sport/football/17988895

whilst Koeman prompted attacks from the back. With the vast majority of the 54,000 crowd assembled in Cologne's Mungersdorfer Stadion, bedecked in orange and offering raucous support, *The Times* suggested that 'victory had seemed a formality as the Dutch teased the Soviets with their fluent skills.'[340] If there's a set of players that should appreciate the difference between being the better team and winning the game, however, they surely wear Oranje shirts. Soviet Union goalkeeper and captain Rinat Dasayev made two outstanding saves, first from Koeman and then Gullit to send the teams in level at the break. Seven minutes after the restart, things changed.

A cross by Hennadiy Lytovchenko from the Soviet Union right flank was overhit and running away from the Dutch area. But closing in, exploiting the wide space exposed by the Dutch three-man back line, Vasyl Rats struck the ball first time, across Van Breukelen and into the far corner. It was a strike of rare quality and it put the Soviet Union ahead. Now Lobanovskyi's tactics came to the fore. Minutes later, Michels threw on Van Basten, removing Vanenburg and dropping Gullit deeper to accommodate a front line of Bosman and the substitute. It was to no great avail, however, and despite their earlier comments, *The Times* reported that 'it was the traditional Soviet virtues of organisation and discipline that won the day.'[341]

The Soviet Union would go on to draw with the Republic of Ireland, before defeating England 3-1, to top the group and send Bobby Robson's team home with the wooden spoon. In contrast, the Dutch road to any kind of successful tournament had suddenly become much trickier. Three days after the defeat to the Soviet Union, they would face England in a game that, following opening-day defeats, both teams needed to win.

340 Soviets thrive in hostile environment, *The Times,* 13 June 1988.
341 Soviets thrive in hostile environment, *The Times*, 13 June 1988.

Before the game there was plenty to keep the newspapers busy. The expected hooliganism broke out among England fans, prompting some doyens of Fleet Street to suggest that the FA should withdraw the England team from the tournament.[342] It was a surely a facile suggestion, with not the slightest hope of being accepted. In *The Times*, Stuart Jones carried an article with quotes from Arnold Muhren, who was apparently mystified why Robson, his old club manager at Ipswich Town, hadn't deployed the skills of Glenn Hoddle in the tournament. 'I don't understand the reason for not playing Hoddle. They say he doesn't defend enough but England have five other players who can defend and not one who can do the same job as him.'[343] Whether Muhren's comments were innocent meandering thoughts, or some plan to influence the England manager's selection for the upcoming game is unclear, but when the teams were announced, there were significant changes to both. Robson had removed Neil Webb to slot in Hoddle, with the more dependable Trevor Steven replacing Chris Waddle. Michels had left Van't Schip out for Erwin Koeman and, more importantly, selected Van Basten from the start, replacing Bosman despite apparently having been assured by Michels, '…before the tournament that he was the principal forward. His role and his position has been taken away.'[344] And, given the outcome of the change, Bosman wasn't getting the role back any time soon.

England's main concern may have been Van Basten's Milan team-mate Ruud Gullit. Whilst the striker carried the greater goal threat, it was the dreadlocked skipper of the Oranje who was more likely to take command of the game, much as he had done for long periods against the Soviet Union. There was also the traumatic memory of that night back in March when

342 England should be brought home now, *The Times*, 14 June 1988
343 Dutch advocate makes case for Hoddle's return, *The Times*, 14 June 1988
344 England ditched by the Dutch, *The Times*, 16 June 1988

a Gullit-inspired Oranje all but destroyed England, despite only drawing 2-2 at Wembley. As Stuart Jones suggested in *The Times*, 'Should Gullit, the European Footballer of the Year, again dictate the pattern, England's hopes will be threadbare.'[345] It was a prescient warning.

Managers often lament ill fortune after defeats, but, after losing 3-1, Bobby Robson's claims that 'We have not qualified because we missed chances in the first half'[346] does at least have some semblance of merit. In the first half, they struck the post twice and, after Bryan Robson had equalised Van Basten's opening goal, the balance of play was fairly even. The difference was that, in Van Basten, the Dutch had a cutting edge so razor-sharp that it sliced the young Tony Adams's reputation to shreds, saddling him with the 'donkey' nickname that haunted him for years. The Milan striker's first came two minutes before half-time. The ball was played in by Gullit. He controlled and turned, less than perfectly, but still too adroitly for Adams to intervene, before driving past Shilton.

Robson bundled the ball home for the equaliser ten minutes of playing time later, but when the Dutch stepped up a gear in retaliation, England were left wanting. Both managers then made changes; Vanenburg was again withdrawn to be replaced by a striker, with Gullit dropping back into midfield. This time, with Van Basten already on the field, Bosman was overlooked for Wim Kieft. Minutes later Robson played his card, removing Steven and sending on the attacking talents of Waddle. Three minutes later, came the decisive moment. It was hardly the result of a flowing Dutch move, as Bobby Robson described it. 'Their second was the sort of goal you see every week in the third division.'[347] Even allowing for a little poetic licence by a frustrated manager, it's a harsh assessment.

---

345 Balancing on a knife edge, *The Times*, 15 June 1988
346 England ditched by the Dutch, *The Times*, 16 June 1988
347 England ditched by the Dutch, *The Times*, 16 June 1988

Not many third division clubs have a striker like Van Basten among their number. If they had, they wouldn't be in the third division for long.

A period of head tennis in the England box ended as Gullit again was the architect, neatly controlling, then rolling a pass on to his *Rossoneri* team-mate, who never looked like squandering the opening, drilling the ball inside Shilton's far post ... Robson immediately sent on Mark Hateley for Peter Beardsley, but four minutes later it was all over as Van Basten stabbed home his hat-trick goal at the far post after a right-wing corner was headed on. None of the striker's goals were breathtaking, but each deflated England in their own way. It was a master craftsman at work.

The final two games of the group would be played simultaneously on 18 June. England's sorry venture ended in a humiliating 3-0 defeat to the Soviet Union in Frankfurt, while the Dutch faced Jack Charlton's Republic of Ireland side to see who would progress to the last four along with Lobanovskyi's Soviet Union. Ahead of kick-off the Dutch trailed the Irish by a point, meaning only a win would be good enough for Michels to keep his team on track. It would be a mighty close thing.

The Irish were in a confident frame of mind. Having led the Soviet Union after Ronnie Whelan's spectacular hooked volley, and beating England, the Irish could have been set for the semi-finals already, but for Protasov's equaliser inside the final 15 minutes. They also had a secret weapon, a kind of man on the inside of Dutch football, and much of that was also down to Van Basten. Frank Stapleton, the former Arsenal and Manchester United forward, had joined Ajax at the end of the 1986/87 season as the Amsterdam club sought a replacement after Van Basten's move to Milan. It was a brief stay before returning to England and Derby County on loan after a stopover in Brussels with Anderlecht. Four league games without scoring seems like a paltry amount of time to assess Dutch capabilities but, ahead of the game, Stapleton was happy to discuss his thoughts and, according to Clive White in *The Times*, '… saw enough of Dutch football, before being loaned to Derby County to respect it but not fear it.'[348]

As fate would have it though, that's pretty much how the game panned out. The Dutch had much of the ball and controlled the game for long periods but failed to break down the Irish defence. As time ticked on, the unlikely prospect of the green shirts progressing to the final four grew. Five minutes after the break, Michels sent on Kieft in what was now becoming a regular ploy. This time it was Erwin Koeman who was replaced to allow Gullit to drop back into midfield and add some muscular urgency. Ahead of the game, Jack Charlton had identified the danger of Gullit, but also acknowledged an impotence to do a great deal about it by deploying a man-marker to nullify the danger. 'I learned a long time ago that you can't mark runners, they run where they want to. Besides, we haven't got anyone fast enough to mark Gullit and I doubt whether anyone has in Europe.'[349]

Michels would later declare himself unimpressed by the rugged defensive determination of the Irish, complaining that they attacked less against his team than when facing England and the Soviet Union. It was true, and Charlton would be the last to deny it. It was hardly surprising, as the Irish just needed a draw. They knew their strengths, and played to them. Conversely, it was the Dutch who deserted their normal pattern of play first.

Approaching the last ten minutes, and with the Irish on the cusp on qualification, Michels played his last card. Bosman was sent from the bench to form a three-man strike force with Kieft and Van Basten. The craft of Arnold Muhren was

348 Charlton's men tackle the Dutch, *The Times*, 13 June 1988
349 Reluctant Charlton must leave players to seek bigger fish, *The Times*, 14 June 1988

discarded in favour of an aerial assault on the Irish goal. It had echoes of Michels's forlorn tactic in Munich 14 years earlier, and now he was reprising the plan against a team containing the likes of Moran, McCarthy and McGrath, who had cut their teeth on defending Route One football. It felt a little like desperation. In 1974, the Oranje were deserted by the fates. This time, the fickle caprice of fortune would work in their favour.

With just eight minutes remaining, Gullit was now also thrown forward to join the crowded Ireland penalty area. Receiving the ball, he played it back out to the right flank, from where Wouters swung another hopeful cross into the box. For the umpteenth time, Moran headed clear. The ball fell to Ronald Koeman, whose sweeper role was now largely redundant as the Irish called all hands back to man the redoubt, some 25 metres or so from goal.

Shaping for a right-foot volley, Koeman mishit the effort, driving the ball into the ground directly in front of him, from where it ballooned up into the air. As the Irish advanced to catch the Dutch forwards offside, the ball prescribed a perfect arc towards the fair-headed Kieft who, under pressure, managed to get a glancing header on the ball towards Packie Bonner's goal. Initially, there seemed little danger as the ball's aerial trajectory suggested it would drift wide of the target. As it bounced though, the spin – either imparted by Koeman's scuffed shot, Kieft's head or a combination of both – caused the ball to jag back towards goal, beyond Bonner and inside the post. If a deviation on a bouncing ball had thwarted Rensenbrink in those dramatic last minutes of the 1978 World Cup Final, now it favoured the Oranje.

The Dutch celebrated as much with relief as joy, as the green-shirted players fell to the floor, their defences finally breached. A young Ruud van Nistelrooy witnessed the moment. 'That Ireland game was massive. We won that and I was 12 years old at the time. Euro '88 is still very clear in my mind and the game against Ireland. Wim Kieft scored in the last minutes with this weird header that went in. It was a bit lucky.'[350] It was indeed. If fate owed a debt to the Dutch from 1978, here was a little payback. As Clive White commented in *The Times*, the goal was '… wickedly timed, but thoroughly deserved,'[351] on the balance of play. The Irish may have cursed their luck a little as 'Van Basten was offside as well when Kieft rerouted Koeman's mishit volley past Bonner in goal,'[352] *The Guardian* asserted.

Such fine points meant little as the four semi-finalists lined up. The Dutch had slipped into second place behind the Soviet Union, and would play the winners of the other group. Now under the coaching of Franz Beckenbauer, West Germany had drawn with Italy and beaten both Spain and Denmark, as the cult Danish Dynamite team of the World Cup two years earlier suddenly looked a spent force. It meant that the hosts topped the group with Italy in second place. The *Azzurri* fell to Lobanovskyi's team as the Soviet Union booked a place in the Munich final with a 2-0 win in Stuttgart. The other semi-final would pit the Oranje against old foes, West Germany. Revenge is a dish best served cold, as the old adage goes. It was time for the Dutch to tuck in.

The Dutch had failed to overcome West Germany for 32 years; the last victory coming in 1956 as the burgeoning legend of Abe Lenstra was given extra lustre by scoring both goals in a 2-1 friendly win in Dusseldorf. Since then, across ten games, the Germans had won seven times, drawing the remaining three. The most recent reverse was that 3-1 defeat in Dortmund's Westfalenstadion. For Michels, who was to take

---

350 https://www.the42.ie/wim-kieft-ireland-holland-euro-88-956511-Jun2013/

351 Nature of Dutch goal makes Irish defeat hard to swallow, *The Times*, 19 June 1988

352 https://www.theguardian.com/football/2016/jun/05/france-holland-spain-best-ever-euros-team

up a coaching position with Bundesliga club Bayer Leverkusen at the end of the tournament, *The Times* ventured that it was the opportunity to deliver a victory that his country had 'been waiting a long time,'[353] for. He believed he had the team to achieve it. 'As well as having the necessary skills, they are all clever individuals. It would not have been possible to develop our style if they didn't all have footballing brains. I have taken advantage of that,'[354] the same article continued.

Like Michels, Beckenbauer had enjoyed a rise in popularity since the start of the tournament. He had been hugely criticised for his squad and initial team selection but, after struggling in the early part of their opening game against Italy, they found their stride and comfortably overcame both the Spaniards and Danes 2-0. It meant they qualified unbeaten and having conceded only a single goal. In typically efficient Teutonic use of technology, Beckenbauer had used a helicopter to zip him quickly around the country, allowing him to observe his opponents both in games and training. As Michels remarked, 'He knows more about our side than I do. He has been watching us from the stands.'[355]

Would Beckenbauer's insight allow him to predict Michels's line-up? Some in the press were certainly prepared to indulge in a little prophesying, suggesting that the Dutch had seemed to improve when Michels switched during games to drop Gullit into midfield and add Bosman or Kieft to support Van Basten. Perhaps that was the right way to go from the start in the semi-final. Michels had little care for press speculation, and when the teams were announced, his line-up was unchanged.

Back in 1974, the German press had played a part in upsetting Dutch serenity with the stories of shenanigans in the team hotel. Would there be a repeat? Some thought not. 'In

353 Michels plots a win over his adopted homeland, *The Times*, 21 June 1988
354 Michels plots a win over his adopted homeland, *The Times*, 21 June 1988
355 Michels plots a win over his adopted homeland, *The Times*, 21 June 1988

'88 the press was friendly,'[356] Jan-Hermen de Bruijn recalled. Perhaps that was true with regards to stories in the newspapers, but other methods were less equitable. In *Football against the Enemy*, Simon Kuper related: 'At 1am on the night before the match, a German journalist rang Gullit, the Dutch captain, in his [hotel] room to ask which club he had played for before joining AC Milan. Later than night the phone rang again, and as Gullit reported, "someone made a ridiculous remark". Then a German journalist knocked on his door.'[357] Perhaps not so "friendly" after all.

But it was the Germans who suffered a problem ahead of kick-off, when Pierre Littbarski, who has started every game so far, was taken ill during the warm-up. Borussia Dortmund's Frank Mill was drafted in as a replacement, and Littbarski wouldn't feature in the game until the last ten minutes.

Around this era, and for some time to come, any games between these two countries always carried more than a little extra baggage; add in any tournament consequences, and the elastic tension would be stretched to snapping point. This was no exception. Although the first half of the game passed without any scoring, it was clearly the Dutch in control. Despite only around 7,000 of the 56,000 fans in Hamburg's Volksparkstadion being official Dutch supporters, many more had garnered tickets from unofficial sources. Oranje voices chanting 'Give us back our bicycles', a comment based on the German requisition of all Dutch bicycles during the occupation, both confirmed their number in the stadium and that there was still plenty of animosity. 'Holland played some of the best football seen in Europe that decade. They treated the Germans as if they were Luxembourgeois, but failed to score,'[358] Simon Kuper said in *Football against the*

356 De Bruijn, Jan-Hermen – Interview with the author
357 Kuper, Simon, *Football against the Enemy* (London: Orion, 1994)
358 Kuper, Simon, *Football against the Enemy* (London: Orion, 1994)

Enemy. Only a late intervention by Jurgen Kohler foiled Van Basten a dozen minutes into the game, and then Gullit lifted a clear chance over the bar. Possession was protected jealously, and the interchange of positions, with Gullit dropping deep on occasions, caused problems for the German midfield, but the back line held firm. Just a minute before the break, that defensive solidity was threatened when the German sweeper Matthias Herget collided with Gullit, and tore a thigh muscle. He was replaced by the inexperienced Hans Pflugler.

The second half began with the Germans adopting a more robust stance. Perhaps believing they had allowed the Dutch too much latitude in the first period, Beckenbauer had sent his team out in determined fashion, and with a will to impose themselves on the game. In his book, Simon Kuper suggested that, 'The Germans came out for the second half with a new tactic; kicking Dutchmen. The Dutch retaliated, and the match grew even more intense.'[359] It led to some hefty challenges, that the Dutch weren't slow in returning. Raphael Honigstein understood the significance of the game to the Dutch. 'I think 1988 mattered to the Dutch because of 1974.'[360] If the game was important to the Dutch, it also mattered to the Germans of course, and they were never going to bend the knee in their own backyard without a fight.

In contrast, it was the lightest of contacts that led to the opening goal, as the composure of Michels's team melted away in the ferocious heat of the battle. Eight minutes after the restart, Jurgen Klinsmann drove into the Netherlands' penalty area, drawing Rijkaard forward to meet the threat. As he did so, the striker stumbled over the Dutchman's leg and plunged to the turf. It was certainly not a clear *schwalbe*, but given Klinsmann's well-established reputation in such matters, there's plenty of room for conjecture. Romanian referee Ioan

359 Kuper, Simon, *Football against the Enemy* (London: Orion, 1994)
360 Honigstein, Raphael – Interview with the author

Igna was in an ideal position to judge the incident, and he had little hesitation in pointing to the spot.

Michels stood on the touchline, arms akimbo, oozing frustration that his team had been led away from the established pattern and suckered into a period of play always likely to end this way. Lothar Matthaus, the 'most German player'[361] in Simon Kuper's words, was already a figure of hate for many Dutch fans and, as he and Igna debated the precise place from which the penalty should be struck, hopes rose that perhaps the delay would distract the German captain's concentration. Such hopes were forlorn. Despite Van Breukelen getting a firm hand to the ball, it still found the back of the net. Through all of the delay, Beckenbauer had stood impassively observing, serene with arms folded. He had expected nothing less from his skipper. Three minutes later, Kieft arrived in exchange for Arnold Muhren.

For the following 20 minutes, the Dutch only confirmed that they had lost their sense of direction. Frustration bubbled up and discipline disappeared in the froth of emotion. For a period, it looked like the pattern of the last three decades would be repeated. It took another controversial moment to turn things back in favour of the Dutch. Edging towards the final 25 minutes, a long ball found Van Basten on the edge of the penalty area policed by Brehme and Kohler. Controlling, he dragged the ball into the right-hand side of the area, with the Bayern Munich centre-back in dutiful attendance. Seeing a chance to tackle, Kohler jabbed out a foot to divert the ball away and Van Basten stumbled to the floor.

For the avoidance of any doubt, perhaps the key second was when Van Basten sought to regain his footing and possession. He was stopped by a blast from Igna's whistle. The Romanian may have been the only man in the stadium

---

361 Kuper, Simon, *Football against the Enemy* (London: Orion, 1994)

who saw an offence committed. Simon Kuper related that there had been a warning of kinds. 'UEFA should have spotted the referee's deficient powers of observation before, when they had mistakenly given him and his linesmen plane tickets for Stuttgart instead of Hamburg, the trio dutifully flew to the wrong city.'[362]

Again, there was no question of a *schwalbe*, just as there was no question of a penalty. Ronald Koeman was unmoved by any doubts, and he sent Immel the wrong way to equalise. The mind quickly raced back 12 years. 'The semi-final ... had weird echoes of the 1974 final, and not just because of the Second World War; there were penalties at both ends and the winners got back into the match through a dodgy spot kick,'[363] *The Guardian* reported. To borrow a quotation from the late commentator Brian Moore, who was giving the game his avid attention for ITV viewers, as the game headed towards a dramatic climax: 'It's all up for grabs now.'

Then came the moment, inside the final couple of minutes, and fittingly, it was a goal of quality. *The Guardian* painted the picture. 'Van Basten's last-minute winner could have been scripted by Hitchcock; a sudden, shocking thrust after a seemingly innocuous move. It came from the back, where Holland won Total Football bingo throughout the tournament by playing a central-defensive pair of Koeman and Rijkaard. At a time when everyone else had stoppers at the back, they had starters – as Koeman showed with the penetrative pass to Jan Wouters that led to Van Basten's goal.'[364] Racing on to Wouters' slide-rule pass, the striker stretched out a long right leg and hooked the ball ahead of Kohler, past Immel and into the far corner of the net.

362 Kuper, Simon, *Football against the Enemy* (London: Orion, 1994)
363 https://www.theguardian.com/football/2016/jun/05/france-holland-spain-best-ever-euros-team
364 https://www.theguardian.com/football/2016/jun/05/france-holland-spain-best-ever-euros-team

On a night with so many echoes of that final in Munich back in 1974 – on German soil, two penalties, one highly dubious, a team going ahead and then losing out, even the winning goals had similarities, the only difference being this time all the goals came in the second half, rather than the first period – only the most poetic of words can capture the moment. 'A night of dark memories and seeming redemption unfolded, with the intensity of a final duel in a Sergio Leone revenge Western,'[365] David Winner said in *Brilliant Orange*. Commentating for Dutch television, Evert ten Napel summed up Dutch emotion. 'Justice, at last!'[366]

The victory was more important to the Dutch than defeat was to the Germans, if Raphael Honigstein's recollections of the time are valid. 'Hamburg was full of Dutch fans, and Hamburg being quite a reserved city, it didn't seem to be providing much support for the German team. I don't remember it as such a big deal that they lost in the semi-final. Perhaps because I wasn't such a big fan of the national team at the time. They didn't have the same kind of support in Germany at the time, simply because in the '80s they were playing pretty crap football.'[367]

If 'Thirty years of hurt, never stopped me dreaming,'[368] imagine what remembering a hated period of history and 32 years without a victory can do to inspire a team, and indeed celebrations. David Winner again, this time when speaking to the Irish website www.the42.ie. 'The Dutch grew to despise [the Germans]. After the … the semi-final … Ronald Koeman wiped his backside with Olaf Thon's jersey. The next year, when the teams clashed in Rotterdam, a banner in the home section likened Lothar Matthaus to Hitler.'[369] Whilst the

365 Winner, David, *Brilliant Orange* (London: Bloomsbury, 2000)
366 https://dutchreview.com/culture/history/dutch-german-football-rivalry/
367 Honigstein, Raphael – Interview with the author
368 'Three Lions' was a song by The Lightning Seeds, Frank Skinner and David Baddiel
369 https://www.the42.ie/holland-1974-world-cup-tragedy-1488354-Mar2016/

banner is perhaps the most personally offensive, the Koeman incident seemed more of an egregious affront to Germans in general. Raphael Honigstein suggested that most Germans took a more mature view of the incident. 'I don't think it was seen very much as an insult to the nation, as just bad sportsmanship.'[370]

It was hardly neighbourly, but neither were the events that had fuelled the animosity and there was still plenty of reflections about the past. *The Independent* reported the emotions of some Dutch players. Still, much bitterness lurked in some Dutch hearts. Goalkeeper Hans van Breukelen declared, 'I had been waiting for that moment for 14 years. Before the game I remembered my feelings watching TV as a teenager, and that boosted my anger. I am happy to have given a gift to the older generation who lived through the war.' Even the relaxed and philosophical Gullit said, 'We gave joy to the older generation, I saw their emotion, I saw their tears.'[371]

There was plenty of joy for the players as well, as David Winner wrote in *Brilliant Orange*, 'After the match, they danced the conga and sang "We're going to Munich." ... While back at the Intercontinental [the team hotel], Prince John-Friso, the Queen's second son, joined in for the Dutch version of "Can you hear the Germans sing?"'[372] It was festival time back home in the Netherlands too – Winner continued his account of the celebrations. 'The men in orange had beaten the hated Germans 2-1 and the Dutch – the sober, sensible, calm and careful Dutch – went completely, utterly, entirely out of their minds with joy. In the minutes after the game, most of the population on the Netherlands spilled out on to the tidy streets, drinking, singing, blowing bicycles into the

---

370 Honigstein, Raphael – Interview with the author
371 A Holland v Germany final? Fate may hand the Dutch a chance to settle old scores, *The Independent*, 6 July 2010
372 Winner, David, *Brilliant Orange* (London: Bloomsbury, 2000)

air, setting off fireworks, cavorting in anything orange they could lay their hands on. About nine million of them threw the biggest party the country had seen since the Liberation. The celebrations went on for four days.'[373] On the fourth day of celebrations, the final would follow.

The problem was that they hadn't won anything yet and, while it was difficult to rein in the understandable excitement of beating the Germans, there was still the final to play, and that against a team that had beaten them earlier in the tournament. Finals and the Dutch were already ill-suited bedfellows, as Rob Smyth wrote in *The Guardian*. 'After the World Cup misery of the 1970s, the Dutch had an understandable fear of finals, which made it even crueller that they had to play two of them to win Euro '88. The historical importance of the semi-final against West Germany was such that, to some of the players and most of the country, the final against the USSR was almost an afterthought.'[374] Michels had first-hand experience of losing a final, and was wary that his players should keep their eyes on the prize. On the eve of the final, the players had presented him with a gold watch as a memento of the victory over Germany. The coach accepted the gift with all good grace, but cautioned them that if they lost the final he would return it. Additionally, five members of the squad had already experienced more recent final disappointments. Muhren, Winter, Wouters, Van't Schip and Bosman, coached by Hulshoff, had been part of the Ajax team that lost the Cup Winners' Cup Final to KV Mechelen.

The Soviet Union side also had issues to contend with. Kuvnetsov's unfortunate yellow card, added to one sustained in the early rounds of the qualifying competition, made him ineligible to play in the final. The man who had successfully

373 Winner, David, *Brilliant Orange* (London: Bloomsbury, 2000)
374 https://www.theguardian.com/football/2016/jun/05/france-holland-spain-best-ever-euros-team Rob Smyth

policed Luca Vialli in the semi-final would have doubtless been detailed to perform a similar function against Van Basten, but that option was lost to Lobanovskyi. His solution was to drop Sergei Aleinikov back. It was a Michels-esque move, not too dissimilar to his decision to move Haan into a centre-back role for the 1974 World Cup. Just as in 1974, when Haan's defensive frailties were finally exposed, the gamble would fail. As well as missing Aleinikov in midfield, he was a less than suitable replacement for Kuvnetsov. The other problem was that Protasov was not fully fit following an injury sustained against the Italians. His importance to the Soviets' pattern of play meant that he was risked but the decision backfired. With his leg heavily strapped, he lasted for a mainly ineffectual 70 minutes before being replaced, by which time the game was, to all intents and purposes, lost.

At 3.30pm on 25 June 1988, the Oranje and Rinus Michels returned to Munich's Olympiastadion. In 1974, the better final would have been the Netherlands against Poland; four years later, the two best footballing sides were the Dutch and Brazil, but the latter were denied by highly debatable means. This time, the two best teams, led by the best coaches in the tournament, would contest the final.

It would be wrong to say the sides were evenly matched, as they had different strengths, but when the game began it quickly became clear that there was plenty of mutual respect. If anything, the Soviets had the better of the opening exchanges, with Lytovchenko impressive. Clear-cut chances were few and far between, but each team took tender care of possession. Long passes, other than when accurately driven, were almost non-existent, as short, crisp passing dominated. Once more, it was Rijkaard stepping forward as the dominant figure in the Dutch back line each time Lobanovskyi's side pressed, and when the first goal came, it was slightly against the run of play.

'For 30 minutes they were the better team,'[375] Michels later conceded, but goals change games, and that's what happened.

Midway through the first period, Belanov created a chance for Lytovchenko, but his shot was saved by Van Breukelen. A goal was coming, though. Approaching the half-hour mark, Dasayev acrobatically tipped a Gullit free kick over the bar. Erwin Koeman swung the corner in from the right. At the near post, Gullit tried to flick the ball on, but it struck a defender and was blocked back out towards Koeman. Delivering another cross on the run, the ball flighted towards Van Basten a dozen yards or so from Dasayev's goal. The tournament's top scorer had been fairly anonymous up to that point, but when the ball came to him, he realised that trying to score with his head from that range was hopeful at best. Instead he nodded the ball back across goal. Reading his intention, after retreating to avoid any offside decision, Gullit turned and homed in on the ball as it floated towards him. In their rush to clear the area, the Dutch captain had been left unmarked by the defenders. He leapt on the six-yard line and thumped a header into the net. There was little finesse about the strike, with dreadlocks flying as if adding extra impetus, but the power of the header defeated Dasayev. The players piled on top of their ecstatic skipper. Orange shirts, scarves, hats and banners exalted and, on the bench, Michels stood and applauded. It felt like a dam – or perhaps more appropriately a dyke – had been breached, and relief as much as joy was now flooding over the Dutch.

It was a severe blow for the Soviet Union, and they battled to get back into the game. For the remainder of the half the Dutch midfield assumed a measure of control with Wouters working hard and Gullit dropping in to support. It ensured the score stayed the same at half-time, and ten minutes into the second period, the game was all but settled with one of

375 Jones, Stuart, Dutch unveil final masterpiece, *The Times,* 26 June 1988

the most spectacular goals ever scored in a major final. A poor touch by Olexandr Zavarov allowed Adri van Tiggelen to intercept and feed Arnold Muhren, advancing in the Soviet Union half of the field, wide on the left flank. He hit the ball first time, crossing towards the far post. The pass looked to be overhit, most probably because it was.

Watching the ball, Van Basten dropped deeper and deeper towards the right-hand side of the area, eventually almost standing on the line of the box, a couple of metres from the goal line when the ball reached him. As with his assist for Gullit's strike, any effort on goal would surely be fatally compromised by both distance and the most acute of angles. A ball back across the box was surely the only option. Gullit was already in the box, with support arriving from Van Tiggelen. They wouldn't be needed. Admitting afterwards that he was too tired to do much else, instead he lashed his right foot at the ball on the volley. With all the accuracy of a cruise missile, the ball flew towards goal, then dipped over Dasayev's head to find the far side of the net. It was impulsive. It was impudent. It was incredible. Dasayev seemed stunned by the turn of events – who wasn't? – as he staggered around his goal line as if struck by a knockout blow.

On the bench, well actually now off the bench, the Dutch coach who had suffered as he watched his team lose 14 years earlier, was overcome by Van Basten's strike. He turned away, arms in the air, lost in ecstasy, as reflected by an article from *The Guardian*. '[That] astonishing volley left Michels staggering around dazed on the touchline, his hand over his face in gratitude and disbelief. He was the Godfather of Total Football and a culture obsessed with striving for perfection, but not even he thought it could actually be achieved.'[376] It was now highly unlikely that he would be returning that

376 https://www.theguardian.com/football/2016/jun/05/france-holland-spain-best-ever-euros-team

gold watch. There would be a heart-stopping, if not watch-stopping, moment or two to endure before everything was confirmed though.

As in the first period, the Soviet Union had probably come out of the break the better side, but were now two goals astray. To have any hopes of redemption, they needed a rapid riposte, and if they could choose who the chances should fall to, they would surely have nominated Belanov. It wasn't their day, though. Nothing was going to dislodge the iron-clad grip the Dutch now had on their destiny. First the Dynamo Kiev player struck a post then, minutes later, a rush of blood to the head led Van Breukelen into an ill-judged chase of the ball and a foul on Sergey Gotsmanov. It gave French referee Michel Vautrot the easiest of decisions, and he pointed to the penalty spot.

Belanov was forced to wait while Gotsmanov received treatment. If he scored, there would be enough time for the Soviet Union to chase down an equaliser. They had played well, and on the balance of the game probably deserved to at least be level. It was a pressure moment, both for Belanov who, in his entire professional career would take 12 penalties, and would only fail to score once, and Van Breukelen, whose impulsive error had thrown his opponents a lifeline. The PSV goalkeeper had a trick up his sleeve.

Back in the 1970s, an aspiring Dutch coach named Jan Reker began compiling a series of index cards detailing players and their penalty techniques. In 1980, he took over as caretaker coach at PSV after Kees Rijvers left, and was then officially appointed to the position when Thijs Libregts moved to Feyenoord in 1983. Van Breukelen joined the club the season after, and worked under Reker for a couple of years. It gave him the opportunity to utilise the data on his coach's index cards. Even after Reker left in 1986, Van Breukelen often called on him ahead of international games to check out the data on potential opponents should a penalty be awarded against him.

A month earlier in a shoot-out, against Benfica, his penalty save from Veloso had won the European Cup for PSV Eindhoven, with Reker's help. 'I always wanted to know as much as possible about the opponent. That's why I always called Jan briefly. That is how Veloso was also in the box of Jan. Reker had indicated that he often shot to the right of the keeper. That is why I deliberately kept that angle a bit bigger. When he took his run, he only looked at the ball. That allowed me to go into the corner earlier and to stop his effort quite simply.'[377] Now he was tapping into what he had been told about Belanov.

As the striker waited, a number of Dutch players took the opportunity to whisper into his ear. What they were saying isn't known, but it was unlikely to be encouragement. Eventually, minutes later, everything was ready. Belanov took a long run-up and struck the ball hard and low to the goalkeeper's right. Watching the video again, it looks like Van Breukelen is already committed to throwing himself low to the right before the ball is kicked. The early movement makes the save look so much simpler than it surely was. Had Reker been able to tip the wink to Van Breukelen? The goalkeeper seems happy enough to suggest that he had. 'The same went for Belanov's penalty kick in the European Championship Final against the Soviet Union. I knew where Belanov was going to shoot. I also had information about this from Jan Reker.'[378]

The two misses put paid to the Soviet Union's hopes. Lobanovskyi removed the struggling Protasov in what was almost an acceptance of defeat ... In the last part of the game, the Dutch could even have scored again as all the fight

377 https://nos.nl/artikel/231028-van-breukelen-klem-moeten-hebben.html
378 http://thegreatmatch.com/great-matches/hans-breukelen-geinformeerde-penaltykiller/

appeared to drain away from their opponents. The great irony was that in the two World Cup Finals they had lost, the Dutch had been the better team. In 1988, when they lifted the trophy, many would argue that the Soviet Union were superior.

'It was the best chance for the Soviet Union to win a trophy,' Sergei Baltacha said. 'At that time, we were a good team, most of our players were from Kiev and we dominated Europe. We really thought we could win that tournament in Germany.'[379]

Instead, it was the Dutch, triumphant in Munich at last. In his last game before moving on to take up a coaching role at Bayer Leverkusen, Michels had led the Dutch to a major international title, European champions. He would return for one final mission a couple of years later, but for now his job was done. He would hand over the squad as winners, boosted by the huge talents of Gullit, Rijkaard, Koeman and Van Basten, all of whom were approaching the peak of their powers.

They were the team of the moment, if not perhaps the greatest of Dutch teams, certainly in the opinions of Rob Smyth. 'I'd say the 1988 team had more luck than the 1970s teams. They could, probably should, have gone out in the group stage, and even in the final they weren't particularly dominant. Their best performance was against West Germany in the semi-final. But style can create the illusion of substance, and the astonishing quality of Marco van Basten's goal in particular has altered memories of what went before. They were still a lovely side to watch – and any team with a centre-back pairing of Koeman and Rijkaard deserves to succeed – but I think 1974 was a slightly superior team.'[380] Jan-Willem Bult does not disagree. Perhaps winning isn't the only definition of greatness. Beauty has a virtue all of its own. 'Even though the

379 https://spielverlagerung.com/2016/04/01/team-analysis-valeriy-lobanovskyis-ussr/?doing_wp_cron=1591608575.0741200447082519531250
380 Smyth, Rob, Author and journalist – Interview with the author

generation Gullit, Van Basten, Rijkaard, Koeman was the first to win an international prize with the national team, they are always saying that the 1974 team was the best.'[381]

In typical Dutch fashion, the title had been won after three consecutive qualification failures, the World Cups in 1982 and 1986, and the European Championship in 1984. Running up until 2020, they would only fail to qualify for one more major tournament, the World Cup of 2002. Two years after the success in Germany, the World Cup was to be held in Italy, and the Oranje would surely be among the favourites to win the trophy. They could finally shake off the bridesmaids trappings. It would be their big day … When the Dutch returned home to Amsterdam, they were greeted by around a million people. They were all looking forward to an even bigger party in Italy.

… and tomorrow 1988–2000

The man charged with getting the Oranje to the church on time was former PSV coach, Thijs Libregts; although, as with Fadrhonc and Zwartkruis, he would be denied the opportunity to walk them up the aisle.

Libregts had left Eindhoven in 1983, to be replaced by Reker, and spent a season with Feyenoord, where he delivered the league and cup double. His time in Rotterdam also included an unsavoury episode involving Ruud Gullit. Reports suggest that the coach criticised Gullit for being lazy and apparently used a racist description for the player that he later defended as merely being a nickname, bereft of any insulting or discriminatory intent.[382] Gullit was understandably unimpressed by the explanation. It was a simmering issue that would come to the boil years later.

---

381 Bult, Jan-Willem – Interview with the author
382 Glanville, Brian, *Footballers Don't Cry* (London: Virgin 1999)

In November 1984, Libregts left Dutch domestic football for an odyssey around Greece. First, he joined Aris Thessaloniki for two seasons, before moving on to PAOK for a brief period and then Olympiacos, without enjoying outstanding success at any of the clubs. It was therefore a typical left-field sort of appointment when, in 1987, under the chairmanship of Andre van der Louw, the KNVB contracted him to take over the national team following the 1988 European Championship.

Despite the opportunity to take over a successful team, brimming with confidence and with potential to improve, Libregts was less than enthusiastic about picking up the baton from Michels, given the success he and the team had enjoyed. Following the great man suddenly looked an insurmountable challenge.

Nevertheless, on 14 September 1988, Libregts took charge of the Netherlands in pursuit of qualification for the 1990 World Cup. With the fickle fancy of fortune up to its mischievous best, the Dutch were placed into Group Four, alongside Wales, Finland and as if merely to stir up trouble, West Germany. With two teams qualifying, though, perhaps the omens were in fact pretty positive. The two strong teams were likely to win most of their matches against the pair of weaker teams.

In the first of the qualifiers, the new man appeared to have changed very little. Ten of the starting XI that had beaten the Soviet Union were on the team sheet. The only absentee was Arnold Muhren, who had brought down the curtain on his international career. In his place, Libregts drafted in Hendrie Kruzen, signed by champions PSV from Den Bosch. When the team took the field it wasn't in the 4-4-2 formation of Michels. Instead, Ronald Koeman, Rijkaard and Van Tiggelen formed a back three with Wouters at the base of a midfield diamond, Gullit at its point and Erwin Koeman and Van Aerle on the flanks. Further forward, Van Basten was supported by

Vanenburg and Kruzen. It looked an unnecessarily careful set-up for a home match against Wales, who had six players from outside the top tier of English football, including two from the third tier.

The Dutch started well and dominated the game for the first 45 minutes, but the Welsh defended resolutely, with Barry Horne dogging the steps of Gullit. Despite a few half-chances, the scoreline was blank at the break. For the second period, Libregts shuffled things around, pushing Ronald Koeman into an advanced midfield position, leaving just Rijkaard and Van Tiggelen to deal with any sporadic Welsh forays. It also meant that Gullit could push further forward to support Van Basten. Past the hour mark, Kieft came on for Vanenburg, but still Wales held firm. The breakthrough finally came inside the final ten minutes when Ronald Koeman crossed to an unmarked Gullit from a quickly taken free kick. His header smashed against Neville Southall's crossbar, but he was quickest to the rebound to notch the winning goal.

Then came the return to Munich's Olympiastadion to face a West German side bent on revenge in front of nearly 70,000 fans. Sonny Silooy was at the time playing for French team Racing Club, although later that same year he would join Ajax, and Libregts brought him into the starting XI in place of Kruzen. Using a 3-5-2 formation, the coach hoped to cover for Gullit, absent through injury as would repeatedly be the case throughout a troubled season for the Dutch skipper, by overloading in midfield with Wouters, Van Aerle and Silooy forming a solid line behind Vanenburg and Erwin Koeman, with Bosman joining Van Basten in attack.

It was an understandably tense battle, but the opening phase clearly favoured the Germans and when Van Aerle had to leave the field inside 20 minutes, to be replaced by Aron Winter, it hardly improved the Dutch coach's state of mind. This was the game when the banner comparing Matthaus to

Hitler was unveiled. The game would continue to see the home side press more, but at the final whistle, it was the Dutch who were the happier to take home a point.

In a break from the rigours of qualification, the Dutch played three successive friendly games, offering a chance for Libregts to experiment a little. They visited Italy in November and the coach gave debuts to four players, and second caps to two more, as the *Azzurri* triumphed thanks to a Vialli goal. Four days into the New Year, another friendly, this time against Israel, saw another new cap as Rob Witschge came off the bench, and the debutants from the Italy game added another cap. Finally, a slightly more recognisable team defeated Lobanovskyi's Soviet Union 2-0 at Eindhoven's Philips Sportpark in a repeat of the European Championship Final. The next game would also carry memories of that championship, as West Germany visited the Stadion de Kuip on 26 April.

Injury deprived Libregts of Van Breukelen, Wouters and Gullit for what was the pivotal game of the group, and the coach switched back to a 3-4-3 formation. Feyenoord's Joop Hiele earned the fifth cap of his truncated international career, almost nine years after his debut. In front of the regular back three, the selection of Aron Winter and Wim Hofkens, both known more for their obdurate defensive abilities than any forward flair, formed the centre of the midfield, flanked by Erwin Koeman and Van Aerle. Van Basten was supported by Vanenburg and Pieter Huistra, who had featured in all of the recent friendlies.

In another tense game, this time it was the Dutch who enjoyed the greater share of possession. A shot on the turn by Karl-Heinz Riedle nearly gave the Germans a chance as the ball appeared to strike the hand of a falling Ronald Koeman. Swedish referee Erik Fredriksson was unimpressed and play was waved on. The Dutch continued to press, but the break was reached without any score. After the restart, Hiele unnecessarily chased a pass to Riedle that appeared to be running out of play, and then slid in on a challenge, catching the striker near the junction of penalty area and goal line ... Replays suggest a penalty may well have been given, but the goalkeeper escaped as Fredriksson placed the ball outside of the area.

There would be no escape as the game passed the 70-minute mark. A series of niggly fouls had broken up any semblance of flow and, when Erwin Koeman tumbled Reuter midway into the Netherlands half, the price would be paid. Andreas Moller delivered the perfect cross for Riedle to power home a diving header. Libregts responded by sending on Groningen's in-form striker Rene Eijkelkamp. Time was now on the Germans' side and they guarded possession as the Dutch chased and harried with increased urgency. Committing more and more men forward, a killer second goal nearly came on the break as Thomas Hassler fed Moller into space with just Hiele to beat, but he dragged his shot wide of the far post. It would be a costly miss. Just as in Hamburg ten months earlier, the 88th minute would be decisive, and it would be Van Basten's time again.

Three minutes earlier, Graeme Rutjes had entered the field to replace Hofkens, but it would be the earlier substitute who rolled a pass for Ronald Koeman to shoot from distance. Standing in as captain for Gullit, Koeman pulled it well wide of Bodo Illgner's goal. Unerringly, however, it travelled directly towards Van Basten, lurking some eight metres from goal, who turned it home joyously.

The Dutch escaped with a point and when, in the next round of games, the Germans could only achieve a goalless draw in Cardiff, it meant that if the Dutch could win their remaining fixtures, they would top the group. They duly did, winning 1-0 in Finland, 2-1 against Wales in Wrexham and 3-0 at home to the Finns. Qualification was achieved as they topped the group with an unbeaten record. The Netherlands were heading for Italy, but Libregts would not be going with them. In November the Oranje lost a friendly 1-0 to Brazil. It was Libregts' last game as coach of the Netherlands.

In reality, the die had probably been cast before the away game in Finland, when the relationship with Gullit was laid bare. A couple of incidents later reported by the Dutch press told the story. '[In] an absolute highlight of his position of power ... on the eve of Finland [v] the Netherlands Gullit [sent] Libregts out of the hall after a tactical discussion as [if the coach was] a schoolboy, because he only [wanted] to deliberate with the players of the Dutch national team. The rest of the group of players [agreed with] the behaviour of· the [captain].'[383] In football parlance, the coach had 'lost the dressing-room' or at least the respect of the players in it. According to Gullit, Libregts was also ridiculed by team-mates. 'During a conversation, Frank Rijkaard and Marco van Basten suddenly burst out laughing. Gullit didn't know why at first. "I had been sleeping on the plane. Later I found out that [they] had been [mocking] Libregts all the time during the flight."'[384]

The next fixture would be a visit to Kiev for a friendly against the Soviet Union on 28 March. With the players' respect for the coach diminished, the outcome appeared inevitable. As Jan-Hermen de Bruijn related, it came as the players assembled at the Hilton Hotel at Schiphol International Airport, three days earlier. A meeting was called and a vote taken as to whether the squad wanted Libregts to continue in his role.[385] No one voted in his favour. 'The decision was made ... by 15 international players from the selection of

383 https://www.nrc.nl/nieuws/1990/04/02/de-ondergang-van-thijs-libregts-carriere-van-bondscoachgehinderd-6926891-a616134
384 https://www.rtlnieuws.nl/node/2313476
385 De Bruijn, Jan-Hermen – Interview with the author

23 called up for the friendly match. Among the footballers who exercised their right to vote in the team is captain Ruud Gullit, despite being injured and his participation in the Italian World Cup being in doubt, the brothers Ronald and Erwin Koeman, Marco van Basten and Frank Rijkaard, from Milan, Van Breukelen, the goalkeeper of PSV Eindhoven, and Hiele, of Feyenoord. Gullit was the first international to rebel against the coach and his differences date back to his time as a Feyenoord player, where he [clashed] with Libregts six years ago. He [had] already launched harsh criticism against him [during the previous] season.'[386]

The coach had never enjoyed an easy relationship with the press or many of the squad. 'Since his appointment as national coach, Libregts has been bombarded with often nuanced criticism both in the press and from the player group. Libregts was portrayed in those comments as arrogant, distant, cynical. … Time and time again stories were raised about discriminatory remarks that Libregts made about Ruud Gullit. The national team coach denied this at an early stage: "They call me grey, Rinus Israel cross-eyed, Waslander red. Maybe someone yells at Gullit black. The smear makes me sick." The usually friendly Gullit [based] his irreconcilable attitude on Libregts' harrowing, discriminatory statements,'[387] the www. nrc.nl news website reported. History was coming back to haunt the coach. Another news website, http://rtlnieuws.nl, suggested that differences between Gullit and Libregts were irreconcilable. 'Libregts had said in an interview that black footballers were somewhat lazy. He meant me by that,' Gullit explained. He said it was not the only incident. 'There was no chemistry and the national coach was not above the players.'[388]

386 https://elpais.com/diario/1990/03/27/deportes/638488807_850215.html

387 https://www.nrc.nl/nieuws/1990/04/02/de-ondergang-van-thijs-libregts-carriere-van-bondscoachgehinderd-6926891-a616134

388 https://rtlnieuws.nl/?html5=true&referrer=https%3A%2F%2Fwww.rtlnieuws.nl%2Fnode%2F2313476

Weeks earlier, aware of disquiet, the coach had said that he would only resign if all of the players were in favour of him going. That criteria had now been fulfilled. A further ballot was then taken on who should be appointed in his place. The information from both votes was passed to the KNVB. The problem for Libregts was the widely held perception that Gullit was far more important to the success of the team than the coach; a position strengthened by the votes of the players. Gullit's influence was now at its zenith, as the www.nrc.nl website confirmed. 'At Feyenoord, Gullit was no more than a good football player under Libregts, but via PSV and AC Milan he has now been transformed into one of the absolute stars in football. Such players have the power to behead a national team coach.'[389]

A couple of days later, information released by the KNVB was carried in newspapers across Europe. 'The Royal Dutch Football Federation (KNVB) yesterday informed Thijs Libregts, coach of the national team, of the negative and unanimous vote of the team against his presence as starting coach during the upcoming World Cup in Italy. Libregts will file a complaint against the KNVB on Friday, as he intends to fulfil his contract until July 1, the date it expires, and accompany the team to Italy. The coach himself assured a few weeks ago that he would only resign if all the players rejected him, a promise that he is now not ready to fulfil.'[390]

The simmering argument had come to the boil. Libregts was removed from his post. The www.nrc.nl website suggested that it was a 'difficult matter to digest for a trainer like Libregts, who has qualified unbeaten – above West Germany – for the World Championship in Italy and for whom the

389 https://www.nrc.nl/nieuws/1990/04/02/de-ondergang-van-thijs-libregts-carriere-
     van-bondscoachgehinderd-6926891-a616134
390 https://elpais.com/diario/1990/03/27/deportes/638488807_850215.html

lucrative offers from abroad were waiting. In view of the events at the moment, he should actually be a folk hero. Rather, the opposite is the case.'[391] The court case would be messy and serve no great purpose to any party, other than to top up the bulging bank accounts of lawyers. There was no chance of Libregts returning.

If an eleventh-hour change of coach sounds like a typical example of Dutch football plucking the potential chaos of change from the comfort of an unbeaten qualifying process, there's more than a grain of logic to having a new coach come in ahead of a tournament. In the World Cups of 1974 and 1978, Michels and then Happel were parachuted in to take over and the Oranje prospered to reach successive finals. Again, in the 1988 European Championship, Michels' late return had a similar effect. Only in the European Championship of 1976 did they enter the tournament with the same coach who had seen them through the entire qualification process. The outcome was not encouraging. The big question now was who would be in charge when the team went to Italy.

That second vote taken at the Hilton suggested the players had a strong preference. After serving three years as coach at Ajax, twice winning the KNVB Cup and then the Cup Winners' Cup, Johan Cruyff returned to Catalunya taking up the coach's position at the Camp Nou in 1988. Success quickly followed as the *Blaugrana* won the Cup Winners' Cup in his first season, followed by the Copa del Rey in 1990, before launching into a period of domestic dominance and continental success with his Barcelona 'Dream Team'. In 1974 the KNVB had appointed a Barcelona coach to lead the team into the World Cup; the votes cast suggested this squad was keen on a repeat. Jan-Hermen de Bruijn related that the count

391 https://www.nrc.nl/nieuws/1990/04/02/de-ondergang-van-thijs-libregts-carriere-van-bondscoachgehinderd-6926891-a616134

was 'Cruyff 8 votes, Beenhakker [coach at Ajax] 3 votes and Aad de Mos [coach at Mechelen] 2.'[392]

By this time, Michels had returned to the KNVB as technical director and was charged with appointing the coach to take the Oranje into the World Cup. Given his success at tournaments, he was surely the right man for the task, and many expected his long-time disciple to be anointed, as the players had clearly indicated would be the popular choice. They would be disappointed, Jan-Hermen de Bruijn suggested. 'Michels only spoke to Beenhakker and ignored Cruyff.'[393]

After leaving his brief tenure with the Oranje, Beenhakker had enjoyed enormous success with Real Madrid, delivering three successive La Liga titles, a Copa del Rey and two Supercopa de Espana victories. On his return to the Netherlands he had won the Eredivisie with Ajax. It was an impressive CV, but the players wanted Cruyff. Some have suggested that, off the record, Cruyff 'was game'[394] for the move. His autobiography suggests the same. 'I wanted that to happen, because it would have allowed us to bring our strengths together and finally become world champions, as we should have done in 1974 and 1978. But it didn't happen, because Michels had other ideas. Against the wishes of major internationals like Ruud Gullit, Marco van Basten, Frank Rijkaard and Ronald Koeman, he left me to one side.'[395] The job went to Beenhakker.

The man who had slated his team after the draw with Belgium four years earlier was back in charge of a group of players, many of whom he had hung out to dry. Ruud Gullit recalled the disappointment of many players upon hearing the news. 'I can't remember what Rinus said to justify this, but it was along the lines of "Leo is more experienced, Johan is an

392 De Bruijn, Jan-Hermen – Interview with the author
393 De Bruijn, Jan-Hermen – Interview with the author
394 https://dutchsoccersite.org/the-1990-world-cup-debacle-revisited/
395 Cruyff, Johan, *My Turn* (London: Macmillan, 2016)

inexperienced coach. He never did the course. And Johan will cause problems with the KNVB, because Johan is expensive and he wants to pick his own staff. It's not good to pick Johan.'"[396]

Back in the mid-1980s, Beenhakker's time with the Oranje had lasted six games, ending with a failure to qualify for the 1986 World Cup. His tenure five years later would be no longer and, arguably, even less successful. The first fixture, a friendly against Austria with what was arguably a first-choice team on the last day of May 1990, was hardly encouraging. Three goals down with an hour played, strikes by Koeman and Van Basten added a veneer of respectability, but only just. Three days later, a victory over Yugoslavia in Zagreb, with Rijkaard and Van Basten netting without reply, was an improvement, but with the opening game of the World Cup a mere nine days away, off the pitch, things were already beginning to unravel for the new coach.

In their wisdom, the KNVB had sent the players to an almost monastic retreat in an isolated spot of Yugoslavia. With the tournament on the horizon, and following a long season, the players, some carrying niggling injuries, were probably looking forward to a period of relaxation and recuperation. Instead of a beach and visits from wives and girlfriends, they were dropped into isolation and full-on training sessions. If that sort of thing had worked for Beenhakker in Spain, in *Brilliant Orange*, David Winner stated how the coach would later reflect on the difference in attitude with Dutch players. 'When you go to a hotel with the Dutch, one player says, "Hey, it's too big", and the other says it's too small. "It's too hot", "It's too cold", "It's too ..." We are busy with everything, ev-er-y-thing! But when you go to a hotel with a Spanish team – and they're all big stars, Hugo Sanchez, Camacho, Juanito, great players – they come in and it's: "OK, this is fine. Where's my

396 https://dutchsoccersite.org/the-1990-world-cup-debacle-revisited/

room? OK. Bye." They sit quietly and don't talk about the bus, and about the driver, and the driver's wife. No! Come on! They think: "We are here to play a football match. We play and we kill them. And then we go home." That's the difference.'[397] The frustration drips from his words, but surely it shouldn't have been a surprise. The consequences though were once more terminal for the Oranje's pursuit of the World Cup.

Three successive draws in the group games against Egypt, England and the Republic of Ireland saw the team limp into the knockout stages. For the recently crowned champions of Europe it was tepid at best, uninspired and flat. It brought a last-16 confrontation with West Germany at the San Siro, home to both the Internazionale contingent of German players, and the Dutch trio of AC Milan. The latter hardly looked to be comfortable in the surroundings and in a typically bad-tempered game, with Rudi Völler and Rijkaard dismissed midway through the first period, the latter compounding his offences by spitting into the German's permed locks, the Dutch fell to an ignominious 2-1 defeat and elimination.

The Rijkaard incident was another milestone in the long-running feud between the teams. Raphael Honigstein recalled that, 'By 1990, especially with Rijkaard, people think "there's something going on here that's bigger than football". By that time, the rivalry is firmly established. Fortunately, things would improve. The relationship between Holland and Germany has changed, the football relationship, over the last 15 to 20 years or so. There's been a lot of cross-pollination between German and Dutch coaches and players in each other's country ... The relationship now is a lot friendlier as a result. Also, politically we're closely aligned in the EU.'[398]

Beenhakker left again, undertaking a varied series of coaching appointments before once more returning to the

397 Winner, David, *Brilliant Orange* (London: Bloomsbury, 2000)
398 Honigstein, Raphael – Interview with the author

colours 16 years later. The Oranje sloped off home, and blame was cast around with abandon. There was even talk of Van Basten having punched Beenhakker, or hurling a handily-placed ashtray at him in the dressing-room. To rub salt into the wounds, the Germans went on to lift the trophy. Did things really fall apart from the moment Michels decided not to speak to Cruyff and appointed Beenhakker instead? It should have been the Oranje's best opportunity to claim their big day since 1978. No one can defeat the Dutch like they can themselves. Careful aim was taken and the bullet delivered directly into the foot.

To whom should the KNVB turn now? Cruyff? Would he even be interested after the apparent snub? Instead, in September 1990, as the Dutch played their first friendly game following the debacle in Italy, a 1-0 defeat to the *Azzurri* in Sicily, sitting in the coach's chair was none other than Rinus Michels. Could he coax one more triumph from the players? It was the only friendly game before qualification for the 1992 European Championship, to be held in Sweden, began. It was significant for the debut of a young, talented forward who joined the action from the bench in the 70th minute. It was the first international appearance for 21-year-old Dennis Bergkamp.

In a group of five, comprising Portugal, Greece, Finland and Malta, with only the winners progressing to the eight-team finals, the Dutch got off to a stumbling start, losing in Porto. From there, though, only a 1-1 draw in Helsinki blotted their otherwise perfect copybook and when the defeat to the Portuguese was avenged in October, Oranje dreams of retaining their title in Sweden were building. A 2-0 victory in Greece confirmed qualification and with Van Basten netting eight goals in the group games, and Bergkamp's four confirming his emerging status, things were looking up again. At the end of the 1991/92 season, Ajax returned to European glory, defeating Torino on away goals to lift the UEFA Cup with a team comprising ten Dutchmen, the exception being Sweden's Stefan Pettersson. Was it a herald of good things to come in Sweden?

The group stages offered hope. A scrappy opening game against Scotland was settled by a late Bergkamp goal, followed by a goalless draw against a CIS team, the interim successor to the Soviet Union. As is so often the case, the key fixture was against Germany. Rijkaard and Rob Witschge had the Oranje two goals clear inside the first 15 minutes. Klinsmann gave the Germans hope shortly after the restart, but Bergkamp added a third with 15 minutes left, and the Dutch topped the group. Germany qualified in second place.

Although Yugoslavia had qualified, the civil war ravaging the country prevented their participation and Denmark were promoted in their place. They provided the opposition for the Dutch in the semi-final … The Danes were now a pale shadow of the Dynamite team that had exploded on to the world football stage a few years earlier. Preben Elkjaer and Michael Laudrup were absent, although the latter's younger brother Brian was keeping the family tradition alive, but the latecomers were still a potent force. Twice trailing, it was only a late goal from Rijkaard that took the game into a penalty shoot-out, and when Van Basten's effort was saved by Peter Schmeichel, it marked the end of another great generation of Dutch talent who could have ditched that World Cup Bridesmaids tag, but fell short. It would be Van Basten's final major tournament, as injury ravaged his latter years. It would also be the last time that Rinus Michels coached the Oranje.

Two years later, with Dick Advocaat now in charge, and Gullit either dropped or on strike depending on whose account you believed, the Dutch would reach the quarter-finals of USA 94 before tumbling to Brazil in the last eight. The same year marked the end of both Rijkaard and Gullit's international careers. The performance in the USA had been inconsistent at best. Narrow victories over Saudi Arabia and Morocco were just sufficient to counteract a 1-0 defeat to Belgium, before a 2-0 victory over the Republic of Ireland took them to the confrontation with Brazil. There was reason for hope. This was a different shade of Oranje, shorn of their ageing stars. *The Guardian* offered up hope of a bright future. 'The Dutch didn't just have better tactics or better players. There was something brittle and individualistic about their style, their way of carrying themselves. This was football of the left bank, the unfiltered cigarette, the gap-year poncho. It might not have been enough to progress regularly through the late stages of knockout tournaments [...] But the Dutch were if anything a deeper, stronger group now.'[399]

Could this shade of Oranje shine as brightly though?

... and tomorrow: 1996–2010

On 24 May 1995, Ajax ended more than two decades of absence from European club football's top table when they defeated AC Milan to win the now rebranded Champions League. For the first time since 1973, the club could call themselves champions of Europe. A new generation of Dutch talent was breaking through and there was an added piquancy in the fact that the triumph took place in Vienna's Ernst-Happel-Stadion. The man who had taken the Oranje to the World Cup Final in 1978 had passed away two years earlier. The following year, Ajax again reached the final, but any burgeoning hopes of emulating the great teams of Michels and Kovacs were stymied when Juventus triumphed on penalties after a goalless game. Although this time there were only eight Dutchman in the final line-up, it still suggested that perhaps Dutch football was on the upward swing again.

399 https://www.theguardian.com/football/2020/apr/13/world-cup-questions-why-didnt-the-great-dutch-teams-of-the-1990s-win-it?CMP=Share_iOSApp_Other

Could this be replicated at international level at the 1996 European Championship?

Guus Hiddink took over as coach in January 1995, but started with two friendly home defeats, first to France and then to Portugal, each time by the only goal of the game. With the tournament being extended to 16 teams, the task of reaching the finals in England was eased. Grouped with the Dutch were the Czech Republic, Belarus, Norway, Luxembourg and Malta. With two qualifying, it shouldn't have been too much of a problem, but only in the final game of the group, when the Dutch triumphed over Norway 3-0 at the Stadion De Kuip, was qualification secured, and then only on goal difference. Hiddink's team would rely on similar calculations for progress once arriving in England for the tournament.

A draw with Scotland and a 2-0 win over Switzerland put the Oranje into, what amounted to, a last-group-game play-off against England. The winners would top the group and, assuming any defeat was not too large, the other team would probably finish second. In what is still regarded as one of England's finest performances, Terry Venables's team were four goals clear and coasting when Patrick Kluivert scored what at the time seemed to be a late consolation goal for the Dutch. It later turned out to be key, however. Scotland's 1-0 victory against Switzerland put them on identical records with the Dutch for points and goal difference. The fact that they had scored three, to the Scots' one, however, saw them progress, although they were eliminated by France on penalties in the quarter-finals.

Hiddink would also take the Oranje to the 1998 World Cup in France. Qualification was achieved, with Belgium being the main opposition, but a 3-1 home win over their neighbours in the penultimate fixture meant that only a point was needed from the home game against Turkey to secure top spot. At the Amsterdam ArenA, Hiddink's team achieved that result, although not without a few scares. For the tournament proper the Oranje were grouped with Mexico, South Korea and, almost inevitably, Belgium.

A goalless draw with the Belgians, a five-goal romp against the Asians and 2-2 draw with Mexico was sufficient for top spot, on goal difference from the Mexicans, and progress to the last 16. A 2-1 win over FR Yugoslavia thanks to an injury-time winner from Edgar Davids sent the Dutch into a last-eight confrontation with Argentina. Again, a late goal did for their opponents, but this strike by Bergkamp was of the highest order. Controlling a long pass, he hypnotised the South American defence with his skill before firing home. It was a goal to put on a par with Cruyff's first strike against the same opponents way back in 1974.

Sadly, in the semi-final, it was penalties again that saw the Dutch eliminated by Brazil. It would be harsh to describe the performance in France as any kind of failure, and in his two tournaments with the national team Hiddink had outperformed many of his predecessors. He would now move on, though, taking charge of Real Madrid briefly, and would be replaced by the first of Michels's players to take on the top job, as Frank Rijkaard assumed control, charged with taking the team to the 2000 European Championship and improving on Hiddink's semi-final placing in France.

As co-hosts, alongside Belgium, Rijkaard had no concerns about qualification tournaments, but that so often proves to be a double-edged sword. A lack of competitive games whilst rivals harden and hone their squads can prove to be counterproductive. Between October 1998 and the start of the tournament in June 2000, Rijkaard led the Dutch in 17 friendlies, seeking to establish the team and system he wanted, to be ready for the finals. Understandably, given the location of the tournament, all but five of the games were played at home, with one each located in neighbouring Belgium, Denmark and

Germany. The remaining two were on tour in South America, against Brazil.

Results of these types of games are hardly the object of the exercise, but it's worth noting that Rijkaard only suffered two defeats. One was away to Brazil, and the other, a 2-1 home loss to Morocco with a largely experimental team. Understandably, when the real action started, the Dutch and their young coach were favoured by many to win the title. A clean sweep in the group games did little to dissuade such opinion. Following an edgy opening game against the Czechs, settled by a late Frank de Boer penalty, three goals without reply against Denmark and a 3-2 win over France meant a last-eight game with FR Yugoslavia. In this game, the Dutch underscored their potential by scoring six times before Savo Milosevic secured the thinnest fig-leaf of consolation in injury time.

Kluivert's team was one to avoid in the semi-finals. With Edwin van der Sar in goal, Rijkaard employed a flexible 4-4-2 formation. The back line was made up of Paul Bosvelt, Jaap Stam, skipper De Boer and Giovanni van Bronckhurst. Phillip Cocu and Edgar Davids were a combative midfield pairing, flanked by Marc Overmars and Boudewijn Zenden. In attack, Bergkamp and Kluivert were a potent force. The former was the creator and the latter the finisher, already with five goals in the tournament. Their semi-final opponents were the Italians and, whereas the Dutch had been free-scoring after that opening game, Dino Zoff's *Azzurri* had been solid and efficient. The Oranje failed to break down Zoff's five-man defence and after a goalless game, penalties again proved to be the Dutch Achilles' heel with three out of four spot kicks missed. Another chance had passed the Dutch by.

After leading Ajax to those two successive Champions League Finals, Louis van Gaal had taken that well-trodden path for Ajax coaches and moved to Barcelona, where he won successive La Liga titles as well as a Copa del Rey. His final term in Catalunya had not been a happy one, though, as things began to fall apart. Never slow to rise to his own defence, after losing the title to Deportivo de La Coruna, he delivered his farewell to the press in typically robust style. 'Amigos de la prensa. Yo me voy. Felicidades. [Friends of the press. I am leaving. Congratulations.]'[400]

Van Gaal was heading home to become head coach of the Netherlands. Radomir Antic took temporary charge of the Barcelona team but, a few months later, the Dutch 'Switcheroo' was completed when Rijkaard took over at the Camp Nou. The former Barca coach took charge of his first game on 2 September 2000 and, typically, had little time for modesty or studied introspection, as David Winner related in *Brilliant Orange*. 'In his first press conference he announced his intention to make Holland World Champions in Japan.'[401] A little over 14 months, and the same number of games later, before the tournament had even begun in Asia, Van Gaal was gone.

Beginning the trail of qualification for the 2002 World Cup to be held jointly by Japan and South Korea, the Netherlands were placed into a group with Portugal, the Republic of Ireland, Estonia, Cyprus and Andorra. Only the group winners were guaranteed a place in the finals, with the runners-up facing a play-off. With both the Dutch and Portuguese being losing semi-finalists in the European Championship two years earlier, the Republic missing out on qualification and the others surely makeweights, it appeared likely that the pair would dispute the top two places. The first game of the programme suggested trouble ahead.

Facing the Republic of Ireland at the Amsterdam ArenA, inside the final 20 minutes the Dutch were struggling and two goals behind. Van Gaal had made all of his permitted changes, with Internazionale's Clarence Seedorf replacing

400 https://www.espn.com/
401 Winner, David, *Brilliant Orange* (London: Bloomsbury, 2000)

Michael Reiziger at half-time, PSV's Arnold Bruggink coming on for his debut instead of Witschge, and Jeffrey Talan of SC Heerenveen taking over from Bert Konterman five minutes later. Fortunately for the coach, it was Talan, making the sixth appearance of his eight-cap career, who scored his sole goal in Oranje to give the home side some hope on 71 minutes, before Van Bronckhorst equalised with five minutes to play, rescuing a point.

Five weeks later, a regulation 4-0 victory in Cyprus was the minimum requirement before the daunting, and now increasingly significant, visit of Portugal to Rotterdam. The result in Strovolos offers a somewhat false impression of the performance. It took the Dutch 68 minutes to score their first goal, and only three more in the final dozen minutes gave the scoreline any kind of semblance of respectability, with the Cypriots feeling more than a little hard done by.

On the same day, the Irish had overturned the formbook again, returning from their visit to Lisbon's Estadio da Luz with a point. If the result inflated Irish hopes, it put the Portuguese squarely into the same situation as the Dutch. Things were going to be tight now for the two supposedly favoured teams in the group.

More than 44,000 fans filled the Stadion de Kuip, hoping and indeed expecting the Dutch to re-establish their credentials as not only strong qualifiers, but also serious contenders for the trophy. The team Van Gaal selected was a mixture of the new and the experienced. Mario Melchiot of Chelsea was making his debut, with Mark van Bommel winning his second cap and Wilfred Bouma his third. This contrasted with the experienced quartet of Van der Sar, Frank de Boer, Overmars and Kluivert, totalling a shade less than 250 caps between them.

On occasions, such mixing of extremes can produce perfectly balanced performances. At others, there's a tendency for them to fall, and this game fell into the latter case. This was the Portugal of Figo, Rui Costa and Sergio Conceicao, and inside a dozen minutes, it was the latter, running on to a slide-rule pass from Pauletta, to place the ball through the legs of Van der Sar and give the visitors the lead. Things went from bad to worse with the break approaching.

A lapse in concentration from Reiziger saw his loose pass intercepted by Pauletta. There were still defenders between him and the Dutch goal, but the Bordeaux striker weaved elegantly away from any challenges before firing powerfully home. The now regular slew of substitutes in the second 45 minutes made little difference, and Portugal had resuscitated their hopes of qualification, whilst wheeling Dutch aspirations into Intensive Care. Portugal were on seven points from their three games, with the Irish on five having played the same number. The Dutch were only a point behind them, but the bare statistics hardly reflected the true balance of the group. The Irish had completed their away fixtures against both Portugal and the Netherlands, taking a point from each. The Dutch, on the other hand, had played Portugal and the Irish at home, accumulating just a single point, and still had to visit Lisbon and Dublin. Qualification would now be an uphill task for Van Gaal.

In the middle of November, a temporary respite of sorts came with an encouraging 2-1 friendly victory over Spain in Seville. It at least closed the year out on a hopeful note, but much of that optimism evaporated in the New Year when a goalless draw at home to Turkey in another friendly confirmed there were still plenty of problems to be addressed.

In March, five unanswered goals in Andorra were little balm to soothe the troubled Dutch soul. Four days later came a much sterner test, against Portugal in Lisbon. After just seven minutes, things were swinging back in favour of the Dutch ... Chelsea's Jimmy Floyd Hasselbaink chased a hopeful lofted ball that the home defenders assumed would run on to the safety of goalkeeper Quim's arms. The rapacious goalscorer got there first, tumbled as the goalkeeper challenged, got to his feet and hammered home from the penalty spot. Three minutes after the break, Kluivert drove home a pass from Overmars to double the lead. With just seven minutes remaining the lead was still intact, but not for much longer. First Pauletta scored, and then, in injury time, a Figo penalty brought the scores level.

The result was a hammer blow and neither a four-goal romp at home to Cyprus the following month, nor a 4-2 victory in Estonia in June, were likely to solve the problems that the profligacy in Portugal had caused. The Irish and Portuguese had also been hoovering up the low-hanging fruit of points against the lesser teams. The big test would come in September, with Van Gaal taking his team to Dublin. A draw would barely be sufficient; a defeat unthinkable, with the remaining fixtures massively favouring their rivals. Before that a 2-0 victory over England at White Hart Lane offered a little encouragement, but in a knockabout game where 19 substitutions were made, it barely served any great purpose at all.

The game in Dublin came on the day before Van Gaal's first anniversary as coach of the Oranje, but Mick McCarthy's team were in no mood to offer congratulations. A second-half goal from Jason McAteer won the game and, as the Irish and Portuguese played out their remaining fixtures without mishap, the Dutch were eliminated. Van Gaal's troubled reign was over. After leaving the Oranje in 1994, Dick Advocaat had spent successful periods with PSV and Rangers, but returned to the national colours to replace Van Gaal.

In 2004, the European Championship was held in Portugal and, under Advocaat, the Dutch skated through qualification, finishing three points behind the Czech Republic, but ten points clear of third-placed Austria. A seven-goal aggregate win over Scotland in the play-off confirmed their passage to the Iberian peninsula. Curiously, the Czechs were placed in the same group as the Dutch in Portugal, alongside, somewhat inevitably, Germany and Latvia. Another second place behind the Czechs advanced them into the knockout rounds, where they overcame Sweden on penalties, before losing out to the hosts in the last four.

The year was also significant for the publication of a book, that seemed to offer a cathartic moment for Dutch football. *1974: Wij Waren de Besten* [1974: We Were the Best][402] became a bestseller in the country. It won the Nico Scheepmaker Beker for the best sports book of 2004, and was also nominated as the best journalistic book of the year. The shadow of 1974 had hung over the country for three decades. Like some dark cloud that refused to allow the sun to shine through, it was the Dutchman's burden.

So many games with Germany since, both victories and defeats, had failed to lance that festering wound, but this book allowed the bile to be spilt. 'The World Cup in 1974. The Dutch national team amazes friend and foe with a daring and successful attacking game until on the Black Sunday of July 7 everything goes wrong: the artful team that teaches the world a game of football is confronted in the final in an apparently immoral way by West Germany. For the Netherlands, that match is therefore called the end of the sixties: it is over with the illusions, a trauma with gradually mythological dimensions is born.'[403] Author Auke Kok unravelled the myth of the Oranje's invincibility and allowed a flawed humanity into the argument. He painted the often-uncomfortable scenes around Michels, Cruyff and the squad in a compelling way. They lost not because of chicanery, but because of a lack of experience, a lack of discipline, and an overdose of arrogance. Germany deserved to win and it was because of self-destruction that Holland failed to win the World Cup.

402 Kok, Auke, *1974: Wij Waren de Besten* (Amsterdam: Thomas Rap, 2004)
403 Kok, Auke, *1974: Wij Waren de Besten* (Amsterdam: Thomas Rap, 2004)

After the European Championship, another of Michels's players took over as coach of the Oranje. Marco van Basten's apprenticeship had been a single term as assistant coach to Jong Ajax, the Amsterdam club's second team. Now he was promoted to lead the national team, and the next World Cup would be back in Germany. If Kok's book had compelled the Dutch to face reality, another opportunity for revenge on their old foes remained something to relish.

Van Basten achieved qualification with consummate ease, winning ten of the dozen group games and drawing the other two. The Oranje were already on their way to qualification when news broke on 3 March 2005 that Rinus Michels had passed away at the age of 77, after heart surgery. Van Basten said, 'Michels was the father of Dutch soccer.'[404] On the UEFA website, Berend Scholten lamented that, 'With the passing of Rinus Michels, the football family has suffered the loss of a legend who played an essential role in putting Dutch football on the map by introducing the world to Total Football.'[405] For others, the truth was much simpler. 'Michels was the greatest ever football coach,'[406] said Jan-Hermen de Bruijn. The Netherlands continued on to Germany, qualifying out of the group, but lost to Portugal in the last 16.

In 2008, Van Basten led the Dutch to the quarter-finals of the European Championship, before leaving to take over at Ajax. In his place, the KNVB appointed the little-known Bert van Marwijk from Feyenoord. He would lead the Dutch to another World Cup Final but, in doing so, would be accused by many of betraying the legacy of those Beautiful Bridesmaids, replacing them with something more akin to Ugly Sisters.

404 https://www.independent.co.uk/news/obituaries/rinus-michels-527100.html
405 https://www.uefa.com/insideuefa/about-uefa/news/01a7-0f846a5fe573-
      c90524e99f26-1000 – michels-a-total-footballing-legend/?referrer=%2Finsideuefa
      %2Fnews%2Fnewsid%3D285010
406 De Bruijn, Jan-Hermen – Interview with the author

Pinning labels on coaches is often a perilous pursuit, but it is safe to say that Van Marwijk's style was more informed by pragmatism than a desire to foster the beautiful game. Years later, when he took over as coach of the Australia football team, an article in *The Guardian* suggested that his approach was driven by 'a pragmatic approach to football, physicality and a focus on results over style.'[407] Perhaps it was a case of the right man at the right time. Dutch football had seen two glorious failures as the Beautiful Bridesmaids of 1974 and 1978 had fallen short. Michels had proven that Europe could be conquered with the traditional Dutch values of innovation and enterprise, but that global prize remained tantalisingly out of reach. Was it time to lock away such fanciful ideals of triumph coupled with exuberance, and decant dreams into realism? If so, the new coach may have been the man to deliver.

Van Marwijk had only recently returned to Dutch domestic football following two seasons in the Bundesliga with Borussia Dortmund, but his credentials were stamped by lifting the KNVB Cup once back in Rotterdam. He was quick to build his coaching team. 'When I became national coach, I immediately thought of them,' Van Marwijk said, referring to assistants Phillip Cocu and Frank de Boer. 'They said very sensible things about football ... and had the qualities and positions in the field to read the game. Their age meant that they kept enough distance from the group, but were still so close to enjoy respect.'[408]

Before launching into the qualification process for the 2010 World Cup to be held in South Africa, Van Marwijk had two friendly fixtures to firm up thoughts about his team. Travelling to Moscow on 20 August 2008 with an experienced squad, he returned with a satisfactory 1-1 draw, but followed

407 https://www.theguardian.com/football/2018/feb/01/bert-van-marwijk-vows-to-do-it-his-way-as-socceroos-coach
408 Van Marwijk: 'Frank ziet tactisch ongelooflijk veel', *De Telegraaf*, 15 May 2002

that up with a worrying 2-1 home defeat to Australia, despite being given an early lead by Klaas-Jan Huntelaar, a couple of weeks later. Four days after that disappointing defeat in Eindhoven, the Dutch travelled to Skopje to begin their World Cup qualification programme against Macedonia. The other members of the group were Norway, Scotland and Iceland. If the preparation games had been less than perfect, the same could not be said when the real business started.

The Oranje went through the qualification process with a 100% record, scoring 17 goals and conceding only two across the eight games. Their total of 24 points put them 14 ahead of the runners-up. Perhaps a little perspective is added, though, by considering that including games home and away against Iceland, the Dutch were only averaging very slightly over two goals per game.

Interspersed amongst the qualifiers, they also played four friendlies, defeating Sweden at home and drawing in Tunisia at the end of 2008, before defeating Norway in June and drawing with England in August 2009. Add in three draws and four wins after qualification was completed, and the Dutch were on the way to South Africa on a run of 19 unbeaten games, following that loss to Australia. Heading to South Africa, confidence was in full bloom, and the tournament's early results did little to burst the Oranje balloon.

Placed in Group E, alongside Denmark, Japan and Cameroon, the Dutch kicked off their campaign against the Danes in Johannesburg on 14 June. Van Marwijk's selection was typical of his approach. A four-man defence in front of Maarten Stekelenburg comprised Gregory van der Wiel, John Heitinga, Joris Mathijsen and skipper Van Bronckhorst. A combative midfield duo of Van Bommel and Nigel de Jong acted as a shield for the defence with the industrious Dirk Kuyt, the creative Wesley Sneijder and the innovative Rafael van der Vaart to supply opportunities for Robin van Persie. An own goal by Daniel Agger just after the restart gave the Dutch the advantage, and Kuyt added the second to round out the win with five minutes remaining.

On paper, the second game, against Japan looked an easier prospect, but it didn't turn out that way. Takeshi Okada's team were organised and disciplined, with their energetic approach disrupting any semblance of rhythm that the Dutch tried to create, and had Tanaka or Matsui been more clinical as the first period drifted to a close, Japan could easily have led at the break. Early in the second period, Sneijder punished their profligacy with the only goal of the game. In the final group encounter a 2-1 win over Cameroon kept up the 100% record, thanks to a late winning strike by Huntelaar. It may have been relevant for the future that the five Dutch goals were outnumbered by the total of six yellow cards.

The last-16 game paired the Dutch with Slovakia, runners-up in Group F. In the first change to his starting XI, Van Marwijk introduced Arjen Robben to replace Van der Vaart. The Bayern Munich winger repaid the coach's faith by scoring the opening goal after 18 minutes and, when Sneijder netted the second with time running out, Vittek's injury-time penalty was purely academic. The Dutch were into the last eight, and would face Brazil.

The game took place on the second day of July, in the early afternoon heat of Port Elizabeth's Nelson Mandela Stadium. Another change was forced on Van Marwijk when Mathijsen was ruled out with injury, meaning a late call-up for Andre Ooijer. A mistake by Ooijer's defensive partner Heitinga allowed Robinho to put the South Americans ahead on ten minutes. It set the pattern of play, with the Dutch being frustrated by the resolute Brazilian defence and prey to being caught again on the break. Eight minutes into the second period, though, it was Sneijder again who got the important goal, and then repeated the trick 15 minutes later, heading home a corner to put the Dutch ahead. They held out until the end to reach the semi-finals, accumulating a further four yellow cards that reflected the physicality of the match, with Brazil's Melo being dismissed towards the end.

The final four teams were made up of the Dutch, Uruguay, Spain and Germany, with the Netherlands paired with the South Americans in the semi-final. What price another Germany v Netherlands final? The Dutch fulfilled their part, defeating Uruguay 3-2, although the South Americans' second goal came well into injury time, offering the scoreline a flavour it hardly warranted. After the game, Dirk Kuyt summed up the Dutch emotions. 'It's an amazing feeling. We said before the tournament that we could do this and get to the final, but we knew it would be a long journey. Holland have been in two finals before [in 1974 and 1978] but we have not managed to go the extra yard and win it.'[409] De Jong's yellow card against Brazil had made him ineligible for the semi-final, but Demy de Zeeuw was a satisfactory replacement. An injury following a blow to the mouth ruled him out of the final, but De Jong would surely have returned anyway. The other option for the coach would be to return Van der Vaart to the starting line-up, but he was always far more likely to go with the muscular Manchester City player.

Van Marwijk's pragmatic approach had taken the Dutch that 'long way', but he acknowledged that the next step would be bigger. 'In the last five weeks I have talked a lot with Ruud Gullit, and I have talked a lot with Johan Cruyff. And from the first time we trained here, Ruud Krol has been here for every session. We talked a lot about everything, the past, the way we played. But I will not think about our legacy at the moment. We have to play the game first.'[410]

409 Orange blossom time for Dutch, *The Times*, 7 July 2010
410 I want to stay with Inter says Sneijder, *The Times*, 9 July 2010

In the other semi-final, the Dutch were denied the opportunity to put their unbeaten run on the line against Germany, when Carles Puyol's late goal sent Spain into the final. The 2010 World Cup Final would be between Spain and the Netherlands in Johannesburg's Soccer City on 11 July. Refereeing the game would be Howard Webb.

The Englishman would not have a quiet time of it, and after the final many would feel compelled to speak out. Ahead of the game, *The Times* suggested that Johan Cruyff may have mixed feelings about who he would prefer to win, 'because Vicente del Bosque's [Spain] team are more Dutch than the Dutch themselves. Every intricate move from Spain should be stamped "made in Amsterdam" because it will owe everything to the Dutch influence.'[411] If Cruyff was indeed in two minds ahead of the final, after it, his opinion would be unclouded.

The match was a lamentable parody of the games played by the Dutch in the 1970s. Despite flailing around to blame anyone bar themselves for a display that tore the heart from the legacy left by Cruyff, Krol, Rensenbrink *et al*, few would dispute not only that the best team won, but also that the nine yellow cards, plus one red, handed out by Webb to the Dutch team was, if anything, a tad restrained. Heitinga was dismissed, but so too could have been De Jong and Van Bommel. For the record, Spain won by a single extra time goal by Andres Iniesta, but although the history books merely show the Netherlands as losing the game, the legacy of the Beautiful Bridesmaids was also lost.

The Guardian suggested that Cruyff was direct and unabashed in his criticism. 'On Thursday they asked me from Holland "Can we play like Inter? Can we stop Spain in the same way Mourinho eliminated Barca?"' Cruyff told *El Periódico*, in reference to the way Internazionale defended their

---

411 Johan Cruyff will be thrilled by a Spain victory and masterclass by the disciple of his art, *The Times*, 11 July 2010

way to a Champions League semi-final victory over Barcelona. 'I said no, no way at all. I said no, not because I hate this style – I said no because I thought that my country wouldn't dare to and would never renounce their style. I said no because, without having great players like those of the past, the team has its own style. I was wrong. Of course, I'm not hanging all 11 of them by the same rope, but almost. They didn't want the ball. And regrettably, sadly, they played very dirty. So much so that they should have been down to nine immediately, then they made two [such] ugly and hard tackles that even I felt the damage. It hurts me that I was wrong in my disagreement that instead Holland chose an ugly path to aim for the title. This ugly, vulgar, hard, hermetic, hardly eye-catching, hardly football style, yes it served the Dutch to unsettle Spain. If with this they got satisfaction, fine, but they ended up losing. They were playing anti-football."[412]

Where many people would have been led by patriotic emotions, clouding their judgement, Cruyff delivered a damning verdict, saddened by his country's team taking the 'ugly path'. On the same day, *The Times* World Cup supplement led with the simple headline 'Cloggers'[413], following up with a report headed 'A victory for anti-thuggery.'[414] The football world was hoping for a rebirth of the Netherlands team of 1974. Instead they got Brazil in the same tournament. Spain won. Football won. The Netherlands lost, and the Beautiful Bridesmaids were abandoned.

Other tournaments both for European glory and world titles would come and go, but in 2010, the Netherlands became the only team in the history of the tournament to lose three World Cup Finals. Two were agonisingly lost when the best team didn't win. The third felt like a betrayal and, strangely,

412 'Johan Cruyff hits out at "anti-football" Holland", *The Guardian* 12 July 2010
413 'Cloggers', *The Times* 12 July 2010
414 'A victory for anti-thuggery', *The Times* 12 July 2010

made the loss easier to bear. Jan-Willem Bult reflected that, 'When Netherlands impresses with attractive football, but doesn't win a cup or reach a final, [it] is less seen as a failure in the eyes of the Dutch. There is pride that such a small country 'teaches' the world how to play football. When there is success, like the final of the World Cup in 2010, but the team doesn't play the attractive Dutch football, there is less sadness about a lost final.'[415]

415 Bult, Jan-Willem – Interview with the author

PART 7

Is the Future Oranje?

Growing from the great days of Ajax and Feyenoord in the early years of the 1970s, Dutch football dazzled magnificently, with vividly bright colours emerging as a butterfly from a chrysalis of 36 years' hibernation away from the international game's biggest prize. And, as with such Lepidoptera, their game was drawn to the bright light of Total Football, a vision of the game that embraced innovation, talent and an abundance of flair. It took the Oranje so close to the ultimate prize, before falling tragically short and leaving not only a nation, but a generation of football dreamers unfulfilled.

There were no winners' medals for the players who lost out on the fields of Munich and Buenos Aires, just silver tears. Instead, what those Beautiful Bridesmaids bequeathed to football was a legacy, a spirit of enlightenment, and a path to be followed. According to Greek mythology, when Pandora opened her box, all of the evils of the world escaped, leaving but one thing remaining: hope.[416] In *1984*, George Orwell wrote that, 'If there was hope, it must lie in the proles.'[417] He meant the workers, the labourers, the artisans who could rise up and overturn a dictatorship. In footballing terms at least, he was surely wrong. If there's any hope for the promise of the unfulfilled glory of the Beautiful Bridesmaids to at last have their big day, it lies not with 'the proles' but with the artists, with the creators of beauty, with the dreamers.

'The world is a better place when there's a strong Netherlands side,'[418] Rob Smyth asserted and, in 2019, it looked like the world was on its way to being that 'better place'. Along with England, Switzerland and Portugal, the Netherlands had qualified for the semi-finals of UEFA's nascent Nations League tournament. By this time coached by Ronald Koeman, another of Rinus Michels's former players,

416 Hesiod, *Works and Days,* approx 700BC
417 Orwell, George, *Nineteen Eighty-Four* (London: Secker & Warburg, 1949)
418 Smyth, Rob – Interview with the author

a young Dutch team defeated England in extra time, but lost out to Portugal in the final. Bridesmaids again? Perhaps, but this team also carried hope for the future. They had picked up from another disappointing time.

Jan-Willem Bult said, 'In the last decade, the Netherlands had another golden generation – Robben, Van Persie, Sneijder, Van der Vaart ('the Big Four'). Impressively, they [reached the] quarter-final at the 2008 European Championship, finalists at the 2010 World Cup, although a disaster in the European Championship of 2012. Then Van Gaal added new young players such as Depay, Blind, De Vrij and reached the semi-final of the World Cup in 2014.[419] Then came the inevitable disappointment. 'The team [had] performed above expectation and failed to qualify for the European Championship of 2016 and World Cup of 2018. Only when Ronald Koeman became the coach and the Big Four was completely replaced by Ajax youngsters such as De Ligt, De Jong, Van de Beek, surrounded by players from top leagues such as Van Dijk, Wijnaldum the performance went up again and the Netherlands qualified for the European Championship of 2020 and reached the final of the Nations League. Meanwhile, the Ajax youngsters are with top European teams and new talents such as Stengs, Boadu arrive.'[420]

Was the delayed European Championship a lost opportunity for Koeman's team? Bult suggests it perhaps was. '[It] would have been the perfect moment for this team to grow on the highest competition and become a favourite for the World Cup of 2022. Yes, this team could grow to that level, the circumstances are good: great coach, great defence, young on average. But vulnerable if one or two key players would get injured, the base is small.'[421]

419 Bult, Jan-Willem – Interview with the author
420 Bult, Jan-Willem – Interview with the author
421 Bult, Jan-Willem – Interview with the author

A central defensive partnership of Liverpool's towering Virgil van Dijk and Matthijs de Ligt, then with Ajax, but completing his education in Serie A with Juventus, may well become the best in the world. In midfield, the burgeoning talent of Frenkie de Jong, who joined Barcelona, also from Ajax, all swaying runs and changes of pace, offered a tantalising glimpse of a rare potential often compared to that of Cruyff himself. On the bench then, but a star now, Donny van de Beek is the perfect foil for De Jong. With the enigmatic Memphis Depay, the energetic Georginio Wijnaldum and the enterprising Steven Bergwijn, there's a promise of an emerging new Oranje that could take on the world. Might they get to the altar?

Ahead of the 2019 final, Koeman was enthusiastic. 'We have a great future. In the last few years, it is the best generation. But they are just starting. They have great talent. We always brought good young players through the system from what we have in Holland. We are a country that will always produce good young players. Always. Sometimes in football it's like this: talented young players coming through the system. The atmosphere around the national team has changed and that was down to the players and how we started in the Nations League. We have the best central defenders with De Ligt and Virgil. They are top defence players. That's great because you build the house, always, from downstairs. You don't start with the roof. We are on a good way back to where we would like to stay as a country.'[422]

How quickly things change. The previous year, interviewed on Sky Sports, Frank de Boer was less optimistic. 'We had the generation with Johan Cruyff. We had the generation with Marco van Basten. We had the generation with Patrick Kluivert. We had the generation with Arjen Robben, Rafael van der Vaart and Wesley Sneijder. Now we have been in a

422 'We're a country that will always produce good young players' *The Guardian*, 3 June 2019

little bit of a situation where we have only had Robben really. He has been the only one to make a difference. So, I think the problem has been 80 per cent down to a lack of quality. Now is the time where we have to be patient.'[423] How can things change so quickly?

A big part of the answer to that question may lie in the success of the youth systems operated at some of the Netherlands' top clubs. The Ajax Academy, for example, is world famous for bringing young players through the ranks to the first team as outstanding talents. In the 1970s, that led to the glorious years of European club hegemony; of late, however, it more usually leads to them being sold on to the Continent's top clubs.

The 2018/19 Champions League tournament offered a brief glimpse of what could be achieved if Ajax were able to resist the big-money bids offered for their star players on an almost annual basis. A window of opportunity was opened when a group of the club's young players were performing at exalted levels before the club was compelled to sell them. After going through the indignity of two qualifying rounds, and progressing from the group stage, they produced a series of outstanding performances.

Losing 2-1 at home to Real Madrid, Ajax then went to the Santiago Bernabeu Stadium and won an astonishing game 4-1. In the next round, a 1-1 draw at home to Juventus looked to have left a mountain to climb in Turin, but again a wonderful away performance saw them prevail, this time winning 2-1. In the semi-final, another exceptional performance away from home brought a 1-0 victory against Tottenham Hotspur in north London, and it was only a goal six minutes into injury time in the home leg that saw them miss out on what would have been a mouth-watering final encounter with Liverpool.

423 De Boer, Frank, Sky Sports, 13 October 2018

Perhaps there's a reason to think that the window may remain open for a while longer. Michael Statham suggested that, 'Players are now leaving the Dutch Eredivisie in their twenties rather than escaping for a big-money move abroad when they are only teenagers, which has helped to develop some fantastic players in the domestic league, where younger players almost always earn playing time. The Dutch are much closer than they were before Koeman took charge, and they have the potential to become a stronger team than the one who reached the final in 2010.'[424] All this is to the benefit of the Oranje, and aspirations for success on the biggest stage.

De Ligt and De Jong are more recent examples of Ajax's production line of talent but the academy's rich history also includes the likes of Johan Cruyff, Marco van Basten, Frank Rijkaard, Dennis Bergkamp and Patrick Kluivert. The club's emphasis on player development has reaped rich dividends. Their website states: 'At AFC Ajax, the training of top football players takes centre stage. That is why the youth academy is also known as the breeding ground of Dutch football.'[425] It's therefore quite apt that the academy is known as 'De Toekomst' (The Future).

The brief opportunity for a dalliance with European club success for Ajax fans was doused when De Jong and De Ligt were both sold on, and others will doubtless follow. Van de Beek has joined Manchester United. As with Cruyff and Neeskens moving to Barcelona in the early 1970s, however, perhaps even these moves aren't entirely bad news for the Oranje, if a little frustrating for Ajax fans. Many players who wear the Oranje now are at Europe's most successful clubs. Such education can surely only aid their development. 'Dutch football is like a fire. It simmers away for a while, then it

424 Statham, Michael – Interview with the author
425 https://english.ajax.nl/

bursts into flame,'[426] Jan-Hermen de Bruijn offered. The international stage may just be about to witness that flaring again. Can the Dutch win the World Cup soon?

If so, it may depend on more than a group of talented players. 'A lot of players from the current national team are young and on the way up. Perhaps we can win it in six years,' Jan-Hermen De Bruijn suggested when he spoke with the author in 2020. 'But it is history that you can only win it when luck is combined with class. In 1988 they had the necessary luck to win a title and every team that has won the World Cup, with perhaps the exception of Brazil in 1970, had their moments of luck. We could do it in two years' time, or in six years' time, more realistically.'[427] The feeling in the Netherlands is one of growing hope, even expectation, and the group of players certainly look to be in place, or very nearly so. Jan-Hermen de Bruijn was optimistic. 'The players like De Ligt, De Jong and Van de Beek. Some amazing players coming out of Ajax again. They are all at the beginning of their careers and they will surely dominate European and world football for six, eight, ten years to come. Especially at this moment, the defence and midfield are OK for the coming decade, but not yet as an attacking force.'[428]

Perhaps it's inevitable that hope springs eternal for football fans in a country who have seen their team lose out in a World Cup Final on three occasions, and twice after being widely lauded as the best team in the tournament For football fans the world over, there remains a mystique, an unfulfilled desire not only to see the best team win global football's greatest prize, but to see it do so in a style yet to be repeated since perhaps the Brazilian triumph of 1970. Failure to qualify for the European Championship in 2016 and then the World

426 De Bruijn, Jan-Hermen – Interview with the author
427 De Bruijn, Jan-Hermen – Interview with the author
428 De Bruijn, Jan-Hermen – Interview with the author

Cup in 2018 would, for so many countries, suggest that any redemption is some way off. Things simply don't work that way for Dutch football, though.

The flame that bursts into life with a scorching vivid orange has never enjoyed an extended run of success. By its very nature it is ephemeral. It burns bright, but briefly. 'Not many teams in world football have such a distinct identity, and because of that they add so much to any tournament. Their failure to qualify in 2016 and 2018 was pretty shocking, but it looks like it was just a blip. And while you can never be completely sure in football – who would have thought Hungary would become an irrelevance – the culture [in Dutch football] is so strong that they should keep regenerating and producing players like Virgil van Dijk and Frenkie de Jong. They're the greatest football nation never to win the World Cup, but there's no reason that can't change,'[429] Rob Smyth suggested.

What would it mean for the country if that 'change' occurred and the Oranje could finally reach the summit of world football? Jan-Willem Bult offered his analysis. 'In the Netherlands [it] is felt that the world thinks that one day it deserves to win. That in good times the teams play attractive football that everybody likes to see. But even though Ajax, Feyenoord and PSV won European Cups and World [Club] Cups, the real gold is still missing. [People of the] Netherlands think that they deserve it and is longing already 45 years for it. One World Cup for the Netherlands would have the same impact as it had for France. Instead of being a sympathetic football country as it is now, it would forever become a member of the Big Nine: Brazil, Germany, Italy, France, Argentina, Netherlands, Spain, England, Uruguay. And generally, the Dutch already think they deserve that

429 Smyth, Rob – Interview with the author

place.'[430] To do so in the style of those teams of the 1970s would raise them even higher.

In 2017, a hint of that 'impact' was felt when the Dutch women's team hosted and won the UEFA Women's Championship, turning many of their players into overnight celebrities. 'There are boys in the country who now choose to wear Miedema [Vivianne Miedema – Dutch international forward] on the back of their shirt over many famous Netherlands men players. Should the Dutch lift the World Cup, it would mean so much for the country, for the fans, the league, and it would vindicate the ways of Dutch clubs to spend money in developing their own youth for future success,'[431] said Michael Statham.

Can it happen? The KNVB certainly believe they are playing their part as their director of football Nico-Jan Hoogma explained as he answered a few questions from the author. Firstly, asked how the KNVB views the future of the Dutch national team, and what do they think they can do to assist clubs to maintain the production and development of world-class players such as De Jong and De Ligt, the answer was both robust and determined. 'We see our future as a bright one. We qualified with Oranje [men] for Euro 2020 after an absence in 2018 and 2016. We have back a lot of top players in several ages. We, as an association, worked a lot to make progression in the way we develop and scout our players and trainers. In fact, that is the task we have for football in general and specially for Dutch football. What we do is helping our clubs, in education, in developing programmes, organise seminars, organise exchanging between Football Associations and so on. In the meantime we raised a state of the art Football Campus in Zeist Holland in which a football player and trainer finds everything he needs; from hotel accommodation, to a fully

430 Bult, Jan-Willem – Interview with the author
431 Statham, Michael – Interview with the author

equipped and manned medical centre and grass and artificial playfields.'[432]

There is also a belief in the organisation that the best way to ensure a continuation of the legacy of Dutch football is to keep former players involved. Hoogma himself played more than 500 games in the Eredivisie and German Bundesliga. Unsurprisingly, he promotes the philosophy. 'We prefer to have good "football-people" in our organisation at any level in any discussion. Practically that means that several former internationals work for and with us Ronald Koeman, head coach of the Nederlands Elftal, [was] a good example of this policy.'[433]

Hoogma is also acutely aware of the importance of the World Cup to Dutch football, and what it would mean for the country to win the World Cup, but without sacrificing the things with which the Oranje shirt is associated. 'We hope that one time we will win it. When we qualify for a tournament, we want to win it. Winning is the very first goal. Nevertheless, I want to emphasise that we want to play good and attractive, winning football. We want to let the stadiums and TV spectators enjoy the way we play the game … That is what professional football also is made for.'[434]

Take a look inside the box that Pandora left open, and there you'll find hope. There's also hope in the work of the academies of Dutch football clubs, identifying, cherishing and developing talent. There's hope in all the words of the journalists and football lovers who wish only the best for the beautiful game, and there's hope in the words of the top man at the KNVB.

I have hope and, if you're a lover of the beautiful game, you should too. 'You may say I'm a dreamer, but I'm not the only

432 Hoogma, Nico-Jan, KNVB director of top football – Interview with the author
433 Hoogma, Nico-Jan, KNVB director of top football – Interview with the author
434 Hoogma, Nico-Jan, KNVB director of top football – Interview with the author

one,[435] as Lennon sang. Perhaps in 2022, perhaps four years later, but as Jan-Hermen de Bruijn said, 'You can only win it when luck is combined with class.' The class has been there, the passions, the ability, but only to have been forsaken by fortune. The Dutch teams of 1974 and 1978 set standards, put down markers and laid a trail for others to follow. One day, in the not too distant future, a new Oranje will follow that trail, but instead of Beautiful Bridesmaids dressed in Oranje, they'll be the Beautiful Brides. I only hope that I'm there to see it.

Let's end, as we began, with a quote from a member of the Beat Generation, this time Allen Ginsberg. 'My fault, my failure, is not in the passions I have, but in my lack of control of them.'[436] It's not a bad description of the Dutch national team of the 1970s, and the continuing aspirations of the Oranje ever since, 'On the Road', as it were, but never quite arriving. Not yet anyway.

435 'Imagine', a song by John Lennon and Yoko Ono, Apple Records, 1971
436 Ginsberg, Allen, *The Book of Martyrdom and Artifice,* (New York: Da Capo Press, 2008 Edition)

INDEX

INDEX